Beginning ASP.NET 2.0

G000141906

Beginning
ASP.NET 2.0 AJAX

Beginning
ASP.NET 2.0 AJAX

Wallace B. McClure

Paul Glavich

Steve C. Orr

Craig Shoemaker

Steven A. Smith

Jim Zimmerman

Wiley Publishing, Inc.

Beginning ASP.NET 2.0 AJAX

Published by
Wiley Publishing, Inc.
10475 Crosspoint Boulevard
Indianapolis, IN 46256
www.wiley.com

Copyright © 2007 by Wiley Publishing, Inc., Indianapolis, Indiana

Published simultaneously in Canada

ISBN: 978-0-470-11283-0

Manufactured in the United States of America

10 9 8 7 6 5 4 3 2 1

Library of Congress Cataloging-in-Publication Data:
Beginning asp.net 2.0 AJAX / Wallace B. McClure ... [et al.].
    p. cm.
  Includes index.
  ISBN 978-0-470-11283-0 (paper/website)
  1. Active server pages. 2. Web sites—Design. 3. Microsoft .NET. I. McClure, Wallace B.
  TK5105.8885.A26B4534 2007
  005.2'76—dc22

For my wife, Ronda; my two children, Kirsten and Bradley; and the rest of my family.

— *Wallace B. McClure*

To my wonderful wife, Michele, for her enduring love and patience; my three children, Kristy, Marc, and Elizabeth, for being so lovable and great people; my two grandchildren, Olivia and William, for just being themselves; my loving parents for all their support; and to everyone else I have met on the way to getting where I am, good or bad, thank you for helping me get here.

— *Paul Glavich*

To my wife, Judie, and the rest of my family. Thanks for all your help!

— *Steve C. Orr*

Thanks to my wife and family for supporting me in work and writing.

— *Craig Shoemaker*

For Michelle, for putting up with me longer than anybody should have to do so.

— *Steven A. Smith*

To my wonderful and patient wife, Chama; my wonderful children, Teryn, Quinn, and Kylin; and my mom.

— *Jim Zimmerman*

About the Authors

Wallace B. "Wally" McClure graduated from the Georgia Institute of Technology in 1990 with a bachelor of science degree in electrical engineering. He continued his education there, receiving a master's degree in the same field in 1991. Since that time, he has done consulting and development for such companies as The United States Department of Education, Coca-Cola, Magnatron, and Lucent Technologies, a web search engine, a web 2.0 company among others. Products and services have included work with ASP, ADO, XML, and SQL Server, as well as numerous applications in the Microsoft .NET Framework. Wally has been working with the .NET Framework since the summer of 2000. Wally McClure specializes in building applications that have large numbers of users and large amounts of data. He is a Microsoft MVP, an ASPInsider, a member of the INETA Speaker's Bureau, and a partner in Scalable Development, Inc. You can read Wally's blog at http://weblogs.asp.net/wallym/ and www.morewally .com. Wally and co-author Paul Glavich also co-host the ASP.NET Podcast. You can listen to it at www.aspnetpodcast.com/. In addition, Wally travels around the southeast United States doing user group talks and sessions at various CodeCamps.

When not working or playing with technology, Wally tries to spend time with his wife Ronda and their two children, Kirsten and Bradley. Occasionally, Wally plays golf and on July 30, 2005, broke par on a real golf course for the first time in his life. If he hadn't been there, he would not have believed it.

Paul Glavich is currently an ASP.NET MVP and works as a senior consultant for Readify. Previously he was a technical architect for EDS Australia and he has more than 15 years of industry experience ranging from PICK, C, C++, Delphi, and Visual Basic 3/4/5/6 to his current specialty in .NET with C#, COM+, and ASP.NET.

Paul has been developing in .NET technologies since .NET was first in beta and was technical architect for one of the world's first Internet banking solutions using .NET technology.

Paul can be seen on various .NET-related newsgroups, has presented at the Sydney .NET user group (www.sdnug.org) and TechEd, and is also a board member of ASPInsiders (www.aspinsiders.com). He has also written some technical articles that can be seen on community sites such as ASPAlliance.com (www.aspalliance.com). Paul has authored a book on Beginning AJAX in ASP.NET, is co-authoring a second book on Microsoft ASP.NET AJAX, and is currently focusing on Microsoft ASP.NET AJAX and Windows Communication Foundation technologies.

On a more personal note, Paul is married with three children, two grandkids, and holds a 4th-degree black belt in Budo-Jitsu.

Steve C. Orr is an ASP Insider, Microsoft Certified Solutions Developer (MCSD), Certified ScrumMaster (CSM), and Microsoft MVP in ASP.NET. He specializes in Microsoft technologies such as ASP.NET, Visual Basic.NET, C#, and SQL Server. He's infamous for his monthly "Control Freak" column in *ASP.NET Pro Magazine*, and has been developing software solutions for leading companies in the Seattle area for nearly two decades. When he's not busy designing software systems or writing about it, Steve can often be found loitering at local user groups and habitually lurking in the ASP.NET newsgroup.

Craig Shoemaker teaches software developers about object-oriented development, architecture, and best practices in .NET. Along with that, he is the host of the Polymorphic Podcast (polymorphicpodcast.com). Always active in the .NET developer community, Craig is a co-author for *Beginning Ajax with ASP.NET* (Wrox), he is featured in *Ajax Design Patterns* (O'Reilly), writes for *CoDe Magazine, ASP Alliance*, and the

PDSA eBook series. Craig's personal appearances include talks given at VSLive!, Southern California Code Camp, Southern California .NET Architecture User Group, and the Podcast and Portable Media Expo. As a full-time Software Engineer for PDSA, Inc. (pdsa.com) Craig's development experience ranges from the entertainment and financial sectors. Working with PDSA's clients has allowed him to consult for banner organizations such as the Twentieth Century Fox Film Corporation and the City of Hope Cancer Research Center.

Steven A. Smith is president of ASPAlliance.com and DevAdvice.com. He is a Microsoft Regional Developer, a Microsoft ASP.NET MVP, and an ASPInsiders Board Member. He is an International .NET Association (INETA) Speaker Bureau member, and author of two books on ASP.NET. Steve is also an Army Engineer officer and veteran of Operation Iraqi Freedom, where he spent six months locating and neutralizing munitions in 2004. He lives in Kent, Ohio, with his wife and business partner Michelle and their daughter Ilyana. When he is not attached to a computer, Steve enjoys spending time with his family hiking, biking, and playing games.

Jim Zimmerman is currently a Visual Developer – ASP/ASP.NET MVP. He speaks on various .NET-related topics including AJAX and Code Generation at Code Camps and .NET user groups in Florida. Jim is a member of the Ajax Control Toolkit (www.codeplex.com/AtlasControlToolkit) and tries to blog when the kids are sleeping at www.jimzimmerman.com/blog. He has a software consulting company that works with several online web properties including one of which he is part owner, CarCentral (www.carcentral.com). He also has more than 10 years experience in web development with past experience using languages such as Perl, PHP, Java, and Visual Basic. For the past three years Jim has been writing most web apps with C# and currently specializes in scalable web application development using ASP.NET 2.0, SQL Server 2005, C#, AJAX, and Team Foundation Server.

When not glued to the computer, Jim likes to play with his wife and children at the beach in Tampa, Florida and play guitar every once in a while.

Credits

Executive Editor
Robert Elliott

Development Editor
John Sleeva

Technical Editor
Ryan Trudelle-Schwartz

Production Editor
Eric Charbonneau

Copy Editor
Kim Cofer

Editorial Manager
Mary Beth Wakefield

Production Manager
Tim Tate

Vice President and Executive Group Publisher
Richard Swadley

Vice President and Executive Publisher
Joseph B. Wikert

Compositor
Laurie Stewart, Happenstance Type-O-Rama

Proofreader
Nancy Hanger

Indexer
Johnna VanHoose Dinse

Anniversary Logo Design
Richard Pacifico

Acknowledgments

I am always amazed at the path to get a book published. As the acronym AJAX started to grow in 2005, I started to think that it would be a good topic for a book. After Scott Guthrie posted a blog entry on June 28, 2005 announcing Microsoft "Atlas" to the world, we started talking with Bob Elliott of Wiley about AJAX and Atlas. Due to the newness of AJAX and projected shipment dates of Atlas, we worked on *Beginning Ajax with ASP.NET*, which discussed how to use AJAX with ASP.NET in general. Even in the early stage of the Atlas technology, that book contained more than 100 pages on the technology. From there we have expanded our coverage to create a full book on ASP.NET AJAX.

We thank Bob Elliott for keeping us focused on what was going on and working with us to develop this book. Our thanks also go out to the editorial staff at Wiley. Their help keeping us on track as "life happened" was appreciated. The work of our technical editor, Ryan Trudelle-Schwartz, was impressive, and his attention to detail was great. Many other people behind the scenes have worked hard on the book. By pulling this group together, Wiley created a team that was dedicated to creating the best possible book on ASP.NET AJAX. For that, we are truly appreciative.

— *Wallace B. McClure and the author team*

Contents

Contents

Contents

Contents

Introduction

Thank you for purchasing *Beginning ASP.NET 2.0 AJAX*. We know that you have a lot of options when selecting a programming book and are glad that you have chosen ours. We're sure you will be pleased with the relevant content and high quality you have come to expect from the Wrox line of books.

The ASP.NET 2.0 AJAX framework is a set of web browser–based technologies that will revolutionize the way web-based applications are designed. It revolutionizes the way applications are used, provides users a responsive application, and provides developers with the alternatives in building their applications. We look at the ASP.NET 2.0 AJAX framework and see a browser-based .NET framework that integrates the ASP.NET server-side programming methodology and provides client-side services at the same time. We believe that this book will meet your needs regarding programming ASP.NET 2.0 AJAX framework on the ASP.NET platform.

Whom This Book Is For

People interested in this book will be developers that are working in the ASP.NET environment and are looking to create a more responsive and modern application using AJAX technologies that are very similar to existing desktop methodologies. Developers that are looking to improve the user experience of their existing applications, develop new applications, develop internal line-of-business applications, and those that want to bulk up with the latest technology that developers all over the world are talking about will find what they are looking for here.

This book is for programmers who use ASP.NET and are starting to use ASP.NET 2.0 AJAX framework technologies. This book will assist developers working on ASP.NET-based applications that want to improve their applications and skills by providing a background in the ASP.NET 2.0 AJAX framework for them and then delving into how to apply the ASP.NET 2.0 AJAX framework to their applications.

What This Book Covers

This is a book for those who are new to the ASP.NET 2.0 AJAX framework. You know and understand ASP.NET, however, you may or may not have much experience with any AJAX frameworks. There are two major parts of the book: the printed book and the online content.

We feel that the printed book needs to work all of the time. You as a user want to purchase the book and have the code work the first day the book is out as well as 18 months after the book is released. Our decision is to only place code within the book that is guaranteed to run as long as possible. As a result, the printed book is divided into the following sections:

❏   Architecture of the ASP.NET 2.0 AJAX framework.

❏   How to add the ASP.NET 2.0 AJAX framework to an existing application.

❑ Basic use of the Microsoft AJAX framework. In this section, you look at how to perform basic AJAX-style operations with web services, using the UpdatePanel, the AJAX Control Toolkit, and other features that are new to developers new to the ASP.NET 2.0 AJAX framework.

❑ Advanced use of the Microsoft AJAX framework. This section includes security, integration with the ASP.NET Services, and debugging.

What about those developers that want to use some of the features of the ASP.NET 2.0 AJAX framework that are included in the CTP? You are not out of luck. The authors feel that including material that is not guaranteed to run in 12 months is not appropriate. At the same time, there is a desire to cover that material and many developers want to learn about these features. As a result, we are going to include some online content. This online content will include the material on the following:

❑ XML-Script

❑ Client-side data binding

❑ Drag and drop

❑ Bridging

In addition to having the online content, it is our goal to keep the content updated based on updates to the product.

How This Book Is Structured

This book is divided into the following chapters:

❑ Chapter 1, "Introduction to ASP.NET AJAX" — What is the ASP.NET 2.0 AJAX framework? The ASP.NET 2.0 AJAX framework is explained from the standpoint of what the product is, what is happening in the industry, and how this book is organized.

❑ Chapter 2, "Creating an ASP.NET AJAX Application" — This chapter discusses how to create an ASP.NET AJAX application and how to add ASP.NET AJAX to an existing application.

❑ Chapter 3, "ASP.NET AJAX Architecture" — This chapter looks at how the features of the ASP.NET AJAX framework work together.

❑ Chapter 4, "Calling Web Services" — Calling logic on the web server without posting back to a web server is the heart and soul of what the ASP.NET AJAX framework provides. This chapter explains how to set up a web service, call a web service, what the proxy looks like at the client, the calling sequence at the client, and sending the data back and forth.

❑ Chapter 5, "The UpdatePanel" — The UpdatePanel control provides an easy mechanism to integrate AJAX with ASP.NET server controls and the page life cycle. This control allows AJAX functionality to be added to an application without the need to radically change an application. The UpdatePanel provides easy AJAX functionality with applications while providing the server-side programming model that ASP.NET developers are familiar with.

❑ Chapter 6, "Control Toolkit" — Although the ASP.NET AJAX framework contains a set of graphical user interface controls in the box, there are a secondary set of controls. These are included in a separate download but are considered to be a companion part of ASP.NET AJAX. As a result, there will be a demand in knowing how to use them.

❑ Chapter 7, "Control Extenders" — Control extenders are used to add (extend) the functionality of server-side controls when running on the client web browser. This allows developers to add functionality to client-side controls and integrate with server-side data.

❑ Chapter 8, "JavaScript Enhancements" — When doing any significant programming with ASP.NET AJAX, it is important to have an understanding of the JavaScript language and the new features that ASP.NET AJAX provides to JavaScript programmers.

❑ Chapter 9, "Microsoft AJAX Library" — ASP.NET AJAX provides a set of objects that build on top of the existing JavaScript objects and extensions provided with the ASP.NET AJAX framework. These objects provide support similar to many of the features in the .NET framework. Two things that come to mind are the event calling mechanism and the low-level http calling sequence.

❑ Chapter 10, "User Interface Design" — ASP.NET AJAX makes calls asynchronously. Because a user can continue to work while an ASP.NET AJAX operation is happening, it is important to provide feedback to the user that something is happening. This chapter looks at several strategies for providing the user with feedback that something is happening.

❑ Chapter 11, "Security and Integration" — Security is on everyone's mind. ASP.NET has a set of services (Profile, membership, authentication). Working with these services and using the ASP.NET 2.0 AJAX framework securely is examined.

❑ Chapter 12, "Debugging" — No code is perfect. The ability to figure out what is going on and removing bugs is critical to all developers.

❑ Chapter 13, "ASP.NET AJAX Futures CTP: Online Content" — This chapter provides a brief description of what you'll find online.

What You Need to Use This Book

To run the examples in this book, you will need the following items:

❑ Visual Studio .NET 2005 or the free Visual Web Developer

❑ Windows Vista, Windows XP, or Windows 2003 Server

❑ A modern web browser, such as the latest version of Internet Explorer, Mozilla Firefox, or Apple's Safari.

❑ ASP.NET 2.0 AJAX framework add-ins — For information regarding the add-ins and getting copies, check out http://ajax.asp.net/

The samples that you will see are written with the following guidelines:

❑ All server-side code is written in C#.

❑ All client-side code is written in JavaScript.

❑ All ASP.NET examples are loadable in the Visual Web Developer for .NET 2.0.

Conventions

To help you get the most from the text and keep track of what's happening, we've used a number of conventions throughout the book.

Try It Out

The *Try It Out* is an exercise you should work through, following the text in the book.

1. They usually consist of a set of steps.

2. Each step has a number.

3. Follow the steps through with your copy of the database.

How It Works

After each *Try It Out*, the code you've typed will be explained in detail.

> **Boxes like this one hold important, not-to-be forgotten information that is directly relevant to the surrounding text.**

Tips, hints, tricks, and asides to the current discussion are offset and placed in italics like this.

As for styles in the text:

❑ We *highlight* new terms and important words when we introduce them.

❑ We show keyboard strokes like this: Ctrl+A.

❑ We show filenames, URLs, and code within the text like so: `persistence.properties`.

❑ We present code in two different ways:

```
In code examples we highlight new and important code with a gray background.
The gray highlighting is not used for code that's less important in the present
context, or has been shown before.
```

Source Code

As you work through the examples in this book, you may choose either to type in all the code manually or to use the source code files that accompany the book. All of the source code used in this book is available for download at `http://www.wrox.com`. Once at the site, simply locate the book's title (either by using the Search box or by using one of the title lists) and click the Download Code link on the book's detail page to obtain all the source code for the book.

Because many books have similar titles, you may find it easiest to search by ISBN; this book's ISBN is 978-0-470-1-1283-0.

Once you download the code, just decompress it with your favorite compression tool. Alternatively, you can go to the main Wrox code download page at `http://www.wrox.com/dynamic/books/download .aspx` to see the code available for this book and all other Wrox books.

Errata

We make every effort to ensure that there are no errors in the text or in the code. However, no one is perfect, and mistakes do occur. If you find an error in one of our books, like a spelling mistake or faulty piece of code, we would be very grateful for your feedback. By sending in errata you may save another reader hours of frustration and at the same time you will be helping us provide even higher quality information.

To find the errata page for this book, go to `http://www.wrox.com` and locate the title using the Search box or one of the title lists. Then, on the book details page, click the Book Errata link. On this page you can view all errata that has been submitted for this book and posted by Wrox editors. A complete book list including links to each book's errata is also available at `www.wrox.com/misc-pages/booklist.shtml`.

If you don't spot "your" error on the Book Errata page, go to `www.wrox.com/contact/techsupport .shtml` and complete the form there to send us the error you have found. We'll check the information and, if appropriate, post a message to the book's errata page and fix the problem in subsequent editions of the book.

p2p.wrox.com

For author and peer discussion, join the P2P forums at `p2p.wrox.com`. The forums are a web-based system for you to post messages relating to Wrox books and related technologies and interact with other readers and technology users. The forums offer a subscription feature to e-mail you topics of interest of your choosing when new posts are made to the forums. Wrox authors, editors, other industry experts, and your fellow readers are present on these forums.

At `http://p2p.wrox.com` you will find a number of different forums that will help you not only as you read this book, but also as you develop your own applications. To join the forums, just follow these steps:

1. Go to `p2p.wrox.com` and click the Register link.
2. Read the terms of use and click Agree.
3. Complete the required information to join as well as any optional information you wish to provide and click Submit.
4. You will receive an e-mail with information describing how to verify your account and complete the joining process.

You can read messages in the forums without joining P2P but in order to post your own messages, you must join.

Once you join, you can post new messages and respond to messages other users post. You can read messages at any time on the Web. If you would like to have new messages from a particular forum e-mailed to you, click the Subscribe to this Forum icon by the forum name in the forum listing.

For more information about how to use the Wrox P2P, be sure to read the P2P FAQs for answers to questions about how the forum software works as well as many common questions specific to P2P and Wrox books. To read the FAQs, click the FAQ link on any P2P page.

Beginning
ASP.NET 2.0 AJAX

Introduction to ASP.NET AJAX

Over the years, we developers have seen many changes in terms of how development occurs. We have gone from terminal-based programming to PC-based programming to Windows-based programming and to the Web. Now we are on the verge of another programming revolution — one that will bring about more interactive user interfaces to web applications. This programming revolution is brought to developers courtesy of a set of technologies that are generally known as AJAX (Asynchronous JavaScript And XML). No longer will users see the annoying flash with the clicking of a button to submit data. No longer will users lose the context of where they are located and be thrown back up to the top of a page. With AJAX, developers can build applications that step out of the traditional postback model of the Web, provide an improved user interface to users, and allow developers to develop applications that are much friendlier to use.

This chapter looks at the following:

- ❑ ASP.NET development and how it led to AJAX
- ❑ What AJAX is and a high-level overview of some of its base technologies
- ❑ The advantages of AJAX
- ❑ What ASP.NET AJAX is
- ❑ Some things that it might not make sense to do with AJAX

Development Trends

If you have been developing for a while, like us old guys, you have gone through several iterations of development — from terminals connected to mainframes and mini-computers to personal computers and then to client-server development. Client-server development allowed for the minimization of back-end resources, network resources, and the front-end PC by sending only the necessary data between back end and front end. Intelligent client-server development allowed for building applications that were responsive to the user and made efficient use of network and back-end resources. As the web development methodology took off in the late 1990s, we unfortunately returned to the terminal-style development. In this methodology, any major operation between the client and server requires that all data be sent in what is called a *round trip*. With a round trip, all data from the form is sent from the client to the web server. The web server processes data and then sends it back to the client. The result of a round trip is that a lot of data is sent back and forth between the client and server. Given the circumstances, these operations may result in more data transfer and CPU utilization than a web application and server can really tolerate.

ASP.NET Development

ASP.NET is a set of web development technologies produced by Microsoft that is used to build dynamic web sites, web applications, and XML-based web applications. ASP.NET is a part of the .NET framework and allows for developers to build applications in multiple languages, such as Visual Basic .NET, JScript .NET, and C#.

Design Methodology

ASP.NET attempts to make the web development methodology like the GUI development methodology by allowing developers to build pages made up of controls similar to a GUI. Server controls in ASP.NET function similarly to GUI controls in other environments. Buttons, text boxes, labels, and datagrids have properties that can be modified and expose events that may be processed. The ASP.NET server controls know how to display their content in an HTML page just like GUI-based user controls know how to display themselves in their GUI environment. An added benefit of ASP.NET is that the properties and methods of the web server controls are similar, and in some cases the same as the comparable controls in the Windows GUI/Windows Forms environment.

Problems ASP.NET Solves

Microsoft has released various web application development methodologies since the shipment of IIS in Windows. Why do developers need ASP.NET? What problems does ASP.NET solve that the previous development methodologies did not solve?

Microsoft's first popular web development technology was the Internet Database Connector (IDC). The IDC methodology provided only database access; it did not provide access to any other resource programmatically. For example, there was no way to programmatically send email or do other non-database operations. Another issue was that it seemed to be somewhat different from the traditional programming languages that most developers were used to (Visual Basic and C++ being two popular ones). Along with this problem was the fact that the development experience was not very attractive within Microsoft FrontPage. Along with the development experience, IDC had no debugging experience worth mentioning. Overall, IDC was nothing more than a stopgap measure to get to an improved environment.

The next web development methodology from Microsoft was Active Server Pages (ASP). ASP was a scripting environment that allowed developers to work with a Visual Basic–like or JavaScript-type environment. Unfortunately, this type of environment came with several problems:

❑ **Prevalence of spaghetti code** — ASP code does not provide a structured development environment, often contributing to the creation of twisted and tangled "spaghetti code." ASP code is literally a file with some basic configuration information at the top of every page. Each page is executed from the top of the page to the bottom of the page. Although it is possible to use Component Object Model (COM) objects to eliminate some of the spaghetti code, this introduces more complexity in the form of another development tool.

❏ **Lack of code separation** — The code tends to be intermixed with display code. Intermixing the code and the display logic requires that the tools developers and designers use work well together. This was often not the case. For example, it was well known that various visual development tools could take a properly running ASP page, rearrange some of the code, and render the ASP page broken.

❏ **Lack of code reusability** — There is very little ability to reuse code within the ASP environment. Code reusability in classic ASP is a function of providing logic in the form of COM objects, as opposed to something within the ASP environment.

❏ **Lack of debugging support** — Debugging an ASP application typically involves the use of `Response.Write`. This is in sharp contrast to an integrated development environment (IDE) developed within a GUI environment.

❏ **Problems of COM** — ASP is based on the Component Object Model and suffers from many of the problems associated with COM. There were two major problems with COM:

  ❏ The first was that updating COM objects tended to overwrite one object with the new one. This could be problematic if a programming method call changed or any other new behavior was introduced.

  ❏ The second major problem with COM was that it was a binary standard. This binary standard was based on a 32-bit programming model. As a result, COM objects would not scale up to run natively within an environment that was an Intel-based, 64-bit environment. Although this might not have been a big deal in the early to middle 1990s when COM was designed and built, by the early 2000s and the introduction of inexpensive 64-bit systems, this was seen as a possible bottleneck.

❏ **Problems with being interpreted** — ASP is interpreted. Each time an ASP file is loaded, the ASP environment parses the ASP file, compiles the code, and then executes the file. This process is repeated on each call to an ASP file. The result is wasted processing on the server.

❏ **Presence of the state machine** — ASP applications typically have a state machine at the top of every ASP page that processes the state of the user and then displays code. (In software code, a state machine is a section of code that depends on both its direct inputs and inputs made during previous calls.) Given that most client-side applications are built based on events, which is a similar concept to a state machine, this is an unfamiliar way to develop for those not well versed in ASP.

After getting feedback from developers, Microsoft developed ASP.NET, which greatly simplifies the web development methodology:

❏ Developers no longer need to worry about processing state. With ASP.NET, actions are performed within a series of events that provide state machine-like functionality.

❏ With the use of a code-behind/beside model, code is separated from display. By separating code and display files, there is less of a chance of designer and developer tools interfering with each other.

❏ A single development tool may be used for building the application and business logic. By having a single integrated development suite, developers are able to more easily interact with the application logic. This results in more code reuse and fewer errors.

❏ With the Visual Studio 2005 IDE, ASP.NET supports many methods to debug and track a running ASP.NET application.

❏ Because ASP.NET is based on the common language runtime (CLR) and .NET, ASP.NET does not suffer from the versioning problems of COM. The .NET framework allows for multiple versions of components to be on a system without their interacting with each other.

❏ ASP.NET is compiled. The first time that a file is loaded, it is compiled and then processed. The compiled file is then saved into a temporary directory. Subsequent calls to the ASP.NET file are processed from the compiled file. The execution of the compiled file on requests is faster than the interpreted environment of classic ASP.

All in all, ASP.NET is a dramatic improvement over ASP and has become widely accepted in the development community.

So, What's the Problem?

Based on what you have just read regarding ASP.NET, it may sound really good to you. You may be asking yourself, "Why is there a need for something else? What's the problem?"

The truth is that ASP.NET has several issues that need to be addressed:

❏ **Round trips** — The server events in ASP.NET require round trips to the server to process these events. These round trips result in all form elements being sent between client and server as well as images and other data files being sent back to the client from the server. Though some web browsers will cache images, there can still be significant data transfer.

❏ **Speed/network data transfer** — Because of the ViewState hidden form element, the amount of data that is transferred during a postback is relatively large. The more data and controls on the page, the larger the ViewState will be and the more data that must be processed on the server and transmitted back to the client.

❏ **Waiting on the result** — When a user clicks a button or some other visual element that posts back data to the server, the user must wait for a full round trip to complete. This takes time when the processing is done on the server and all the data, including images and ViewState, are returned to the client. During that time, even if the user attempts to do something with the user interface, that action is not actually processed on the client.

❏ **User context** — Unless an application is able to properly use the SMARTNAVIGATION feature of ASP.NET, the user is redirected to the top of a page by default on a postback. Though there are ways around this issue, this is the default behavior.

❏ **Processing** — The number of server round trips, amount of data that is transferred, and the ViewState element's size result in processing on the server that is not really necessary.

Users typically do something, data is sent to the server, the web server processes it, and the result is finally sent to back to the user. While the server is processing the data, the user interface is "locked" so that additional operations don't happen until a result is returned to the user.

Improving the User Experience

Based on the preceding issues, several options are available for improving the user experience:

❑ **Java** — Java applets are cross-platform applications. While being used as a cross-platform mechanism to display data and improve the user experience, Java development on the client has not been accepted with open arms by the development community and is primarily used for user interface gee-whiz features as opposed to improving the experience of the user application. (As a side note, Java has been widely accepted for building server-side applications.)

❑ **XML-based languages** — XML User Interface Language (XUL) and Extensible Application Markup Language (XAML) are two of several languages that can provide an improved user experience. The problem with XUL is that it has been used only in the Mozilla/Firefox line of browsers. Silverlight (formerly WPF/e), an associated product, is an interpreter for a subset of XAML. Currently, there is support for Silverlight on Windows and the Apple Macintosh.

❑ **Flash** — Although Flash has been used and there are cross-platform versions, the product has been used only in the area of graphic UI needs and has not been accepted by the development community as a whole for building line of business applications. Recently, Adobe has released a pre-release version of an Internet technology referred to as Apollo. Apollo is a runtime that allows web skillsets to be used to develop rich desktop applications.

❑ **AJAX** — AJAX is a set of client technologies that provide for asynchronous communication between the user interface and the web server, along with fairly easy integration with existing technologies.

Given the amount of recent discussion among developers regarding AJAX, it appears that AJAX has the greatest chance among these technologies of gaining market acceptance.

Current Drivers

Interest in web-based development has grown over the past few years. With that interest, Microsoft has gone from classical ASP to ASP.NET development. ASP.NET development has grown to the point that it is the most popular development platform for web-based applications. Even with its popularity, it has to continually improve or it will get left in the dust of a more modern technology.

Over the past few years, building client-side web-based applications has grown in popularity. Users have liked the applications because of the increased client-side functionality, such as keeping a common user context during a "post" to the server and drag-and-drop features common to typical client applications. This functionality was popularized by several applications from Google, including Gmail, Google Suggest, and Google Maps.

In February 2005, this functionality got the name Asynchronous JavaScript And XML (AJAX) thanks to an essay by Jesse James Garrett. At about this time, several .NET libraries started to show up. These libraries hid many of the complexities of interfacing with web services and allowed developers to concentrate on the application as opposed to creating the plumbing to talk to the web services.

ASP.NET needs to add this functionality. The question becomes, how does one add client-side functionality to a development methodology that is mostly a server-side technology?

From a network standpoint, these applications are more efficient because they communicate back only the necessary pieces of information and get back only the necessary updates from the server. From a web server standpoint, these applications tend to use less CPU on the server. As a result, these types of applications are highly desirable.

What Is AJAX?

So into this development environment comes a set of technologies that are collectively referred to as AJAX. If you are an "old guy" developer like me, then AJAX represents a similar concept to the client-server development mentioned earlier in the chapter. With client-server development, the amount of data transferred is minimized over a terminal application by transferring only the necessary data back and forth. Similarly, with AJAX, only the necessary data is transferred back and forth between the client and the web server. This minimizes the network utilization and processing on the client.

Advantages of AJAX

The advantages of AJAX over classical web-based applications include:

❑ **Asynchronous calls** — AJAX allows for the ability to make asynchronous calls to a web server. This allows the client browser to avoid waiting for all data to arrive before allowing the user to act once more.

❑ **Minimal data transfer** — By not performing a full postback and sending all form data to the server, network utilization is minimized and quicker operations occur. In sites and locations with restricted pipes for data transfer, this can greatly improve network performance.

❑ **Limited processing on the server** — Along with the fact that only the necessary data is sent to the server, the server is not required to process all form elements. By sending only the necessary data, there is limited processing on the server. There is no need to process all form elements, process the ViewState, send images back to the client, or send a full page back to the client.

❑ **Responsiveness** — Because AJAX applications are asynchronous on the client, they are perceived to be very responsive.

❑ **Context** — With a full postback, users may lose the context of where they are. Users may be at the bottom of a page, hit the Submit button, and be redirected back to the top of the page. With AJAX there is no full postback. Clicking the Submit button in an application that uses AJAX will allow users to maintain their location. The user state is maintained, and the users are no longer required to scroll down to the location they were at before clicking Submit.

History of AJAX

For all its perceived newness and sexiness, the technologies that make up AJAX are really not new. The ability to communicate back to the server through a hidden frame without posting the main page back to the server has been around for a long time. Communication between client and server has been available — back to the release of Internet Explorer's ability to script ActiveX controls on the client browser and to the MSXML component, both of which date back into the late 1990s. Personally, I saw the first formal usage of client script and MSXML in 2003. The problem with the technology at that time was the need to manually create the necessary client-side JavaScript. In 2003, there was too much code overall that had to be written and too much custom code that had to be written to get this to work. Only since the second half of 2005 have client-side libraries and server-side support for ASP.NET started to make their presence felt and been used significantly.

The mainstream development community has only recently started using the technique. The release of Google's Suggest and Maps are what really opened the eyes of the users to the development technologies. These applications sent a shockwave through the development community.

Technologies That Make Up AJAX

AJAX is a general umbrella term. AJAX itself stands for Asynchronous JavaScript And XML. The term was coined by Jesse James Garret of Adaptive Path in an essay published in February 2005 (`http://www.adaptivepath.com/publications/essays/archives/000385.php`) and was quickly accepted by the development community.

Based on this general umbrella term, take a look at the specific items that make up AJAX:

❑ **XMLHttpRequest** — `XMLHttpRequest` allows the browser to communicate to a back-end server. This object allows for the browser to talk to the server without requiring a postback of the entire web page. With Internet Explorer 5 and 6, this capability is provided by the MSXML ActiveX component. With the Mozilla Firefox, IE 7, and other web browsers, this capability is provided by an object literally called `XmlHttpRequest`. The `XmlHttpRequest` object is modeled after the MSXML component and defined by the XMLHttpRequest standard from the W3C. The ASP.NET 2.0 AJAX client-side JavaScript libraries hide the differences between the various browsers.

❑ **JavaScript** — JavaScript provides the capability to communicate with the back-end server. The version of JavaScript must be version 1.5 or later. Though JavaScript is not specifically required, it is needed from the standpoint that JavaScript is the only client-side scripting environment supported across the major modern web browsers. There are other client script languages; however, these are not supported across all browsers.

❑ **DHTML/DOM support** — The browser must support the ability to dynamically update form elements, and the ability to do this in a standard way comes through the support for the Document Object Model (DOM). By supporting the DOM, it becomes easy for developers to write a single piece of code that targets multiple browsers.

❑ **Data transport with XML or JSON** — Using XML allows for the ability to communicate with the web server in a standard mechanism. The default data format with ASP.NET AJAX is JSON.

What Is ASP.NET 2.0 AJAX?

On June 28, 2005, Microsoft announced "ASP.NET 2.0 AJAX." ASP.NET 2.0 AJAX is an AJAX-oriented .NET library that runs on .NET 2.0. Though ASP.NET 2.0 AJAX is an AJAX library and can be used to perform AJAX operations, it is really much more. ASP.NET 2.0 AJAX offers many of the same types of features of the server-side ASP.NET, but it is directed at the client side. Because ASP.NET 2.0 AJAX is fully integrated with ASP.NET, it provides rich integration with the services provided by ASP.NET.

ASP.NET 2.0 AJAX provides the following features (and much more):

❑ AJAX-style communications between client and server. This communication is over web services.

❑ Asynchronous communication. All client-to-server communication in the ASP.NET 2.0 AJAX framework is asynchronous.

❑ A set of server-side controls that enable rich client-side functionality.

❑ A set of client-side controls and classes that further enable client-side functionality.

❑ A framework for encapsulating client-logic through the creation of namespaces and classes.

❑ Cross browser support. Although there is no official matrix of web browsers that ASP.NET 2.0 AJAX supports, the latest versions of Internet Explorer, Firefox, and Safari are supported. In addition, Opera is thought to be supported; however, we have not been able to find an official statement from Microsoft regarding this.

Running ASP.NET AJAX Applications

Unfortunately, not all web browsers ever produced will support ASP.NET AJAX. To run an ASP.NET AJAX application, a web browser must:

❑ **Be relatively modern** — ASP.NET AJAX applications are not available in all versions of all web browsers. Though Internet Explorer version 6 and later, Firefox version 1.5 and later, and Safari provide support for these applications, older versions may be problematic because of their support for different versions of the other requirements.

❑ **Support the DOM** — The capability to update form elements on a page based on new data is important. Accessing the controls in a standard way means that writing code that runs over a majority of web browsers is easier than having code that has a large number of if/then/else statements that are dependent on the browser version.

❑ **Support JavaScript** — ASP.NET AJAX requires some amount of actions to occur out on the client. These actions are done using the JavaScript programming language. Because the major web browsers support JavaScript, it makes sense for JavaScript to be used for the client-side programming language.

❑ **Possibly have ActiveX enabled on the client** — If you are using the Internet Explorer 6 browser while running on Windows, you may have problems if ActiveX is not enabled.

Who's Using AJAX?

Great, now that you have seen that there is this technology called AJAX, are you alone in not having seen or talked about this before? Absolutely not! AJAX has just recently taken off in the second half of 2005 from a mindshare standpoint. As discussions have gone on with counterparts in the development community, many developers are just now looking to what AJAX can do for their applications and ultimately their customers. So, just who is using AJAX publicly?

❑ **Google Suggest** — Google Suggest features a dynamic drop-down list box that provides possible items to search on along with the approximate number of search results.

- ❑ **Google Maps** — The ability to grab a map and zoom around without requiring a postback is just amazing. This app/service took the development world by storm when it came out.

- ❑ **Google Gmail** — Google Gmail is a web-based email system.

- ❑ **Live.com** — The local.live.com service from Microsoft is actively using the ASP.NET AJAX framework, as is nearly the entire Live.com service. Hotmail, the email service for Live.com, has updated its service and uses AJAX.

- ❑ **Outlook web access** — The web interface into Microsoft Exchange 2000 was one of the early AJAX applications.

- ❑ **Easy Search Component** — The ASP.NET Easy Search Component provides support for searching a single web site similar to the Google Suggest service.

- ❑ **Other component vendors** — Component vendors such as ComponentArt, Dart, and others are providing controls that provide a rich user experience without forcing a full postback.

To go along with the third-party interest, the amount of developer interest is tremendous. For example, one only has to put the word *AJAX* into a blog title to receive an increase in the number of web views. Based on the amount of third-party support and the interest of developers, it is only a matter of time before everyone is doing it.

Currently

At this time, the first version of the ASP.NET 2.0 AJAX framework is an add-on to the existing .NET 2.0. It runs on top of the framework with no changes to the underlying "bits."

ASP.NET 2.0 AJAX falls into four areas:

- ❑ **Server-side controls** — Server-side controls generate the appropriate client-side markup and script to perform client-side operations without the need for a postback. These controls provide a fairly easy environment to debug. For example, debugging with the UpdatePanel is fairly easy. Besides the UpdatePanel, other controls that work similarly are the ASP.NET AJAX Control Toolkit.

- ❑ **Client-side classes** — These classes provide additional functionality to the client-side browser. This type of functionality is similar in concept to the base class libraries included in the .NET framework. An example would be the whole Sys.Net namespace along with the extensions to the base JavaScript objects.

- ❑ **Web services integration** — This functionality allows a developer to use web services as the communication channel between the web browser and the web server without having to understand the differences between the MSXML component in IE and the XmlHttpRequest object in Firefox.

Packaging

The packaging of ASP.NET 2.0 AJAX can be fairly confusing. The basics of the packaging are:

- ❑ **ASP.NET 2.0 AJAX Extensions 1.0** — The ASP.NET 2.0 AJAX Extensions 1.0, also referred to as the RTM/Core code, is an independent download. This contains the functionality that will receive support from Microsoft in the initial release of the product. The source code is available.

❑ **ASP.NET AJAX Futures Community Technology Preview (CTP)** — The ASP.NET 2.0 AJAX framework contains a set of functionality that is experimental in nature. This functionality will eventually become integrated with the RTM/Core code. During the initial release, the Futures CTP functionality will be a separate download from the RTM/Core bits. This will not receive specific support from Microsoft beyond community-based support. The CTP bits require that the RTM/Core bits already be installed for the CTP bits to be installed. The CTP is also referred to as *Value-Added Bits*.

❑ **Microsoft AJAX Library** — The Microsoft AJAX Library is a set of JavaScript client libraries that make up the standard download to a web browser and provide much of the support for AJAX in the client. These libraries will work with a non-IIS server and are available as a separate download. This library is included in the ASP.NET 2.0 AJAX Extensions 1.0 download as well as being available as a separate download.

❑ **ASP.NET AJAX Control Toolkit** — The AJAX Control Toolkit is a separate download that provides a set of client-side GUI widgets that integrate with the ASP.NET 2.0 AJAX framework. The toolkit is licensed separately from the framework and includes the source code for developers who would like to review the source.

Futures

It has already been announced that ASP.NET 2.0 AJAX will be integrated into the .NET framework and Visual Studio in the Orcas versions of these products. Future versions will undoubtedly have more integration between ASP.NET 2.0 AJAX, ASP.NET, and Visual Studio.

Summary

AJAX provides developers a foundation to build web-based applications with an improved user experience. In this introductory chapter, you have looked at the following:

❑ Development from a historical perspective

❑ Web development methodologies

❑ Some of the features that ASP.NET AJAX provides, such as improved user responsiveness and decreased load on the web server

❑ Multiple technologies that can improve the user experience

❑ The general components in the ASP.NET 2.0 AJAX packaging

❑ The problems ASP.NET AJAX solves, and who is using it

The next chapter looks at creating an ASP.NET AJAX application.

Creating an ASP.NET AJAX Application

ASP.NET AJAX installs templates that make it quick and easy to create new web applications that leverage its features. In addition, it is fairly straightforward to update existing ASP.NET applications to allow them to support ASP.NET AJAX controls and functionality. The biggest challenge in setting up an application to use ASP.NET AJAX involves adding a number of settings to the web.config file. In the case of a new application, project templates are installed with the ASP.NET AJAX installation to make this task easy. For existing applications, follow the steps in this chapter to ensure they are properly configured to take advantage of ASP.NET AJAX's features.

In this chapter, you learn about the following:

❑ Installing ASP.NET AJAX

❑ Creating an ASP.NET AJAX application

❑ Adding ASP.NET AJAX to an existing ASP.NET application

Installing ASP.NET AJAX

Before you can start using ASP.NET AJAX, you need to install it. You can find the latest installation at the official Microsoft ASP.NET AJAX web site, http://ajax.asp.net/. From there, click the Download link. You may also wish to download the latest ASP.NET AJAX Control Toolkit and ASP.NET 2.0 AJAX Futures CTP, because these provide additional features beyond the ASP.NET AJAX core installation.

After you have downloaded the installation files for ASP.NET AJAX, run the installer (ASPAJAXExtSetup.msi). You should see the installation wizard with an initial screen (similar to Figure 2-1).

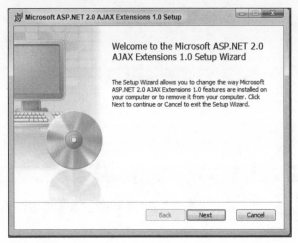

Figure 2-1

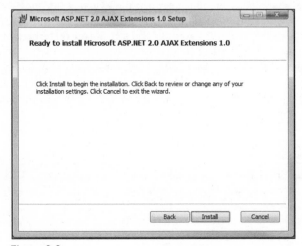

Figure 2-2

After accepting the End User License Agreement, click the Install button, as shown in Figure 2-2.

Wait for the installer to complete, which should take just a few minutes. When it has completed, you should see a screen confirming that the installation was successful. You may wish to read the Release Notes at this time; if so, just leave the Display Microsoft ASP.NET 2.0 AJAX Extensions 1.0 Release Notes check box checked. Click the Finish button to complete the setup process.

The installation process installs ASP.NET AJAX in the Global Assembly Cache (GAC) of the computer. In most environments, the ASP.NET AJAX assembly (System.Web.Extensions.dll) should not be included in the /bin folder of your web site, but rather ASP.NET AJAX should be installed for the entire server.

You can find additional installation documentation at `http://ajax.asp.net/docs/InstallingASPNETAJAX.aspx`.

Creating an ASP.NET AJAX Application

Creating a new ASP.NET AJAX-enabled web site can be done with Visual Studio using the templates that were installed with ASP.NET AJAX. If you installed Web Application Projects or Visual Studio 2005 SP1, you have two options for creating an AJAX-enabled web application: web site or web application.

Try It Out   **Creating a New ASP.NET AJAX Web Site**

To create a new ASP.NET AJAX web site, open Visual Studio and follow these steps:

1. Choose New Web Site from the File menu. The New Web Site dialog box is displayed, as shown in Figure 2-3.

2. Select ASP.NET AJAX-Enabled Web Site from under the Visual Studio Installed Templates section. This creates a basic web site with the necessary configuration files. Verify the programming language for the site and that the web site will be created in the folder where you would like it, and click OK.

3. Alternatively, if you prefer to use the Web Application Project structure for your web application, you may do so using a similar project template. Simply open Visual Studio and choose New Project from the File menu. When the New Project dialog box is displayed, as shown in Figure 2-4, select ASP.NET AJAX-Enabled Web Application from under the Visual Studio Installed Templates section.

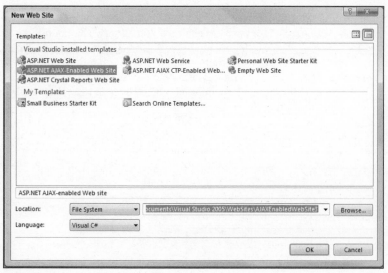

Figure 2-3

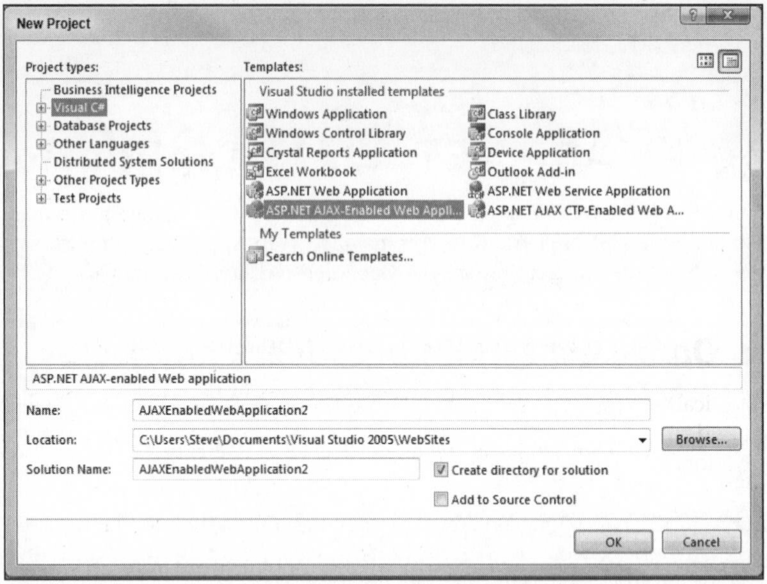

Figure 2-4

How It Works

Regardless of whether you choose to structure your web site as a Visual Studio Web Site or as a Visual Studio Web Application Project, the rest of the steps involved in getting started with ASP.NET AJAX are the same. The rest of the walkthrough in this section uses a web site. Figure 2-5 shows the initial files created when a new web site called BeginningASPNETAJAX is created.

When the project opens, `Default.aspx` is open in the IDE. Notice that it includes the `<asp:ScriptManager ID="ScriptManager1" runat="server" />` control automatically. This control is described in Chapter 3, and is required for ASP.NET AJAX functionality to work correctly on an ASP.NET page. This is one key difference between the ASP.NET AJAX web site template and the standard ASP.NET web site template. The other difference is the `web.config` file that is included with the project automatically. If you open the `web.config` file, you will find that it includes about 100 lines of text. The details of these configuration settings are covered in Chapter 3.

Once ASP.NET AJAX is successfully installed, you should see a new addition to your Toolbox in Visual Studio. This new section is called AJAX Extensions and includes several new controls, as shown in Figure 2-6.

Figure 2-5

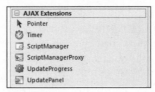

Figure 2-6

Creating a Database to Manage Users and Roles

The sample application you are creating manages some data in a sample database used by ASP.NET to manage users and roles. This database, called ASPNETDB.MDF, can be created using the ASP.NET Web Site Administration Tool.

Try It Out   Creating a Sample Database

To create the ASPNETDB.MDF database, perform the following steps:

1. Access the ASP.NET Web Site Administration Tool by clicking the ASP.NET Configuration icon at the top of Solution Explorer (on the far right). It is available as an option only when your ASP.NET web site is the active item in the solution (which shouldn't be an issue if you only have the one web site open).

2. A new web application is launched. Your browser should launch to show you the ASP.NET Web Site Administration Tool, as shown in Figure 2-7.

Figure 2-7

3. In the browser, click Security. This copies a fresh version of ASPNETDB.MDF to your application's App_Data folder. (The process might take a few moments.) You can confirm that the database was created by refreshing the web site in Solution Explorer (click the refresh icon). You should see the ASPNETDB.MDF file in the App_Data folder. For this application, you need some sample data, so you're going to enable roles and then add several roles.

4. Click Enable Roles, and then Create or Manage Roles. Next, add roles for Developers, Managers, and Administrators. When you've finished, you should see a screen similar to the one in Figure 2-8.

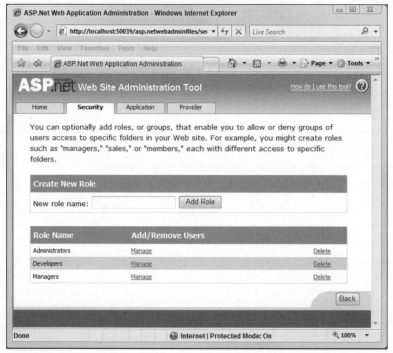

Figure 2-8

Creating a Data Access Layer

Now you're ready to build an application that uses ASP.NET AJAX capabilities to manage data. In accordance with best practices, you connect to the database using a data access layer that you create by means of a DataSet. As you try out the following steps, you will first open the table in the database and view the data to confirm it is what you expect, and then you'll create a DataSet with a TableAdapter to access the data in your application.

Try It Out   Creating a Data Access Layer

To create a data access layer, perform the following steps:

1. Double-click `ASPNETDB.MDF` in the Solution Explorer (recall that it is in the `App_Data` folder; refresh the folder if necessary). This connects to the database in your Server Explorer.

2. In the tree view, expand Tables and then expand aspnet_Roles. Right-click aspnet_Roles and select Show Table Data. You should see three rows of data, with the column RoleName containing the names of the three roles you just added using the Web Site Administration Tool.

3. Close the window showing the aspnet_Roles table contents. Next you add a DataSet to your web site to manage talking to the database.

4. Right-click the web site name in Solution Explorer and select Add New Item. Choose DataSet and name it **Roles.xsd**. If you are prompted to create an `App_Code` folder, click Yes. When the `Roles.xsd` file has been added to the project, a TableAdapter Configuration Wizard appears.

5. The first step is to choose your data connection. This should default to `ASPNETDB.MDF`, which is fine. Click Next.

6. The next step prompts you to save the connection string, with a name defaulting to `ASPNETDBConnectionString`. Click Next.

7. The third step allows you to choose a command type, with the default being Use SQL Statements. Click Next. Now enter the following SQL statement:

```
SELECT * FROM aspnet_Roles
```

8. Click Next, click Finish, and save the `Roles.xsd` file.

9. You now have a TableAdapter for the aspnet_Roles table that you can use to manipulate the data in the table. Before saving the file, there is one more change that must be made to allow editing to work properly. Right-click the aspnet_RolesTableAdapter and select Properties. In the Properties box, expand the `UpdateCommand` property and edit the `CommandText` so that it matches the following:

```
UPDATE      aspnet_Roles
SET             RoleId = @RoleId, RoleName = @RoleName, Description = @Description
WHERE      (ApplicationId = @Original_ApplicationId) AND (LoweredRoleName =
@Original_LoweredRoleName)
```

10. Next, open the `UpdateCommand`'s Parameters collection and Remove the `@ApplicationId` and `@LoweredRoleName` parameters. When you are finished, the Parameters collection should include `@RoleId`, `@RoleName`, `@Description`, `@Original_ApplicationId`, and `@Original_LoweredRoleName`.

11. Save the file, which should look similar to Figure 2-9.

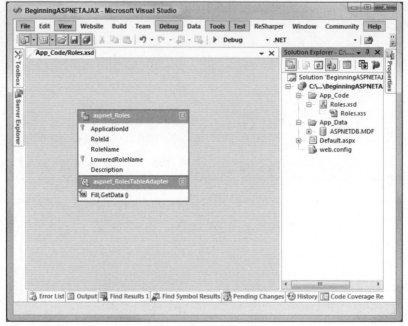

Figure 2-9

Building a Roles Manager Page

Next you build a simple Roles Manager page. A typical non-AJAX ASP.NET page uses frequent post-backs to make updates to the server. Your page will take advantage of ASP.NET AJAX functionality to eliminate postbacks, resulting in a less jarring and more responsive user experience.

Try It Out　　**Building a Roles Manager Page**

To create a Roles Manager page, perform the following steps:

1. To begin, open `Default.aspx`. Switch to Design view if it is not already there. Drag a `GridView` control from the Visual Studio Toolbox onto the page.

2. From its Tasks Smart Tag, select the Choose Data Source option, and choose <New Data Source>. The Data Source Configuration Wizard is displayed. From here, choose Object as the type of Data Source, and specify the ID for the data source as RolesDataSource, as shown in Figure 2-10.

3. Click OK and select RolesTableAdapters.aspnet_RolesTableAdapter from the drop-down list on the next page of the wizard. Click Next.

4. On the next page, Define Data Methods, leave everything as the default and click Finish. The wizard closes, and the `GridView` is now shown with the appropriate columns from the aspnet_Roles table. In the GridView Tasks Smart Tag, select the Enable Sorting and Enable Editing check boxes, and press Ctrl+F5 to launch the page in your browser.

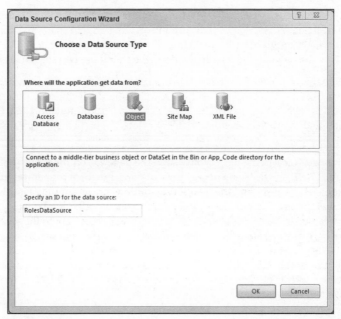

Figure 2-10

5. You should be able to click Edit for any given row, apply changes, and select Update to see those changes made to the database. The page should also support bidirectional sorting via clicking on each column's header text. The page is functional, but it does not include any AJAX functionality. I include the server time on the page by adding `<%= DateTime.Now.ToLongTimeString() %>` to the top of the page (just after `<body>`).

6. You can see that the time updates on every request. Figure 2-11 shows how the page should look after these steps have been completed.

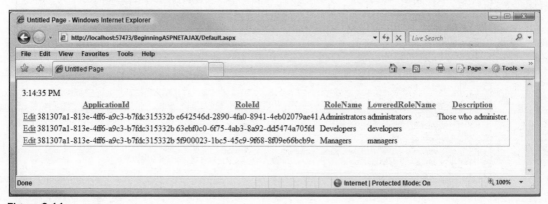

Figure 2-11

7. To enable this page to perform its functions without reloading the entire page on every request, you use the ASP.NET AJAX `UpdatePanel` control. Drag an `UpdatePanel` control from the Toolbox onto the page's design surface. Next, drag the `GridView` control into the `UpdatePanel`. Figure 2-12 shows how the page should look in the designer after these two steps have been completed.

8. Save the page and view it in the browser once again (Ctrl+F5, or right-click and choose View in Browser). Sort the columns and edit the rows (using the techniques described in step 5), noting the time displayed at the top of the page. The page should function just as it did before, with the exception that the time does not update, nor does the page flicker or reload.

By adding an `UpdatePanel` to the page, you enable the page to communicate with the web server asynchronously via ASP.NET AJAX. There are a variety of ways in which asynchronous communication can occur between the web browser and the web server, but few are as simple to implement as the ASP.NET AJAX `UpdatePanel` control. The `UpdatePanel` works together with the `ScriptManager` control to detect when controls contained in the `UpdatePanel` are attempting to post back to the server. The `ScriptManager` control, when partial-page updates are enabled (the default), will communicate with the server and return updated content to any `UpdatePanels` on the page that are marked to be updated. The web server, in this scenario, returns only the contents of the `UpdatePanels` that need to be updated, not the entire page. Thus, it is best to limit the contents of `UpdatePanels` to those controls that need to be dynamically updated in response to server communication.

You can disable partial-page update support by setting the `EnablePartialRendering` property of the `ScriptManager` control to `false`.

Most users are accustomed to some web-based user interface behaviors, such as page flicker or browser update animations. Thus, they may not notice that the application has responded without these familiar cues. Another important control that ships with ASP.NET AJAX is the `UpdateProgress` control.

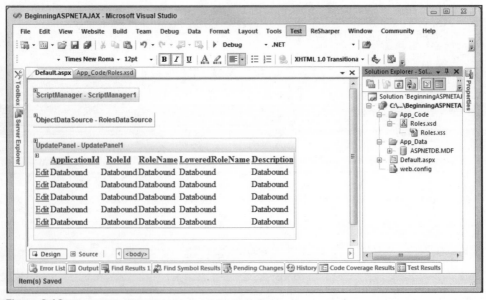

Figure 2-12

Adding an UpdateProgress Control

The `UpdateProgress` control provides users with an indication that server communication is taking place even though the browser is not refreshing the page.

Adding an UpdateProgress Control

Perform the following steps to add an `UpdateProgress` control to the page:

1. Drag the `UpdateProgess` control from the Toolbox and place it directly above the `GridView`.

2. Inside the `UpdateProgess` control, type **Updating…**. This is the text that will be displayed when an update is occurring.

3. Each `UpdateProgess` control is typically associated with an `UpdatePanel`. (If no `UpdatePanel` is associated, the `UpdateProgess` control will be shown when *any* `UpdatePanel` updates.) To do so, open the `UpdateProgess` control's properties, and choose UpdatePanel1 (or whatever ID you provided for the `UpdatePanel` added previously) for its `AssociatedUpdatePanelID` property.

4. If you view the page in the browser at this point, you most likely will not notice any difference in its behavior. This is because the page and the server are responding too quickly for the `UpdateProgress` control to be displayed. To introduce some latency to the application, simulating a real-world scenario in which the user and the web server are not using the same hardware, add the following line to the `Page_Load` method in `Default.aspx.cs`:

    ```
    System.Threading.Thread.Sleep(1000);
    ```

    This causes the page to sleep for one second before rendering.

    Obviously, you do not want to include this in production code; this is only to simulate real-world response times!

5. View the page in the browser and you should notice the `Updating...` text appear briefly as you complete each sorting or editing operation.

6. In addition to text, it is also common practice to use an animated graphic for the `UpdateProgress` control. You can find many common and freely usable images for this purpose at `http://ajaxload.info/`. I recommend saving the image locally to ensure it doesn't disappear, to improve your site's performance, and as proper netiquette. In the following code, I have downloaded the image used from `http://ajaxload.info` and saved it locally.

7. Add one of these images to the `UpdateProgress` control, as follows:

    ```
    <asp:UpdateProgress ID="UpdateProgress1" runat="server"
    AssociatedUpdatePanelID="UpdatePanel1">
        <ProgressTemplate>
            Updating...<img src="5-1.gif" />
        </ProgressTemplate>
    </asp:UpdateProgress>
    ```

How It Works

The UpdateProgress control uses client-side script to hook into the associated UpdatePanel control (or all UpdatePanel controls and their triggers). When an update is fired, the contents of the ProgressTemplate are made visible. Likewise, when the update has completed, the ProgressTemplate is hidden once again. This provides a very easy way to notify users that an update is taking place without the usual browser flicker behavior that defines most non-AJAX web applications.

The page now clearly indicates to the user when server-side activity is taking place, while remaining very responsive. Figure 2-13 illustrates the page during an update, showing the UpdateProgress control in action.

Figure 2-13

This page now uses the ScriptManager, UpdatePanel, and UpdateProgress controls that ship with ASP.NET AJAX 1.0. The only other controls included in this release are the Timer and ScriptManagerProxy controls, which are covered in later chapters. In addition to these controls, many others are included in the CTP releases of ASP.NET AJAX, and in the AJAX Control Toolkit. Some of these other controls are shown later in this chapter as AJAX functionality is added to an existing web site, and others are shown later in the book.

Adding ASP.NET AJAX to an Existing ASP.NET Application

ASP.NET AJAX provides an easy starting point for users in the form of web site and web application templates for Visual Studio. However, most organizations already have existing web applications to which they would like to add AJAX functionality, and in most cases starting over with a new project type is not an ideal solution. For these cases, the solution is to add ASP.NET AJAX functionality to the site. Initial setup is the same as for a new application — install ASP.NET AJAX using the instructions given earlier in this chapter. Once installed, open Visual Studio and load the web project to which you wish to add ASP.NET AJAX functionality.

To demonstrate this process in this chapter, you use an existing application that is freely available and simulates a real-world application. The PayPal eCommerce Starter Kit (also known simply as the Commerce Starter Kit) is available from the `www.asp.net` web site at `asp.net/downloads/starterkits/PaypalEcommerce.aspx`. If you wish to follow along with the rest of this chapter, download and install the PayPal eCommerce Starter Kit (also available from the book's web site).

Once the starter kit is installed, you can create the PayPal eCommerce web site by opening Visual Studio and choosing a New Web Site. Under My Templates, select Commerce Starter Kit 2, as shown in Figure 2-14. Choose a location in IIS where you would like the starter kit to be installed (it has dependencies on IIS and would not run for me using a file system–based web site) and click OK.

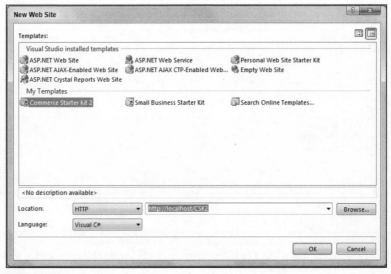

Figure 2-14

Once you click OK, the starter kit is unzipped into the folder you specified and opens up with a web site project. You must complete the starter kit installation by running the web site. View `Default.aspx` in your web browser, and specify the location of your database. Once the install is complete, restart the application and view `Default.aspx` once more, and you should see the home page as shown in Figure 2-15.

If you are unfamiliar with the application, browse through it. There are several areas of the application that could benefit from additional AJAX functionality (it has some already, including for ratings), such as shopping cart management and search. You will focus on adding AJAX functionality to this area of the site, once you have configured the web site to support ASP.NET AJAX.

Figure 2-15

Try It Out   **Configuring the Web.Config File to Support ASP.NET AJAX**

In Visual Studio, find the `web.config` file in the Solution Explorer and open it. You can find the modifications required to enable this application to support ASP.NET AJAX in the sample `web.config` file provided when ASP.NET AJAX was installed — by default at `C:\Program Files\Microsoft ASP.NET\ASP.NET 2.0 AJAX Extensions\v1.0.61025`.

Seven sections of the `web.config` must be updated to support ASP.NET AJAX. It is often easiest to copy and paste these sections from the sample `web.config` provided at the path shown previously. You are simply updating the file without examining the functionality of these changes. (These are explained further in Chapter 3.)

1.   The first modification is to the `<configSections>` element, which defines additional configuration sections needed by ASP.NET AJAX. If your application already has a `<configSections>` element, you should simply add the `<sectionGroup>` elements to your existing `<configSections>` element. The complete `<configSections>` element required for ASP.NET AJAX is shown in the following code:

```
<configSections>
  <sectionGroup name="system.web.extensions"
type="System.Web.Configuration.SystemWebExtensionsSectionGroup,
System.Web.Extensions, Version=1.0.61025.0, Culture=neutral,
PublicKeyToken=31bf3856ad364e35">
    <sectionGroup name="scripting"
type="System.Web.Configuration.ScriptingSectionGroup, System.Web.Extensions,
Version=1.0.61025.0, Culture=neutral, PublicKeyToken=31bf3856ad364e35">
      <section name="scriptResourceHandler"
type="System.Web.Configuration.ScriptingScriptResourceHandlerSection,
System.Web.Extensions, Version=1.0.61025.0, Culture=neutral,
PublicKeyToken=31bf3856ad364e35" requirePermission="false"
allowDefinition="MachineToApplication"/>
      <sectionGroup name="webServices"
type="System.Web.Configuration.ScriptingWebServicesSectionGroup,
System.Web.Extensions, Version=1.0.61025.0, Culture=neutral,
PublicKeyToken=31bf3856ad364e35">
        <section name="jsonSerialization"
type="System.Web.Configuration.ScriptingJsonSerializationSection,
System.Web.Extensions, Version=1.0.61025.0, Culture=neutral,
PublicKeyToken=31bf3856ad364e35" requirePermission="false"
allowDefinition="Everywhere" />
        <section name="profileService"
type="System.Web.Configuration.ScriptingProfileServiceSection,
System.Web.Extensions, Version=1.0.61025.0, Culture=neutral,
PublicKeyToken=31bf3856ad364e35" requirePermission="false"
allowDefinition="MachineToApplication" />
        <section name="authenticationService"
type="System.Web.Configuration.ScriptingAuthenticationServiceSection,
System.Web.Extensions, Version=1.0.61025.0, Culture=neutral,
PublicKeyToken=31bf3856ad364e35" requirePermission="false"
allowDefinition="MachineToApplication" />
      </sectionGroup>
    </sectionGroup>
  </sectionGroup>
</configSections>
```

2. The `<controls>` element within `<pages>` within `<system.web>` must be updated to map the asp prefix to the `System.Web.Extensions` assembly, which houses the ASP.NET AJAX controls. If your `web.config` file already includes any of these elements, you need only add the child elements. It is important not to duplicate any of the elements. The following code shows the complete `<pages>` element (which again would reside within the `<system.web>` element):

```
<pages>
  <controls>
    <add tagPrefix="asp" namespace="System.Web.UI" assembly="System.Web.Extensions,
Version=1.0.61025.0, Culture=neutral, PublicKeyToken=31bf3856ad364e35"/>
  </controls>
</pages>
```

3. For this to work, of course, the application must be able to locate the `System.Web.Extensions` assembly. This reference is provided in the `<assemblies>` element within the `<compilation>` element, which is also part of the `<system.web>` element. The following code shows the required assembly configuration:

```
<compilation debug="false">
  <assemblies>
    <add assembly="System.Web.Extensions, Version=1.0.61025.0, Culture=neutral,
PublicKeyToken=31bf3856ad364e35"/>
  </assemblies>
</compilation>
```

4. ASP.NET AJAX requires several HTTP handlers for script and web service requests. Add or update the `<httpHandlers>` section within the `<system.web>` element, as follows:

```
<httpHandlers>
  <remove verb="*" path="*.asmx"/>
  <add verb="*" path="*.asmx" validate="false"
type="System.Web.Script.Services.ScriptHandlerFactory, System.Web.Extensions,
Version=1.0.61025.0, Culture=neutral, PublicKeyToken=31bf3856ad364e35"/>
  <add verb="*" path="*_AppService.axd" validate="false"
type="System.Web.Script.Services.ScriptHandlerFactory, System.Web.Extensions,
Version=1.0.61025.0, Culture=neutral, PublicKeyToken=31bf3856ad364e35"/>
  <add verb="GET,HEAD" path="ScriptResource.axd"
type="System.Web.Handlers.ScriptResourceHandler, System.Web.Extensions,
Version=1.0.61025.0, Culture=neutral, PublicKeyToken=31bf3856ad364e35"
validate="false"/>
</httpHandlers>
```

5. In addition, ASP.NET AJAX depends on an HTTP Module to manage some of its script functionality. Add or update the `<httpModules>` section within the `<system.web>` element, as shown here:

```
<httpModules>
  <add name="ScriptModule" type="System.Web.Handlers.ScriptModule,
System.Web.Extensions, Version=1.0.61025.0, Culture=neutral,
PublicKeyToken=31bf3856ad364e35"/>
</httpModules>
```

6. Next, the `<system.web.extensions>` section can be added if you desire additional configuration options, but by default its contents are commented out. Note you don't add this section within `<web.config>`, but within the root `<configuration>` element. An empty `<system.web .extensions>` element is shown here. (Note that this section is not required for this example; I mention it here only for the sake of completeness.)

```
<system.web.extensions>
  <scripting>
    <webServices>
    </webServices>
  </scripting>
</system.web.extensions>
```

7. Finally, the `<system.webServer>` element is used to provide additional configuration settings to IIS 7. It is optional, especially if the web site will be deployed on an earlier version of IIS. The default `<system.webServer>` element, which you add to the root `<configuration>` element, is shown here:

```
<system.webServer>
  <validation validateIntegratedModeConfiguration="false"/>
  <modules>
    <add name="ScriptModule" preCondition="integratedMode"
type="System.Web.Handlers.ScriptModule, System.Web.Extensions, Version=1.0.61025.0,
Culture=neutral, PublicKeyToken=31bf3856ad364e35"/>
  </modules>
  <handlers>
    <remove name="WebServiceHandlerFactory-Integrated" />
    <add name="ScriptHandlerFactory" verb="*" path="*.asmx"
preCondition="integratedMode"
        type="System.Web.Script.Services.ScriptHandlerFactory,
System.Web.Extensions, Version=1.0.61025.0, Culture=neutral,
PublicKeyToken=31bf3856ad364e35"/>
    <add name="ScriptHandlerFactoryAppServices" verb="*" path="*_AppService.axd"
preCondition="integratedMode"
        type="System.Web.Script.Services.ScriptHandlerFactory,
System.Web.Extensions, Version=1.0.61025.0, Culture=neutral,
PublicKeyToken=31bf3856ad364e35"/>
    <add name="ScriptResource" preCondition="integratedMode" verb="GET,HEAD"
path="ScriptResource.axd" type="System.Web.Handlers.ScriptResourceHandler,
System.Web.Extensions, Version=1.0.61025.0, Culture=neutral,
PublicKeyToken=31bf3856ad364e35" />
  </handlers>
</system.webServer>
```

The `<system.webServer>` section is for IIS 7, which, at the time of this writing, has not been released. It is not anticipated that this section will change; however, if you are running this under IIS 7, check the book's web site for updated information.

After you have added or updated these seven configuration sections within the `web.config` file of the web site, ASP.NET AJAX controls can be used within the site.

How It Works

The details of the configuration changes and their effects are covered in Chapter 3. At a high level, these changes provide the ASP.NET application with the information it needs to process ASP.NET AJAX requests, mainly for JavaScript files that are required to enable dynamic client functionality. Additionally, web service requests are modified to provide dynamic proxy script files upon request from ASP.NET AJAX controls, allowing client-side scripts to call these proxy functions as local page functions. The last thing these configuration changes do, specifically in step 2, is to add the ASP.NET AJAX controls like the `UpdatePanel` to the standard `<asp: >` prefix for server controls, making their use consistent with other ASP.NET server controls.

Adding a ScriptManager Control

The Commerce Starter Kit, like many real-world web sites, uses master pages for its primary layout. Because all ASP.NET AJAX controls require a `ScriptManager` control to function, it makes sense to add a `ScriptManager` control to the site's master page, `site.master` (as well as `admin.master` if any AJAX functionality will be added to the admin features of the site). To do this, open `site.master` in Source view and drag a `ScriptManager` control from the Toolbox onto the master page, just below the `<form>` element, as follows:

```
<body>
    <form id="elForm" runat="server" defaultbutton="btnSearch">
    <asp:ScriptManager ID="ScriptManager1" runat="server">
    </asp:ScriptManager>
    <div id="header">
```

Note that because some pages might need to customize the behavior of the `ScriptManager` control, and because only one instance of the `ScriptManager` control can exist on a given page, the `ScriptManagerProxy` control should be used by any ASP.NET page that needs to specify additional scripts or properties. Figure 2-16 shows how these pages and controls should be organized.

For now you do not need to worry about using the `ScriptManagerProxy` control, but keep it in mind for your own applications, which may require its use. Now that the site's master page has an instance of the `ScriptManager` control on it, any page that uses the master page can take advantage of ASP.NET AJAX controls. It's time for you to look at how you can add AJAX features to this application.

First, update the shopping cart management page so that it doesn't require a postback whenever the users update the items in their cart. The page you change is `basket.aspx`, and it allows users to delete or update the quantity of each item in the shopping cart. Each of these is accomplished with a postback — a perfect opportunity to add an `UpdatePanel`.

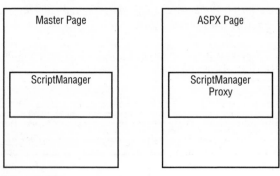

Figure 2-16

Adding an UpdatePanel Control

The page includes a label showing the total amount for all items currently in the cart, a button to update the cart with changes, and a repeater that includes a delete button for each item and a text box with the item quantity for each item. To capture all the dynamic portions of the page you want your `UpdatePanel` to wrap all the controls. To achieve this, drag an `UpdatePanel` control onto the page and then drag all the controls just mentioned into it. (If you're in Source view, add a `<ContentTemplate>` element to the `UpdatePanel` and move all the other controls into this template.) Save your changes and test the page. Now as you update quantities and add or remove items, the cart is updated immediately, without a page refresh. Because all the controls that can update the `UpdatePanel` are inside its `ContentTemplate`, no `<Triggers>` element is needed.

The `UpdatePanel` *control is covered in detail in Chapter 5.*

Adding an AutoCompleteExtender Control

Next consider updating the Search box with an `AutoCompleteExtender` control, which ships with the ASP.NET AJAX Control Toolkit. The `AutoCompleteExtender` control enhances the behavior of a standard `TextBox` control by providing the user with a list of possible matches based on what they have typed in the text box. These appear below the text box, similar to a drop-down list, and the user can select any of these options to complete the text box rather than typing the complete text. To use the `AutoCompleteExtender` control, you need to download and install the Control Toolkit from `http://ajax.asp.net/downloads/`.

The Control Toolkit is covered in detail in Chapter 6.

Try It Out   Adding AutoCompleteExtender

After the Control Toolkit is installed, adding the `AutoCompleteExtender` to the Search text box in the `site.master` page is fairly straightforward:

1. Locate the `txtSearch` control in `site.master`, and add the extender control:

```
Search:
<asp:TextBox ID="txtSearch" runat="server"></asp:TextBox>
<ajaxToolkit:AutoCompleteExtender
    runat="server"
    ID="autoComplete1"
    TargetControlID="txtSearch"
    ServicePath="SearchWebService.asmx"
    ServiceMethod="GetSearchCompletionList"
    MinimumPrefixLength="2"
    CompletionInterval="1000"
    EnableCaching="true"
    CompletionSetCount="12" />
<asp:ImageButton ID="btnSearch" runat="server" SkinID="doSearch"
ImageAlign="AbsMiddle" OnClick="btnSearch_Click" />
```

2. Add a new web service to the web site, called `SearchWebService.asmx`, and check the Place Code in Separate File check box. Next, open the `SearchWebService.cs` file from within the `App_Code` folder, and modify it as follows:

```
[System.Web.Script.Services.ScriptService]
public class SearchWebService : System.Web.Services.WebService
{
    [WebMethod]
    public string[] GetSearchCompletionList(string prefixText, int count)
```

```
    {
        if (count == 0) count = 10;

        ProductCollection myProducts = new ProductCollection().Where("productName",
SubSonic.Comparison.Like, prefixText + "%").OrderByAsc("productName").Load();

        List<string> items = new List<string>(count);
        for (int i = 0; i < count; i++)
        {
            if (i > myProducts.Count - 1) break;
            items.Add(myProducts[i].ProductName);
        }

        return items.ToArray();
    }

}
```

The `GetSearchCompletionList` returns an array of strings containing `productName` values for any products in the store with names that begin with the prefix specified in the Search text box. For example, typing in "sam" results in all products that start with "Samsung" being returned. Figure 2-17 shows the `AutoCompleteExtender` in action.

Figure 2-17

How It Works

Adding auto-completion behavior to a text box on a web page that is powered by a web service is an extremely powerful technique. However, using the AJAX Control Toolkit and ASP.NET AJAX, you added this behavior to an existing web site with just a small amount of web service code and a single ASP.NET web control. The `AutoCompleteExtender` web control adds script events to the targeted `TextBox` control and detects when the total number of characters in the `TextBox` is at least `MinimumPrefixLength` long. Then, it calls the web service asynchronously, returning the list of results and displaying the results in a list attached to the bottom of the text box. Some more client-side code allows the user to select an item from the list and have that item become the text within the text box. Extender controls like the `AutoCompleteExtender` are very powerful because they allow you to add additional behavior to existing controls, rather than requiring you to replace your standard controls with new, improved ones.

There are many other places in the Commerce Starter Kit where AJAX functionality can be added to improve the user's experience. I'm sure you can think of areas in your own applications that could also benefit from such enhancements. Now that you've seen how simple it is to configure an ASP.NET web site to support ASP.NET AJAX, you're ready to learn more about everything ASP.NET AJAX has to offer.

Summary

In this chapter you've learned how to create an ASP.NET AJAX web application from scratch, and how to add ASP.NET AJAX capabilities to existing ASP.NET web applications. Most of the initial work involved with setting up ASP.NET AJAX involves downloading and running the installation, which takes just a few minutes, and then for existing applications, updating the `web.config` to support the new ASP.NET AJAX features.

Once set up, ASP.NET AJAX can quickly be included in many ASP.NET pages, especially those that rely heavily on postbacks. Common scenarios for integrating ASP.NET AJAX functionality into ASP.NET pages include wrapping data updates inside `UpdatePanels` and enhancing the usability of search features through extenders like `AutoCompleteExtender`.

Don't forget to check out the latest ASP.NET AJAX Control Toolkit to see what kinds of new controls have been added. This project is a joint venture between Microsoft and many community contributors, and is being updated frequently with new controls. Find out more at `http://ajax.asp.net/ajaxtoolkit/`. You learn about many more useful applications of ASP.NET AJAX controls as you go through the rest of this book.

If you are going through the book's chapters in order, you should now have two sample ASP.NET AJAX applications (one very small one and one based on a starter kit) with which to apply the concepts that are presented in the rest of the book.

ASP.NET AJAX Architecture

ASP.NET AJAX has a unique, yet familiar architecture that builds on the foundations of ASP.NET 2.0 to strengthen its weak points. This chapter begins by discussing those weak points and describing how ASP.NET AJAX strengthens ASP.NET with powerful new features.

In this chapter you also learn key conceptual details about the ASP.NET AJAX framework, including client-side and server-side development and configuration details. Before you build a house (or a web site), you should have a solid foundation, and this chapter provides you with the foundational details you need to become a skilled ASP.NET AJAX developer.

Specifically, this chapter covers a variety of topics, including:

❑ Analyzing the foundations of ASP.NET AJAX

❑ Understanding the code library

❑ Working with the compatibility layer

❑ Exploring the Microsoft AJAX Library

❑ Stepping through the client-side event life cycle

❑ Investigating server-side components and controls

❑ Learning about the JavaScript files that get downloaded to the client

❑ Understanding how handlers are used

❑ Working with ASP.NET AJAX `web.config` files

Analyzing the Foundations of ASP.NET AJAX

One day HTML was born, and thus was the World Wide Web. HTML was good and highly useful, although it had its limitations. One significant limitation was that the basic web servers of the time (such as IIS) could serve only static HTML by default. Eventually ASP came along to solve this issue fairly efficiently with a rudimentary system that generated HTML dynamically. ASP was also good and highly useful, but also had limitations centered around its scripted nature and lack of truly object-oriented capabilities.

Because of those limitations ASP.NET eventually overpowered and replaced ASP, bringing along a thick server-side library based on the highly extensible .NET framework. It also included a light layer of client-side functionality mainly intended to smooth minor browser differences. This client-side layer was mostly hidden from developer view and was not especially designed for extensibility. As AJAX became the hot buzzword, and capable new browsers eroded Internet Explorer's once dominant market share, this lack of flexible client-side support turned out to be one of ASP.NET's biggest limitations.

Fatefully, ASP.NET AJAX came along to enhance ASP.NET with a sophisticated client-side library and a significant server-side layer to complement it.

Figure 3-1 illustrates the layers and relationships built between these technologies over time. It's important to note that each technology has both client-side and server-side elements, although they vary in the amount of functionality they provide. Some layers are thin and simple (from a web developer's perspective), whereas thicker layers provide significantly more meat.

ASP.NET AJAX is implemented primarily as client-side functionality to fill in for the lack of such functionality in ASP.NET 2.0. Its related server-side features are nearly as impressive even though they delegate many tasks to the client-side library.

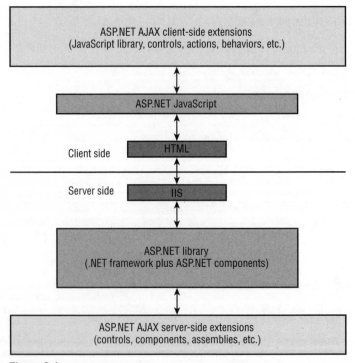

Figure 3-1

Understanding the Code Library

The code library of ASP.NET AJAX is split into two main physical parts: the client-side functionality and the server-side functionality.

The "Microsoft AJAX Library" contains all the client-side functionality. It consists of all the JavaScript files required to make ASP.NET AJAX work its magic. This JavaScript library contains a rich object model that in many ways mimics the server-side object model of ASP.NET. Although the server-side functionality of ASP.NET AJAX requires the Microsoft AJAX Library in order to function, the reverse is not necessarily true. The Microsoft AJAX Library does not rely on ASP.NET and can be used independently with any back-end server, including Linux, Apache, and so on.

ASP.NET AJAX includes a fairly rich server-side library, including components and controls such as the `UpdatePanel` that make AJAX development a breeze even for developers who are complete novices at client-side development.

When ASP.NET AJAX is installed, the Microsoft AJAX Library is automatically installed with it, so no separate installation is necessary. Alternatively, if you don't want or need to work with the server-side elements of ASP.NET AJAX, you can download the Microsoft AJAX Library by itself.

From a development perspective these two layers often work together behind the scenes transparently.

For example, you can take a server-side development approach, use the server-side controls, and potentially never touch any client-side code directly. Controls like `UpdatePanel` use both client and server-side code, but you might work directly with only server-side code and leave the client-side handling up to the ASP.NET AJAX framework.

Conversely, you might take a client-centric approach to development, exclusively using the Microsoft AJAX Library. Both techniques are detailed in upcoming chapters.

Attaining Cross-Browser Compatibility

The JavaScript code of the Microsoft AJAX Library has been carefully written to be cross-browser compatible with all major browsers such as Internet Explorer, Safari, and Mozilla (which includes Firefox and Netscape).

Internally a variety of tricks are used to keep things compatible, such as browser detection, internal branching, and choosing functions that are naturally cross-browser friendly. But you don't generally need to worry about that because, for server-centric development anyway, it all works automatically.

If you're doing direct client-side development, however, you may be interested in these details to keep your JavaScript code cross-browser (and cross-version) compatible. The source code for these JavaScript files is available (as detailed later) so you can study it in depth. After you learn to use Microsoft's AJAX Library to its fullest extent, your code will be cross-browser compatible by default. Experienced JavaScript developers might need to take a little time to un-learn old browser-specific programming habits and instead learn the new cross-browser classes and techniques that are now available in the Microsoft AJAX Library.

For example, the `$get` function is the cross-browser replacement for the JavaScript `document` `.getElementById` function.

So instead of this JavaScript:

```
var a = document.getElementById("Label1");
```

You'd write this new cross-browser compatible script:

```
var a = $get("Label1");
```

Aside from the few minor syntactical differences such as this, the learning curve for the Microsoft AJAX Library primarily consists of getting to know the classes contained in its object model. I recommend that you learn the new client-side object model as thoroughly as you can. The more you use it (instead of old-fashioned JavaScript coding techniques) the more cross-browser compatible your client-side script will be by default.

Exploring the Microsoft AJAX Library

The Microsoft AJAX Library effectively extends JavaScript with capabilities that it never had before. For example, when creating client-side script you'll now have new object-oriented features at your disposal such as classes, inheritance, interfaces, namespaces, enumerations, and reflection.

See Chapter 8 for additional JavaScript enhancements.

JavaScript has also been extended with types familiar to C# developers, such as `StringBuilders` and `Timers`. Even existing JavaScript types such as strings, arrays, and booleans have been extended to function more like their C# counterparts. The following table summarizes the major namespaces of the Microsoft AJAX Library.

Client Namespace	Description
Global	Global classes include extensions to JavaScript intrinsic types such as Array, Boolean, String, Error, Number, and Object.
Sys	The root namespace that's the client-side equivalent of the "System" namespace in the .NET framework. Contains some foundational classes such as Application and StringBuilder. Also contains useful interfaces such as IDisposable and INotifyPropertyChange.
Sys.Net	Contains classes useful for executing network-related tasks, such as the WebRequest class and the XmlHttpExecutor class. This namespace encapsulates virtually all client/server communication.
Sys.Serialization	Used for serializing objects between the client and server.

Client Namespace	Description
`Sys.WebForms`	Compartmentalizes functionality related to the partial page postback technology of ASP.NET AJAX. Contains classes such as the `PageRequestManager` class.
`Sys.UI`	Contains user interface–related features, such as controls, events, and enumerations.
`Sys.Services`	Provides access to ASP.NET server-side services such as authentication, and the profile service.

In general, an attempt has been made to make JavaScript more like C# so that developers can spend more time creating valuable functionality and less time massaging syntactical differences between software layers. This also makes it easier for C# objects to be serialized to and from JavaScript, which now happens automatically in many cases.

You might assume that XML is used to serialize such objects, and that would be a logical assumption. However, the verbosity of XML prompted Microsoft to instead use JavaScript Object Notation (JSON) serialization, which is described in more detail in Chapter 4. This reduces network bandwidth requirements, making ASP.NET AJAX more efficient than it would otherwise be.

In fact, because so little XML is actually used directly by ASP.NET AJAX, it can be debated whether ASP.NET AJAX is a true AJAX technology at all! After all, since AJAX stands for "Asynchronous JavaScript And XML," it seems we may be missing the key XML ingredient. Though such a debate might be philosophically interesting to get into with your peers, from a user standpoint, ASP.NET AJAX fulfills the same basic functional requirements as other AJAX libraries.

If you search through the source code of the Microsoft AJAX Library (covered in more detail in Chapter 9), you'll find virtually all instances of the letters "XML" are referring to the `XmlHttp` browser object that is used for client/server communication.

Using the client-side framework now becomes a lot more like developing with C# code in the .NET framework, as shown in the following example. String concatenation in JavaScript is often slow. What's really needed is a client-side `StringBuilder` object, and now we have one. The following example uses the new client-side `StringBuilder` object to efficiently concatenate a message together for display to the user.

In this example, the client-side `StringBuilder` object has a virtually identical interface to the classic server-side .NET `StringBuilder` object.

Try It Out   Using the Script Library

1. Create a new Visual Studio ASP.NET AJAX-enabled web site.

2. Add a `ScriptManager` to a new web form:

```
<asp:ScriptManager ID="ScriptManager1" runat="server"/>
```

3.   Add this block of JavaScript to the end of the page:

```
<script type="text/javascript">
    var sb = new Sys.StringBuilder("In the beginning");
    sb.append("\r\n"); //carriage return
    sb.append("Microsoft Created ASP");
    alert(sb.toString());
</script>
```

4.   Now run the application and see the message appear.

How It Works

Creating a new web project using the ASP.NET AJAX-Enabled Web Site Template ensures that all the required ASP.NET AJAX references are included in the web.config file. Adding the ScriptManager to the page ensures that ASP.NET AJAX will download the required JavaScript files that include the Microsoft AJAX Library, which in turn define the object model used in the custom JavaScript code block. The JavaScript code block takes advantage of this object model by using the client-side StringBuilder object to efficiently concatenate together a string for display to the user.

Stepping through the Client-Side Event Life Cycle

Just as ASP.NET 2.0 has a server-side event life cycle (the OnPreLoad event is fired before the OnLoad event, and so on), the ASP.NET AJAX framework exposes events in a particular order as well. Having a full understanding of these events gives you a definite advantage. The ASP.NET 2.0 AJAX client-side event life cycle is documented in the following table. The events are listed in the order in which they occur during an asynchronous (partial-page) postback.

Event Name	Event Description
initializeRequest	This event is raised when an asynchronous postback is first initiated. It's a good place to evaluate postbacks to determine whether they should be cancelled or permitted to proceed.
beginRequest	This event is raised when ASP.NET AJAX is fully prepared to execute the call to the server, and just before it does so. It's useful for displaying a processing notification to the user. (See Chapter 10 for an example.)
pageLoading	This event gets called when the client receives a response from the server, but before the page display is updated.

Event Name	Event Description
pageLoaded	This is the only event that gets called during the initial page load, not just after an asynchronous postback. When it's raised, you can be assured that the client-side framework is fully loaded and initialized.
endRequest	This event gets called after the page display has been fully updated to reflect the server's response from an asynchronous postback. It's a good place to hide any processing notification that may have been displayed during the beginRequest event.

These events can be accessed via the PageRequestManager class. Chapter 10 shows an example of wiring up these events to display and hide a processing notification during asynchronous postbacks.

Investigating Server-Side Controls and Components

The server-side portion of ASP.NET AJAX consists of many new components, controls, and classes. This server-side functionality relies heavily upon the JavaScript classes in the Microsoft AJAX Library.

After installing ASP.NET AJAX, the System.Web.Extensions assembly can be found in the Global Assembly Cache, as shown in Figure 3-2.

This server-side library provides functionality in the form of the System.Web namespace that can be used in any web application that has a reference to the System.Web.Extensions assembly.

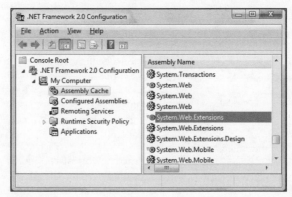

Figure 3-2

Within the server-side `System.Web` namespace are many useful nested namespaces, as detailed in the following table.

Server-side Namespace	Namespace Description
`System.Web.Configuration`	Supplies programmatic access to ASP.NET AJAX-related sections of the `web.config` file.
`System.Web.Handlers`	Provides optimized pre-fetching functionality for script downloads.
`System.Web.Script.Serlialization`	Provides extensible JSON serialization and deserialization features.
`System.Web.Script.Services`	Defines classes that are used for calling web services.
`System.Web.UI`	Contains script management features and network communication code as well as all server controls and control designers.

The `System.Web.UI` namespace contains most of the server-side functionality of ASP.NET AJAX. It contains several important nested namespaces such as `System.Web.UI.Compatability` that extends the standard ASP.NET validation controls with support for ASP.NET AJAX. The `System.Web.UI.Design` namespace can be useful for creating custom extensions to ASP.NET AJAX.

The new server-side controls included with ASP.NET AJAX are listed in the following table.

Server Control Name	Control Description
`ScriptManager`	Non-visible at runtime. Required for every ASP.NET AJAX-enabled web form. Manages client-side scripts. Only one instance allowed per page.
`ScriptManagerProxy`	Non-visible at runtime. If a master page contains the `ScriptManager` control and its content page wishes to use ASP.NET AJAX functionality, the content page must use a `ScriptManagerProxy` control that coordinates script management with the `ScriptManager` control.
`UpdatePanel`	Any controls placed inside an `UpdatePanel` can be easily refreshed via AJAX-style partial postbacks. (For more details, see Chapter 5.)
`UpdateProgress`	Displays a status bar or other animation to give feedback to users during long-running AJAX requests.
`Timer`	The `Timer` control can execute client-side events at precise intervals, such as refreshing an `UpdatePanel` every *x* seconds.

The `ScriptManager` control should be considered required for any ASP.NET page that uses ASP.NET AJAX functionality because it manages and coordinates all required script files. Though it is technically possible to reference required scripts manually without the use of this control, it would be an error-prone process that likely results in less efficient script loading. While this control manages the ASP.NET AJAX script files by default, it is also usually best to let it manage any custom script files you may have as well. Such configuration is covered in more detail later in this chapter.

If you're using ASP.NET master pages in your site and your master page needs to use AJAX functionality, it will need an instance of the `ScriptManager` control. If one of its content pages also needs to use AJAX functionality, it will also need an instance of the `ScriptManager` control. The problem here is that a page may have no more than one instance of the `ScriptManager` control and this situation would technically be putting two instances on the same page. The solution is to use the `ScriptManagerProxy` control in the content page instead of the `ScriptManager` control. The `ScriptManagerProxy` control acts as a substitute `ScriptManager` control, delegating most of its functionality to its parent `ScriptManager` control contained in the Master Page.

By now you likely know that AJAX enables parts of pages to be updated independently of the rest of the page. The `UpdatePanel` control is used to specify which parts of the page get updated. Any controls placed inside an `UpdatePanel` are automatically enhanced with easy AJAX updates. Updates can be triggered by a variety of events, such as client-side click events or the tick event of a `Timer` control. The `UpdatePanel` is covered in full detail in Chapter 5.

Some AJAX calls may take longer than others. If an AJAX call triggers a long-running SQL query, for example, you may want to provide feedback to the user during that process. The `UpdateProgress` control is intended to supply just such functionality. It can display static text, animations, flash content, or virtually any bit of HTML. The `UpdateProgress` control can be set to display as soon as an AJAX call begins, or alternatively when an AJAX call fails to return after a configurable time period. Chapter 10 covers the `UpdateProgress` control in more detail.

The `Timer` control is useful for executing events at regular intervals. Typically, it is used for updating an `UpdatePanel` on a recurring basis. The `Timer`'s integer `Interval` property is intended to be set in milliseconds, so a setting of 10,000 would cause an `UpdatePanel` to update every 10 seconds. The easiest way to configure a `Timer` control to update a specific `UpdatePanel` is to drag the `Timer` control inside of the `UpdatePanel`. (It's invisible at runtime.) Alternatively, more complex scenarios are possible such as using triggers to cause a `Timer` control to update multiple `UpdatePanels`:

```
<asp:ScriptManager ID="ScriptManager1" runat="server" />
<asp:Timer ID="Timer1" OnTick="Timer1_Tick"
    runat="server" Interval="5000" />
<br />
<asp:UpdatePanel ID="UpdatePanel1"
    UpdateMode="Conditional" runat="server">
    <ContentTemplate>
        <asp:Label ID="Label1" runat="server" Text="Label1" />
    </ContentTemplate>
    <Triggers>
        <asp:AsyncPostBackTrigger
            ControlID="Timer1" EventName="Tick" />
    </Triggers>
</asp:UpdatePanel>
<asp:UpdatePanel ID="UpdatePanel2"
    UpdateMode="Conditional" runat="server">
```

```
    <ContentTemplate>
        <asp:Label ID="Label2" runat="server" Text="Label2" />
    </ContentTemplate>
    <Triggers>
        <asp:AsyncPostBackTrigger
            ControlID="Timer1" EventName="Tick" />
    </Triggers>
</asp:UpdatePanel>
```

Examining the JavaScript Files

You may recall from earlier in this chapter that the client-side components of ASP.NET AJAX are called the Microsoft AJAX Library. They can be used with or without the support of the server-side components of ASP.NET AJAX. The Microsoft AJAX Library consists of three primary JavaScript files.

When installed with the full ASP.NET AJAX installation package, these JavaScript files can be found by default in the `Program Files\Microsoft ASP.NET\ASP.NET 2.0 AJAX Extensions\v1.0.x\ MicrosoftAjaxLibrary\System.Web.Extensions\v1.0.x\` folder. There are both debug and release versions of these files. Although functionally identical, the release versions are not for human consumption because they have all comments and white space removed for optimal download size. Though prerelease versions of ASP.NET AJAX (codenamed "Atlas") had been criticized for their dubious reputation of being large and bloated, I'm happy to report that the release versions are a tiny fraction of the size, weighing in at only around 100KB total. The library also contains its own intelligent pre-fetching techniques that can silently download and cache scripts in the background via HTTP handlers for optimum download efficiency.

You can learn a lot by examining the more readable debug version of these files — not just about ASP.NET AJAX but also about advanced JavaScript coding techniques in general. Make sure that you have a lot of time on your hands if you want to do an in-depth analysis of these files, because together they contain more than 9000 lines of JavaScript code!

Such a large code base obviously contains a lot of power, and all this functionality is exposed in such intuitive ways that it is possible to take advantage of its abilities while barely needing to be aware of its existence.

The following table summarizes the three primary JavaScript files of the Microsoft AJAX Library.

File	Description
MicrosoftAjax.js	This is the most commonly used JavaScript file, which contains the bulk of the Microsoft AJAX Library.
MicrosoftAjaxWebForms.js	Contains the code for the Microsoft AJAX ASP.NET WebForms Framework.
MicrosoftAjaxTimer.js	This relatively small file contains only the code needed for the timer functionality of the Microsoft AJAX Library.

`MicrosoftAjax.js` is the main JavaScript file in the Microsoft AJAX Library. It extends JavaScript with simulated object-oriented capabilities and provides a client-side object model reminiscent the .NET framework.

`MicrosoftAjaxWebForms.js` contains the Microsoft AJAX ASP.NET WebForms Framework. It defines the client-side `Sys.WebForm` namespace that provides support for partial-page postbacks. It also defines the client-side functionality for the new `UpdateProgress` server control that's detailed in Chapter 10.

As you might have guessed, the `MicrosoftAjaxTimer.js` file contains all the client-side code related to the new `Timer` server control.

Handling HTTP Handlers

As you may know, ASP.NET Http Handlers can intercept requests for certain configurable file types and redirect the processing of those files to specified custom code modules. ASP.NET 2.0 built on this capability by allowing otherwise external resources to be compiled directly into assemblies and retrieved dynamically via a feature called *ASP.NET 2.0 Embedded Web Resources*.

By default, ASP.NET AJAX downloads its main JavaScript files from embedded web resources, so altering the source script files directly in the file system folders mentioned previously would be pointless. Instead of altering these files, it is recommended that you extend the library as needed with your own server-side code, client-side scripts, and custom controls. (However, if you're determined to update the ASP.NET AJAX JavaScript files directly, you can point ASP.NET AJAX to your updated versions of the files using the `ScriptManager`'s `ScriptPath` property.)

As mentioned earlier, the `ScriptManager` control is in charge of managing and downloading scripts to the client. It intelligently queues and sequentially downloads scripts. It has a variety of properties to allow the addition of static or dynamic scripts at design time and runtime. Additionally, the client-side `Sys.Application` namespace has a variety of events that allow you to deal gracefully with expected or unexpected script loading actions. Using these, timeouts and other script load failures can be trapped and dealt with elegantly. The `ScriptLoadTimeout` property of the `ScriptManager` control can be used to specify how long to wait for script downloads. The `ScriptPath` property can be used to specify in which folder script files are located by default. Individual scripts can be configured to ignore this property for cases where a particular script file is stored elsewhere, as shown in the ScriptReference Collection Editor of Figure 3-3. This collection editor can be invoked at design time by clicking the ellipsis button of the `Scripts` property of the `ScriptManager` control in the Visual Studio properties window.

As you can see, a variety of useful properties can be set in this dialog box for customizing script loading in a variety of ways:

❑ The `ScriptMode` property can be used to specify whether debug or release versions of the script files should be downloaded.

❑ The `Assembly` property can be used in cases where a script file is provided as an embedded web resource.

❑ The `ResourceUICultures` property can be used to specify which UI cultures are available.

Figure 3-3

In Source view of the ASPX page, the properties from the ScriptReference Collection Editor are serialized into the following definition:

```
<asp:ScriptManager ID="ScriptManager1" runat="server" >
    <Scripts>
        <asp:ScriptReference IgnoreScriptPath="True"
            Name="MyCustom.js" Path="/scripts/"
            ResourceUICultures=""
        />
    </Scripts>
</asp:ScriptManager>
```

Of course, you can type such definitions manually if you prefer this user interface instead of using the ScriptReference Collection Editor dialog.

This entire design-time configuration culminates at runtime through the ScriptResource HTTP handler. The ScriptResource handler is responsible for serving up script references at runtime. It optionally appends any localized script references if the `EnableScriptLocalization` property of the `ScriptManager` control is set to `true`.

This ScriptResource functionality requires a reference in the `web.config` file to an HTTP handler named `ScriptResource.axd` (as detailed in the next section.) If you're missing this important ASP.NET AJAX reference you may see a client-side error message such as "'Sys' is undefined" because the client-side script files that define the Microsoft AJAX Library won't have been downloaded as they should have been. Such an error might also occur if you're trying to interact with the ASP.NET AJAX library before it's been fully loaded and initialized, as is signaled by the `pageLoaded` event.

Working with the Web.Config File

In the `Program Files\Microsoft ASP.NET\ASP.NET 2.0 AJAX Extensions\v1.x\` folder you'll find a `web.config` file, as shown in the following code. This file contains all the settings the ASP.NET AJAX library could possibly require from an ASP.NET AJAX-enabled web site. Depending on which ASP.NET AJAX features your application uses, it's likely that your web application `web.config` file won't need every one of these settings.

```xml
<?xml version="1.0"?>
<configuration>
  <configSections>
    <sectionGroup name="system.web.extensions"
type="System.Web.Configuration.SystemWebExtensionsSectionGroup,
System.Web.Extensions, Version=1.0.61025.0, Culture=neutral,
PublicKeyToken=31bf3856ad364e35">
      <sectionGroup name="scripting"
type="System.Web.Configuration.ScriptingSectionGroup, System.Web.Extensions,
Version=1.0.61025.0, Culture=neutral, PublicKeyToken=31bf3856ad364e35">
        <section name="scriptResourceHandler"
type="System.Web.Configuration.ScriptingScriptResourceHandlerSection,
System.Web.Extensions, Version=1.0.61025.0, Culture=neutral,
PublicKeyToken=31bf3856ad364e35" requirePermission="false"
allowDefinition="MachineToApplication"/>
        <sectionGroup name="webServices"
type="System.Web.Configuration.ScriptingWebServicesSectionGroup,
System.Web.Extensions, Version=1.0.61025.0, Culture=neutral,
PublicKeyToken=31bf3856ad364e35">
          <section name="jsonSerialization"
type="System.Web.Configuration.ScriptingJsonSerializationSection,
System.Web.Extensions, Version=1.0.61025.0, Culture=neutral,
PublicKeyToken=31bf3856ad364e35" requirePermission="false"
allowDefinition="Everywhere" />
          <section name="authenticationService"
type="System.Web.Configuration.ScriptingAuthenticationServiceSection,
System.Web.Extensions, Version=1.0.61025.0, Culture=neutral,
PublicKeyToken=31bf3856ad364e35" requirePermission="false"
allowDefinition="MachineToApplication" />
          <section name="profileService"
type="System.Web.Configuration.ScriptingProfileServiceSection,
System.Web.Extensions, Version=1.0.61025.0, Culture=neutral,
PublicKeyToken=31bf3856ad364e35" requirePermission="false"
allowDefinition="MachineToApplication" />
        </sectionGroup>
      </sectionGroup>
    </sectionGroup>
  </configSections>
```

```
  <system.web>
    <pages>
      <controls>
        <add tagPrefix="asp" namespace="System.Web.UI"
assembly="System.Web.Extensions, Version=1.0.61025.0, Culture=neutral,
PublicKeyToken=31bf3856ad364e35"/>
      </controls>
    </pages>
    <!--
          Set compilation debug="true" to insert debugging
          symbols into the compiled page. Because this
          affects performance, set this value to true only
          during development.
    -->
    <compilation debug="false">
      <assemblies>
        <add assembly="System.Web.Extensions, Version=1.0.61025.0, Culture=neutral,
PublicKeyToken=31bf3856ad364e35"/>
      </assemblies>
    </compilation>

    <httpHandlers>
      <remove verb="*" path="*.asmx"/>
      <add verb="*" path="*.asmx" validate="false"
type="System.Web.Script.Services.ScriptHandlerFactory, System.Web.Extensions,
Version=1.0.61025.0, Culture=neutral, PublicKeyToken=31bf3856ad364e35"/>
      <add verb="*" path="*_AppService.axd" validate="false"
type="System.Web.Script.Services.ScriptHandlerFactory, System.Web.Extensions,
Version=1.0.61025.0, Culture=neutral, PublicKeyToken=31bf3856ad364e35"/>
      <add verb="GET,HEAD" path="ScriptResource.axd"
type="System.Web.Handlers.ScriptResourceHandler, System.Web.Extensions,
Version=1.0.61025.0, Culture=neutral, PublicKeyToken=31bf3856ad364e35"
validate="false"/>
    </httpHandlers>

    <httpModules>
      <add name="ScriptModule" type="System.Web.Handlers.ScriptModule,
System.Web.Extensions, Version=1.0.61025.0, Culture=neutral,
PublicKeyToken=31bf3856ad364e35"/>
    </httpModules>
  </system.web>

  <system.web.extensions>
    <scripting>
      <webServices>
      <!-- Uncomment this line to customize maxJsonLength and add a custom
converter -->
      <!--
      <jsonSerialization maxJsonLength="500">
        <converters>
          <add name="ConvertMe" type="Acme.SubAcme.ConvertMeTypeConverter"/>
        </converters>
      </jsonSerialization>
```

```
  -->
      <!-- Uncomment this line to enable the authentication service. Include
requireSSL="true" if appropriate. -->
      <!--
        <authenticationService enabled="true" requireSSL = "true|false"/>
      -->

      <!-- Uncomment these lines to enable the profile service. To allow profile
properties to be retrieved and modified in ASP.NET AJAX applications, you need to
add each property name to the readAccessProperties and writeAccessProperties
attributes. -->
      <!--
      <profileService enabled="true"
                      readAccessProperties="propertyname1,propertyname2"
                      writeAccessProperties="propertyname1,propertyname2" />
      -->
      </webServices>
      <!--
      <scriptResourceHandler enableCompression="true" enableCaching="true" />
      -->
    </scripting>
  </system.web.extensions>

  <system.webServer>
    <validation validateIntegratedModeConfiguration="false"/>
    <modules>
      <add name="ScriptModule" preCondition="integratedMode"
type="System.Web.Handlers.ScriptModule, System.Web.Extensions, Version=1.0.61025.0,
Culture=neutral, PublicKeyToken=31bf3856ad364e35"/>
    </modules>
    <handlers>
      <remove name="WebServiceHandlerFactory-Integrated" />
      <add name="ScriptHandlerFactory" verb="*" path="*.asmx"
preCondition="integratedMode"
          type="System.Web.Script.Services.ScriptHandlerFactory,
System.Web.Extensions, Version=1.0.61025.0, Culture=neutral,
PublicKeyToken=31bf3856ad364e35"/>
      <add name="ScriptHandlerFactoryAppServices" verb="*" path="*_AppService.axd"
preCondition="integratedMode"
          type="System.Web.Script.Services.ScriptHandlerFactory,
System.Web.Extensions, Version=1.0.61025.0, Culture=neutral,
PublicKeyToken=31bf3856ad364e35"/>
      <add name="ScriptResource" preCondition="integratedMode" verb="GET,HEAD"
path="ScriptResource.axd" type="System.Web.Handlers.ScriptResourceHandler,
System.Web.Extensions, Version=1.0.61025.0, Culture=neutral,
PublicKeyToken=31bf3856ad364e35" />
    </handlers>
  </system.webServer>
</configuration>
```

This `web.config` file is included in a new web application by default when the "ASP.NET AJAX-Enabled Web Site" template is chosen from Visual Studio, as shown in Figure 3-4.

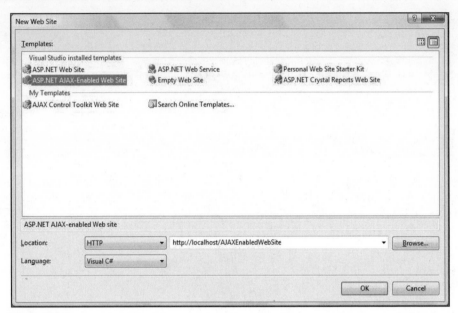

Figure 3-4

There are quite a few interesting sections in that `web.config` file, so let's break it down a bit. The `configSections` part of the `web.config` file contains these entries:

```
<configSections>
    <sectionGroup name="system.web.extensions"
type="System.Web.Configuration.SystemWebExtensionsSectionGroup,
System.Web.Extensions, Version=1.0.61025.0, Culture=neutral,
PublicKeyToken=31bf3856ad364e35">
      <sectionGroup name="scripting"
type="System.Web.Configuration.ScriptingSectionGroup, System.Web.Extensions,
Version=1.0.61025.0, Culture=neutral, PublicKeyToken=31bf3856ad364e35">
        <section name="scriptResourceHandler"
type="System.Web.Configuration.ScriptingScriptResourceHandlerSection,
System.Web.Extensions, Version=1.0.61025.0, Culture=neutral,
PublicKeyToken=31bf3856ad364e35" requirePermission="false"
allowDefinition="MachineToApplication"/>
        <sectionGroup name="webServices"
type="System.Web.Configuration.ScriptingWebServicesSectionGroup,
System.Web.Extensions, Version=1.0.61025.0, Culture=neutral,
PublicKeyToken=31bf3856ad364e35">
          <section name="jsonSerialization"
type="System.Web.Configuration.ScriptingJsonSerializationSection,
System.Web.Extensions, Version=1.0.61025.0, Culture=neutral,
PublicKeyToken=31bf3856ad364e35" requirePermission="false"
allowDefinition="Everywhere" />
          <section name="authenticationService"
type="System.Web.Configuration.ScriptingAuthenticationServiceSection,
System.Web.Extensions, Version=1.0.61025.0, Culture=neutral,
```

```
    PublicKeyToken=31bf3856ad364e35" requirePermission="false"
    allowDefinition="MachineToApplication" />
            <section name="profileService"
    type="System.Web.Configuration.ScriptingProfileServiceSection,
    System.Web.Extensions, Version=1.0.61025.0, Culture=neutral,
    PublicKeyToken=31bf3856ad364e35" requirePermission="false"
    allowDefinition="MachineToApplication" />
            </sectionGroup>
        </sectionGroup>
      </sectionGroup>
    </configSections>
```

Starting at the bottom, the `profileService` entry is only needed if your application takes advantage of ASP.NET profiles and also its ASP.NET AJAX functionality uses this service. For example, profile services can be useful to remember where a particular user dragged a user interface element so that it can appear to remain there the next time the user logs in. If configured properly, this can happen with zero lines of code, with ASP.NET AJAX and ASP.NET taking care of all the work.

Similarly, the `authenticationService` is useful only for web sites that manage accounts and it is likely unneeded for a general news and information web site that only deals with anonymous users.

The rest of the `configSections` entries are not very optional, and should be left as-is.

The following `System.Web` section associates the `System.Web.Extensions` namespace with the `asp` tag prefix. Additionally, it globally registers the AJAX server controls so that they can be used on every page without having to register the controls on each page:

```
    <controls>
        <add tagPrefix="asp" namespace="System.Web.UI"
    assembly="System.Web.Extensions, Version=1.0.61025.0, Culture=neutral,
    PublicKeyToken=31bf3856ad364e35"/>
        </controls>
```

The `Compilation` section should have its `Debug` attribute set to `true` during development because it inserts extra debugging code and symbols, which can be quite useful. However, this attribute should be set to `false` in production scenarios because of the potential drag on performance:

```
    <compilation debug="false">
      <assemblies>
        <add assembly="System.Web.Extensions, Version=1.0.61025.0, Culture=neutral,
    PublicKeyToken=31bf3856ad364e35"/>
      </assemblies>
    </compilation>
```

The `HttpHandler` section enables several useful ASP.NET AJAX features. The first line removes the standard ASP.NET association with web services (`*.asmx`) files so it can instead be associated with the ASP.NET AJAX server-side library. The final `add` element specifies that script files should be downloaded through the ASP.NET AJAX HTTP handler for efficient, sequential background downloading:

```
    <httpHandlers>
      <remove verb="*" path="*.asmx"/>
```

```
        <add verb="*" path="*.asmx" validate="false"
type="System.Web.Script.Services.ScriptHandlerFactory, System.Web.Extensions,
Version=1.0.61025.0, Culture=neutral, PublicKeyToken=31bf3856ad364e35"/>
        <add verb="*" path="*_AppService.axd" validate="false"
type="System.Web.Script.Services.ScriptHandlerFactory, System.Web.Extensions,
Version=1.0.61025.0, Culture=neutral, PublicKeyToken=31bf3856ad364e35"/>
        <add verb="GET,HEAD" path="ScriptResource.axd"
type="System.Web.Handlers.ScriptResourceHandler, System.Web.Extensions,
Version=1.0.61025.0, Culture=neutral, PublicKeyToken=31bf3856ad364e35"
validate="false"/>
    </httpHandlers>
```

If you're missing these important references to `ScriptResource.axd` and `AppService.axd`, you may see an error message such as "'Sys' is undefined."

Similarly, there is a section that registers the Http Modules used by ASP.NET AJAX:

```
    <httpModules>
        <add name="ScriptModule" type="System.Web.Handlers.ScriptModule,
System.Web.Extensions, Version=1.0.61025.0, Culture=neutral,
PublicKeyToken=31bf3856ad364e35"/>
    </httpModules>
```

The `webServices` element of the `web.config` file defines several optional nuggets of potentially useful functionality:

```
    <system.web.extensions>
      <scripting>
        <webServices>
        <!-- Uncomment this line to customize maxJsonLength and add a custom
converter -->
        <!--
        <jsonSerialization maxJsonLength="500">
          <converters>
            <add name="ConvertMe" type="Acme.SubAcme.ConvertMeTypeConverter"/>
          </converters>
        </jsonSerialization>
        -->
        <!-- Uncomment this line to enable the authentication service. Include
requireSSL="true" if appropriate. -->
        <!--
        <authenticationService enabled="true" requireSSL = "true|false"/>
        -->

        <!-- Uncomment these lines to enable the profile service. To allow profile
properties to be retrieved and modified in ASP.NET AJAX applications, you need to
add each property name to the readAccessProperties and writeAccessProperties
attributes. -->
```

```
    <!--
    <profileService enabled="true"
readAccessProperties="propertyname1,propertyname2"
writeAccessProperties="propertyname1,propertyname2" />
    -->
    </webServices>
  </scripting>
</system.web.extensions>
```

Again working from the bottom up, the system.web.extensions section contains a couple sections that are required only for client-side support of ASP.NET personalization and authentication. Above that is a section that allows customization of the JSON serialization functionality of ASP.NET AJAX. Because JSON can only serialize simple data types by default, you can add your own type converters here to handle more complex types manually. JSON is detailed in the next chapter.

The final section is intended specifically for the consumption of IIS 7, and will be ignored by earlier versions of IIS. This section allows IIS 7 to handle ASP.NET AJAX functionality in a more efficient and compartmentalized fashion:

```
    <system.webServer>
      <validation validateIntegratedModeConfiguration="false"/>
      <modules>
        <add name="ScriptModule" preCondition="integratedMode"
type="System.Web.Handlers.ScriptModule, System.Web.Extensions, Version=1.0.61025.0,
Culture=neutral, PublicKeyToken=31bf3856ad364e35"/>
      </modules>
      <handlers>
        <remove name="WebServiceHandlerFactory-Integrated" />
        <add name="ScriptHandlerFactory" verb="*" path="*.asmx"
preCondition="integratedMode"
          type="System.Web.Script.Services.ScriptHandlerFactory,
System.Web.Extensions, Version=1.0.61025.0, Culture=neutral,
PublicKeyToken=31bf3856ad364e35"/>
        <add name="ScriptHandlerFactoryAppServices" verb="*" path="*_AppService.axd"
preCondition="integratedMode"
          type="System.Web.Script.Services.ScriptHandlerFactory,
System.Web.Extensions, Version=1.0.61025.0, Culture=neutral,
PublicKeyToken=31bf3856ad364e35"/>
        <add name="ScriptResource" preCondition="integratedMode" verb="GET,HEAD"
path="ScriptResource.axd" type="System.Web.Handlers.ScriptResourceHandler,
System.Web.Extensions, Version=1.0.61025.0, Culture=neutral,
PublicKeyToken=31bf3856ad364e35" />
      </handlers>
    </system.webServer>
```

Now that you understand the various sections of the ASP.NET AJAX web.config file you can feel confident using it as-is or extracting the required pieces into a pre-existing ASP.NET application's web.config file to enhance it with AJAX capabilities.

Summary

In this chapter you learned about the structure of ASP.NET AJAX and how it came to be. You learned about the client- and server-side components, controls, classes, namespaces, and related syntax. The standard Java-Script source files have been examined, as well as the client-side event life cycle. You should now have a solid foundation on which to build your future ASP.NET AJAX-enabled applications.

In the next chapter you learn more about using client-side script, including basic web service calls and error handling. As promised, you also learn more about the magic that is JSON. Data types play a key role in all this; read on to learn how to use them gracefully and consistently across all application layers.

Calling Web Services

Calling web services is an important part of AJAX. Web services are the base mechanism used to transmit data between the client and the browser without the need for a postback. Calling a web service instead of performing a postback has several advantages, including less network traffic and generally higher performance.

Microsoft's ASP.NET AJAX framework provides mechanisms that allow for AJAX-style operations. With this type of support, asynchronous commands can be sent between the client web browser and the web server. This communication is made through web services. This chapter looks at the following topics:

❑ Understanding AJAX

❑ Using client-side JavaScript

❑ Sending and receiving data with client-side JavaScript

❑ Setting up web services to be called

Introducing AJAX

AJAX is the acronym for Asynchronous JavaScript and XML. The acronym was coined by Jesse James Garrett in February 2005 in an essay about building rich, interactive, web-based applications that can rival much of the functionality of client-side GUI applications.

Although the term AJAX is relatively new, the technologies that make up AJAX are not. Several technologies have been available for a number of years to enable these types of operations. However, it wasn't until Microsoft packaged the MSXML component (also known as the XMLHttpRequest object) as an ActiveX object and shipped it with Internet Explorer that what resembles modern AJAX became available. After Microsoft shipped the MSXML component, other browser vendors created the JavaScript-based XMLHttpRequest object for inclusion in their browser. The XMLHttpRequest object produced by the other browser vendors had the same type of programming interface as the MSXML object.

In addition to this similar XML programming model, major browser vendors have been adding support for the Document Object Model (DOM) to their browsers. With the addition of support for the DOM, it has become easier for developers to perform the same operations across various browsers. No longer is there a need to create an IE, Firefox, Safari, and other version of a site.

With the creation of a similar programming model in XML requests, it became fairly simple to create a library that used the same programming methodologies and hides the differences between various browsers. Numerous libraries have been created that assist in creating AJAX-style applications. These libraries vary from purely client-side libraries like Sarissa to libraries that integrate the client and server, such as AJAX.NET Pro and Microsoft's ASP.NET AJAX Library.

AJAX-type programming has gained a significant amount of interest in the web development community with the release of several properties from Google, starting with Google Maps. With this interest, users became interested in the features and rich applications and wanted these types of features added to their applications.

Advantages of Developing with ASP.NET AJAX

Developing rich client-side applications with ASP.NET AJAX has several advantages over traditional ASP.NET applications. These advantages are as follows:

❑ **Bandwidth utilization** — With a traditional ASP.NET application, all form elements (including ViewState) are packaged and sent to the server, the server processes the information, and all of the page information is sent back to the web browser. This is known as a *postback*. With an AJAX-style request, only the necessary information is sent from the browser to the server, processed on the server, and then sent back to the client. The data is then processed on the client.

❑ **Server utilization** — Because there is less data being sent from the client to the server and less processing done on the server, the server is utilized less than it is during a full postback.

❑ **User experience** — The user experience with AJAX applications is much improved over traditional ASP.NET applications. Processing occurs quicker because

   ❑ less data is sent to the server for processing.

   ❑ there is no postback.

   ❑ the page's server events are not processed.

   ❑ there is no reload of the page.

   ❑ the user stays at the same location within the page and thus stays within the same context.

   ❑ there is no flash of a page reloading.

   ❑ the user interface is not blocked from additional operations on the client.

❑ **Interactivity** — ASP.NET AJAX calls are made independent of a page postback. They are made over the XMLHttpRequest/MSXML object. They have a request and a callback mechanism and are therefore made asynchronously. Therefore, the browser does not lock out user input during the call and additional things can be done at the browser.

As a result of these advantages, the growth in interest in AJAX-oriented applications has been tremendous. When Google shipped Google Maps (`http://maps.google.com/`), the resulting discussion in the development community was tremendous and really lit a fire under many developers to add this level of functionality to their applications.

Disadvantages of Developing with ASP.NET AJAX

Although AJAX applications have many advantages, they also have several disadvantages at this time. These disadvantages must be weighed against the perceived advantages. Some of the disadvantages are as follows:

❑   **Back button** — Users expect that a browser back button will take them to the previous page or state of that page. Unfortunately, with the browser back button in an ASP.NET AJAX page, the user is not necessarily redirected to the previous state of the page, but to the previous page. This can be confusing for users.

❑   **Accessibility/Section 508** — Although many ASP.NET AJAX features are accessible, much like any coding paradigm, some issues are involved in accessing the application. With the U.S. government, there are a set of standards for accessing information that are referred to as *Section 508*. There is much confusion of Section 508 applications and ASP.NET AJAX. Some features are accessible, some are only accessible when coded certain ways, and some features are not accessible. This has led to confusion in the marketplace. When programming with ASP.NET AJAX, a developer must make sure that the application supports Section 508, as necessary.

❑   **MSXML** — With Internet Explorer Version 6 and earlier, the MSXML support is provided by an ActiveX object. If ActiveX is turned off at the client, there will be no support for ASP.NET AJAX. This problem has been resolved with Internet Explorer Version 7 and later; however, that version of the browser is not available on every platform that Version 6 is.

AJAX Libraries

Several libraries besides ASP.NET AJAX provide support for AJAX operations. Here are some of the more popular ones:

❑   **Sarissa** — Sarissa is a purely client-side JavaScript library. It hides the differences with programming to the client browser. Because Sarissa is a client-side library, it provides very little support for integrating directly with the web server.

❑   **AJAX.NET Professional** — The AJAX.NET Professional library allows for integrating ASP.NET applications with AJAX. It is an open source library that works with both ASP.NET 1.1 and 2.0. Because it is a .NET-focused library, it provides integration with the backend IIS Server. The library is similar to ASP.NET AJAX and provides the necessary client-side proxies to call into ASP.NET servers.

❑   **ASP.NET AJAX** — The ASP.NET AJAX Library is a library from Microsoft for supporting AJAX-style operations. The library integrates with ASP.NET 2.0 including full support for integrating the client, the web server, and Visual Studio .NET. By integrating with Visual Studio .NET, ASP.NET AJAX provides a level of integration that is not readily available in other libraries.

With probably four to five other .NET libraries and many other client-side JavaScript libraries around, you can see that AJAX is definitely gaining traction among developers inside and outside of the .NET community. With ASP.NET AJAX, Microsoft will provide a level of integration with Visual Studio that third-party vendors of frameworks and libraries will be hard-pressed to match.

Client-Side JavaScript Overview

With JavaScript within the acronym, you can see that JavaScript is an important part of AJAX and thus ASP.NET AJAX. Though client-side JavaScript is important for us in looking at ASP.NET AJAX, there is no way that this chapter can adequately cover all parts of JavaScript. As a result, this chapter just looks at some of the basics of dealing with JavaScript on the client and how to interact with controls.

If you are looking for a full book on client-side JavaScript, check out Professional JavaScript for Web Developers, *by Nicholas C. Zakas, ISBN: 0-7645-7908-8.*

What Is JavaScript?

JavaScript was developed by Netscape in the mid-1990s and is loosely based on the syntax of the Java and C programming languages. Developers are most familiar with its use as a scripting language in a web browser. This scripting language can be used to write functions that interact with elements in a web page. This interaction is performed through the Document Object Model (DOM), which is a standardized way to interact with controls in a web page. Most modern browsers provide some level of support for the DOM.

For more information about the Document Object Model, check out entries at Wikepedia.org at `http://en.wikipedia.org/wiki/Document_Object_Model` *and at the World Wide Web Consortium at* `www.w3.org/DOM/`.

Why Do You Need JavaScript?

You may be familiar with the ASP.NET design model. With ASP.NET, applications depend on the client for very little; the majority of work occurs on the server. This work is done in the form of a postback of all client form elements and a full page being sent to the web. As a result, very little is required at the client. With ASP.NET AJAX, the client is able to do more operations, but to perform these operations, you need to have some type of programmability support in the client browser. This programmability support is provided by JavaScript and as a result, client-side JavaScript is a requirement for ASP.NET AJAX.

Common Control References

With ASP.NET AJAX, there are several client-side references that you should be familiar with. There are code references that access client-side controls fairly regularly. These references are for a `<div>` tag, textbox, and a drop-down list box. Here's a look at the references:

❑   **<DIV> tag** — Referencing a `<div>` tag is a very important item. This is the mechanism to put text onto a form without the user being able to easily edit it. This is similar to a .NET `Label` control in a GUI application. To reference the control, you can use:

```
document.getElementById(ControlName).innerHTML
```

❑ In this example, the `ControlName` is merely a string representing the ID value of a control. With this code, a program can get/set the values of a text onscreen that users cannot change on their own. Though `innerHTML` is commonly used, it is a non-standard DOM command.

❑ To write to a `<div>` tag in a standard way, the following code, which is a little more complex, will work:

```
var strVal = 'This is text content.';
var div = document.getElementById( 'divStandard' );
var divtext = document.createTextNode( strVal );
if ( null == div.firstChild )
{
    div.appendChild( divtext );
}
else
{
    div.childNodes[0].data = strVal + "-2";
}
```

❑ In this code, the first time it is run, the value of `This is text content.` is placed within the `<div>` tag with an ID of `divStandard`. The second time that the code is run, the value of `This is text content.-2` is placed within the `<div>` tag with an ID of `divStandard`. Because this is fairly cumbersome, the `innerHTML` method is typically used.

❑ **Textbox** — Referencing a textbox is an important requirement of JavaScript. Textboxes are a form element used to enable a user to change data. The data can be any textual input data that a user would like to enter. To get/set the textual values of a textbox, use the following code to reference the textbox:

```
document.getElementById(ControlName).value
```

❑ In this example, `ControlName` is a string that represents the name of the control. Just like the `<div>` tag, this code example can be used to get or set the value in the textbox.

❑ **Drop-down list box** — A drop-down list box is a form element that is used to allow a user to enter one or more predefined pieces of data. For example, the drop-down list box can contain a list of states or provinces within a country. There are several mechanisms used to reference a drop-down list box. To reference the selected index, the code is:

```
document.getElementById(ControlName).selectedIndex
```

❑ This command gets the selected index of the drop-down list box.

❑ To reference the value of selected item within a drop-down list box, use the following code:

```
document.getElementById(ControlName).options[document.getElementById(ControlName)
.selectedIndex].value
```

❑ This command will get the actual value of the item within the selected drop-down list box.

❑ The final feature of importance with a drop-down list box is the ability to add items to it. This is done by the following command:

```
document.getElementById(ControlName).options.add( new Option(stringText,
stringTextValue));
```

- ❑ With this command, an option is added to the drop-down list box named `ControlName`. With this example, the user will see the contents of `stringText` and it will have a value of `stringTextValue`.

❑ **Server control** — Referencing an ASP.NET server control from client-side JavaScript can be somewhat confusing. Within the client and server, a control ID is designed to be unique. One would think that a client-side ID would map directly to a server-side control, but this is not always the case. There are many situations where a server control is defined once and repeated within another control. ASP.NET will create a unique client-side ID. This client-side ID is more than just the server-side ID; it is a combination of the container, the server-side ID, and an interater. To reference the client-side ID of a server-side element, the following code will generate the necessary reference:

```
document.getElementById("<%=EventDate.ClientID%>").innerHTML
```

- ❑ In this example, the text of a `<div>` tag can be processed. The server-side ID is handed to the client by some in-place ASP.NET code and uses the `.ClientID` property of a server control.

❑ **ASP.NET AJAX shortcut ($get())** — AJAX code tends to contain a significant amount of code that is `document.getElementById()`. ASP.NET AJAX provides a shortcut to use `document.getElementById()`; this shortcut is the dollar symbol with the word get (`$get()`).

Browsers Supported

One of the more interesting design requirements of ASP.NET AJAX is that it should work across the latest versions of major browsers. This includes support for the latest versions of Internet Explorer, Firefox, and the Apple Safari browser. Due to the client-side requirement for an object capable of working with web services (MSXML or `XMLHttpRequest`), many older browsers are not supported and along with many embedded browsers for mobile devices. Figure 4-1 shows one of the ASP.NET AJAX examples from this chapter running in Firefox.

Though not specifically a web browser, many of the latest versions of screen readers will work properly; however, each application and feature should be tested to ensure that it works properly for the necessary users.

Figure 4-1

What Is at the Client?

Now that you have looked at some of the technologies for performing ASP.NET AJAX operations, you need to look at the specifics. This section looks at the ScriptManager, proxies for web services, error processing, and other pieces involved in the process of making ASP.NET AJAX calls work.

The ScriptManager

The ScriptManager control is the key to getting ASP.NET AJAX to load on the client. The following code sets up the ScriptManager:

```
<asp:ScriptManager ID="ScriptManager1" runat="server" >
    <services>
        <asp:ServiceReference
Path="WebServices/DataTypes.asmx"></asp:ServiceReference>
    </services>
</asp:ScriptManager>
```

The ScriptManager then produces something similar to the following JavaScript include. This JavaScript include the source data through an httphandler.

The scripts that are supplied with ASP.NET AJAX run against several web servers besides Microsoft IIS, however, examples along those lines are outside the scope of this book.

The handler reads the inputs, determines the AJAX libraries that need to be sent to the client, and then sends the appropriate libraries to the client web browser:

```
<script src="/WebServicesIntegration/WebResource.axd?d=eOVOaSz5OiQZUM8HaT8OgA2&amp;
t=632968892944906146" type="text/javascript"></script>
<script src="/WebServicesIntegration/ScriptResource.axd?d=J7pvNve2eJUy-P88c1qUNwg
-C8pjXTS3t8uIej_rVvlIAamu2zBKU252EPaa4h7LLFGu5TGJGfDN68NMlFJxHYT1-
9FkOu_BvLS5heZAUno1&amp;t=633061042199201228" type="text/javascript"></script>
<script src="/WebServicesIntegration/ScriptResource.axd?d=J7pvNve2eJUy-P88c1qUNwg-
C8pjXTS3t8uIej_rVvlIAamu2zBKU252EPaa4h7LLFGu5TGJGfDN68NMlFJxHQMZGas09QaxqqtLF61b4e0
1&amp;t=633061042199201228" type="text/javascript"></script>
<script src="WebServices/DataTypes.asmx/js" type="text/javascript"></script>
    <script type="text/javascript">
//<![CDATA[
Sys.WebForms.PageRequestManager._initialize('ScriptManager1',
document.getElementById('form1'));
Sys.WebForms.PageRequestManager.getInstance()._updateControls([], [], [], 90);
//]]>
</script>
<script type="text/javascript">
<!--
Sys.Application.initialize();
// -->
</script>
```

The `ScriptManager` has the following important properties that can be set:

❑ `AllowCustomErrorsRedirect` — The `AllowCustomErrorsRedirect` property sets whether or not custom error redirects can occur during an asynchronous postback by an `UpdatePanel`.

❑ `AsyncPostBackErrorMessage` — The `AsyncPostBackErrorMessage` property sets the error message that will be displayed during an asynchronous postback by an `UpdatePanel`.

❑ `AsyncPostBackTimeout` — The `AsyncPostBackTimeout` property sets the time before a time-out occurs during an asynchronous postback by an `UpdatePanel`.

❑ `AuthenticationService` — The `AuthenticationService` property provides settings for the client-side authentication service.

❑ `EnablePageMethods` — The `EnablePageMethods` property provides for enabling page-based web services.

❑ `EnablePartialRendering` — The `EnablePartialRendering` property instructs the AJAX client-side libraries to set up support for the `UpdatePanel`. (The `UpdatePanel` is discussed in Chapter 5.) A value of `true` enables support for the `UpdatePanel`. A value of `false` disables support for the `UpdatePanel`.

❑ `EnableScriptGlobalization` — The `EnableScriptGlobalization` property enables globalization of script.

❑ `EnableScriptLocalization` — The `EnableScriptLocalization` property enables localization of script.

❑ `LoadScriptBeforeUI` — The `LocalScriptBeforeUI` property sets whether or not the script references should be loaded before the UI is displayed by the browser.

❑ `ProfileService` — The `ProfileService` property provides settings for the client-side profile service.

❑ `ScriptMode` — The `ScriptMode` property specifies the types of script (Debug or Release) to load.

❑ `ScriptPath` — The `ScriptPath` property specifies the path that should be used if the scripts are not loaded from an assembly web resource.

❑ `Scripts` — The `Scripts` property is a collection of JavaScript files that will be included in the page.

❑ `Services` — The `Services` property is a collection of web services that will be made available within a page.

Services

The `<services>` tag loads up the set of web services that the web browser is going to use as follows:

```
<script src="WebServices/DataTypes.asmx/js" type="text/javascript"></script>
```

From the preceding JavaScript, a web service proxy is generated. This web service proxy is created by calling the web service with `"/js"` on the end of the URL from the web browser. To see what various data types look like, this code calls the `\WebServices\DataTypes.asmx` file because it has several different data types being used within it. The following code is loaded into the web browser:

```
var DataTypes=function() {
```

```
DataTypes.initializeBase(this);
this._timeout = 0;
this._userContext = null;
this._succeeded = null;
this._failed = null;
}
DataTypes.prototype={
ReturnString:function(succeededCallback, failedCallback, userContext) {
return this._invoke(DataTypes.get_path(),
'ReturnString',false,{},succeededCallback,failedCallback,userContext); },
ReturnBoolean:function(succeededCallback, failedCallback, userContext) {
return this._invoke(DataTypes.get_path(),
'ReturnBoolean',false,{},succeededCallback,failedCallback,userContext); },
AddTwoNumbers:function(a,b,succeededCallback, failedCallback, userContext) {
return this._invoke(DataTypes.get_path(),
'AddTwoNumbers',false,{a:a,b:b},succeededCallback,failedCallback,userContext); },
CodeCampInfo:function(CodeCampId,succeededCallback, failedCallback, userContext) {
return this._invoke(DataTypes.get_path(),
'CodeCampInfo',false,{CodeCampId:CodeCampId},succeededCallback,failedCallback,userC
ontext); }}
DataTypes.registerClass('DataTypes',Sys.Net.WebServiceProxy);
DataTypes._staticInstance = new DataTypes();
DataTypes.set_path = function(value) { DataTypes._staticInstance._path = value; }
DataTypes.get_path = function() { return DataTypes._staticInstance._path; }
DataTypes.set_timeout = function(value) { DataTypes._staticInstance._timeout =
value; }
DataTypes.get_timeout = function() { return DataTypes._staticInstance._timeout; }
DataTypes.set_defaultUserContext = function(value) {
DataTypes._staticInstance._userContext = value; }
DataTypes.get_defaultUserContext = function() { return
DataTypes._staticInstance._userContext; }
DataTypes.set_defaultSucceededCallback = function(value) {
DataTypes._staticInstance._succeeded = value; }
DataTypes.get_defaultSucceededCallback = function() { return
DataTypes._staticInstance._succeeded; }
DataTypes.set_defaultFailedCallback = function(value) {
DataTypes._staticInstance._failed = value; }
DataTypes.get_defaultFailedCallback = function() { return
DataTypes._staticInstance._failed; }
DataTypes.set_path("/WebServicesIntegration/WebServices/DataTypes.asmx");
DataTypes.ReturnString= function(onSuccess,onFailed,userContext)
{DataTypes._staticInstance.ReturnString(onSuccess,onFailed,userContext); }
DataTypes.ReturnBoolean= function(onSuccess,onFailed,userContext)
{DataTypes._staticInstance.ReturnBoolean(onSuccess,onFailed,userContext); }
DataTypes.AddTwoNumbers= function(a,b,onSuccess,onFailed,userContext)
{DataTypes._staticInstance.AddTwoNumbers(a,b,onSuccess,onFailed,userContext); }
DataTypes.CodeCampInfo= function(CodeCampId,onSuccess,onFailed,userContext)
{DataTypes._staticInstance.CodeCampInfo(CodeCampId,onSuccess,onFailed,userContext);
}
var gtc = Sys.Net.WebServiceProxy._generateTypedConstructor;
if (typeof(CodeCampInformation) === 'undefined') {
var CodeCampInformation=gtc("CodeCampInformation");
CodeCampInformation.registerClass('CodeCampInformation');
}
```

This code shows several interesting things:

❑　A proxy method is created by the calls to:

```
var DataTypes=function() {
DataTypes.initializeBase(this);
this._timeout = 0;
this._userContext = null;
this._succeeded = null;
this._failed = null;
}
```

❑　The JavaScript proxy shows the options for calling a method as well as the parameters used for those calls.

HTTP Calling Options

The JavaScript proxy to call a web service is created automatically by ASP.NET AJAX. There are two options to call the methods within the web service: HTTP Post and HTTP Get.

An HTTP Post is the default mechanism to call a web service. With an HTTP Post, a body of data is sent from the browser to the server. The body of data does not have a size limit; thus, a Post is a better choice than a Get when a large amount of data is sent to the server during the request. The client puts the data into a JSON format and sends that to the server. The server takes the JSON data, translates it to the appropriate .NET data types, and then performs the call to the web service. The server will translate the return data into the JSON format and send it down to the browser. The browser is then responsible for processing the data.

With an HTTP Get, the processing steps are the same, except that the initial communications is different. The initial communication is made through an HTTP Get. As a result, the browser will send the parameters as a query string to the server. Therefore, size limitations must be considered on both the browser and the server. In addition, sending data as an HTTP Get is considered to expose a security risk. An HTTP Get is an easier target for tampering, so care should be taken when using it. To use an HTTP Get, the ScriptMethod attribute should be modified to use the following attribute:

```
[ScriptMethod(UseHttpGet=true)]
```

Scripts

The <Scripts> section is a collection of JavaScript files included for processing on a web page. An example ScriptManager is shown here:

```
<asp:ScriptManager ID="ScriptManager1" runat="server" >
    <scripts>
        <asp:ScriptReference Path="TestScriptFile.js"></asp:ScriptReference>
    </scripts>
    <services>
        <asp:ServiceReference Path="WebServices/GetData.asmx"
></asp:ServiceReference>
    </services>
</asp:ScriptManager>
```

The preceding ScriptManager control has a reference to the JavaScript file TestScriptFile.js as well as the web service file WebServices/GetData.asmx.

This `<scripts>` tag results in the following code being generated:

```
<script src="TestScriptFile.js" type="text/javascript"></script>
<script src="WebServices/GetData.asmx/js" type="text/javascript"></script>
```

Shortcuts

ASP.NET AJAX provides a set of shortcuts for commonly used commands:

❏ `$get(ControlName)` — `$get` is a shortcut to `Sys.UI.DomElement.getElementById` and functions exactly like the `document.getElementById` DOM method. `$get(ControlName)` is used to obtain a reference to a form element on a web page.

❏ `$addhandler(Element, EventName, HandlerMethod)` — `$addHandler` is a shortcut to `Sys.UI.DomEvent.addHandler`. `Element` is the form element that will be assigned the event. `EventName` is the name of the event that will be processed. For example, processing the `click` event would have its name of `"click"` be used. `Handler` is the name of the client-side method that will be called.

❏ `$clearHandlers(Element)` — `$clearHandlers` is a shortcut to `Sys.UI.DomElement` `.clearHandlers`. `Element` is a form element that will have all handlers removed from it.

❏ `$create()` — `$create` is a shortcut to `Sys.Component.create`.

❏ `$find()` — `$find` is a shortcut to `Sys.Application.findComponent`.

❏ `$removeHandler()` — `$removeHandler` is a shortcut to `Sys.UI.DomEvent.removeHandler`.

ScriptManagerProxy

A page with ASP.NET AJAX can have only one `ScriptManager` control. Attempting to put multiple `ScriptManagers` onto a single page will result in an error. What is a developer going to do with a page that is actually a master page along with content sections? If the master page has the `ScriptManager`, how can the content sections modify the settings for that particular page and its needs? The answer is the `ScriptManagerProxy` class. The `ScriptManagerProxy` class allows for a content page or control to add services and scripts that are needed on that particular page.

XML-Script

XML-Script is something that is common to every page that loads up the ASP.NET AJAX `ScriptManager`. For this example, the XML-Script merely loads the appropriate references for calling into the JavaScript and the web services it references. XML-Script does much more. For more information on the XML-Script code, refer to Chapter 14 regarding the online content, as well as the online content itself.

Server-Side Operations

Communicating back to a web server is at the very core of ASP.NET AJAX. When performing AJAX-style operations, communication to the web service is critical. The next question is what is needed on the server? There are a few things necessary on the web server. Obviously, a web server is needed with the `System.Web.Extensions.dll` file configured in the `web.config`. A web service to call against is the other thing needed. The web service does not need to be configured in any special way. The following is an example web service that is used:

```csharp
using System;
using System.Data;
using System.Data.SqlClient;
using System.Collections;
using System.Collections.Generic;
using System.Web;
using System.Web.Services;
using System.Web.Services.Protocols;
using System.Web.Script.Services;
  [WebService(Namespace = "http://tempuri.org/")]
[WebServiceBinding(ConformsTo = WsiProfiles.BasicProfile1_1)]
[ScriptService]
public class GetData : System.Web.Services.WebService
{
    public GetData()
    {
        //Uncomment the following line if using designed components
        //InitializeComponent();
    }
    [WebMethod]
    [GenerateScriptType(typeof(CodeCamp))]
    public CodeCamp[] CodeCampList()
    {
        CodeCamp lSpec;
        List<CodeCamp> lData = new List<CodeCamp>();
        DataTable dtData;
        CCData CodeCampData = new CCData();
        dtData = CodeCampData.GetCodeCamps();
        foreach (DataRow drData in dtData.Rows)
        {
            lSpec = new CodeCamp(Convert.ToInt32(drData["CodeCampId"]),
                Convert.ToString(drData["Name"]));
            lData.Add(lSpec);
        }
        return (lData.ToArray());
    }
    [WebMethod]
    [GenerateScriptType(typeof(CodeCampInformation))]
    public CodeCampInformation[] CodeCampInfo(int CodeCampId)
    {
        CodeCampInformation lSpec;
        List<CodeCampInformation> lData = new List<CodeCampInformation>();
        DataTable dtData;
        CCData CodeCampData = new CCData();
        dtData = CodeCampData.CodeCampInfo(CodeCampId);
        foreach (DataRow drData in dtData.Rows)
        {
            lSpec = new CodeCampInformation(Convert.ToString(drData["City"]),
                Convert.ToDateTime(drData["DateOfEvent"]),
                Convert.ToInt32(drData["NumberOfAttendees"]));
            lData.Add(lSpec);
        }
```

```
        return (lData.ToArray());
    }
    [WebMethod]
    public DataTable CodeCampInfoWithDelay(int CodeCampId)
    {
        CCData CodeCampData = new CCData();
        System.Threading.Thread.Sleep(10000);
        return CodeCampData.CodeCampInfo(CodeCampId);
    }
}
```

As you look at the code, you see that there is nothing special about the code in that web service. This code looks like any other web service code that you might write. The method `CodeCampList()` takes no input and returns a complex object. The method `CodeCampInfo()` takes an integer method as the input, passes that to an instance of a class, and then returns a complex object.

There are two requirements that calling through ASP.NET AJAX imposes on the code:

❑   The `[ScriptService]` attribute must be applied to any web service class.

❑   When a complex object is returned, the information about that object must be communicated to the calling method. This is done through the `[GenerateScriptType(typeof)]` attribute on the individual method.

It might seem strange that there is no mention in this section of using web services that return DataSets and DataTables. After all, all developers are familiar with DataSets and DataTables. Unfortunately, Microsoft was not able to schedule enough time to get DataSet and DataTable support into the ASP.NET 2.0 AJAX Extensions 1.0 release. Support for DataSets and DataTables is in the ASP.NET AJAX Futures CTP. DataSet and DataTable support is discussed in Chapter 14 and in the online content.

Putting the Client and Server Together

As you can see by now, there are many moving parts to an ASP.NET AJAX application. As a result, there are many places where things can go wrong. This section ties these pieces together so that you can make a call out to a web service in your application and get things started.

Using the ASP.NET Calling Convention

The calling convention for ASP.NET AJAX is to make a call into a web service, pass the necessary parameters, and then to process returned data in various callbacks that are passed to the web service call. Look at the first code sample for calling into a web service using ASP.NET AJAX:

```
function pageLoad()
{
    GetCodeCampList();
}
function GetCodeCampList()
{
    GetData.CodeCampList(CodeCampListOnCompleteCallBack,
        CodeCampOnServerException);
}
```

```
function GetCodeCampInfo()
{
    var iCodeCamp;
    iCodeCamp = $get("CodeCamp").options[$get("CodeCamp").selectedIndex].value;
    GetData.CodeCampInfo(iCodeCamp, CodeCampInfoOnCallBack,
CodeCampOnServerException);
}
function CodeCampListOnCompleteCallBack(result)
{
    var iLength = document.getElementById("CodeCamp").options.length;
    for(i=0; i<iLength; i++)
    {
        $get("CodeCamp").options[0] = null;
    }
    document.getElementById("CodeCamp").options.add(new Option("", ""));
    for(i=0;i<result.length;i++)
    {
        $get("CodeCamp").options.add(
            new Option(result[i].Name,
            result[i].CodeCampId));
    }
    $get("ExceptionInfo").style.visibility = "hidden";
}
function CodeCampOnServerException(result)
{
    var ExceptionOutput;
    var Return = "<br />";
    if ( null != result )
    {
        ExceptionOutput = "Message: " + result.get_message() + Return;
        ExceptionOutput += "Stack Trace: " + result.get_stackTrace() + Return;
        ExceptionOutput += "Exception Type: " + result.get_exceptionType() +
Return;
        $get("ExceptionInfo").innerHTML = ExceptionOutput;
        $get("ExceptionInfo").style.visibility = "visible";
    }
}
function CodeCampInfoOnCallBack(result)
{
    if ( null != result )
    {
        if ( result.length == 1 )
        {
            $get("<%=CityInfo.ClientID%>").innerHTML = result[0].City;
            $get("<%=EventDate.ClientID%>").innerHTML = result[0].DateOfEvent;
            $get("<%=AttendeeNum.ClientID%>").innerHTML =
result[0].NumberOfAttendees;
        }
        else{
            alert(result.get_length() + " number of rows were returned.");
        }
    }
}
```

In this specific example, the page and code do the following things:

1. When a page loads, the `pageLoad()` method is fired. This method is a special ASP.NET AJAX event that is called if the method exists on a page.

2. The `pageLoad()` method calls out to a web service. When the data is returned, the data is formatted and placed within a `<select>` tag/drop-down list box showing a set of codecamp events.

3. The user is expected to select one of the items from the drop-down list box.

4. When the user clicks the button, a call is made to a web service to get data about a codecamp.

There are a couple of things to look at in the preceding code:

❑ The method call `GetData.CodeCampInfo(iCodeCamp, CodeCampInfoOnCallBack, CodeCampOnTimeOutCallBack, CodeCampOnServerException);` calls out to the web service. Examination of the web service shows that the `CodeCampInfo()` method takes one paramater; however, this code call passes three parameters. The first parameter matches the `CodeCampInfo()` integer parameter.

❑ The second parameter is not actually passed to the web service. The second parameter is the method that will be called when the web service returns the data to the client.

❑ The final parameter is not passed to the web service but is the name of the method that will be called if there is an unhandled exception in the web service. The method `CodeCampOnServerException` is not shown in this section but is shown later in this chapter when discussing error processing.

❑ The callbacks that handle the timeout and the server exception are not required.

❑ Note the use of `<%=CityInfo.ClientID%>`. This is done to get the name of the ASP.NET control as it will be generated on the client. This is not absolutely necessary unless you are using ASP.NET controls that are embedded inside of some other container. If the controls on the page are purely client-side controls, there is no need to reference them this way. You can reference them through the client-side ID attribute of the control.

Figure 4-2 shows some example output from the previous code running in Internet Explorer.

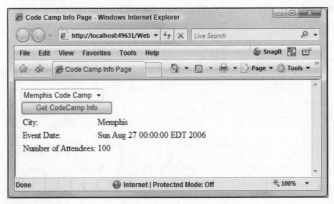

Figure 4-2

Performing Asynchronous Operations

Typically, developers work on a programming model that involves commands being executed one at a time. This is referred to as *synchronous programming*. In this situation, a command is made along with passing some parameters. The command executes and any necessary data is passed back to whoever executed. Command execution continues after a method is called. This is fairly simple to implement, however there are several problems with this scenario:

❑ It tends to lock the calling programming at a point waiting on command execution to return. For commands that execute fairly quickly, that is not an issue. For commands that run a long time, this can be a problem. This is further compounded by the fact that this type of programming tends to lock the user interface. A command goes out and a user does not necessarily know whether the command is running or a problem has occurred.

❑ With web browsers, the default action of animating the browser logo in the top-right corner is typically not enough to instruct the user that a command is happening. The user may think that the browser has locked up.

❑ Operations that might take several minutes result in the application being completely unresponsive.

Figure 4-3 shows how synchronous processing results in a problem in a web browser. In this scenario, a web browser must go back and forth between the web client and the web server to do any meaningful processing. During that time, a user is unable to make any changes to the user interface of the application and must wait on a result to come back from the server. If a user makes a change while waiting, that change will most likely be overwritten by the new data that comes back from the server.

Into this problem steps the concept of asynchronous operations. With asynchronous operations, a command can be called and work can continue on the client. Waiting on long-running operations to complete is not a problem when using asynchronous operations. Figure 4-4 shows conceptually that a user can continue working at the client while a request happens at the server. Once the server request is done, the server sends the response back to the client and the client browser processes the request while the user works. During this process, users can usually continue doing work while server work is performed and work continues at the client. Please remember that due to a lack of threading in JavaScript within a browser, there may be some instances where the user is still blocked from performing some operations. However, this situation is still an improvement over a standard postback where any data that the user inputs after a postback is initiated is ignored.

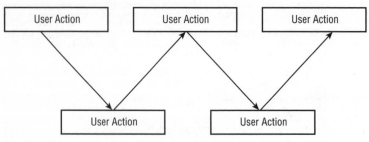

Figure 4-3

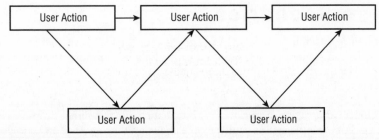

Figure 4-4

Because ASP.NET AJAX runs asynchronously, let's take a moment to mention ASP.NET AJAX's asynchronous communications layers. With client architecture for ASP.NET AJAX sits in five basic layers. These layers are as follows:

❏ **Client application** — The client application is what developers are primarily building.

❏ **Script core library** — The script core library contains the building blocks that are available to a developer.

❏ **Client asynchronous communications layer** — The client asynchronous communications layer contains the various communications methods.

❏ **Browser compatibility layer** — This layer handles the differences between the various browsers, such as Internet Explorer, Firefox, and Safari.

❏ **The browser itself** — The browser can be Internet Explorer, Firefox, or Safari.

The most complicated part is the client asynchronous communications layer. This layer contains the following five sub-layers:

❏ **The proxy layer** — The proxy layer contains the web service proxies, page method proxies, profile proxy, and the authentication proxy. These are the services exposed by the web services and services on the server.

❏ **WebRequest** — The `WebRequest` class is responsible for making HTTP requests.

❏ **WebRequestManager** — The `WebRequestManager` class is responsible for managing the relationship between web requests and the object that made the call.

❏ **XmlHttpExecutor** — The `XmlHttpExecutor` class performs network requests using the browser's support.

❏ **XmlHttp** — The `XmlHttp` object is the low-level object that performs the XML HTTP request.

In parallel with the `XmlHttpExecutor` and the `XmlHttp` objects is the JSON serializer, which is discussed later in this chapter.

AJAX-Type Scenarios

Calling a web service through ASP.NET AJAX is going to be the main way that a developer will use ASP.NET AJAX. In that scenario, a web service is called with one or more parameters and some type of data is returned. The question is which scenarios make sense and which do not. Here are some of the scenarios that make sense:

❑ Choosing a value in one drop-down list box that results in another drop-down list box being updated. For example, a user could select a state and then another drop-down list box could be filled with the major cities of that state.

❑ Although it is possible to validate simple data within the ASP.NET controls, there are situations where it is necessary to validate against business rules that exist on the server. Data can be handed to a web service and the web service can return a true or false depending on whether the data meets the defined business rule.

❑ In many situations where data needs to be paged through. This could be a grid of data or just individual records.

❑ How would you like to have an application that saved data to a centralized web server periodically? That way, you could restart at the latest save point in case something goes wrong.

❑ If bandwidth is constrained, asynchronous processing can limit the bandwidth utilization of an application. With a full postback, all form elements are sent to the server and then the page is reformed and sent from the server to the client. With an AJAX operation, only the data that is necessary is sent to the server and only the necessary return values are sent.

❑ If CPU utilization on the server is constrained, asynchronous processing can limit the use of the server CPU. With a regular postback, all form data, including the ViewState, are processed along with all necessary events on the server. With an AJAX call, only the necessary web service methods are called.

❑ If a high degree of user interaction is necessary, asynchronous processing can assist. With an AJAX-style interface, the user perceives an increased level of interactivity.

As you can see, using AJAX-type operations often makes a lot of sense in web-based applications.

Returning Data

ASP.NET AJAX would not be of much interest if it could not work with data. Luckily, ASP.NET AJAX has support for working with data. This data can be in the form of simple data types like integers, strings, Booleans, and such along with DataTables/DataSets, and also custom business objects. This section looks at passing data back and forth.

Simple Data Types

Several data types can easily be passed between the browser and a web service in ASP.NET AJAX. These data types can be integers, strings, Booleans, and other simple data types. These data types work because they can be serialized and shipped from the browser to the server and back through the JSON serialization/deserialization process. Take a look at some example code:

```
[WebMethod]
public double AddTwoNumbers(double a, double b)
{
    return (a + b);
}
```

This code demonstrates a web service that merely takes two numbers and returns the added value back to the caller.

The client-side code JavaScript looks like this on the .aspx page:

```
function AddNumbers()
{
    DataTypes.AddTwoNumbers(3.3, 4.8888, AddTwoNumbersComplete);
}
function AddTwoNumbersComplete(result)
{
    alert("Number returned: " + result);
}
```

The result of running this code is that 8.1888 is returned to the calling browser, as shown in Figure 4-5.

Figure 4-5

Working with Custom Business Objects

Some applications make use of custom data objects, also called custom business objects. These business objects may contain more custom logic than a DataSet/DataTable. Luckily, ASP.NET AJAX can handle the data contained within a custom business object.

The client-side JavaScript code looks like this:

```
function CallComplexObject()
{
    var objCat = new BeginningAJAXWithASPNET.AnimalClass();
    objCat.Name = "Fluff";
    objCat.Address = "Washington, DC";
    objCat.Parents = "Fred Smith";
    BeginningAJAXWithASPNET.WebServiceAnimal.ReturnAnimal( objCat,
AnimalCompleteEvent);
}
function AnimalCompleteEvent(result)
{
    var str = "";
    var strReturn = "<br />";
    str += "Name: " + result.Name + strReturn;
    str += "Address: " + result.Address + strReturn;
    str += "Parents: " + result.Parents + strReturn;
    $get("Output").innerHTML = str;
}
function AnimalServerException(result)
{
    alert("Exception Message: " + result.get_message());
    alert("Server Exception Occurred.");
}
```

The server-side code that holds the `AnimalClass()` is as follows:

```
public class AnimalClass
{
    public AnimalClass()
    {
        //
        // TODO: Add constructor logic here
        //
    }
    private string _Name = String.Empty;
    private string _Address = String.Empty;
    private string _Parents = String.Empty;
    public String Name
    {
        get { return (_Name); }
        set { _Name = value; }
    }
    public String Address
    {
        get { return (_Address); }
        set { _Address = value; }
```

```
    }
    public String Parents
    {
        get { return (_Parents); }
        set { _Parents = value; }
    }
}

[WebMethod]
[GenerateScriptType(typeof(AnimalClass))]
public AnimalClass ReturnAnimal(AnimalClass AnimalObj)
{
    return AnimalObj;
}
```

Figure 4-6 shows the output from the example application returning a custom business object. In this example, several properties of the object are read and shown to the user.

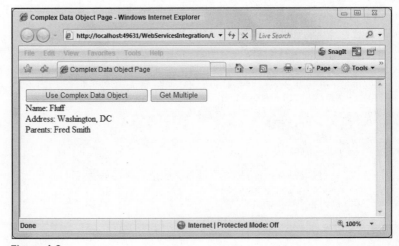

Figure 4-6

Now that you have seen that ASP.NET AJAX can handle a complex business object, the question becomes: what about multiple objects? It can handle them also. This example builds on the previous `AnimalClass()` example. It returns multiple `AnimalClass()` objects in the form of an array of objects.

Take a look at the server-side code:

```
[WebMethod]
[GenerateScriptType(typeof(AnimalClass))]
public AnimalClass[] ReturnAnimals()
{
    List<AnimalClass> AnimalArray = new List<AnimalClass>();
    AnimalClass obj = new AnimalClass();
    obj.Name = "Wells";
    obj.Address = "Knoxville, TN";
    obj.Parents = "Wally and Ronda";
```

```
        AnimalArray.Add(obj);
        AnimalClass obj2 = new AnimalClass();
        obj2.Name = "Spot";
        obj2.Address = "Atlanta, GA";
        obj2.Parents = "Mom and Dad";
        AnimalArray.Add(obj2);
        return (AnimalArray.ToArray());
    }
```

The client-side web browser code looks like this:

```
function GetMultipleObjects()
{
BeginningAJAXWithASPNET.WebServiceAnimal.ReturnAnimals(ReturnMultipleCompletedEvent
);
}
function ReturnMultipleCompletedEvent(result)
{
    var str = "";
    var strReturn = "<br />";
    for(i=0;i<result.length;i++)
    {
        str += "Name: " + result[i].Name + strReturn;
        str += "Address: " + result[i].Address + strReturn;
        str += "Parents: " + result[i].Parents + strReturn;
        str += strReturn;
    }
    $get("Output").innerHTML = str;
}
function CallComplexObject()
{
    var objCat = new BeginningAJAXWithASPNET.AnimalClass();
    objCat.Name = "Fluff";
    objCat.Address = "Washington, DC";
    objCat.Parents = "Fred Smith";
    BeginningAJAXWithASPNET.WebServiceAnimal.ReturnAnimal( objCat,
AnimalCompleteEvent);
}
function AnimalCompleteEvent(result)
{
    var str = "";
    var strReturn = "<br />";
    str += "Name: " + result.Name + strReturn;
    str += "Address: " + result.Address + strReturn;
    str += "Parents: " + result.Parents + strReturn;
    $get("Output").innerHTML = str;
}
function AnimalServerException(result)
{
    alert("Exception Message: " + result.get_message());
    alert("Server Exception Occurred.");
}
```

Figure 4-7 shows the output from handling multiple custom business objects returned from a web service call.

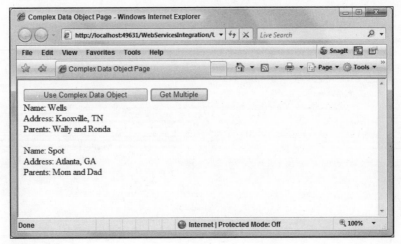

Figure 4-7

Page-Based Web Services

Although most web services in ASP.NET are encapsulated within an .asmx page, it is possible to encapsulate a web service within an .aspx page. When a page-based web service is included with ASP.NET AJAX, it provides a convenient single distribution mechanism for an application. The following Try It Out shows some example code.

Try It Out   **Encapsulating a Web Service in an .aspx Page**

```
<%@ Page Language="C#" %>
<%@ Import Namespace="System.Web.Services" %>
    <script language="c#" runat="server">

        [WebMethod]
        public static string CallMethod(string UserName)
        {
            return ("Hi " + UserName);
        }
    </script>
<!DOCTYPE html PUBLIC "-//W3C//DTD XHTML 1.0 Transitional//EN"
"http://www.w3.org/TR/xhtml1/DTD/xhtml1-transitional.dtd">

<html xmlns="http://www.w3.org/1999/xhtml" >
<head runat="server">
    <title>Page Methods Page</title>
</head>

<body>
    <form id="form1" runat="server">
    <asp:ScriptManager ID="ScriptManager1" runat="server"
EnablePageMethods="true"></asp:ScriptManager>
    <div>
```

```
    <input type="button" value="Click Me" id="btnClickMe"
onclick="CallPageMethod()" />
    </div>
    </form>
    <script type="text/javascript">
        function CallPageMethod()
        {
            PageMethods.CallMethod("Wally", CallPageMethodOnComplete);
        }
        function CallPageMethodOnComplete(result)
        {
            alert("Value returned: " + result);
        }
    </script>
</body>
</html>
```

How It Works

Here are the steps to get this example to work:

1. On the `<ScriptManager>` tag, the `EnablePageMethod` property must be set to `true`.

2. A server-side method must be created. This method must be marked with the `[WebMethod]` attribute and must be static. Even though the server-side method is most likely "private" to the given page, the method must be marked as public.

3. In the calling JavaScript, instead of using the calling convention of `ClassName.MethodName`, the calling convention is `PageMethods.MethodName`. In this calling convention, `PageMethods` is a defined name that takes the place of the `ClassName`, and `MethodName` is the name of the method that is to be called.

Data Format with JSON

The term "AJAX," which stands for Asynchronous JavaScript And XML, has caught on in the development community. It is implied that XML is used for the data format. However, ASP.NET AJAX does not use XML for its data transport when working with web services. Rather, it uses a slightly different format, called the *JavaScript Object Notation* (JSON) by default.

What Is JSON?

JSON is a data-interchange format that is fairly easy for machines to use and create. JSON is a text format that is based on C language conventions. It is built on two items:

❑ A list of values, such as an array

❑ A collection of name/values pairs, such as an object

This might not make a lot of sense, so look at a quick example. Say you have an object defined like this:

```
public class CodeCampInformation
{
    private string _City;
    private DateTime _DateOfEvent;
    private int _NumberOfAttendees;
    public CodeCampInformation()
    {
    }
    public CodeCampInformation(string City, DateTime DateOfEvent, int
NumberOfAttendees)
    {
        _City = City;
        _DateOfEvent = DateOfEvent;
        _NumberOfAttendees = NumberOfAttendees;
    }
    public string City
    {
        get { return (_City); }
        set { _City = value; }
    }
    public DateTime DateOfEvent
    {
        get { return (_DateOfEvent); }
        set { _DateOfEvent = value; }
    }
    public int NumberOfAttendees
    {
        get { return (_NumberOfAttendees); }
        set { _NumberOfAttendees = value; }
    }
}
```

The preceding class definition defines an object called CodeCampInformation. This object has properties of City, DateOfEvent, and NumberOfAttendees. These values can be read and assigned through the gets and sets defined or the object's constructor.

Based on the preceding class definition, look at an example object. In the test object, the example code is going to create an object that has a City value of "Orlando", a DateOfEvent value of March 26, 2006, and a NumberOfAttendees value of 150. Based on these values, the following JSON object was created:

```
[{"City":"Orlando","DateOfEvent":"\/Date(1143345600000)\/","NumberOfAttendees":150}
]
```

Why Use JSON?

Now that you have seen what JSON is, why should you use it? Isn't JSON just a different format from XML? JSON has one major advantage over XML when it is used in a web environment: JavaScript supports an eval(string) method that will evaluate the included string value and run it as if it is code. This is somewhat easier than processing XML on the client. As a result, JSON is used by default within the Microsoft AJAX Library.

JSON is the default format for ASP.NET AJAX. However, it is not the only format supported by ASP.NET AJAX. XML is also supported. XML output from a web service can be performed by adding the following attribute to a web service:

```
[ScriptMethod(ResponseFormat.XML)]
```

Problem Areas

You have looked at calling out to a web service and have seen all of the advantages of this scenario, but there are some areas that can trip you up. I have already discussed the issue of being asynchronous, but integrating client-side and server-side processing with the ViewState can be a very daunting task, for example.

Invalid Postback or Callback Argument

Consider the following scenario:

1. There is a server-side drop-down list box.

2. Another form element makes an ASP.NET AJAX call and brings back data.

3. This data is then populated into the drop-down list box.

4. A user then clicks a button, which results in a server-side button click event being called.

The result of these four steps is the exception shown in Figure 4-8. This exception occurs because the ASP.NET runtime did not know about this new value in the ASP.NET drop-down list box.

This is the first problem that developers will likely run into: the Invalid postback or callback argument exception. This argument exception is generated because ASP.NET attempts to check the data that is sent to it. The data in the drop-down list box is tested against the data that was shipped out through the initial web request. The ASP.NET runtime sees that the data that is coming back to it in the drop-down list box is not the same as the data that it sent out. Therefore, the ASP.NET runtime throws the argument exception. Several workarounds help you resolve this issue:

❑   The `EnableEventValidation` property of the page or the web application can be set to `false`. Due to the security hole that this opens up, it is best to do this only on the page necessary. Even then, enabling this feature on the page opens up the page to an injection attack. As a result, this option should only be used when other forms of security are taken.

❑   Within the `Render` event of the page, the ASP.NET runtime can be told that there are allowed values. The problem with this scenario is that the other allowed values must also be known at the time of the `Render` event. This could mean potentially adding hundreds, thousands, or hundreds of thousands of values. The following source code that shows what must be done:

```
protected override void Render(HtmlTextWriter writer)
{
    ClientScript.RegisterForEventValidation(
```

```
        this.ddlName.UniqueID, "Fred Smith" );
ClientScript.RegisterForEventValidation(
        this.ddlName.UniqueID, String.Empty);
base.Render(writer);
}
```

In this code, the values are statically added. A developer could easily make a call to a method that returns a DataTable and the results could be dynamically added. The problem with this scenario is that this must be done with such a large number of potential values. These values are stored in the ViewState, which results in more data being sent to the client and back on a postback in addition to more processing being done on the server to check whether a value that is returned is valid. Figure 4-8 shows the argument exception.

❑   Instead of using ASP.NET server controls, use the ASP.NET HtmlControls. The HtmlControls do not keep their state between postbacks in AJAX; however, they do not validate the data either. As a quick reminder, an HtmlControl appears to be the same as an HTML form element with the attribute of `runat="server"` added to it. Here is an example:

```
<select id="ddlName2" runat="server" />
```

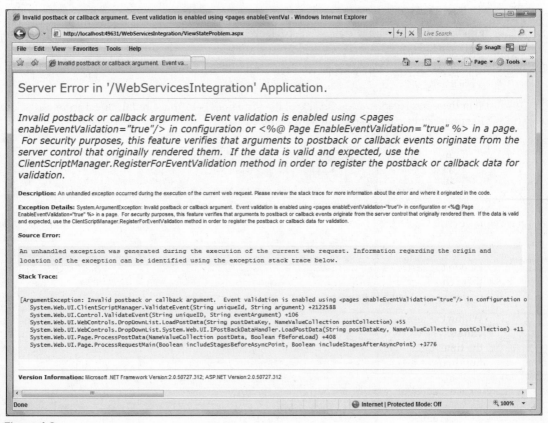

Figure 4-8

One last thought on this is that the argument exception issue greatly depends on the control being used. If the field to be updated is a textbox, an exception is not thrown. Why, you might ask? Well, the textbox can accept just about any textual information; therefore, updating a textbox does not cause this problem.

Synchronizing ViewState

One of the things that is integral to ASP.NET is the ViewState. The ViewState is encoded data that saves important data about a page in a special hidden form element called __ViewState. This data includes values that are bound to a grid, drop-down list, or other form element. This information is used to keep the data consistent between page postbacks as well as allow for change events to occur on this page. The problem with this is that with ASP.NET AJAX calls can be made to the server and controls can be updated without control changes being reflected in the ViewState. Thus, control elements can now get out of sync with the ViewState.

Look at the steps of how this can happen:

1. Create a page with a drop-down list box with an ID of ddlName, a client-side button that performs an ASP.NET AJAX callback to the server with an ID of btnGetName, value of "Get Name", an onclick value of GetName(), and a server-side button that will perform a server-side postback, with an ID of btnRoundTrip and text of Round Trip.

2. On the client-side button, create an onclick event that will fill the drop-down list box. An example is shown in Figure 4-9.

3. On the server-side button, create a postback method named btnRoundTrip_Click and perform a postback.

4. When the server-side button is clicked, the page goes back to its initial state. Figure 4-10 shows the initial state and the state after a round trip.

Figure 4-9

Figure 4-10

The question with this issue is why does the drop-down list box get reset to its initial state? The reason for this is the ViewState. When a postback occurs, the contents of the drop-down list box are reset to the values that are within the ViewState.

Now that you have seen the problem with the ViewState, the question becomes how to resolve this issue. The following are two possible approaches to resolve this problem:

❑ You need to manage the state on your own. This state must be "serialized" on the client, stored in a hidden form element, and then "deserialized" and the data placed into the appropriate client controls. This presents additional problems when saving ViewState information to a location besides the default location on an ASP.NET web page.

❑ After performing ASP.NET AJAX operations, a page can perform only ASP.NET AJAX operations. In this scenario, using ASP.NET AJAX becomes a one-way operation on a page level. This is a simple way to resolve the issue; however, it may or may not be workable given the complexity of a page and the functionality required by the user.

Much like the problem with the argument exception discussed previously, the problem with the ViewState is dependent on the control that is being used. When an ASP.NET AJAX operation updates a textbox, the control keeps its value during a postback. So, once again the ViewState issue is dependent on the controls that are used.

Handling Errors

Although we all believe that we are great developers, we can't handle every situation. As a result, errors and exceptions can occur within any application. Handling errors/exceptions is a very important part of any application. Users and developers need to be notified when errors have occurred within an application. With ASP.NET AJAX, it is possible to perform some type of processing of the exception on the client. This section looks at the information that is returned to the client browser.

When an exception occurs on the server, that exception can be bubbled up to the ASP.NET AJAX client. Web applications can then process the error and provide some type of diagnostic or other information.

In JavaScript, the standard syntax for calling to a web service is as follows:

```
WebServiceClass.MethodName( p1, p2, ...., pN, OnCompleteCallBack,
OnServerExceptionCallBack);
```

The final parameter is a callback to a method that processes any server-side exception that is unhandled within the web service that is called. The `OnServerExceptionCallBack` is a JavaScript method that accepts an object containing exception information. Take a look at the calling syntax for the `OnServerExceptionCallBack` method:

```
function CodeCampListOnServerException(result)
{
var ExceptionOutput;
var Return = "<br />";
if ( null != result )
    {
        ExceptionOutput = "Message: " + result.get_message() + Return;
        ExceptionOutput += "Stack Trace: " + result.get_stackTrace() + Return;
```

```
        ExceptionOutput += "Exception Type: " + result.get_exceptionType() + Return;
        $get("ExceptionInfo").innerHTML = ExceptionOutput;
        $get("ExceptionInfo").style.visibility = "visible";
    }
}
```

By inserting a command to generate an `ApplicationException()` on the server, you are able to generate the following result, as shown in Figure 4-11. The command to generate the error is

```
throw (new ApplicationException("Exception in method CodeCampInformation.  Data
passed: " + Convert.ToString(CodeCampId)));.
```

The following is the complete code for generating the exception:

```
[WebMethod]
[GenerateScriptType(typeof(CodeCampInformation))]
public CodeCampInformation[] CodeCampInfo(int CodeCampId)
{
    CodeCampInformation lSpec;
    List<CodeCampInformation> lData = new List<CodeCampInformation>();
    DataTable dtData;
    CCData CodeCampData = new CCData();
    dtData = CodeCampData.CodeCampInfo(CodeCampId);
    foreach (DataRow drData in dtData.Rows)
    {
        lSpec = new CodeCampInformation(Convert.ToString(drData["City"]),
            Convert.ToDateTime(drData["DateOfEvent"]),
            Convert.ToInt32(drData["NumberOfAttendees"]));
        lData.Add(lSpec);
    }
    throw (new ApplicationException("Exception in method CodeCampInformation.  Data
passed: " + Convert.ToString(CodeCampId)));
    return (lData.ToArray());
}
```

Figure 4-11 shows data that is returned from an unhandled exception on the server.

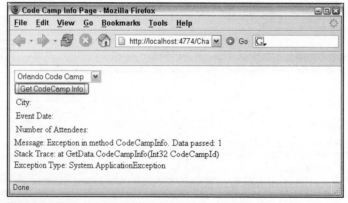

Figure 4-11

get_message()

The get_message() method on the returned result object allows you to get at the message passed from within an exception. In Figure 4-11, the get_message() method returned the text "Exception in method CodeCampInfo. Data passed: 1". This is the message that was passed to the constructor of the ApplicationException() object to create and throw the ApplicationException() object.

get_stackTrace()

The get_stackTrace() method on the returned result object allows a developer to get at the stack trace within an exception. In Figure 4-11, the get_stackTrace() method returned the method name where the topmost unhandled exception has occurred. Typically, this will be the method name where an exception occurred. In the example, the exception occurred within the GetData.CodeCampInfo() method.

get_exceptionType()

The get_exceptionType() method on the returned result object allows you to determine the type of exception that occurred. In Figure 4-11, the get_exceptionType() method returned the exception type of System.ApplicationException. This is the exception type that was thrown in the web method.

get_statusCode()

The get_statusCode() method on the returned result object returns the HTTP status code that is returned.

get_timedOut()

The get_timedOut() method on the exception's returned result object is a binary representing whether or not a timeout occurred on the request.

Futures

As mentioned in the introduction of the book, Microsoft has shipped several downloads that make up ASP.NET AJAX. One of these is the *Futures CTP*. The Futures CTP contains additional web service support for data and data binding. This support will include support for client-side DataSets and DataTables as well as taking that data and binding it to a client-side visual GUI element. For more information, check out Chapter 13 as well as the online material itself.

Summary

As you can see, the ASP.NET AJAX Library contains significant support for calls that are often referred to as AJAX operations. Some of the things that you have learned about in this chapter are:

❑ How to set up the ScriptManager to call out to web services

❑ How to call methods with various data types

❑ How to process the errors on the client

The next chapter looks at the UpdatePanel control. The UpdatePanel provides an easy way to add functionality from the ASP.NET AJAX Library to an application while retaining many of the features of server-centric ASP.NET development.

The UpdatePanel

The UpdatePanel is absolutely the coolest control included in the ASP.NET 2.0 AJAX Extensions 1.0. The UpdatePanel provides support for implementing AJAX-style operations by integrating the server-side development methodology that is well known to ASP.NET developers with the client-side AJAX development paradigm.

This chapter looks at the following topics:

❑ What the UpdatePanel is

❑ How the UpdatePanel works

❑ How to provide full support for all browsers through the UpdatePanel

❑ The client-side web page life cycle

This chapter examines the UpdatePanel control based on an example search form and then the result. Logically, this follows the general form shown in Figure 5-1, which shows the Search box, and Figure 5-2, which shows search results.

Figure 5-1

Figure 5-2

What Is the UpdatePanel?

Development methodologies have changed over the years. In the world of client-server applications, typically the majority of development work has taken place at the client. Everything from business rules to user interface items occur on the client. Web development and ASP.NET uses a different development methodology. With ASP.NET, a postback occurs, which takes form elements and various other pieces of information, sends it to the web server, the web server processes it, formats a page of data, and then sends the result back to the client. Along with this processing, the user notices several things:

❑ Processing at the client tends to stop. Even if the user attempts to change a form element, the change is not reflected in what is sent to the web server. The result is that the page that is returned is based on what the form elements looked like at the moment the form submission occurred.

❑ When the data returns from the web server, there is typically a "flash" of the browser's screen and the user is redirected to the top of the web page, thus typically losing the context of where they are in the application. For pages that are less than one screenful of information, this is not a big deal. For larger pages, this can become a significant issue.

❑ If the processing at the server takes a significant time, the user may become frustrated.

For most postback scenarios in ASP.NET, the complete page does not need to be reloaded. Typically, only sections of the page need to be reloaded. A search page, as shown in Figure 5-1, does not need to have its form elements reloaded. The search page doesn't need the search elements to change along with any existing images to come down. The search page merely needs the data to be sent down in the grid.

The UpdatePanel control, which is a part of the ASP.NET 2.0 AJAX Extensions, allows for the updating of the section of a web page. The UpdatePanel is also a container of other controls. As a result, it is similar to a Panel control. The difference is that the UpdatePanel control allows server methods and events to be called in an asynchronous manner so that data can be sent to the client.

Understanding Asynchronous Postbacks

An asynchronous postback is much like a regular postback. An asynchronous postback sends all textual form elements, with the exception of the FileUpload control, to the server and the server processes all necessary events. The two main differences are as follows:

❑ The client sends the request to the server using the XMLHttpRequest object as a client-side asynchronous request.

❑ The new data is returned to the client as opposed to the complete page. The new data that is sent is not in an XML or JSON format. The new data is in custom textual format.

The data for the asynchronous postback is in the format

```
size|control type|control name|data
```

The following is some example data that is sent back on an asynchronous postback:

```
2871|updatePanel|upSearch|
            <div>
<table cellspacing="0" rules="all" border="1" id="gvSearchResults"
style="border-collapse:collapse;">
</table>
</div>

|3044|hiddenField|__VIEWSTATE||80|hiddenField|__EVENTVALIDATION|/wEWBgLXoIfRDALO+4f
+BgLBlK2QCgLAlK2QCgLDlK2QCgKln
/PuCqRDJk++EvtU8+jTDGyT7B75ioKB|9|asyncPostBackControlIDs||btnSearch|0|postBackCont
rolIDs|||9|updatePanelIDs||tupSearch|0|childUpdatePanelIDs|||8|panelsToRefreshIDs||
upSearch|2|asyncPostBackTimeout||90|18|formAction||SimpleUpdates.aspx|17|pageTitle|
|Update Panel Page|
```

Browsers Supporting the UpdatePanel

Not all web browsers support the UpdatePanel. At the time of this writing, only the following browsers support the UpdatePanel control:

- ❑ **Internet Explorer** — Internet Explorer 6.0 and later web browsers are supported. Based on the design differences between Internet Explorer Version 6 and Version 7, Internet Explorer Version 6 must be checked to make sure that the ActiveX controls are enabled. This is due to the fact that the AJAX callback functionality is enabled by the MSXML control, which is an ActiveX control. Version 7 of Internet Explorer supports AJAX callback functionality through a JavaScript object.

- ❑ **Mozilla/Firefox** — Firefox 1.5 and later along with its affiliated browsers (Mozilla) are supported.

- ❑ **Safari** — The Safari web browser 1.2 and later are supported on the Apple Macintosh.

Several sources state the Opera 9 is a supported browser. At the time of this writing, Opera has not been officially listed as a supported browser.

The following code tests the web browser to verify that it meets the necessary criteria for using the UpdatePanel:

```
public static bool IsValidForUpdatePanel()
{
    bool IsValid = false;
    System.Web.HttpBrowserCapabilities BrowseCaps =
                HttpContext.Current.Request.Browser;
    try
    {
        IsValid = (IsIE6OrLater(BrowseCaps) || IsFF15OrLater(BrowseCaps) ||
            IsSafari(BrowseCaps)) &&
            HttpContext.Current.Request.Browser.JavaScript;
    }
```

```
        catch
        {
            IsValid = false;
        }
        finally
        {}
        return (IsValid);
    }
    private static bool IsIE6OrLater(System.Web.HttpBrowserCapabilities pBrowseCaps)
    {
        return ((pBrowseCaps.IsBrowser("IE")) &&
            (pBrowseCaps.MajorVersion >= 6) &&
            (pBrowseCaps.ActiveXControls)) ||
            ((pBrowseCaps.IsBrowser("IE")) &&
            (pBrowseCaps.MajorVersion >= 7));
    }
    private static bool IsFF15OrLater(System.Web.HttpBrowserCapabilities pBrowseCaps)
    {
        return ((pBrowseCaps.IsBrowser("Firefox")) &&
    ((pBrowseCaps.MajorVersion == 1) &&
            (pBrowseCaps.MinorVersion == .5) ||
            (pBrowseCaps.MajorVersion >= 2)));
    }
    private static bool IsSafari(System.Web.HttpBrowserCapabilities pBrowseCaps)
    {
            return (pBrowseCaps.IsBrowser("Safari")) &&
                (pBrowseCaps.MajorVersion >= 2);
    }
```

This code "sniffs" the web browser. If the browser is Internet Explorer 6 or later, Firefox 1.5 or later, or Safari 2 or later, `true` is returned, and the result is that asynchronous postbacks are turned on or off. The returned value can be passed to the `.EnablePartialRendering` property of the `UpdatePanel`.

> *The `EnablePartialRendering` property is a "special" property on the `ScriptManager`. This property must be set early in the .aspx page's life cycle, typically in the `PreInit` event. Setting the property too late in the page's life cycle results in an error.*

In addition to the ability to manually enable the asynchronous postbacks, the `ScriptManager` provides the `SupportsPartialRendering` property to check the calling browser. The value is set by the `ScriptManager`. The value defaults to `true` under the following conditions:

❑ The `W3CDomVersion` property is set to `1.0` or greater.

❑ The `EcmaScriptVersion` property is set to `1.0` or greater.

❑ The `SupportsCallback` property is set to `true`.

One would think that this property is read only. It is not. It can be set in code based on whatever criteria the developer deems. The `SupportsPartialRendering` property must be set during or before the `Init` event in the server-side page life cycle.

Configuring the UpdatePanel

The UpdatePanel needs to be properly configured for the situation. Several settings on the ScriptManager and the UpdatePanel controls directly affect the UpdatePanel.

ScriptManager

The ScriptManager is required on every ASPX page that uses the UpdatePanel. If the ScriptManager is not on an ASPX page that uses the UpdatePanel, the UpdatePanel throws an exception and processing of that page stops. Not only must the ScriptManager be present on the page, but the ScriptManager must appear before the UpdatePanel control on the page; otherwise, the UpdatePanel throws an error. The following ScriptManager line shows the EnablePartialRendering property:

```
<asp:ScriptManager ID="ScriptManager1" runat="server"
EnablePartialRendering="true">
</asp:ScriptManager>
```

By default, the ScriptManager's EnablePartialRendering *property is set to* true.

The ScriptManager is responsible for adding the appropriate JavaScript support to the ASPX page that is sent to the browser. As a reminder, the code that follows will be different on your system:

```
<script
src="/TestWeb/WebResource.axd?d=AM51VlkQO2XElLdrEXI4tg2&amp;t=632961577701930400"
type="text/javascript"></script><script
src="/TestWeb/ScriptResource.axd?d=7dU46xtleKcv0ogeigzzt6Z10dodjHd2d9nl5WXTf7gPgTZR
pUAwgXfQMBtWPrRcpeb2TL-2Y3EaB6tBpznluNI7myB4flEd5yZs-VgqWA-
TpFfmeki9NrZTwhGfdK4_weufdABHFea6Mx2xsCRvL42DnWwjlCkdzjaqEdG8fDk1&amp;t=63298581393
1443120" type="text/javascript"></script>
<script
src="/TestWeb/ScriptResource.axd?d=7dU46xtleKcv0ogeigzzt6Z10dodjHd2d9nl5WXTf7gPgTZR
pUAwgXfQMBtWPrRcpeb2TL-2Y3EaB6tBpznluNI7myB4flEd5yZs-VgqWA-
TpFfmeki9NrZTwhGfdK4_NldvwElbcU-
ssmFVCSF7_viedDm3yXa8MAomTCTeZxM1&amp;t=632985813931443120"
type="text/javascript"></script>
```

In addition, with the UpdatePanel, there is additional code that is sent to the client. The call to the PageRequestManager and the trigger hookup looks something like the following code:

```
<script type="text/javascript">
//<![CDATA[
Sys.WebForms.PageRequestManager._initialize('ScriptManager1',
document.getElementById('form1'));
Sys.WebForms.PageRequestManager.getInstance()._updateControls(['tup1'],
['btnSubmit','btnSubmitRemove'], [], 90);
//]]>
```

In this example, the buttons btnSubmit and btnSubmitRemove will cause the PageRequestManager to determine that an event occurred on the form element and that the PageRequestManager should intercept this request and go back to the server for the asynchronous postback to be processed.

Methods and Properties of the ScriptManager

The following are the methods and properties of the ScriptManager that are associated with the UpdatePanel:

❑ AsyncPostBackError — The AsyncPostBackError is an event handler that catches errors that occur during an asynchronous update.

❑ AsyncPostBackErrorMessage — The AsyncPostBackErrorMessage property sets the textual message that is displayed on an error to the client browser through an alert().

❑ AsyncPostBackSourceElementID — The AsyncPostBackSourceElementID contains the ID of the element that caused the postback.

❑ AsyncPostBackTimeout — The AsyncPostBackTimeout property sets the timeout in seconds for an asynchronous callback. The default value is 90 seconds.

❑ EnablePartialRendering — The EnablePartialRendering property is a Boolean property. Setting the property to true enables partial rendering. Setting the property to false turns off the partial rendering. This property must be set sometime before the page's Init event. By default, the value of this property is true.

❑ IsInAsyncPostBack — The IsInAsyncPostBack property returns a Boolean value indicating whether or not an asynchronous postback is occurring.

❑ RegisterAsyncPostBackControl() — The RegisterAsyncPostBackControl(ControlName) method adds the ControlName control to the list of controls that may cause an asynchronous postback.

❑ SupportsPartialRendering — The SupportsPartialRendering property gets/sets whether or not the calling browser supports partial page updates through an asynchronous postback.

The following code uses the .EnablePartialRendering property and RegisterAsyncPostBackControl() method to set up the page, ScriptManager, and the HTML that is sent to the browser:

```
protected void Page_PreInit(object sender, EventArgs e)
{
    if (BrowserDetect.IsValidForUpdatePanel() == false)
        this.ScriptManager1.EnablePartialRendering = false;
    else
        this.ScriptManager1.EnablePartialRendering = true;
}
```

The method BrowserDetect.IsValidForUpdatePanel() defined in the code is a custom written static method that returns a Boolean. If the browser supports the UpdatePanel, true is returned. If the browser does not support the UpdatePanel, false is returned.

Triggering the UpdatePanel

The first issue when using the `UpdatePanel` is to figure out when an asynchronous postback should occur. The `UpdatePanel` will be triggered by the `PageRequestManager`. The `PageRequestManager` will check the ID of an element that is performing the form submission. When the postback is attempted by an element that is within the list of controls of the `PageRequestManager`, the postback is "hijacked" and converted into an asynchronous postback. The question then pops up: how to associate a control with the `UpdatePanel`? There are two ways to do this:

❑ **Declaratively** — Control IDs can be specified on the .aspx page as part of the `UpdatePanel` markup.

❑ **Programmatically** — As mentioned previously, controls can also be registered programmatically by calling the `RegisterAsyncPostBackControl()` method on the `ScriptManager` control.

Several types of controls can cause an update. These are controls explicitly listed as asynchronous trigger and child controls within an `UpdatePanel` as well as `UpdatePanels` that have their `Update()` method called.

RegisterAsyncPostBackControl Method

The `ScriptManager.RegisterAsyncPostBackControl()` method associates a control with the `UpdatePanel`. This can be done fairly simply with the following code:

```
ScriptManager1.RegisterAsyncPostBackControl(btnSearch);
```

In this example code, the postback caused by the button `btnSearch` causes an asynchronous postback. This code can placed at any point in the page life cycle.

Explicit Triggers

The `UpdatePanel` supports two types of triggers:

❑ **AsyncPostbackTrigger** — The `AsyncPostbackTrigger` defines the controls and events that cause an asynchronous postback to occur.

❑ **PostbackTrigger** — Within the `UpdatePanel`, child triggers will trigger an asynchronous postback by default. A `PostbackTrigger` defines a child control that will perform a full postback.

The entry in Figure 5-3 results in the following code in the .aspx page:

```
<Triggers>
  <asp:AsyncPostBackTrigger ControlID="btnSearch" EventName="Click" />
</Triggers>
```

The result of this code sample is that a partial postback is triggered on the click event of the element with the ID of `btnSearch` and data is sent to the client.

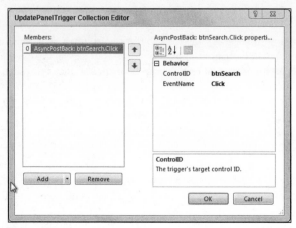

Figure 5-3

<asp:UpdateProgess>

How many times have you built an application and had a user think it was a good idea to hit the submit button multiple times? Though this might be ok when waiting on an elevator, it can cause some scalability issues on a web application. By hitting the submit button multiple times, a request is made against the server each time the submit button is selected. As a result, it is important to notify the user that a long-running request is occurring with code like the following, which causes the output like that shown in Figure 5-4 to display on the user's screen:

```
<asp:UpdateProgress ID="UpdateProgress1" runat="server">
<ProgressTemplate>
    <img src="Images/3MA_processingbar.gif" /><br />
    An update is currently taking place on the server.  Please don't click the stop
button on the browser.
    <asp:Button ID="abortButton" runat="server" Text="Abort Operation" />
</ProgressTemplate>
</asp:UpdateProgress>
```

Abort Button

With an asynchronous operation, it might be appropriate to stop the execution of the request. Although it is not possible to stop the server from completing a long-running request, it is possible to stop the client web browser from listening for the request.

The previous code example and Figure 5-4 include an Abort button. If the user clicks the Abort button while an asynchronous postback is running, the browser stops waiting on the asynchronous operation. This won't stop the process from running on the server, but it does stop the browser from listening for a response.

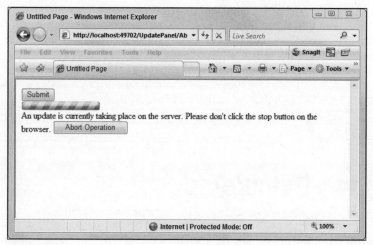

Figure 5-4

ChildrenAsTriggers

The UpdatePanel contains a property called ChildrenAsTriggers. This property is a Boolean property. By default, the child controls of an UpdatePanel cause an asynchronous postback on the UpdatePanel. Setting the ChildrenAsTriggers property to false results in child controls not being set as triggers of the UpdatePanel.

UpdateMode

The UpdatePanel defines two modes to trigger an update:

❑ **Always** — When the UpdateMode of an UpdatePanel is set to Always, the UpdatePanel's content is on each postback that is caused by a control somewhere on the page.

❑ **Conditional** — If the UpdateMode of an UpdatePanel is set to Conditional, there are three instances where an UpdatePanel can be updated:

❑ An UpdatePanel's .Update() method is called.

❑ An asynchronous postback is called by a control that is a trigger for the UpdatePanel.

❑ The ChildrenAsTriggers property is explicitly set to true and a child control of the specific UpdatePanel attempts to perform a postback. A child control of an UpdatePanel further down in the hierarchy will not cause an update to an outer UpdatePanel.

RenderMode

Two types of updates occur with the UpdatePanel. This is set by the RenderMode of the UpdatePanel. The two modes are Block and Inline, which work as follows:

❑   Block — The Block mode is the default rendering mode of the UpdatePanel. The Block mode results in the location of the UpdatePanel being defined by a `<div>` tag.

❑   Inline — The Inline mode results in the location of the UpdatePanel being defined by a `<span>` tag.

Server-Side Debugging

There are a few problems when debugging an AJAX application, including:

❑   **Debugging confusion** — Is an operation going on at the client, server, or where?

❑   **General development experience** — ASP.NET development is primarily a server-side development methodology, but AJAX has a number of client-side features. This can create confusion among developers.

Debugging a full AJAX application is not quite as easy as hitting the F5 key in Visual Studio and walking through the application. The UpdatePanel is designed to marry the client-side AJAX operations to the server-side debugging and development experience of ASP.NET. This works fairly well. The server-side events fire and there is full support for debugging. Figure 5-5 shows the breakpoints that are set in Visual Studio.

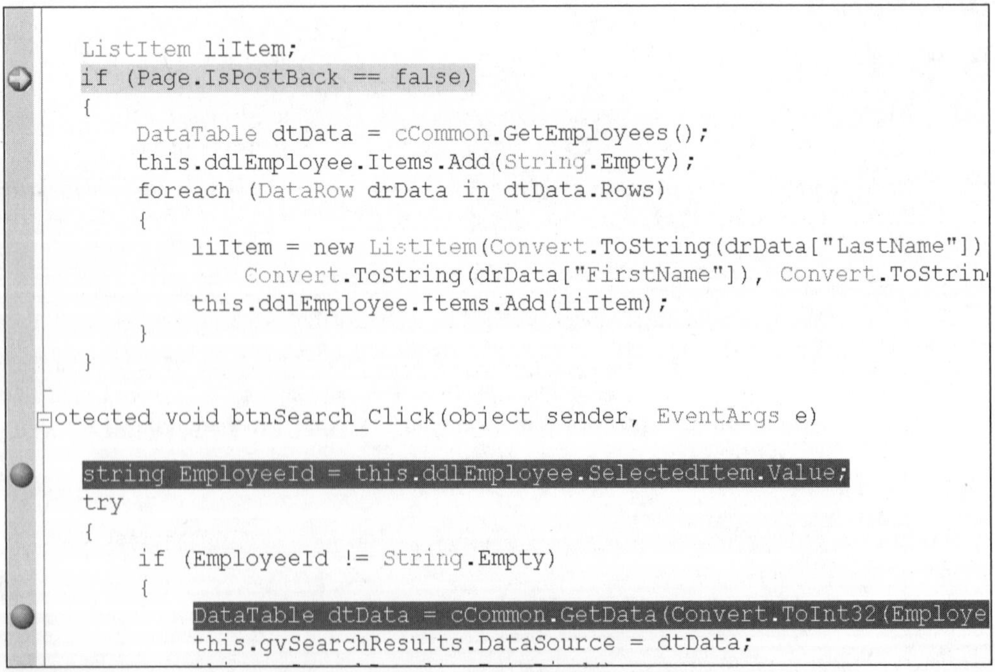

```
ListItem liItem;
if (Page.IsPostBack == false)
{
    DataTable dtData = cCommon.GetEmployees();
    this.ddlEmployee.Items.Add(String.Empty);
    foreach (DataRow drData in dtData.Rows)
    {
        liItem = new ListItem(Convert.ToString(drData["LastName"])
            Convert.ToString(drData["FirstName"]), Convert.ToStrin
        this.ddlEmployee.Items.Add(liItem);
    }
}

otected void btnSearch_Click(object sender, EventArgs e)
{
    string EmployeeId = this.ddlEmployee.SelectedItem.Value;
    try
    {
        if (EmployeeId != String.Empty)
        {
            DataTable dtData = cCommon.GetData(Convert.ToInt32(Employe
            this.gvSearchResults.DataSource = dtData;
```

Figure 5-5

With the UpdatePanel, you can easily add AJAX functionality to your application while debugging it. For more information on debugging, see Chapter 12.

Dynamically Adding an UpdatePanel

It often is advantageous to add UpdatePanels based on specific situations — for example, when additional calls are embedded within a grid of data, custom controls, or other data-bound control situations.

Try It Out   Dynamically Adding an UpdatePanel

Take a look at an example of dynamically adding an UpdatePanel to a page. In this example, individual rows within the search grid contain an UpdatePanel that is added for each individual row. Here is what is happening:

1. An UpdatePanel is defined. The UpdatePanel will be triggered by the button with an ID of btnTest when it is clicked.

2. Within the UpdatePanel, a GridView is defined. The GridView has the ID value of gvSearchResults.

3. Within the GridView, several columns are defined. There are two columns of interest. One is the column with the button with the ID value of btnTest. The other column contains the UpdatePanel. The column with the UpdatePanel has a label with the ID value of lblTest.

4. The button btnTest and UpdatePanel that contains the label lblTest are associated. The button will act as a trigger for the UpdatePanel.

5. When the button btnTest is clicked, the UpdatePanel containing lblTest is updated.

Here is the code for the parent UpdatePanel:

```
<asp:UpdatePanel runat="server" ID="upSearch" UpdateMode="Conditional">
<ContentTemplate>
    <asp:GridView ID="gvSearchResults" runat="server" AutoGenerateColumns="False">
        <Columns>
            <asp:BoundField AccessibleHeaderText="Last Name" DataField="LastName"
HeaderText="Last Name" />
            <asp:BoundField AccessibleHeaderText="First Name" DataField="FirstName"
HeaderText="First Name" />
            <asp:BoundField AccessibleHeaderText="Project Name"
DataField="ProjectName" HeaderText="Project Name" />
            <asp:BoundField AccessibleHeaderText="Date Work Performed"
DataField="DateWorkPerformed"
                DataFormatString="{0:MM-dd-yyyy}" HeaderText="Date Work Performed"
HtmlEncode="False" />
            <asp:TemplateField AccessibleHeaderText="Test 1">
                <ItemTemplate>
                    <asp:Button ID="btnTest" runat="server" Text="Test Call"
OnClick="btnTest_Click"/>
```

```
                    </ItemTemplate>
                </asp:TemplateField>
                <asp:TemplateField AccessibleHeaderText="Test 2">
                    <ItemTemplate>

                        <asp:UpdatePanel ID="up1" runat="server"
    UpdateMode="Conditional">
                            <ContentTemplate>
                                <asp:Label runat="server" ID="lblTest" />
                            </ContentTemplate>
                            <Triggers>
                                <asp:AsyncPostBackTrigger ControlID="btnTest"
    EventName="Click" />
                            </Triggers>
                        </asp:UpdatePanel>
                    </ItemTemplate>
                </asp:TemplateField>
            </Columns>
            <HeaderStyle BackColor="Silver" />
            <AlternatingRowStyle BackColor="Wheat" />
        </asp:GridView>
    </ContentTemplate>
    <Triggers>
        <asp:AsyncPostBackTrigger ControlId="btnSearch" EventName="Click" />
    </Triggers>
</asp:UpdatePanel>
```

The following is the code for the btnTest's click event:

```
protected void btnTest_Click(object sender, EventArgs e)
{
    Button btn = (Button)sender;
    Label lbl = (Label)btn.Parent.FindControl("lblTest");
    lbl.Text = "Client Id: " + btn.ClientID + " Time: " + DateTime.Now.ToString();
}
```

How It Works

When the btnTest's click event occurs, the steps are as follows:

1. Get a reference to the button that was clicked. This is done by casting the sender into a Button.

2. Go to the parent of the button, which is the row. This is done by referencing the parent of the Button.

3. Get a reference to the label called lblTest. A call to FindControl is used to get the reference to the Label and casting the resulting object to be of type Label.

4. Update the lblTest's Text property. This is the final line of code and sets the Label's text property to a value.

Figure 5-6 shows some example output from the previous code. This code demonstrates that an UpdatePanel can be added dynamically and processing can occur on it.

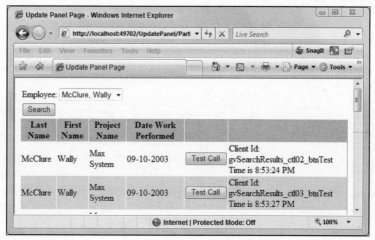

Figure 5-6

Client Page Life Cycle

ASP.NET pages have a processing life cycle. ASP.NET developers are familiar with the concepts of the page load, page init, and other events. These events occur at various points in the processing of an ASP.NET page on the server.

With a client web browser that supports the DOM standard, the web browser will raise the `window.onload` event when a page loads and the `window.onunload` event when a user leaves the current page, performs a refresh of the browser, or a postback. Unfortunately, these events only occur during the processing of full page postbacks and do not occur during an asynchronous processing.

With the `PageRequestManager` class, asynchronous postbacks implement a set of events. These events may have event handlers attached to them.

PageRequestManager

The `PageRequestManager` class within the Microsoft AJAX Library is designed to manage the asynchronous postback feature of the Microsoft AJAX Library. The class coordinates the work between the `ScriptManager` and the `UpdatePanel`. `PageRequestManager` exposes a set of methods, properties, and events that allow you to integrate the asynchronous postbacks within the client-side programming environment.

The `PageRequestManager` requires that the `EnablePartialRendering` property of the `ScriptManager` be set to `true`. When this property is set to `true`, the contents of the `MicrosoftAjaxWebForms.js` file are sent to the client browser. The next step is to get an instance of the object. This is performed by calling the `.getInstance()` method. There is only one instance of the `PageRequestManager` per page.

initializeRequest

The `initializeRequest` event is raised before a request is initialized for an asynchronous postback. The data for the event is passed as the `InitializeRequestEventArgs` argument. This event argument allows you to check the object that caused the postback and to access the request object. An example setup is

```
Sys.WebForms.PageRequestManager.getInstance().add_initializeRequest
(initializeRequestHandler)
```

In addition to the `add_initializeRequest` method, there is an associated `remove_initializeRequest()` method that can be used to remove the page's initialize handler method. The following is an example remove call:

```
Sys.WebForms.PageRequestManager.getInstance().remove_initializeRequest
(initializeRequestHandler);
```

beginRequest

The `beginRequest` event is raised right before an asynchronous postback request is sent to the server. The data for the event that is passed is the `BeginRequestEventArgs` argument. This event argument allows you to check the object that caused the postback and to access the request object. The following is an example setup in JavaScript:

```
Sys.WebForms.PageRequestManager.getInstance().add_beginRequest(beginRequestHandler)
```

In addition to the `add_beginRequest` method, there is an associated `remove_beginRequest()` method that can be used to remove the page's `beginRequest` handler method. The following is an example remove call:

```
Sys.WebForms.PageRequestManager.getInstance().remove_beginRequest(beginRequestHandler);
```

pageLoading

The `pageLoading` event is raised after the response to the final asynchronous postback has been received from the server but before any updates of the page occur. The data for the event that is passed is the `PageLoadingEventArgs` argument. This event argument allows you to check information about the panels on the page that are modified. The information that is exposed is based on the last asynchronous postback. The following is an example setup in JavaScript:

```
Sys.WebForms.PageRequestManager.getInstance().add_pageLoading(pageLoadingHandler)
```

In addition to the `add_pageLoading` method, there is an associated `remove_pageLoading()` method that can be used to remove the page's `pageLoading` handler method. The following is an example remove call:

```
Sys.WebForms.PageRequestManager.getInstance().remove_pageLoading(pageLoadingHandler);
```

pageLoaded

The `pageLoaded` event fires after all content on a page is refreshed. The content on the page may be refreshed by either an asynchronous or full postback. You can use this event to provide a custom UI effect when content is updated. The following is an example setup in JavaScript:

```
Sys.WebForms.PageRequestManager.getInstance().add_pageLoaded(pageLoadedHandler)
```

In addition to the `add_pageLoaded` method, there is an associated `remove_pageLoaded()` method that can be used to remove the page's `pageLoaded` handler method. The following is an example remove call:

```
Sys.WebForms.PageRequestManager.getInstance().remove_pageLoaded(pageLoadedHandler);
```

endRequest

The `endRequest` is processed after the request is completed. The data for the event is passed as an `EndRequestEventArgs` object. From this object, you can access any information about errors that may have occurred on the server and the response object. The following is an example setup in JavaScript:

```
Sys.WebForms.PageRequestManager.getInstance().add_endRequest(endRequestHandler)
```

In addition to the `add_endRequest` method, there is an associated `remove_endRequest()` method that can be used to remove the page's `endRequest` handler method. The following is an example remove call:

```
Sys.WebForms.PageRequestManager.getInstance().remove_endRequest(endRequestHandler);
```

init

The `init` event is processed after all script has been loaded but before any objects are created. The event is useful for those that are creating components. This event gives a component writer the ability to add a component to a page. This event is raised only once on the initial load of a page; it is not raised on additional partial postbacks. The following is an example setup in JavaScript:

```
Sys.WebForms.PageRequestManager.getInstance().add_init(initHandler);
```

Page-level developers should use the `pageLoad` *event, not the* `init` *event.*

In addition to the `add_init` method, there is an associated `remove_int()` method that can be used to remove the page's `init` handler method. The following is an example remove call:

```
Sys.WebForms.PageRequestManager.getInstance().remove_init(initHandler);
```

pageUnload

The unload event is processed when a page is unloaded. It is processed before objects are disposed and before the `window.unload()` method is called. By default, the unload event is processed by a method named `pageUnload`. A page developer should use this method to release any resources through code. The following is an example setup in JavaScript:

```
Sys.WebForms.PageRequestManager.getInstance().add_unload(pageUnloadHandler);
```

In addition to the `add_unload` method, there is an associated `remove_unload()` method that can be used to remove the page's unload handler method. The following is an example call:

```
Sys.WebForms.PageRequestManager.getInstance().remove_unload(pageUnloadHandler);
```

Try It Out   UpdatePanel Events Demonstration

Now work through an example of the events in the client-side life cycle. In this example, the `beginRequest` and `endRequest` events are being handled by adding the request handler straight in the JavaScript of the page. These requests are going to be used to communicate additional information to a user, such as an asynchronous postback is in process and any error information that has occurred during the asynchronous postback. Once the event happens, two parameters are passed to the handlers: the sender and event arguments.

This example uses the client-side `UpdatePanel` events to communicate to the user that an asynchronous postback is occurring and to communicate any error messages. The initial communication that an asynchronous postback has occurred is handled in the `BeginAsyncPostBackRequestHandler` method. Any error reporting occurs in the `EndAsyncPostBackRequestHandler` method. These methods are set up by referencing the current instance of the `PageRequestManager` and calling the `add_beginRequest()` and `add_endRequest()` methods.

Consider the following code:

```
<script language="javascript" type="text/javascript">
var pageReqMan = Sys.WebForms.PageRequestManager.getInstance();
pageReqMan.add_beginRequest(BeginAsyncPostBackRequestHandler);
pageReqMan.add_endRequest(EndAsyncPostBackRequestHandler);
function BeginAsyncPostBackRequestHandler(sender, args)
{
    var htmlElement = $get("<%=lblError.ClientID %>");
    htmlElement.innerHTML = "An asynchronous postback has started.";
}
function EndAsyncPostBackRequestHandler(sender, args)
{
        var htmlElement = $get("<%=lblError.ClientID %>");
    if (args.get_error() != undefined)
    {
        var eString = args.get_error().message;
        args.set_errorHandled(true);

        if (null != eString)
        {
            htmlElement.innerHTML = eString;
        }
```

```
        else
        {
            htmlElement.innerHTML = "";
        }
    }
}
</script>
```

Figure 5-7 shows the output and processing when handling the server side error and the `endRequest` event.

Figure 5-7

How It Works

Here's how the previous code works:

1. A `beginRequest` event handler is assigned by a call to the `Sys.WebForms` `.PageRequestManager`'s current instance.

2. An `endRequest` event handler is assigned by a call to the `Sys.WebForms` `.PageRequestManager`'s current instance.

3. When the `beginRequest` event is fired, a message is displayed in a label on the page.

4. When the `endRequest` event is fired, a message is displayed in a label if there is an error. If there is not an error, the label is cleared.

5. Within the `endRequest` handler, because you are handling the errors on your own, `args.set_errorHandled(true);` tells the system that it does not need to perform any other error handling.

Adding Controls

Dynamically adding controls to a page in ASP.NET is fairly straightforward. Controls are added through `Page.Controls.Add()`. The `UpdatePanel` is also a container of controls. Adding controls to the `UpdatePanel` is slightly different; however, it is fairly close in its concept.

Try It Out   **Adding Controls to the UpdatePanel**

The steps to add a control to an `UpdatePanel` in this example are as follows:

1. During the `Page_Load` event, check the status of the page. If the page is in an asynchronous postback and the ViewState variable `AsyncControlExists` is set to `true`, the `AddAControlOnAsyncPostBack()` method will be called. This method will add a control to the `UpdatePanel` as a child control.

```
protected void Page_Load(object sender, EventArgs e)
{
    if ((this.ScriptManager1.IsInAsyncPostBack) && (AsyncControlExists = true))
    {
        AddAControlOnAsyncPostBack();
    }
}
protected bool AsyncControlExists
{
    get
    {
        if (null != ViewState["AsyncControlExists"])
        {
            return ((bool)ViewState["AsyncControlExists"]);
        }
        else
        {
            return (false);
        }
    }
    set
    {
        ViewState["AsyncControlExists"] = value;
    }
}
```

2. If the page is in an asynchronous postback and the `ViewState` value of `AsyncControlExists` is set to `true`, the control is added by going through the `UpdatePanel`'s `ContentTemplateContainer` collection. This is shown in the following code:

```
void AddAControlOnAsyncPostBack()
{
    if (AsyncControlExists == true)
```

```
    {
        Button btnA = new Button();
        btnA.Style.Add("position", "absolute");
        btnA.Style.Add("top", "150px");
        btnA.Style.Add("left", "200px");
        btnA.Style.Add("width", "200px");
        btnA.Click += new EventHandler(btnA_Click);
        btnA.Text = "Hi There.  I was just added.";
        upl.ContentTemplateContainer.Controls.Add(btnA);
    }
}
```

3.   When the Remove button is clicked, the added control is removed.

```
protected void btnSubmitRemove_Click(object sender, EventArgs e)
{
    AsyncControlExists = false;
}
```

Take a look at the rest of the code:

```
protected void btnSubmit_Click(object sender, EventArgs e)
{
    this.AsyncControlExists = true;
    AddAControlOnAsyncPostBack();
}

void btnA_Click(object sender, EventArgs e)
{
    throw new Exception("The method or operation is not implemented.");
    //This code could do anything.  The exception
    // is only there to show something happening.
}
```

How It Works

Here's how this code works:

1.   When the page loads, nothing is on the page except for the submit button that adds the control within the UpdatePanel, and the button that removes the control within the UpdatePanel.

2.   When user clicks the Add button, the ViewState property of AsyncControlExists is set to true and the postback state of page is checked. If the page is in an asynchronous postback, which it will be in this situation, a button with an ID of btnA will be added to the UpdatePanel.

3.   If the user clicks the btnA button, the btnA_Click event is fired and a message is returned to the user.

Figure 5-8 shows the dynamically added button.

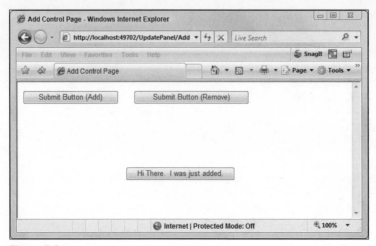

Figure 5-8

Error Reporting

Reporting errors is an important part of an application. With applications that are making asynchronous calls back and forth between the client web browser and the web server, the user may not realize that an activity has occurred, let alone that an error has occurred. The problem then is how to send an error to the client and to process that information. There are several ways to send server-side exceptions to the web client. You can take the default (do nothing) approach, work with the `AsyncPostBackErrorMessage` property of the ScriptManager control, or integrate with the client-side page life cycle.

Minimalist Error Handling

Unfortunately, in many applications, due to time constraints, developers tend to only insert error handling late in an application and sometimes even not at all. The `UpdatePanel` has some capabilities to handle exceptions without input from the user.

Take a look at this in practice. Within the search button, add the following code within your button's click event on the server:

```
throw(new ApplicationException("This is an unhandled ApplicationException."));
```

Once the button is clicked within a regular post, the user gets something similar to a typical ASP.NET error screen, sometimes referred to as the Yellow Screen of Death or an error message that may go unnoticed in the bottom-left corner of the browser window. Instead of either of these types of error messages, the `UpdatePanel` generates a JavaScript `alert()` message box when a user gets an error during an asynchronous postback. The message box displays the message of the unhandled exception.

With a minimalist approach, you don't have to perform any operations or any additional coding. Without making any changes to the `ScriptManager`'s properties, some amount of error handling is built in. Any unhandled exceptions are sent back to the client web browser and the exception message is sent to the user through a browser-based alert (see Figure 5-9).

Figure 5-9

It is good that the user gets feedback and it's fairly easy for you implement, however, sending the message property of the server-side exception may not be what you really want to send. Though this message was relatively benign, some exceptions may have a message that contains information that should not be shown to the user. In addition, these messages might be confusing to the user.

Generic Text

Sometimes when an error occurs, it is necessary to send only a piece of generic text to the client browser. This generic message is set up as a property of the `ScriptManager`. An example is:

```
<asp:ScriptManager ID="ScriptManager1" runat="server" ScriptMode="Auto"
AsyncPostBackErrorMessage="This is an example error message." />
```

If an error occurs on the server, the error message from the `ScriptManager` is displayed in the client, as shown in Figure 5-10.

Figure 5-10

Server-Side Error Handling

Although the first two methods are fairly simple to implement, they don't meet the needs of every application. Some applications need more complicated error processing than these options provide. Handling errors on the server side requires two items to implement on the server side:

❑ The `ScriptManager` must be configured with the error handling method that processes any page-level errors that occur during an asynchronous postback. This is done by registering an event to handle the `OnAsyncPostBackError` property of the `ScriptManager`. In this situation, if an exception occurs on an asynchronous postback, the `ScriptManager1_AsyncPostBackError` method is called.

```
<asp:ScriptManager ID="ScriptManager1" runat="server" ScriptMode="Auto"
OnAsyncPostBackError="ScriptManager1_AsyncPostBackError" />
```

❑ The `ScriptManager1_AsyncPostBackError` is used to format a message to be sent to the client. In this example, the code for the message looks like this:

```
protected void ScriptManager1_AsyncPostBackError(System.Object o,
AsyncPostBackErrorEventArgs e)
{
    this.ScriptManager1.AsyncPostBackErrorMessage = "An error has occurred.
Exception Message: " + e.Exception.Message.ToString();
}
```

 ❑ This is a rather simple example. In this example, the `AsyncPostBackErrorMessage` property of the `ScriptManager1` control is being filled with some information. Specifically, this information is the `e.Exception.Message`, which is the message of the exception that was fired on the asynchronous postback.

 ❑ The result of these two code examples is the output shown in Figure 5-11.

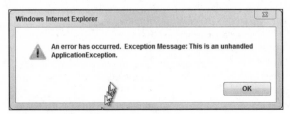

Figure 5-11

Though this example merely returns data in a JavaScript alert window, there other possibilities, such as returning data to the user in a defined field within the `UpdatePanel` or a separate, special `UpdatePanel`, just for returning server status to the user.

Client and Server Error Processing

Although the `window.alert()` method in JavaScript provides some simple error handling, there is often a need for more and different error handling. With Microsoft's AJAX, it is possible to process an error on the client in other ways. Look at the following code:

```
<script language="javascript" type="text/javascript">
var pageReqMan = Sys.WebForms.PageRequestManager.getInstance();
pageReqMan.add_endRequest(EndAsyncPostBackRequestHandler);
function EndAsyncPostBackRequestHandler(sender, args)
{
    var htmlElement = $get("<%=lblError.ClientID %>");
    args.set_errorHandled(true);
    if (null != args.get_error())
    {
        htmlElement.innerHTML = args.get_error().message;
    }
    else
    {
        htmlElement.innerHTML = "";
    }
}
</script>
```

This code sets up a handler for the end request. When the end request handler is called, two arguments are handed into the method. The first argument is the object that fired the event. In this case, that is the instance of the page request manager. The second argument is the argument of the event. From this, it is possible to get error information. This is provided by the `get_error()` method. Once it is determined that the `get_error()` method does not return a `null` value, the message field is called to get the text of the message. The output of that is shown in Figure 5-12.

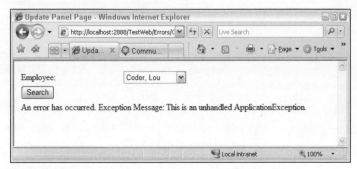

Figure 5-12

Along with the message field, there are other members of interest:

❑   `name` — The `name` property is the client-side name of the exception.

❑   `description` — The `description` is a description of the exception. Depending on the exception, this may or may not be the same as the `.message` property.

❑   `httpStatusCode` — This is the HTTP status code that is returned from the server.

❑   `popStackFrame` — The `popStackFrame` method updates the `filename` and `lineNumber` fields of the error instance based on the next frame in the browser's stack trace.

The result of this is that there are many ways to handle errors that occur during asynchronous postbacks.

Writing Controls

In some situations developers will want to encapsulate common user interface widgets into user controls. These pieces of UI functionality can be put into a component that will be used across projects. For example, you might have a common set of data-binding routines and UI elements that you want to include in multiple pages of a web application. Typically, these controls integrate in with the ASP.NET page. However, the `UpdatePanel` has its own set of requirements. To integrate with the ASP.NET AJAX `UpdatePanel`, a control must be able to do the following:

1.   Register any client-side JavaScript script that the control needs to use on the client.

2.   Initialize and use the client-side JavaScript script that the control will use.

3.   Implement dispose functionality for the client-side JavaScript. This is an important step in cleaning up any possible memory leaks in the browser and should not be forgotten.

Registering Script

The first issue is to register script. If you have authored a control that works with ASP.NET, you are probably familiar with the `Page.ClientScript` registration methods. Unfortunately, the `Page.ClientScript` registration methods won't work correctly. Happily, there is a solution. The ASP.NET AJAX `ScriptManager` provides a set of methods that are very similar to the `Page.ClientScript` registration methods.

Script registration must occur through the `ScriptManager`'s APIs. The script registration can occur through the several static methods in the class `System.Web.UI.ScriptManager()`, as discussed in the following table:

Method	Purpose	Parameters
`RegisterClientScriptBlock (Control, Type, String1, String2, Boolean)`	`RegisterClientScriptBlock` is used to register a client script block to be used with the `UpdatePanel` (partial page rendering).	`Control` — The control that is registering the client script block.
		`Type` — The type of the client script block.
		`String1` — The first string is the key that uniquely identifies the script block.
		`String2` — The second string is the content of the script.
		`Boolean` — Indicates whether to add the `<script>` tags to the script that is sent to the client. A value of `true` sends the `<script>` tag to the client browser.
`RegisterClientScriptInclude (Control, Type, String1, String2)`	The `RegisterClientScriptInclude` method will register a client script to be included as a script file reference.	`Control` — The control that is registering the client script include.
		`Type` — The type of the client script include.
		`String1` — The first string is the key that uniquely identifies the script include.

Method	Purpose	Parameters
		`String2` — The second string is the URL that points to the script file.
`RegisterClientScriptResource` `(Control, Type, String)`	The method takes the parameters listed and adds the script. This method is used when script is embedded within a resource.	`Control` — The control that is registering the client script.
		`Type` — The type of the client script.
		`String` — The client script.

Other items that are important include the following:

❑ If a control has client-side event handlers that are defined, it must implement dispose functionality on the client.

❑ The control's scripts need to provide access to initialization code so that each control instance can be independently initialized. This means that code typically needs to be divided into methods that will be shared among all instances and the initialization code.

Initializing Script

The next problem to solve is initializing the script. This can be done at the `PreRender` event of the control. This will be the time when the initialization events occur and the event handlers are created. This is done through the `ScriptManager`'s `RegisterStartupScript()` method. The `RegisterStartupScript()` method will register the startup script with the `Page` object. A call to the `RegisterStartupScript()` method will look something like this:

```
ScriptManager.RegisterStartupScript(PageOrControl, typeof(UIWidget), ScriptKey,
ScriptToCall, bool);
```

where the parameters are as follows:

❑ `PageOrControl` — The first parameter is either the page or control that is associated with the startup script. Typically, this is the page that will be updated and is passed as `this`. A control can also be passed in; however, it will generally be the page that is passed in.

❑ `typeof(UIWidget)` — The second parameter will be the type of control that is sent to the client.

❑ `ScriptKey` — The third parameter is a string and is the key that marks the name of the script.

- ❑   `ScriptToCall` — The fourth parameter is a string and is the script that will be called on initialization.

- ❑   `bool` — The final parameter is a Boolean indicating whether or not to place the script to call within a `<script>` tag. Typically, `true` will be handed in for this value.

And example would look something like this:

```
ScriptManagerHelper.RegisterStartupScript( this, typeof(MathWidget),  ClientID +
"_Initialize", "UIWidget_InitializeMethod('" + ClientID + "');", true);
```

Implementing Dispose Functionality on the Client

It might seem strange to think that a control in the client web browser needs to be disposed. After all, dispose is a server-side concept. Most programmers believe that when a user navigates away from a page, all items from the page are flushed out of the web browser's memory. Unfortunately, this is not the case. Many web pages don't clean up very well when a user navigates away from them. This can result in memory leaks and the web browser locking up a system. As a result, a programmer needs to implement dispose for code that runs on the client.

The next question you will ask is "What to do within a `Dispose()` type of method?" This is rather easy. Typically, the `Dispose` method will be the opposite of the `Initialization` method. Assuming that a button's click event registers a keypress event, the `UIWidget_Dispose()` event might look something like this:

```
function UIWidget_Dispose(IDOfWidget)
{
    $get(IDOfWidget).detachEvent('onkeypress', UIWidget_KeyPressHandler);
}
```

The final problem is how to get the `UIWidget`'s `Dispose()` method to be called on the client side. This can be done through another call to the `ScriptManager`'s `RegisterStartScript()` method. In this case, this code will take advantage of some little-known functionality of the `UpdatePanel` to automatically call the `Dispose()` method of a client that is within a certain format, referred to as *expando format*. The call to the `RegisterStartupScript` will look something like this:

```
ScriptManager.RegisterStartupScript( this,  typeof(UIWidget),  ClientID +
"_Dispose",@"document.getElementById('" + ClientID + @"').dispose = function() {{
UIWidget_Dispose('" + ClientID + @"');}}",  true);
```

Complementary Controls

Two additional controls are closely associated with the `UpdatePanel` control: `UpdateProgress` and `Timer`.

The UpdateProgress Control

If you don't want to jump into using the client-side page life cycle to communicate that updates are occurring, the `UpdateProgress` control is a good tool for the job. The `UpdateProgress` control is a complementary control to the `UpdatePanel` control. The `UpdateProgress` control is used to provide status information regarding asynchronous postbacks caused by the action of an `UpdatePanel`. The control is good for communicating to the user that an asynchronous postback is occurring during a long-running asynchronous postback.

Associating an UpdateProgress Control with an UpdatePanel

The UpdateProgress control contains a named property called the AssociatedUpdatePanelID. By setting this property to the value of an UpdatePanel's ID, an UpdateProgress is associated with an UpdatePanel. Whenever the specified UpdatePanel is in an asynchronous update, the content from the UpdateProgress control is displayed to the user. If an UpdateProgress's AssociatedUpdatePanelID is not specified, the UpdateProgress's content is displayed for all asynchronous postbacks.

> *In the 1.0 version of the ASP.NET AJAX Extensions, there is a discrepancy between the UpdateProgress documentation and how it acts. It appears to be a bug; however, that is in the eye of the beholder. With the 1.0 version, the UpdateProgress is not displayed unless the UpdatePanel's asynchronous postback is performed by a child control of an UpdatePanel.*

ProgressTemplate

The ProgressTemplate is the container for any messages that will be displayed to the user. The <ProgressTemplate> value can contain HTML markup and text.

In a previous example in this chapter, you saw the AbortButton. The AbortButton is a special button and ID that can be used to stop an asynchronous postback. Along with the AbortButton, the abortPostBack() method of the PageRequestManager can be used to stop a currently running asynchronous postback.

The Timer Control

The Timer control is a server-side control that generates the necessary code on the front end to cause a postback to occur at defined interfaces. Though the Timer control can be used to cause the entire page to postback, when used with the UpdatePanel, it can cause an asynchronous postback to occur to update sections of a web page through the UpdatePanel at regular intervals. The asynchronous update can be set to occur at regular (timed) intervals.

The two members of the Timer control that are of interest are the Interval property and the Tick event. The Interval property is used to set the interval for an update. The Tick event is the event on the server that fires when a postback occurs that is caused by the Timer control.

Take a look at an example with the UpdatePanel, UpdateProgress, and Timer controls in the following Try It Out.

Try It Out   The UpdatePanel, UpdateProgress, and Timer Controls

In this example, the UpdateProgress and Timer controls are used to enhance the asynchronous postback of the UpdatePanel. An UpdateProgress is set to display the data within its ProgressTemplate after the asynchronous postback is away from the browser for 500 milliseconds. The Timer control's Tick event will cause an asynchronous postback after 10 seconds and will continue to update as long as its Enabled property is set to true.

Here's the source code in the .aspx page:

```
<asp:ScriptManager ID="SCM1" runat="server" />
<asp:Timer ID="Timer1" runat="server" Interval="10000" OnTick="Timer1_Tick" />
```

```
<div>
Original Page Load Time: <%=DateTime.Now.ToString() %>
<asp:UpdateProgress ID="UpProgress" runat="server" DisplayAfter="500"
DynamicLayout="true" >
    <ProgressTemplate>
        Update Currently in Progress........
    </ProgressTemplate>
</asp:UpdateProgress>
<asp:UpdatePanel ID="UP1" runat="server" UpdateMode="Conditional">
    <ContentTemplate>
        <asp:Label ID="lbl1" runat="server" Text="" />
    </ContentTemplate>
    <Triggers>
        <asp:AsyncPostBackTrigger ControlID="Timer1" EventName="Tick" />
    </Triggers>
</asp:UpdatePanel>
</div>
```

Along with the source code of the .aspx page, the following is the code in the .cs file:

```
protected void Timer1_Tick(object sender, EventArgs e)
{
    this.lbl1.Text = "Server Time: " + DateTime.Now.ToString();
    System.Threading.Thread.Sleep(15000);
}
```

How It Works

The following steps are performed under the covers:

1. The page loads. During the page load, the initial set of ASP.NET AJAX code occurs, and the time of the page load is displayed to the user. During the page load, the Timer control is set so that the Tick event fires every 10 seconds.

2. Once the Timer control's Tick event fires, an asynchronous postback occurs.

3. Within the asynchronous postback, a delay of 15 seconds is inserted to cause a delay.

4. While the asynchronous postback is occurring, the "Update Currently in Progress…" message is displayed to the user. The message is displayed to the user after a delay of 500 milliseconds. The delay in displaying the message minimizes the flash that a user would get if there was no delay in displaying the message. After all, the UpdateProgress control is used to provide some level of feedback to the user about a potentially long-running asynchronous postback.

5. Once the asynchronous postback is completed, the <div> that contains the message is made invisible and the user sees the output.

Figure 5-13 shows the final output of an asynchronous postback with the UpdatePanel and Timer controls.

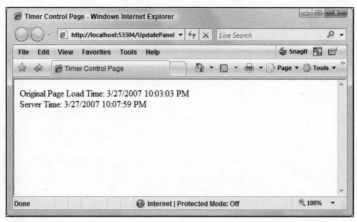

Figure 5-13

Summary

As you can see, the `UpdatePanel` is a very powerful control. It provides a number of useful functions, including:

❑   A simple way to provide AJAX-like functionality to an application. Developers can take advantage of AJAX functionality within their application through a server control.

❑   Integration with the ASP.NET server events.

❑   Simple debugging experience for server-side events. Developers are able to use the familiar debugging experience of Visual Studio 2005.

❑   Client-side page life cycle. Advanced developers are able to integrate with the page life cycle that is exposed through the page request manager.

Control Toolkit

The ASP.NET AJAX Control Toolkit is a community project initiated by Microsoft that provides a set of controls based around the Microsoft AJAX Library and AJAX ASP.NET 2.0 Extensions 1.0. These controls are free for use within your own applications and provide features and behaviors far beyond those supplied in the Microsoft AJAX Library and ASP.NET 2.0 Extensions 1.0. You can think of the Microsoft AJAX Library and ASP.NET 2.0 Extensions 1.0 as the core framework (much like the .NET framework base class library itself), and the ASP.NET AJAX Control Toolkit as a set of controls built on top of that framework (much like the ASP.NET server-based controls or Windows Forms–based controls).

The Control Toolkit is a lot more than just a reusable set of controls, however. Complete with IntelliSense and designer support, it also provides a framework for building your own AJAX extender controls, and alleviates much of the common coding required to implement server-based controls.

It provides comprehensive cross-browser support, much like the ASP.NET 2.0 AJAX Extensions 1.0 and AJAX Library itself. Internet Explorer, Firefox, and Safari are among the major browsers supported with support for browsers such as Opera included where possible.

This chapter covers exactly what the Control Toolkit is from a community project perspective, examines controls within the Toolkit, and also covers the controls provided for developers wishing to create their own extender controls using the Control Toolkit. Specifically, you learn about the following topics:

❑   What a community project managed by Microsoft really means

❑   How to install the Control Toolkit

❑   What an extender control is

❑   How the controls within the Control Toolkit can be used

❑   What features and support the Control Toolkit provides for developers wishing to create their own extender controls

❑   How you can contribute to the Control Toolkit project

A Community Project

The ASP.NET AJAX Control Toolkit (herein referred to as the "Toolkit") is a project initiated by Microsoft that aims to provide a set of ready-to-use controls built using the Microsoft AJAX Library and AJAX ASP.NET 2.0 Extensions 1.0. The Toolkit is a brand new type of development project for Microsoft. It is free for use within your own applications, it comes complete with source code, and it is structured to allow people within the community to contribute to the project, in conjunction with Microsoft developers.

Currently, the project is managed by a team within Microsoft known as the "Agility team," led by Shawn Burke. This team manages who can contribute to the Toolkit, how the development project is structured, new development, issues and bug tracking, as well as release management. Initially, the Toolkit provided around six controls solely developed by Microsoft. Once this initial release was established and made available to the community, Microsoft looked to the community for potential contributors to the Toolkit. Initially, this was only a small set of two community contributors, but as the management process of community contribution was tried, tested, and put to actual use, this number grew. Currently, the number of community contributors totals approximately eight, and this number is constantly increasing.

> Shawn Burke's blog is located at `http://blogs.msdn.com/sburke/` and contains regular information updates relating to the AJAX Control Toolkit.

The project itself is hosted within Microsoft's own CodePlex servers. CodePlex is the home of Microsoft's latest community collaborative-development web site. The location is `www.codeplex.com`. The Toolkit is one of many projects hosted here and utilizes the Team Foundation Server source control mechanism. The latest release of the Toolkit can always be downloaded from here: `www.codeplex.com/Wiki/View .aspx?ProjectName=AtlasControlToolkit`.

Because this type of project is a new frontier for Microsoft, expansion of the Toolkit from a community perspective is carefully managed. Ultimately, the aim is to provide quality reusable controls of a very high standard to the community, free to use within their own applications, complete with source code. Eventually, the aim is to hand off the management process of the Toolkit to the community itself; however, this will again be carefully managed once the structure and management of the project is well established such that the quality of the Toolkit remains constant.

The Toolkit itself provides immense value to developers, and in some ways, even more so than the AJAX Library and extensions themselves. The Toolkit controls are targeted at specific use-case scenarios, provide easy drag-and-drop behavior with designer support, and extend the Microsoft AJAX Library and ASP.NET 2.0 AJAX Extensions frameworks to provide a highly productive way to add rich and dynamic behavior to your web applications. The Toolkit controls utilize a familiar server control design mechanism, which can often alleviate the need entirely for developers to learn the intricacies of the Microsoft AJAX Library and ASP.NET 2.0 AJAX Extensions.

Installing the Toolkit

Before installing the Toolkit, you need to ensure that you have downloaded and installed the ASP.NET AJAX Extensions themselves. These extensions are required because they form the framework upon which the Toolkit itself is based. They can be downloaded from `http://ajax.asp.net`.

To start using the Toolkit, you only need to download the latest release of the Toolkit from the CodePlex servers at `www.codeplex.com/Wiki/View.aspx?ProjectName=AtlasControlToolkit`. On this page is listed the ZIP file `AJAXControlToolkit.zip`, which contains the entire Toolkit, including unit tests and the sample web site. After you download them, decompress the installation files to your local disk, and as a matter of good practice to ensure all files are included and expanded properly, rebuild the Toolkit solution. The following steps outline this process:

1. Download the latest AJAX Control Toolkit package (`AJAXControlToolkit.zip`) from CodePlex (`www.codeplex.com/Wiki/View.aspx?ProjectName= AtlasControlToolkit`).

2. Extract the files to a directory location on your system. To do this you can use several tools such as WinZip (`www.winzip.com/downwz.htm`), WinRAR (`www.rarlab.com/ download.htm`), or the built-in compressed folders functionality of Windows XP and Windows Vista.

3. Using Visual Studio 2005, open the `AjaxControlToolkit.sln` by selecting File ➪ Open Project/Solution and navigate to the location where you extracted the Toolkit files in the previous step. Select the solution file and click Open.

4. Right-click the solution within Visual Studio 2005 Solution Explorer and select Rebuild Solution to rebuild the entire solution. The solution should rebuild successfully and ensure that everything is extracted and set up correctly.

There are two main ways in which you can utilize the Toolkit, depending on your development needs. You can reuse the controls within your own applications, or create your own extender controls to use in your applications or make available to others.

The simplest scenario is using the controls within your own applications. This will save large amounts of development effort and time, and involves the following steps:

1. In Visual Studio 2005, load the application in which you wish to use the Toolkit controls.

2. Add the Toolkit project to your application solution by right-clicking the solution in the Solution Explorer window, selecting Add ➪ Existing Project, browsing to the location you extracted the Toolkit, and selecting the Toolkit project file, `AjaxControlToolkit.csproj`, which exists in the `AjaxControlToolkit` directory.

3. From your main application, add a project reference to the Toolkit project by right-clicking your project in the Solution Explorer in Visual Studio 2005, selecting Add Reference, selecting the Project tab, and then selecting the AjaxControlToolkit project.

   Alternatively, you can add a reference to the Toolkit assembly, `AjaxControlToolkit.dll`, explicitly from within your Visual Studio 2005 project by right-clicking your project in the Solution Explorer window in Visual Studio 2005, selecting Add Reference, selecting the Browse tab, and navigating to the `AjaxControlToolkit.dll`, which should be located in the directory where you extracted the Toolkit files.

The project reference approach, as opposed to the direct assembly reference approach, is the preferred method for including the Toolkit (or any external project). Larger solutions often dictate the need to separate projects and reference only by assembly, however, where possible, a project reference is a better choice.

Although both approaches work equally well from a functional perspective, the project reference allows better debugging and referencing of correct versions of external projects. Referencing the assembly directly does have the advantage of being the simpler approach, though.

The Toolkit is shipped as a single solution that contains four separate projects:

❑ **AJAXControlToolkit** — This is the set of controls and extender control framework that comprises the Toolkit itself. It represents the main deliverable content of the Toolkit and is the main focus of this chapter.

❑ **SampleWebSite** — This is a web site that contains documentation for the Toolkit. A separate web page exists for each control within the Toolkit that shows a simple example of its use and the markup required to render the control on a page. Usage scenarios, full property listings of the control, and general notes about the control are contained within its specific page. In addition, the web site contains general information about how to include the Toolkit into your applications, how to create your own extender controls, setting up the Toolkit, Toolkit framework notes, and extra information on some of the more complex controls such as the `Animation` control extender.

❑ **ToolkitTests** — This project is a set of unit tests designed to run each control through a set of predefined tests to verify that it is functioning as intended. Each control is required to have its own unit test page that exercises its functionality. This is especially important for control authors, but this project provides a fantastic framework with which to test dynamic browser behaviors for which AJAX type controls are well known. Traditionally, it has been very hard and requires substantial effort to test a control to ensure that it dynamically displays content or manipulates the browser without a visual indication. The test framework provided makes this an automated process in a similar fashion to unit tests using traditional server-side programming languages.

Figure 6-1 shows an example test run using the Toolkit test harness solution provided with the Toolkit.

Running the Toolkit tests is easy. Simply load the Toolkit solution into Visual Studio 2005. In the ToolkitTests project, right-click the `Default.aspx` page and select View In Browser. Select the tests to run (as shown in Figure 6-1) and click the Run Tests button.

The unit testing framework provided with the Toolkit is a very powerful tool that can be utilized within your own projects for the purpose of testing your own dynamic controls and dynamic behaviors. Currently, the tests are targeted specifically at the Toolkit controls, but with a little tweaking, you can tailor them to suit your own projects.

❑ **TemplateVSI** — This project was created by the AJAX Control Toolkit team and provides a set of template additions to Visual Studio to aid in the creation of AJAX Control Toolkit web sites, and also new extender controls based on the Toolkit framework.

To install the template additions, simply navigate to the bin directory within this project, and run the `AjaxControlExtender.vsi` file. A set of dialog boxes will be presented that lead you through the installation, after which the templates will be installed within Visual Studio.

Once it is installed, you have some new options to choose from when creating a web site or a new project. Within Visual Studio, select the File ➪ New ➪ Web Site menu option and you will be presented with a dialog box with the various web site templates to choose from, as shown in Figure 6-2.

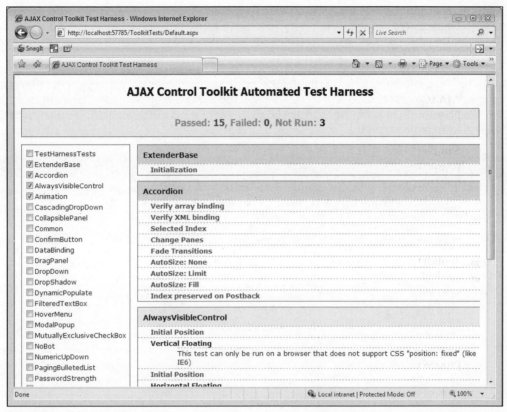

Figure 6-1

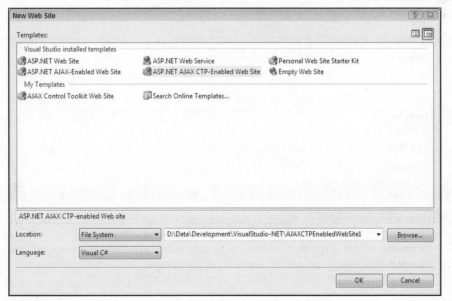

Figure 6-2

Figure 6-2 shows the options available after installing the `AjaxControlToolkit.vsi` file. A new option is provided, the AJAX Control Toolkit Web Site. Selecting this template and clicking the OK button creates a blank web site with all the correct assembly references and `web.config` declarations required to begin creating a web site using the AJAX Control Toolkit.

In addition to the web site template, the Toolkit provides a new template so that you can start creating your own extender controls using the Toolkit framework. This is explored in detail in Chapter 7. This new template can be found by selecting the File ➪ New ➪ Project menu option. This opens a dialog box similar to the one in Figure 6-3.

In this figure, under the My Templates section, a new project template, ASP.NET AJAX Control Project, is shown. If you select a project and click the OK button, a new project is created with the basic set of files required to start creating your own control extender using the Toolkit. As mentioned previously, this is discussed in detail in Chapter 7 where creating extender controls is examined exclusively.

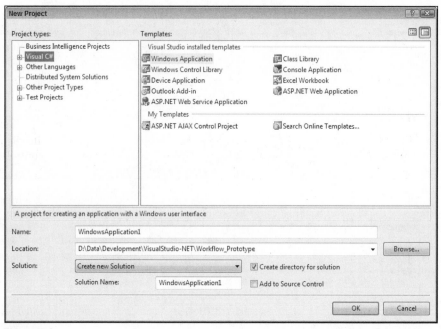

Figure 6-3

Examining the Controls within the Toolkit

The controls within the Toolkit are highly functional controls that can be used to enhance your applications. In most but not all scenarios, these controls will complement the existing behavior of your applications by enhancing or extending them in some way. The framework that is supplied within the Toolkit package provides enhanced functionality for creating controls that extend an existing control or element's behavior. Not surprisingly, these types of controls are called extender controls.

Extender Controls

The Toolkit bases almost all the provided controls around a notion of extender controls. As the name suggests, *extender controls* extend the features and functionality of existing components and controls by supplementing them with new properties and behavior. Understanding this concept is important before moving on to an examination of the controls themselves.

The basis for extender controls are provided by the AJAX ASP.NET 2.0 Extensions framework. This extender class is an abstract class that provides the basic functionality with which to create your own custom extender components that extend existing controls. The fully qualified class name for this is `Microsoft.Web.UI.ExtenderControl`. You can create components based on this class by inheriting from this class; however, because it is abstract, you must supply implementation details. The Toolkit utilizes this class, but builds upon it by providing concrete implementation details that make the task of creating extender controls even easier. The details of this are provided in Chapter 7, which deals exclusively with developing these types of controls.

Developers familiar with Windows Forms programming may be familiar with the extender controls that are shipped with the .NET framework. With Windows Forms development, extender controls are placed onto the form and extend specific controls contained on that form, such as supplying tooltip functionality, but are not explicitly provided by the control itself. This concept is the same used for extender controls within the Toolkit.

Basic Control Usage

Each control within the Toolkit is a server-based control that usually emits the requisite client script to support its functionality. As mentioned previously, the Toolkit controls are extender controls and typically extend an existing element.

Each definition of an extender control requires the declaration of the extender control, with properties contained within the main declaration that reference the elements themselves. The following simple example demonstrates this using the `TextBoxWatermarkExtender` control:

```
<ajaxToolkit:TextBoxWatermarkExtender ID="TextBoxWatermarkExtender1" runat="server"
TargetControlID="TextBox1" WatermarkText="Type First Name Here"
WatermarkCssClass="watermarked" />
```

This code sample was taken from the SampleWebSite provided with the AJAX Control Toolkit package.

The preceding example shows a `TextBoxWatermark` extender control defined within a page. It has an ID and the requisite `runat="server"` attribute that all ASP.NET server controls require. The `TargetControlID` attribute defines what HTML element will be extended, in this case the element with an `ID` of `TextBox1`. This property is common to every single extender control and specifies the element to be extended. Beyond that property are two attributes specific to the `TextBoxWatermark` extender control: the `WatermarkText` and `WatermarkCssClass` attributes. These custom attributes are different for each extender and are discussed later in this chapter when examining the `TextBoxWatermark` extender control and the rest of the controls within the Toolkit. The format of this control declaration is what is important here because this pattern is used with all extender controls in the Toolkit, and provides a consistency that makes it easy to use any control within the Toolkit.

To demonstrate the concept of an extender control, when a normal ASP.NET `Textbox` control is placed onto a Web Form designer surface, the properties of the text box, as shown in the Properties pane, are similar to Figure 6-4.

When an extender control is placed onto the Web Form such as the previous `TextBoxWatermark` declaration, the properties of the text box are extended or supplemented with some new properties to support this extended behavior. This is shown in Figure 6-5.

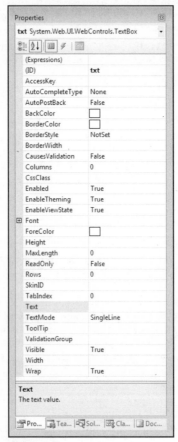

Figure 6-4

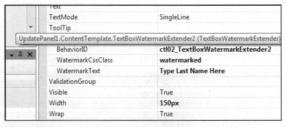

Figure 6-5

The figure shows that there are now a series of `TextBoxWatermarkExtender` attributes where there were none before. This concept is identical for almost all the controls within the Toolkit in that a custom set of attributes are added to the control being targeted and extend the control's functionality.

Examining the Controls

Now that you know what an extender control is, it is time to look at the controls themselves. When the Toolkit is installed on your system, documentation is also installed that describes what each control does and provides basic guidance about development with the controls and Toolkit itself. The following section is not intended to replace this documentation, but rather to supplement it and provide additional examples of intended control usage.

As mentioned previously, the Toolkit ships with a sample web site demonstrating each control in simple situations. Use this chapter in conjunction with the sample web site.

Control List

The following list of controls within the Toolkit gives a brief overview of each control and provides a quick glance at the use of each control. Each control will not be examined nor demonstrated in detail. Following this brief overview, some of the more complex and interesting controls are shown with examples. This approach has been taken to avoid repeating content used by the Toolkit documentation for the simpler controls, and to further explain the usage of the more complex controls. The current set of controls that ship with the Toolkit are as follows:

❑   `Accordion` — Allows displaying of panes of information, stacked together, and selectively expanded when the user clicks them. These panes are animated and expand when clicked, such that it looks like an accordion instrument being expanded and contracted. It is useful when you want to place a large amount of information on a page without displaying it all at once. The user can choose which pane of information to display. Figures 6-6 and 6-7 show how text can be expanded after the `Accordion` control has been applied.

❑   `AlwaysVisibleControl` — Provides a way to display a dialog or frame of information on a page, and have it anchored to a part of the page such as the bottom of the page or along the left border. If the user resizes the browser window, or scrolls to a different part of the page, the control will automatically smoothly scroll the frame or dialog, so that it is always visible in the specified location.

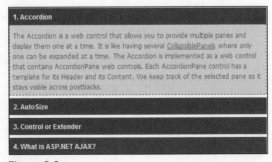

Figure 6-6

123

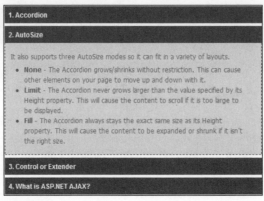

1. Accordion

2. AutoSize

It also supports three AutoSize modes so it can fit in a variety of layouts.

- **None** - The Accordion grows/shrinks without restriction. This can cause other elements on your page to move up and down with it.
- **Limit** - The Accordion never grows larger than the value specified by its Height property. This will cause the content to scroll if it is too large to be displayed.
- **Fill** - The Accordion always stays the exact same size as its Height property. This will cause the content to be expanded or shrunk if it isn't the right size.

3. Control or Extender

4. What is ASP.NET AJAX?

Figure 6-7

❑   `Animation` — The `Animation` control is one of the more complex controls within the Toolkit and is really more than just a control. It is a flexible mechanism for defining many forms of interactive animations on other controls. Effects such as moving, resizing, fading, and color effects (such as cycling through a range of colors) can be easily achieved by using this control's easy declarative programming style. This control is examined in more detail following this section.

❑   `AutoComplete` — This control provides the very popular method of a drop-down box on a textual input field, showing user search matches as the user types text into the field (see Figure 6-8).

❑   `Calendar` — This control is a client-side date picker control that looks very similar to the standard ASP.NET date picker control. However, all functionality is within the client and requires no specific server-side support.

❑   `CascadingDropDown` — This control can be attached to an ASP.NET `DropDownList` control to get automatic population of a set of `DropDownList` controls. Each time the selection of one the `DropDownList` controls changes, a specified web service is called to retrieve the list of values for the next `DropDownList` in the set.

❑   `CollapsiblePanel` — This control is effective at conserving real estate by allowing standard content to be contained within a panel that is expanded and collapsed through user interaction; thus information takes up valuable screen space only when the user requires it.

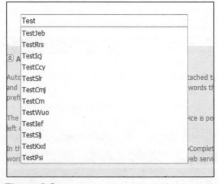

Figure 6-8

❑ ConfirmButton — One of the simpler controls, this allows you to define a confirmation dialog box without resorting to JavaScript. Though not complex, this functionality is extremely common throughout many applications and so this control provides a convenient way to offer confirmation boxes, like the one shown in Figure 6-9, through a single declarative statement.

Figure 6-9

❑ DragPanel — This control extends any ASP.NET panel so that the user can drag it around the browser window and reposition it dynamically.

❑ DropDown — This control emulates the "Sharepoint" style drop-down menu control. A drop-down control is displayed, but when clicked, it displays customized menu items that the user can choose from, rather than the standard list of textual items.

❑ DropShadow — Provides a method of adding drop shadows to a control so that a 3D or perspective type effect is achieved, making the control more visually appealing (see Figure 6-10).

Figure 6-10

❑ DynamicPopulate — This control simply populates an HTML control with the results of a web service or page method call. This is a common requirement and alleviates the need to code JavaScript explicitly for this task. Typically, the result of the server-side operation is HTML content that is appended to the control being targeted.

❑ FilteredTextBox — This control prevents a user from entering invalid characters into a text entry field/text box. The valid characters are completely customizable to suit the application's requirements. For example, entry can be restricted to allowing only numbers to be typed into the text box.

❑ HoverMenu — This control allows a popup menu or dialog to be defined whenever the mouse hovers over a particular control. This is similar to a contextual menu except that no mouse click is required. The popup menu is shown whenever the mouse is situated above the targeted control. The popup dialog or menu is then hidden when the mouse moves away from the targeted control. Figure 6-11 shows an example of a popup message.

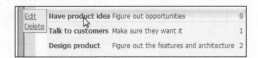

Figure 6-11

❑ ListSearch — The ListSearch control allows you to perform an incremental search within a drop-down list or list box by typing characters, and having the search executed within the drop-down list or list box as you type based on the characters entered so far.

❑ MaskEdit — The MaskEdit control allows formatted and validated input into a text box based on the data type specified for the text box entry (see Figure 6-12). All formatting and validation of the data is performed on the client.

Figure 6-12

❑ ModalPopup — Applications commonly require a modal dialog box to be displayed, requiring input or user interaction before allowing program flow to continue. Traditionally, this is can only natively be achieved with either an "alert" or "confirm" box using JavaScript. This control provides a customizable way of showing almost any form of dialog that can be designed using HTML as a modal popup window. Figure 6-13 shows an example of a modal dialog box.

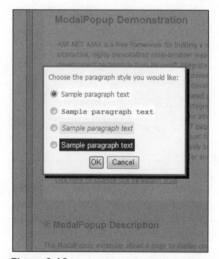

Figure 6-13

❑ MutuallyExclusiveCheckBox — This control can be attached to any traditional ASP.NET check box control and provides the ability for one CheckBox control to deselect other check box controls. This is similar in functionality to a radio button control; however, a radio button control cannot be deselected but requires other radio buttons to be selected, whereas a check box can simply be deselected without affecting other controls.

❑ NoBot — This control provides a simplistic method of reducing the blog-comment spam on sites. Though not guaranteed 100% effective, it can provide an invisible and easy way of reducing the amount of comment spam experienced by sites. This control is targeted at low-to-medium-traffic sites and is similar in concept to CAPTCHA validation; however, it requires no human user intervention.

CAPTCHA is a technique where a distorted image of characters is displayed to the user. The user is required to enter into a text field what the characters are before being allowed to proceed. This procedure is used a lot within blog sites to reduce comment spam by bots. This is effective against bots that try to automate the adding of comments to blog sites because these bots are unable to decipher the distorted characters, and thus are blocked from entering a comment.

❑   NumericUpDown — Allows a user to select a numeric value using visual controls and a click of the mouse. This is typically performed via simply clicking up or down arrows to increase or decrease the numeric value accordingly, as shown in Figure 6-14.

Figure 6-14

❑   PagingBulletedList — As the name suggests, this control can extend a traditional ASP.NET BulletedList control to provide paging functionality where the list of bulleted items is excessive or large. The control also supports the ability to sort the items through configuration attributes.

❑   PasswordStrength — Provides immediate visual indication of the strength of a password as the user is entering it into the text entry field. This control is customizable to use either textual indicators or graphical bar indicators to show the password's strength, as shown in Figure 6-15.

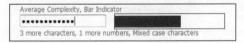

Figure 6-15

❑   PopupControl — This control can be attached to almost any control and will cause a popup window to be displayed to allow further interaction by the user. Complex forms are supported as popup windows with the ability to contain any HTML content.

❑   Rating — Many web sites provide a mechanism by which users can graphically indicate a rating of the associated content. This is often done with a series of five stars, where the user can highlight the number of stars visually representing how good the content is, as shown in Figure 6-16. This control encapsulates this visual rating mechanism and makes it easy to add a visual rating mechanism to your sites.

Figure 6-16

❑ ReorderList — This provides the ability to display a bulleted list of data bound to a data source, but allow the user to interactively change the order of the displayed items by picking up and dragging an item with the mouse to its new location within the displayed list. The newly dragged content triggers an update of the bound data source to reflect the new position of the item.

❑ ResizableControl — Allows content to be stored within a resizable window or frame where the user can dynamically resize the window using the mouse. This is similar to the standard resizable windows on Windows Forms applications but within a web browser. The content within the window or frame is dynamically adjusted as the window is resized. An example is shown in Figure 6-17.

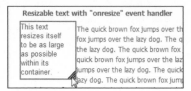

Figure 6-17

❑ RoundedCorners — Enhances the visual appearance of controls that use a traditional 90 degree "hard" angled corners (such as a rectangular panel control), by replacing the corners with softer, rounded corners for a more visually appealing interface (see Figure 6-18).

Figure 6-18

❑ Slider — Provides users the ability to visually "grab and slide" a marker to change a particular value, using the mouse (see Figure 6-19). This is often used in Windows Forms applications where a user might adjust the volume of speakers by sliding a marker bar up or down with a mouse. This control provides this same experience but within the web browser.

Figure 6-19

❑ SlideShow — Extends an image control and provides an easy way to generate a slideshow for a set of images. The slideshow can be configured with a set interval, image transitions, and loop through the images in a round-robin fashion.

❑ Tabs — A completely client-side implementation that provides a set of tab container controls to allow switching between page display content. Each tab can contain its own display controls and is activated by the user clicking the respective tab element. Figure 6-20 shows an example.

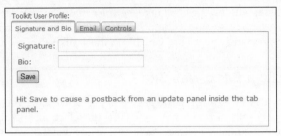

Figure 6-20

❑ TextBoxWatermark — A relatively simple control that adds watermark text to a text input field. When the user enters text within the field, the watermark text is removed. If no data is entered into the text field or is present in the field, the watermark text is redisplayed again.

❑ ToggleButton — Another relatively simple control that switches an image to opposing states (for example, on or off) each time it is clicked. Similar in functionality to a traditional check box, except that customizable images are used.

❑ UpdatePanelAnimation — This control allows sophisticated animation to occur whenever an UpdatePanel control executes an asynchronous postback operation. Similar in concept to the UpdateProgress control provided with the AJAX ASP.NET Extensions, but utilizing the animation framework within the Toolkit to provide more complex animations during an UpdatePanel asynchronous operation.

❑ ValidatorCallout — Provides a visual indicator in the form of a "callout" graphical display to indicate validation messages to the user when inputting data on a form, as shown in Figure 6-21. This "callout" is dynamically displayed and hidden as required during the input process.

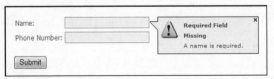

Figure 6-21

As you can see, there are quite a number of controls within the Toolkit and together they provide a broad range of functionality. The controls all have one thing is common though, in that they all aim to make the development experience easier. Almost all controls remove the need to code JavaScript to varying degrees, and all support a more traditional ASP.NET server-side programming model, complete with IntelliSense support and server-side syntax validation.

It should be noted that new controls are constantly being added to the Toolkit by the current set of con-tributors, as well as from new contributors within the community. As a result, the Toolkit is an ever-expanding suite of valuable controls for you to make use of within your applications.

Putting the Controls to Use

To demonstrate the use of some of these controls, you add a selection of Toolkit controls to an existing page. The entire control set won't be utilized here, because many controls are very similar and/or obvious in their usage; however, this section examines some of the more unique controls that require a little more explanation than previously given or available in the Toolkit documentation.

Try It Out   **Creating a Basic Web Site**

For this example, you start by creating a basic page that performs some very basic functions such as searching on a name or staff ID, displaying those results for selection, and also displaying some help information. The assumption here is that you have an existing site that you wish to add functionality to by using the Toolkit controls.

1.   Start by creating a brand new web site from within Visual Studio. Load up Visual Studio, and select the File ➪ New ➪ Web Site menu option. From the dialog presented, select ASP.NET Web Site, specify a location where to create the web site, and click OK.

2.   A `Default.aspx` file is created in the project for you. Double-click the file and the markup for that page is displayed within Visual Studio. Replace the existing content in that page, shown in the following listing:

```
<html xmlns="http://www.w3.org/1999/xhtml" >
<head runat="server">
    <title>Untitled Page</title>
</head>
<body>
    <form id="form1" runat="server">
    <div>

    </div>
    </form>
</body>
</html>
```

with the following content:

```
<html xmlns="http://www.w3.org/1999/xhtml" >
<head runat="server">
    <title>AJAX Control Toolkit Demonstration</title>
    <link href="mainStyle.css" rel="stylesheet" type="text/css" />
</head>
<body>
    <form id="form1" runat="server">
        <asp:Panel ID="panelTitle" runat="server">
            <h3>Exciting Webpages R Us.</h3>
        </asp:Panel>
```

```
    <div>
        <asp:Panel ID="srchPanel" runat="server">
            <h4>Enter Search Criteria</h4>

            <div id="criteria">
                <div class="innerCriteria">
                    <asp:Label ID="lblStaffID" runat="server">Staff ID:</asp:Label>
                    <asp:TextBox ID="txtStaffID" runat="server"></asp:TextBox>
                </div>
                <div class="innerCriteria">
                    <asp:Label ID="lblName" runat="server">Name:</asp:Label>
                    <asp:TextBox ID="txtName" runat="server"></asp:TextBox>
                </div>
            </div>

            <div id="criteriaButtons" class="criteriaButtons">
                <asp:Button ID="btnSearch" runat="server" Text="Search"
CssClass="criteriaButton" OnClick="btnSearch_Click" />
                <asp:Button ID="btnClearForm" runat="server" Text="Clear"
CssClass="criteriaButton" OnClick="btnClearForm_Click"  />
                <asp:Button ID="btnHelp" runat="server" Text="Help"
CssClass="criteriaButton" OnClick="btnHelp_Click"  />
            </div>

        </asp:Panel>

        <asp:Panel ID="srchResults" runat="server">
            <h4>Search Results / Navigation</h4>
            <asp:Panel ID="srchRsltDetail" runat="server">
                <ul>
                <asp:DataList ID="dataView" runat="server" CellPadding="4"
ForeColor="#333333">
                    <HeaderTemplate>
                        <div class="resultLine">
                            <asp:Label ID="rsltStaffNum" runat="server"
CssClass="resultItem" Text='StaffNumber' />
                            <asp:Label ID="rsltName" runat="server"
CssClass="resultItem" Text='Name' />
                            <asp:Label ID="rsltGender" runat="server"
CssClass="resultItem" Text='Super Power' />
                        </div>
                    </HeaderTemplate>
                    <ItemTemplate>
                        <li>
                            <div class="resultLine">
                                <asp:Label ID="rsltStaffNum" runat="server"
CssClass="resultItem" Text='<%# Eval("StaffNumber") %>' />
                                <asp:Label ID="rsltName" runat="server"
CssClass="resultItem" Text='<%# Eval("Name") %>' />
                                <asp:Label ID="rsltGender" runat="server"
CssClass="resultItem" Text='<%# Eval("Power") %>' />
                            </div>
                        </li>
                    </ItemTemplate>
```

```
                        <FooterStyle BackColor="#1C5E55" Font-Bold="True"
ForeColor="White" />
                        <SelectedItemStyle BackColor="#C5BBAF" Font-Bold="True"
ForeColor="#333333" />
                        <AlternatingItemStyle BackColor="White" />
                        <ItemStyle BackColor="#E3EAEB" />
                        <HeaderStyle BackColor="#1C5E55" Font-Bold="True"
ForeColor="White" />
                </asp:DataList>
                </ul>
            </asp:Panel>
        </asp:Panel>

        <asp:Panel ID="helpPanel" runat="server" Visible="false">
            <h5>Help Information</h5>
            <p>The following functionality can be used from within this highly
complex user interface</p>
            <p><b>StaffID & Name</b>: These fields provide a means to enter search
crieria based around the persons StaffID and Name respectively</p>
            <p><b>Search Button</b>: Performs a search using the entered
criteria</p>
            <p><b>Clear Button</b>: Clears the search criteria and search
results.</p>
            <p><b>Help Button</b>: Displays this help text.</p>
            <asp:Button ID="btnClose" runat="server" Text="Close"
OnClick="btnClose_Click" />
        </asp:Panel>

    </div>
    </form>
</body>
</html>
```

3.   Next, double-click the `Default.aspx.cs` code-behind file, and add the following code to the class:

```csharp
protected void btnSearch_Click(object sender, EventArgs e)
{
    System.Threading.Thread.Sleep(2000);

    // perform some search here
    DataTable result = PerformSearch(txtStaffID.Text,txtName.Text,false);
    dataView.DataSource = result;
    dataView.DataBind();
}
protected void btnHelp_Click(object sender, EventArgs e)
{
    System.Threading.Thread.Sleep(2000);

    // show some help text
    helpPanel.Visible = true;

}
protected void btnClose_Click(object sender, EventArgs e)
```

```csharp
{
    helpPanel.Visible = false;
}

protected void btnClearForm_Click(object sender, EventArgs e)
{
    txtName.Text = "";
    txtStaffID.Text = "";
    helpPanel.Visible = false;
    dataView.DataSource = PerformSearch(null, null,true);
    dataView.DataBind();
}

#region PerformSearch - construct dummy search data
private DataTable PerformSearch(string staffNumText, string nameText, bool
returnEmptyData)
{
    // Create a simple 3 column table
    DataTable dt = new DataTable("SearchTable");
    DataColumn col1 = new DataColumn("StaffNumber", typeof(int));
    DataColumn col2 = new DataColumn("Name", typeof(string));
    DataColumn col3 = new DataColumn("Power", typeof(string));

    dt.Columns.Add(col1);
    dt.Columns.Add(col2);
    dt.Columns.Add(col3);

    // Fill in the table with some random data
    if ( !returnEmptyData  )
    {
        Random r = new Random(DateTime.Now.Millisecond);
        string[] names = new string[] { "Joe", "Mary", "Alice", "Paul", "Steve",
"Wally", "Craig", "Superman", "Batman", "Spiderman", "Wonderwoman" };
        string[] superPower = new string[] { "Super Speed", "Super Strength",
"X-Ray Vision", "Super Coolness", "Climbs Walls", "Truth Lasso" };
        int loop = r.Next(2, 10);
        for (int i = 0; i < loop; i++)
        {
            int staffNum = r.Next(100, 9999);
            string namePrefix = null;
            if (string.IsNullOrEmpty(nameText))
                namePrefix = names[r.Next(0, names.Length - 1)];
            else
                namePrefix = nameText;
            string name = string.Format("{0}{1}", namePrefix, r.Next(1, 200));
            string power = superPower[r.Next(0, superPower.Length - 1)];
            dt.Rows.Add(new object[] { staffNum, name, power });
        }
    }
    dt.AcceptChanges();

    return dt;
}
#endregion
```

4. Finally, to complete the basic web site, right-click the project in the Visual Studio Solution Explorer window and select Add New Item. Select Style Sheet from the window of available options and click OK. Replace the contents of the style sheet you just added with the following code:

```
h3
{
    text-align:center;
    padding:6px 3px 6px 3px;
    border: solid 1px black;
}
h5
{
    text-align:center;
}

#srchPanel
{
    border:1px 1px 1px 1px;
    border-style:solid;
    border-color:Navy;
    width:400px;
    height:150px;
    text-align:center;
    float:left;
    margin: 5px 3px 5px 3px;
}
#srchPanel span
{
    padding-right:10px;
    margin-left:40px;
    width:200px;
}
.criteriaBlock
{
    float:inherit;
    clear:both;
    display:block;
}
.innerCriteria
{
    float:left;
}
.criteriaButtons
{
    float:none;
    clear:both;
    display:block;
}
.criteriaButton
{
    margin-left:10px;
    margin-right:10px;
    width:100px;
```

```
    }

#srchResults
{
    width:450px;
    border:1px 1px 1px 1px;
    border-style:double;
    border-color:Gray;
    text-align:center;
    padding: 5px 3px 5px 3px;
    margin: 5px 3px 5px 3px;
}

#helpPanel
{
    clear:both;
    border:1px 1px 1px 1px;
    border-style:double;
    border-color:Gray;
    text-align:left;
    width:350px;
    margin: 3px 5px 3px 5px;
    padding: 2px;
}
.resultItem
{
    width:150px;
    float:left;
}
.resultLine
{
    width:350px;
    text-align:left;
    clear:both;
    vertical-align:middle;
}
```

5. After these files have been created, you can right-click the `Default.aspx` file within the Visual Studio Solution Explorer window, and select View In Browser from the context menu. This will display a browser window that looks similar to Figure 6-22.

How It Works

The Web Form areas are divided into separate panels to make the logical grouping easier. The search panel simply has two text entry fields and buttons to initiate the search, clear the entry form, or invoke the help information.

A second panel contains a `DataList` control to display the results of the search. The `DataList` control is bound to the `StaffNumber`, `Name`, and `Power` fields, respectively.

The third panel is a container for the static help information that is displayed when the Help button is clicked.

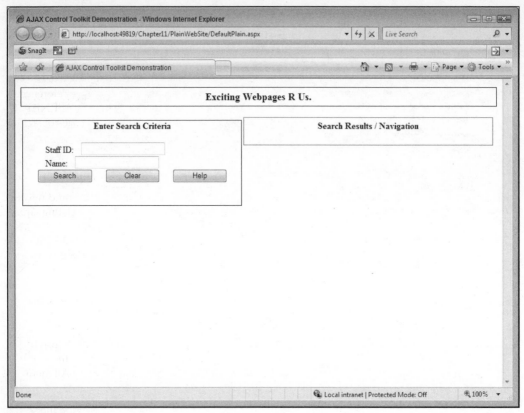

Figure 6-22

When a search is performed, the Search button is clicked and the server-side event first creates a small delay to simulate a database or service call, calls a search method, and then databinds the results of the search method to the `DataList`. This is shown in the following code:

```
System.Threading.Thread.Sleep(2000);

// perform some search here
DataTable result = PerformSearch(txtStaffID.Text,txtName.Text,false);
dataView.DataSource = result;
dataView.DataBind();
```

The `PerformSearch` method simply generates some random results within a `DataTable` object and returns the `DataTable`.

This is a very simplistic and contrived example; however, the site is functional, but not particularly attractive. In addition, the usability of the site could be improved considerably.

Enhancing the Web Page Using Controls from the Toolkit

Now that you have a working web site/page, you can enhance the look and usability of the page using some of the controls from the AJAX Control Toolkit.

Because the AJAX Control Toolkit is based on the foundation of the ASP.NET 2.0 AJAX Extensions 1.0 and Microsoft AJAX Library, you need to enable the site to incorporate the appropriate references and settings to make use of this functionality. If you had initially created the site using the ASP.NET AJAX-Enabled Web Site template that is available when creating a new web site, this next series of steps would not be necessary.

Try It Out   Enabling the Site for ASP.NET AJAX Functionality

Perhaps the easiest way to enable an existing site to use ASP.NET AJAX is to create a brand new site using the ASP.NET AJAX template and merge the settings from the new site to your existing site.

1. To do this, open a new instance of Visual Studio and select the File ➪ New ➪ Web Site menu option. Select ASP.NET AJAX-Enabled Web Site from the list of templates, specify a location to create this web site, and click OK.

   Keep your existing example site that you have created thus far open in the original instance of Visual Studio.

2. A new web site will be created that has all the necessary settings to allow you to use functionality from the ASP.NET 2.0 AJAX Extensions and Microsoft AJAX Library. Open the web.config file, highlight/select all the contents of this file (Ctrl+A or click the Edit ➪ Select All menu option), and copy them to the clipboard (Ctrl+C or click the Edit ➪ Copy menu option).

3. You need to add a web.config file to your example site so that you can provide the settings and references for your example site. Switch to the instance of Visual Studio that contains your example web site. Within the Solution Explorer window, right-click the project and select Add New Item. Select the Web Configuration File option and click Add, as shown in Figure 6-23.

4. All of the changes required to enable AJAX are within the web.config file of your site. After you add the web.config file into your site, it opens in the editor window in Visual Studio. Select the entire contents of the file by using Ctrl+A or by selecting the Edit ➪ Select All menu option. Paste the contents of the clipboard (which you recently populated by copying the web.config contents from your newly created ASP.NET AJAX-Enabled site) by either using Ctrl+V or selecting the Edit ➪ Paste menu option. The contents of the web.config file now match the contents of a newly created ASP.NET AJAX-Enabled web site.

Your site has now been enabled to use the ASP.NET AJAX Extensions. Now you can simply reference the AJAX Control Toolkit assembly and you are ready to go.

Because most existing sites would already contain some customized form of web.config file, it would be necessary to merge contents of the ASP.NET AJAX-Enabled web.config with your custom web.config, making sure to retain the settings from each. This needs to be done manually due to the various customization points that can be performed within a web.config file, but the process can be made a little easier by using a tool such as WinMerge to compare and merge changes from two different files. WinMerge is a free open source tool that you can download from http://winmerge.org/.

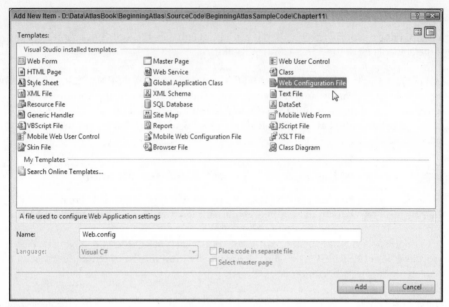

Figure 6-23

How It Works

With this simple example, you are replacing the entire contents of your existing web.config with a newly generated web.config from the ASP.NET AJAX template. The newly generated web.config contains all the necessary handler and section registration to properly ensure that ASP.NET AJAX is enabled for your site. The web.config file can be replaced completely in this case because there have been no specific configuration settings implemented for the existing site.

If you have specific application configuration settings, custom sections, or other custom handlers in the web site you plan to use the ASP.NET AJAX extensions on, you will need to ensure that those custom settings are migrated, and added into the web.config that has all the ASP.NET AJAX settings.

Adding Support for the AJAX Control Toolkit

Now that you have an ASP.NET 2.0 AJAX Extensions 1,0 enabled application, you also need to add support for the AJAX Control toolkit functionality. In order to add support for the Toolkit to your application, you reference the AJAX Control Toolkit assembly directly.

Try It Out   Adding a Reference to the AJAX Control Toolkit

1.   Right-click the web site within the Visual Studio Solution Explorer window and select Add Reference. A dialog box is shown, similar to Figure 6-24.

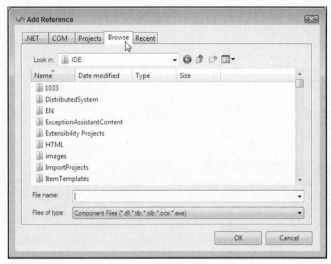

Figure 6-24

2. Select the Browse tab as shown in the preceding figure and navigate to the location of the Toolkit assembly, `AjaxControlToolkit.dll`, on your system. The location will depend on where you chose to extract and install the files from the Toolkit download and will typically be in the `bin\debug` or `bin\release` folder of the AjaxControlToolkit project.

3. There are now two ways to enable the Toolkit controls within the web site. The first is to register the newly referenced assembly for each page that uses any Toolkit controls. This makes sense if you are only utilizing the Toolkit controls on a few pages within your web site. The other is to enable the control registration from within the `web.config` file and make it available to all pages within your application.

In order to register the controls from within the page itself, you need only add the following declaration to your page, near the top of the page where all page-level declarations are stored:

```
<%@ Register Assembly="AjaxControlToolkit" Namespace="AjaxControlToolkit"
TagPrefix="toolkit" %>
```

The `TagPrefix` attribute of the declaration indicates the prefix used when referencing the Toolkit controls and can be any literal string you choose. For example, if you referenced a control within the page using the previous `Register` declaration, you would use syntax similar to the following:

```
<toolkit:TextBoxWatermarkExtender ID="tb1" runat="server" TargetControlID="txt1"
WatermarkText="Enter Text" />
```

The recommendation is to do this from within your `web.config` file to allow all pages to use the Toolkit controls in your application, even if most pages do not use them. This method prevents extra declarative statements in a page should you choose to use the Toolkit controls on your page. Secondly, each page registration can have a different tag prefix. Having a centralized declaration in the `web.config` means all pages will use the same tag prefix and thus be consistent across the site.

5. To add the declaration to your `web.config` file, simply add the following text to the `<system.web>`
    `<pages>`
        `<controls>` section:

```
<add tagPrefix="toolkit" namespace="AjaxControlToolkit"
assembly="AjaxControlToolkit" />
```

The section within your `web.config` file should now look similar to the following:

```
<system.web>
  <pages>
    <controls>
      <add tagPrefix="asp" namespace="System.Web.UI"
assembly="System.Web.Extensions, Version=1.0.61025.0, Culture=neutral,
PublicKeyToken=31bf3856ad364e35"/>
      <add tagPrefix="toolkit" namespace="AjaxControlToolkit"
assembly="AjaxControlToolkit"/>
    </controls>

...rest of file omitted for brevity....
```

How It Works

By adding a reference to the AJAX Control Toolkit assembly, you are including the functionality of that assembly within your application. In order to indicate that a control declaration is intended to be resolved within that assembly, you need to assign a tag prefix to be associated with the assembly and its namespace.

Once this has been done, the tag prefix can be used in your code to indicate that a control declaration is to be resolved with the AJAX Control Toolkit assembly.

Finally, you are ready to add controls to your page.

Try It Out   **Adding the Controls to the Page**

1. Like any ASP.NET AJAX-enabled application, you need to add a `ScriptManager` control to your page before you can add any form of ASP.NET AJAX control to it. You can do this by adding the following code within the `<form>` declaration:

```
<asp:ScriptManager ID="sm1" runat="server"></asp:ScriptManager>
```

2. Start by making your title a little more aesthetic by giving it a drop shadow. It is important to note that you may have to alter the styles of elements to fit your requirements. What may work in a static display may look out of place or wrong when Toolkit controls are added to the page because of the behavior of Cascading Style Sheets (CSS) within web pages. To prepare your title for a drop shadow, make sure it is opaque, and not transparent, otherwise the drop shadow will be visible through the title panel. To do this, add the following CSS declaration to the h3 element of your style sheet:

```
background-color:White;
```

3. Now you can add a `DropShadowExtender` control to your page and target the panel that contains your title:

```
<toolkit:DropShadowExtender ID="ds1" runat="server" TargetControlID="panelTitle"
Opacity=".7" Width="4" />
```

In most instances, Toolkit controls need to target other server controls, and an error is raised if a Toolkit control targets a plain HTML element. This is certainly the case with the `DropShadowExtender`, however this is not always strictly the case and will depend on the implementation of the control itself.

4. You also do the same with the search panel, but because this panel is crucial to the functionality of the page, use an `AlwaysVisibleControlExtender` to ensure that this panel stays visible on the page at all times. Again, you must change the style of the panel to ensure that you won't see the shadow through the panel and add the following style declaration to the `#srchPanel` element in the CSS file:

```
background-color:White;
```

5. Next you add in the Toolkit extender controls themselves, the `DropShadowExtender` and the `AlwaysVisibleControlExtender` controls, respectively:

```
<toolkit:DropShadowExtender ID="ds2" runat="server" TargetControlID="srchPanel"
Opacity=".6" Width="3" TrackPosition="true" />
<toolkit:AlwaysVisibleControlExtender ID="av1" TargetControlID="srchPanel"
runat="server"
        HorizontalSide="Right" VerticalSide="Bottom" HorizontalOffset="5"
VerticalOffset="25" />
```

6. Next, you use a `ModalPopup` extender control to display help text. The `ModalPopup` extender takes care of hiding and displaying the control it is extending. You can do this using the following code:

```
<toolkit:ModalPopupExtender ID="mp1" runat="server" TargetControlID="btnHelp"
PopupControlID="helpPanel"
    OkControlID="btnClose" DropShadow="true"
BackgroundCssClass="inactiveBackground" />
```

7. Previously, the help panel would initially have its `Visible` property set to `false`. When the user clicked the Help button, a postback would occur, and the `Visible` property would be set to `true` so that the help panel would be rendered and displayed in the browser. Now that the `ModalPopup` extender is controlling the display behavior, you can remove the `Visible` attribute from the help panel control. The definition of the help panel is now the following:

```
<asp:Panel ID="helpPanel" runat="server">
    <h5>Help Information</h5>
    <p>The following functionality can be used from within this highly complex user
interface</p>
    <p><b>StaffID & Name</b>: These fields provide a means to enter search crieria
based around the persons StaffID and Name respectively</p>
    <p><b>Search Button</b>: Performs a search using the entered criteria</p>
```

```
<p><b>Clear Button</b>: Clears the search criteria and search results.</p>
<p><b>Help Button</b>: Displays this help text.</p>
<asp:Button ID="btnClose" runat="server" Text="Close" OnClick="btnClose_Click" />
</asp:Panel>
```

8. The `ModalPopup` extender control has an attribute of `BackgroundCssClass`. This CSS class is applied to the page itself while the `ModalPopup` extender control is displaying its content. This presents a useful visual clue because when the `ModalPopup` extender displays its contents, nothing can be selected from the page itself (hence the modal concept). The definition of the CSS class follows:

```
.inactiveBackground {
    background-color:Gray;
    filter:alpha(opacity=70);
    opacity:0.7;
}
```

9. Additionally, because the `ModalPopup` extender control takes care of intercepting the button click events to open and close the window, you can remove both the `OnClick` event handlers for the `btnClose` and `btnClearForm` buttons from the markup in the ASPX page, as well as the handler and associated code from the code-behind file. That is, both the btnClose_Click and the btnClearForm_Click event handlers can be deleted from the code-behind file.

10. Now you enhance the search result display area by using a `DragPanelExtender` to allow the search results to be moved around the screen by the user, as well as applying a `DropShadowExtender` to enhance the visual aspect of the search result panel. You do this using the following code:

```
<toolkit:DragPanelExtender ID="dp1" runat="server" TargetControlID="srchResults" />
<toolkit:DropShadowExtender ID="ds3" runat="server" TargetControlID="srchResults"
TrackPosition="true" Opacity=".6" Width="3" />
```

11. You also need to update the style sheet to include the following element:

```
body
{
    height:600px;
}
```

This allows the search result panel to be dragged around the screen without immediately being repositioned back to its original position. You can think of it as giving the `DragPanelExtender` a "working" area with which to drag around.

12. Because you are using `DropShadowExtender`, you want to make sure you can't see the shadow through the panel control so you need to apply the following style attribute to the search panel CSS class in the style sheet:

```
background-color:White;
```

13. Finally, you wrap the entire search result panel and extenders within an `UpdatePanel` control

UpdateProgress control and associated style sheet entries to ensure the user is aware that an asynchronous operation is occurring. The markup for the search result is now as follows:

```
<asp:UpdatePanel ID="up1" runat="server">
    <ContentTemplate>
        <toolkit:DragPanelExtender ID="dp1" runat="server"
TargetControlID="srchResults" />
        <toolkit:DropShadowExtender ID="ds3" runat="server"
TargetControlID="srchResults" TrackPosition="true" Opacity=".6" Width="3" />
        <asp:Panel ID="srchResults" runat="server">
            <h4>Search Results / Navigation</h4>
            <asp:Panel ID="srchRsltDetail" runat="server">
                <ul>
                <asp:DataList ID="dataView" runat="server" CellPadding="4"
ForeColor="#333333">
                    <HeaderTemplate>
                        <div class="resultLine">
                            <asp:Label ID="rsltStaffNum" runat="server"
CssClass="resultItem" Text='StaffNumber' />
                            <asp:Label ID="rsltName" runat="server"
CssClass="resultItem" Text='Name' />
                            <asp:Label ID="rsltGender" runat="server"
CssClass="resultItem" Text='Super Power' />
                        </div>
                    </HeaderTemplate>
                    <ItemTemplate>
                        <li>
                            <div class="resultLine">
                                <asp:Label ID="rsltStaffNum" runat="server"
CssClass="resultItem" Text='<%# Eval("StaffNumber") %>' />
                                <asp:Label ID="rsltName" runat="server"
CssClass="resultItem" Text='<%# Eval("Name") %>' />
                                <asp:Label ID="rsltGender" runat="server"
CssClass="resultItem" Text='<%# Eval("Power") %>' />
                            </div>
                        </li>
                    </ItemTemplate>
                    <FooterStyle BackColor="#1C5E55" Font-Bold="True"
ForeColor="White" />
                    <SelectedItemStyle BackColor="#C5BBAF" Font-Bold="True"
ForeColor="#333333" />
                    <AlternatingItemStyle BackColor="White" />
                    <ItemStyle BackColor="#E3EAEB" />
                    <HeaderStyle BackColor="#1C5E55" Font-Bold="True"
ForeColor="White" />
                </asp:DataList>
                </ul>
            </asp:Panel>
        </asp:Panel>
    </ContentTemplate>
    <Triggers>
        <asp:AsyncPostBackTrigger ControlID="btnSearch" EventName="Click" />
    </Triggers>
</asp:UpdatePanel>
```

The related `UpdateProgress` control markup comprises the following code:

```
<asp:UpdateProgress ID="pr1" runat="server">
    <ProgressTemplate>
        <div id="progressMessage">... data is being accessed ...</div>
    </ProgressTemplate>
</asp:UpdateProgress>
```

An important fact to note about the preceding code is that the extender controls for the search result panel are all declared within the same update panel. Failure to do this results in an exception when trying to execute the page. All extenders that extend controls within an update panel must also reside within the same update panel. This is due to the way that rendering of the partial content occurs on the client browser.

14. You also include a specific entry in the style sheet to ensure the `UpdateProgress` control is displayed in the right position and in the right color. The following CSS entry shows this:

```
#progressMessage
{
    position:absolute;
    color:Red;
    left:100px;
    top:50px;
}
```

You don't really need the Clear button anymore because a majority of the displayed content is managed separately by each control and its respective extender. You can remove the `btnClear` component from the markup within the page and also remove the `btnClearForm_Click` handler from the code-behind file.

15. To add further usability cues to the page, you can use a `TextBoxWatermarkExtender` control to extend both the text input fields on the screen. To do this, add the following code:

```
<toolkit:TextBoxWatermarkExtender ID="tb1" runat="server"
TargetControlID="txtStaffID" WatermarkText="Enter a Staff ID"
WatermarkCssClass="textBoxWatermark" />
<toolkit:TextBoxWatermarkExtender ID="tb2" runat="server" TargetControlID="txtName"
WatermarkText="Enter Name" WatermarkCssClass="textBoxWatermark" />
```

Here you have specified some text to display as a watermark when no text exists in any of the text fields used for entering search criteria.

16. You specified a CSS class to use when displaying this watermark text, so you must include that definition within the style sheet. The following code is used:

```
.textBoxWatermark
{
    background-color:Silver;
    color:Teal;
}
```

With the addition of the Toolkit controls and associated styles, you have now created a more visually appealing, and more importantly, more usable site for your users. The page itself now utilizes dynamic client-side behavior and effects, all without using a single line of JavaScript.

How It Works

Each logical group of user interface functionality that has been grouped with panels has been extended by an AJAX Control Toolkit extender control.

The title panel has been extended with a `DropShadowExtender` control. This control knows how to determine the size of the targeted element and draw an appropriately sized shape to simulate a shadow, in addition to positioning it appropriately.

The search panel was also the target of a `DropShadowExtender` to enhance its visual appearance. However, you also used an `AlwaysVisibleExtender` to target the same search panel. This control includes the necessary JavaScript to ensure that the search panel is kept on the screen regardless of dimensions, adding an enhanced usability element to the page. You specified the `VerticalSide` and `HorizontalSide` attributes to tell the control where it should be positioned. You also subtly altered its positioning by specifying the `HorizontalOffset` and `VerticalOffset` attributes to adjust the relative positions in pixels. This acts as a type of margin for the specific alignment you are using (for example, horizontal or vertical, respectively).

A `TextBoxWatermarkExtender` has been used to extend the text entry fields of the search panel (one extender per text input control). These provide a usability enhancement with the visual cue to enter data into the text fields. The `TextBoxWatermarkExtender` uses a CSS class to determine how the text is displayed within the text box, and includes the necessary JavaScript functions to dynamically show and hide the watermark text based on whether the user has any data in the text input field.

Additionally, you used a `ModalPopupExtender` and targeted the Help button. This allowed a modal window to be displayed that contained the help text. Using this, you specified that the `OKControl` (which is the control that accepts the `ModalPopup` window, and then closes it) was the Close button within the panel that contained the help text. This control takes care of disallowing interaction by the user with anything else in the browser, except for that window, thus making it modal in relation to the browser. The `BackgroundCssClass` attribute specifies a CSS class that determines what the background page of the browser looks like as the modal popup is displayed.

The search results are wrapped within an `UpdatePanel` so that this operation is executed and updated asynchronously.

You can also make use of advanced animations in your pages, which would typically make extensive use of JavaScript to achieve. You can do this using the `AnimationExtender` control. The `AnimationExtender` control is a complex control that utilizes its own set of inner markup syntax. The properties that it supports are listed within the SampleWebSite provided by the Toolkit. For this example, you only want to add a little glitz to your page.

Try It Out   Adding Glitz to Your Page Using the AnimationExtender Control

1.   When the page loads, it would be nice to cycle the colors in the title panel text to highlight the title when the page first loads. To do this, you can add the following markup that utilizes the `AnimationExtender` control to achieve this effect:

```
<toolkit:AnimationExtender ID="anim2" runat="server" TargetControlID="panelTitle">
```

```
    <Animations>
        <OnLoad>
            <Sequence>
                <Color Duration="1" Fps="15" StartValue="#FFFFFF"
EndValue="#F00B11" Property="style" PropertyKey="color" />
                <Color Duration="1" Fps="15" StartValue="#F00B11"
EndValue="#30CF09" Property="style" PropertyKey="color" />
                <Color Duration="1" Fps="15" StartValue="#30CF09"
EndValue="#000000" Property="style" PropertyKey="color" />
                <Color Duration="1" Fps="15" StartValue="#000000"
EndValue="#230DEE" Property="style" PropertyKey="color" />
            </Sequence>
        </OnLoad>
    </Animations>
</toolkit:AnimationExtender>
```

In this code sample, notice the `<OnLoad>` tag within the `AnimationExtender`, which specifies the animations to execute when the page loads. A `<Sequence>` tag determines which animations are run in sequence. When more than one animation is present inside an animation event, it must be enclosed in either a `<Sequence>` tag to execute the animations in sequence, or a `<Parallel>` tag to execute the animations in parallel with each other (that is, at the same time). The actual animations used in this instance are `<Color>` animations where you specify the time (Duration), speed (frames per second — Fps), the starting color via a color value (StartValue), and the ending color value (EndColor).

`AnimationExtender` supports many event types that trigger the animations enclosed within it, such as `OnClick`, which triggers the animations when the user clicks the target control; and `OnMouseOver` and `OnMouseOut`, which trigger the animations when the user hovers the mouse over the target control and moves the mouse away from the target control, respectively. Again, more definitions exist and are detailed within the SampleWebSite provided by the Toolkit. A thorough examination of this control is beyond the scope of this chapter and warrants a chapter or two on its own.

2. What you can also do is to add a start display panel when the page loads to alert the user to the fact you have created a new and wonderful version of this page, and allow the user to clear the panel and continue work. To do this you first create the markup and associated CSS style to display the panel. The markup is shown in the following code:

```
<asp:Panel ID="intro" runat="server" CssClass="introBox">
    <div id="introText">
        <p>Welcome to the brand new Search Page.</p><p>Click this message to clear
this panel.</p>
    </div>
</asp:Panel>
```

The associated CSS styles are also listed in the following code:

```
.introBox
{
    border:Double 1px Black;
    text-align:center;
    vertical-align:middle;
    margin:auto;
```

```
        width:40%;
        background-color:Silver;
    }
    #introText
    {
        padding:3px 5px 3px 5px;
        color:Fuchsia;
        font-family:Verdana;
        font-size:larger;
        vertical-align:middle;
    }
```

3. This takes care of displaying the panel. Now you associate an animation with the panel so that when the user clicks within it, it nicely fades out and disappears. This is achieved with the following markup:

```
<toolkit:AnimationExtender ID="anim1" runat="server" TargetControlID="intro">
    <Animations>
        <OnClick>
            <Sequence>
                <FadeOut Duration="1" Fps="30" />
                <StyleAction Attribute="display" value="none" />
                <StyleAction Attribute="visibility" value="hidden" />
            </Sequence>
        </OnClick>
    </Animations>
</toolkit:AnimationExtender>
```

Now when the application is viewed within the browser, when the page loads, the title text cycles through a set of colors for approximately four seconds and the initial message panel appears on the page. When the user clicks the panel, it fades and disappears allowing the user to use the page without distraction. The page should look similar to Figure 6-25.

How It Works

The `AnimationExtender` control contains a library of generic animation JavaScript functions and objects to produce animations such as fading in or out, as well as color cycling, object movement, object sizing, and many others. Each of these generic animations is included in the page when you define an `AnimationExtender` and make use of the respective animation via its specific tag. For example, the `<FadeOut>` animation is really a declarative way of specifying properties for the `AjaxControlToolkit` `.Animation.FadeOutAnimation` JavaScript object.

So each declaration of a particular animation simply specifies the properties to a JavaScript object. Each animation object that is defined is also associated with a particular event. In the example code, you have defined animations that are triggered via the loading of the document using the `<onLoad>` tag, and also triggered via an element being clicked using the `<onClick>` tag. Again, these declarative tags take care of generating the JavaScript code necessary to attach the included JavaScript animation objects to the element's or object's event.

Chapter 7 goes into more detail on how to use the `AnimationExtender` *animation objects programmatically via JavaScript in your applications.*

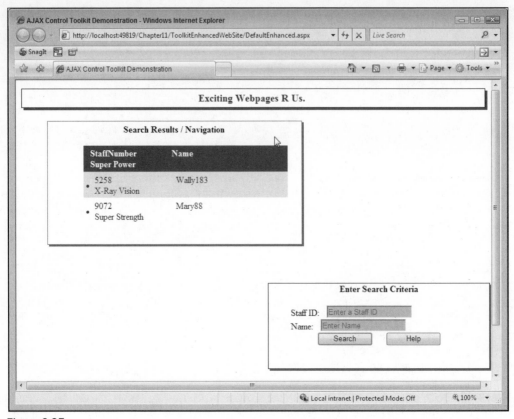

Figure 6-25

As you can see, by adding some simple markup and utilizing the `AnimationExtender` control, you can achieve some advanced animation effects that you would normally be able achieve only if you have a deep understanding of JavaScript, Cascading Style Sheets, and browser document object model semantics. These animation effects would ordinarily require a lot of coding.

There is a lot more to the `AnimationExtender` than this simple example shows and we recommend that you examine this control further. The results will be well worth it in terms of visual appearance of your sites, and the time saved to achieve those effects.

The entire page markup should now look similar to the following code:

```
<%@ Page Language="C#" AutoEventWireup="true"  CodeFile="DefaultEnhanced.aspx.cs"
Inherits="DefaultEnhanced" %>

<!DOCTYPE html PUBLIC "-//W3C//DTD XHTML 1.0 Transitional//EN"
"http://www.w3.org/TR/xhtml1/DTD/xhtml1-transitional.dtd">
```

```
<html xmlns="http://www.w3.org/1999/xhtml" >
<head id="Head1" runat="server">
    <title>AJAX Control Toolkit Demonstration</title>
    <link href="mainStyle.css" rel="stylesheet" type="text/css" />
</head>
<body>
    <form id="form1" runat="server">
        <asp:ScriptManager ID="sm1" runat="server"></asp:ScriptManager>

        <toolkit:AnimationExtender ID="anim2" runat="server"
TargetControlID="panelTitle">
            <Animations>
                <OnLoad>
                    <Sequence>
                        <Color Duration="1" Fps="15" StartValue="#FFFFFF"
EndValue="#F00B11" Property="style" PropertyKey="color" />
                        <Color Duration="1" Fps="15" StartValue="#F00B11"
EndValue="#30CF09" Property="style" PropertyKey="color" />
                        <Color Duration="1" Fps="15" StartValue="#30CF09"
EndValue="#000000" Property="style" PropertyKey="color" />
                        <Color Duration="1" Fps="15" StartValue="#000000"
EndValue="#230DEE" Property="style" PropertyKey="color" />
                    </Sequence>
                </OnLoad>
            </Animations>
        </toolkit:AnimationExtender>

        <toolkit:AnimationExtender ID="anim1" runat="server"
TargetControlID="intro">
            <Animations>
                <OnClick>
                    <Sequence>
                        <FadeOut Duration="1" Fps="30" />
                        <StyleAction Attribute="display" value="none" />
                        <StyleAction Attribute="visibility" value="hidden" />
                    </Sequence>
                </OnClick>
            </Animations>
        </toolkit:AnimationExtender>

        <toolkit:DropShadowExtender ID="ds1" runat="server"
TargetControlID="panelTitle" Opacity=".7" Width="4" />
        <asp:Panel ID="panelTitle" runat="server">
            <h3>Exciting Webpages R Us.</h3>
        </asp:Panel>

        <asp:Panel ID="intro" runat="server" CssClass="introBox">
            <div id="introText">
                <p>Welcome to the brand new Search Page.</p><p>Click this message
to clear this panel.</p>
            </div>
        </asp:Panel>
```

```
        <toolkit:DropShadowExtender ID="ds2" runat="server"
TargetControlID="srchPanel" Opacity=".6" Width="3" TrackPosition="true" />
        <toolkit:AlwaysVisibleControlExtender ID="av1" TargetControlID="srchPanel"
runat="server"
                HorizontalSide="Right" VerticalSide="Bottom" HorizontalOffset="5"
VerticalOffset="25" />
        <toolkit:TextBoxWatermarkExtender ID="tb1" runat="server"
TargetControlID="txtStaffID" WatermarkText="Enter a Staff ID"
WatermarkCssClass="textBoxWatermark" />
        <toolkit:TextBoxWatermarkExtender ID="tb2" runat="server"
TargetControlID="txtName" WatermarkText="Enter Name"
WatermarkCssClass="textBoxWatermark" />

        <asp:Panel ID="srchPanel" runat="server">
            <h4>Enter Search Criteria</h4>

            <div id="criteria">
                <div class="innerCriteria">
                    <asp:Label ID="lblStaffID" runat="server">Staff ID:</asp:Label>
                    <asp:TextBox ID="txtStaffID" runat="server"></asp:TextBox>
                </div>
                <div class="innerCriteria">
                    <asp:Label ID="lblName" runat="server">Name:</asp:Label>
                    <asp:TextBox ID="txtName" runat="server"></asp:TextBox>
                </div>
            </div>

            <div id="criteriaButtons" class="criteriaButtons">
                <asp:Button ID="btnSearch" runat="server" Text="Search"
CssClass="criteriaButton" OnClick="btnSearch_Click" />
                <asp:Button ID="btnHelp" runat="server" Text="Help"
CssClass="criteriaButton"  />
            </div>


        </asp:Panel>

        <asp:UpdatePanel ID="up1" runat="server">
            <ContentTemplate>
                <toolkit:DragPanelExtender ID="dp1" runat="server"
TargetControlID="srchResults" />
                <toolkit:DropShadowExtender ID="ds3" runat="server"
TargetControlID="srchResults" TrackPosition="true" Opacity=".6" Width="3" />
                <asp:Panel ID="srchResults" runat="server">
                    <h4>Search Results / Navigation</h4>
                    <asp:Panel ID="srchRsltDetail" runat="server">
                        <ul>
                        <asp:DataList ID="dataView" runat="server" CellPadding="4"
ForeColor="#333333">
                            <HeaderTemplate>
                                <div class="resultLine">
                                    <asp:Label ID="rsltStaffNum" runat="server"
CssClass="resultItem" Text='StaffNumber' />
                                    <asp:Label ID="rsltName" runat="server"
```

```
                    CssClass="resultItem" Text='Name' />
                                        <asp:Label ID="rsltGender" runat="server"
CssClass="resultItem" Text='Super Power' />
                                </div>
                            </HeaderTemplate>
                            <ItemTemplate>
                              <li>
                                    <div class="resultLine">
                                        <asp:Label ID="rsltStaffNum" runat="server"
CssClass="resultItem" Text='<%# Eval("StaffNumber") %>' />
                                        <asp:Label ID="rsltName" runat="server"
CssClass="resultItem" Text='<%# Eval("Name") %>' />
                                        <asp:Label ID="rsltGender" runat="server"
CssClass="resultItem" Text='<%# Eval("Power") %>' />
                                    </div>
                                </li>
                            </ItemTemplate>
                            <FooterStyle BackColor="#1C5E55" Font-Bold="True"
ForeColor="White" />
                            <SelectedItemStyle BackColor="#C5BBAF" Font-Bold="True"
ForeColor="#333333" />
                            <AlternatingItemStyle BackColor="White" />
                            <ItemStyle BackColor="#E3EAEB" />
                            <HeaderStyle BackColor="#1C5E55" Font-Bold="True"
ForeColor="White" />
                        </asp:DataList>
                        </ul>
                    </asp:Panel>
                </asp:Panel>
            </ContentTemplate>
            <Triggers>
                <asp:AsyncPostBackTrigger ControlID="btnSearch" EventName="Click" />
            </Triggers>
        </asp:UpdatePanel>

        <asp:UpdateProgress ID="pr1" runat="server">
            <ProgressTemplate>
                <div id="progressMessage">... data is being accessed ...</div>
            </ProgressTemplate>
        </asp:UpdateProgress>

        <toolkit:ModalPopupExtender ID="mp1" runat="server"
TargetControlID="btnHelp" PopupControlID="helpPanel"
        OkControlID="btnClose" DropShadow="true"
BackgroundCssClass="inactiveBackground" />

        <asp:Panel ID="helpPanel" runat="server">
            <h5>Help Information</h5>
            <p>The following functionality can be used from within this highly
complex user interface</p>
            <p><b>StaffID & Name</b>: These fields provide a means to enter search
crieria based around the persons StaffID and Name respectively</p>
            <p><b>Search Button</b>: Performs a search using the entered
criteria</p>
```

```
                <p><b>Clear Button</b>: Clears the search criteria and search
    results.</p>
                <p><b>Help Button</b>: Displays this help text.</p>
                <asp:Button ID="btnClose" runat="server" Text="Close" />
            </asp:Panel>
        </form>
    </body>
    </html>
```

Mixing Controls

It is important to realize that the controls that come with the Toolkit utilize dynamic manipulation of positional and display styles, as well as behavioral aspects of HTML elements on a page. Some of the controls constantly monitor and alter these attributes of elements. When multiple extender controls are targeted at the same HTML element, it can sometimes result in unexpected behavior. This depends on the behavior and style aspects being altered, and the elements being targeted.

A good example is the `AnimationExtender` control combined with the `DropShadowExtender` control. Depending on the animation effect applied, the drop shadow that is also applied to the element often makes the effect look incorrect or "odd" because the drop shadow is not being animated, but is dynamically applied by the drop shadow extender control.

These kinds of scenarios can be either specifically avoided, or circumvented by specific combinations of properties, and in some cases writing extra JavaScript to manipulate the properties of the extender controls themselves under certain conditions.

In general, it is best to ensure that extenders with potentially conflicting sets of behaviors are thoroughly tested to verify that the functionality desired is achieved.

Creating Your Own Extender Controls

The AJAX Control Toolkit provides support for control authors wishing to create their own controls. You may want to use controls to provide customized behaviors from some of the existing Toolkit controls, or to create a brand new extender control not already covered by the Toolkit.

As already mentioned at the start of this chapter, the Toolkit comes with a VSI installation file that can be used to install development templates into Visual Studio in the form of ASP.NET AJAX Control Project.

Selecting this template when creating a new project creates a project with the files required to compile and create a blank extender component with no functionality. The component could be added into a page but would do nothing, and it is left up to you to implement the required properties and functionality.

When first looking at the Toolkit, it is best to become familiar with the way the controls are added to a page, their markup syntax, and how they operate in general. When you are familiar with the usage techniques, you can then turn your attention to the details of creating controls. For this, it is recommended to look at the relatively simple controls such as the `TextboxWatermarkExtender` control. This provides a great basis from which to learn and contains enough functionality, in a simple enough use-case scenario, to demonstrate how to leverage the provided extender framework.

Examining an existing control is also best done in conjunction with reading the documentation provided for doing so within the SampleWebSite that accompanies the Toolkit. This provides a brief overview of how to go about creating controls and some of the functionality that support this.

A full examination of creating your own extender controls is covered in detail in the next chapter, which covers creation of extender controls exclusively and looks at the features provided by the Toolkit framework to make it easy. There are a large number of features within the Toolkit that provide common functionality for dealing with script files, resources, exposing properties, IntelliSense support, automatic mapping of server-side properties to script behavior components, and many other features that extend the already comprehensive support within the ASP.NET AJAX framework. This is why an entire chapter is devoted to this topic.

Contributing to the AJAX Control Toolkit Open Source Project

As already mentioned earlier in this chapter, the Toolkit is an open source project that is currently run and managed by Microsoft, with various non-Microsoft community contributors. The Toolkit team is always open to accepting other community members to contribute to the Toolkit.

Currently, the easiest way to do this is to first have a control in some working state that you wish to contribute to the Toolkit, or that you think could be a valuable addition. Secondly, contact Shawn Burke at sburke@microsoft.com and indicate your desire to contribute to the Toolkit, citing the control you would like to contribute. Obviously, ensure that the control you have developed is not covered by an already existing control.

If you join the Toolkit team, you will be given a set of access credentials and a Toolkit contributors document that outlines how to connect to the CodePlex Team Foundation Server source control system. The document also details the methodology behind the structure of the development solution and the process by which controls are initially added to the development solution. This shows the steps in which a control is initially added to the prototype area of the development solution, then migrated to the development branch, and finally to the release branch of the solution.

Summary

The AJAX Control Toolkit is a large project. It is comprised of many sub-projects, the main one being the suite of components provided to enhance and supplement the development experience. Though the ASP.NET AJAX Extensions and Client Library provide a rich base from which to extend, it can arguably be said that the Toolkit provides some of the greatest value to developers. The reason for this is that the hard work has already been done for you. You need only to use the provided controls, set some properties, and enjoy the benefits of a rich, dynamic, and interactive browser user interface. Almost all of the functionality can be achieved with little to no JavaScript knowledge whatsoever. Some developers consider this an immense benefit in itself!

This chapter covered all the aspects of the Toolkit from its community focus, to the controls, their usage, and how you might begin to create your own controls. Specifically, you looked at the following:

❑ The AJAX Control Toolkit as a Microsoft open source community project.

❑ How to install the Toolkit and what you get after installation, beyond just a set of controls. This includes the SampleWebSite, the Test harness framework and associated unit tests for each control, as well as new templates that allow easy creation of Toolkit-enabled web sites and Toolkit controls.

❑ The basic concept of an extender control and how the Toolkit makes use of that.

❑ The controls within the Toolkit. This is a moving target and is always expanding as the community and Microsoft itself continue to add to the Toolkit.

❑ Features and support provided by the Toolkit for developers wishing to create their own extender controls. Extensive details on the technical aspects of this are covered in Chapter 7.

❑ How you can contribute to the AJAX Control Toolkit project. The Toolkit is constantly evolving and welcomes volunteer effort from the community. This makes it a truly collaborative effort between Microsoft and the community at large and allows the Toolkit to become a really useful library for all ASP.NET developers.

This chapter has briefly covered all the controls in the Toolkit and shown how to implement a few specific controls within your pages and web applications. This should provide a good example of how to use some of the simpler controls, as well as the more complex controls such as the `AnimationExtender`. We encourage you to experiment with the various controls listed within the Toolkit. Try changing some properties, adding various controls, and looking at the effects of each. It is through this that a true familiarity with the Toolkit is achieved.

Control Extenders

In the previous chapter, you saw how the ASP.NET AJAX Toolkit controls utilized the concept of an extender control to augment the behavior of existing controls within your application. An extender control is typically targeted at another control, and provides enhanced functionality for that control, and perhaps other controls as well.

There are really two types of controls that form the basis of the control set within ASP.NET AJAX 2.0 Extensions: script controls and extender controls. Both form part of the core framework of ASP.NET 2.0 AJAX Extensions.

Script controls are standalone controls that define their own behavior and operate independently of other controls (although often in conjunction with other controls). A good example of this is the `UpdatePanel` or the `Timer` control.

Extender controls operate in tandem with at least one other control on a page, and extend the functionality of that control. You saw this concept demonstrated extensively in Chapter 6 on the AJAX Control Toolkit. A good example is the `TextboxWatermarkExtender` that ships with the Toolkit, which extends a regular `Textbox` control. You saw how extender controls can be used within your applications in various ways to achieve rich, dynamic behavior, often without the need to write any JavaScript code.

This chapter details concepts and techniques required to build your own extender controls and provide reusable custom behavior for your AJAX applications. Specifically, this chapter covers:

❏ Extender control features within the core framework

❏ Building your own extender control using only the core functionality of ASP.NET 2.0 AJAX Extensions

❏ The enhanced framework and features provided by the AJAX Control Toolkit for building extender controls

❏ Building the same extender control using the AJAX Control Toolkit

❏ Advantages and disadvantages of both approaches

The Core Framework

ASP.NET 2.0 AJAX Extensions provide intrinsic support for building extender controls. Primarily it does this via the `IExtenderControl` interface, which exists in the `System.Web.UI` namespace. Any custom extender controls must implement the `IExtenderControl` interface. This interface has the following two methods:

❑ `GetScriptDescriptors` — This method is used by the AJAX framework to ask the component for a list of operations that describe the behavior and properties of the component.

```
IEnumerable<ScriptDescriptor>GetScriptDescriptors(Control targetControl)
```

❑ `GetScriptReferences` — As the name suggests, this method is called by the AJAX framework to obtain a list of dependent scripts (JavaScript resources) that are required for this component to operate.

```
IEnumerable<ScriptReference> GetScriptReferences()
```

Strictly speaking, these are the only two methods you are required to implement for an extender control. However, these are only interface definitions, and there is no surrounding functionality to aid in the functioning of an extender control. An example is the provision of a target control property. As mentioned previously, an extender typically targets another control to extend its functionality and it seems logical to be able to provide this commonality across all extender controls.

The `System.Web.UI.ExtenderControl` base class provides a level of implementation detail for extender controls that you can use to build your own controls. It cannot be created itself, but is used only as the base class from which to inherit and build upon. It provides two abstract methods that you must provide implementations for. These methods are the two interface methods discussed previously, `GetScriptDescriptors` and `GetScriptReferences`. However, this base class encapsulates much of the common functionality required to make an extender control useful. As suggested previously, this includes the provision of a target control property to specify which control is being extended. The `ExtenderControl` base class itself inherits from the `System.Web.UI.Control` class to provide basic web control functionality. Figure 7-1 shows this simplified class relationship.

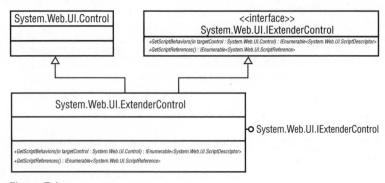

Figure 7-1

Creating a Control

Now that you know what pieces of the core framework you need to use to create an extender control, you can go about actually creating a control. The details of the `ExtenderControl` base class will become clear as we address each area of functionality and implementation.

You will be looking at how to create an extender using both the core ASP.NET 2.0 AJAX Extensions components and the enhanced support provided by the ASP.NET AJAX Control Toolkit. For both of these examples, we chose a relatively simple control so that we can highlight aspects of control creation without confusing the issue with complex implementation details.

Creating the Project

For the control building example, you build an enhancement to the regular `System.Web.UI.WebControls.Button` control. In a lot of applications, particularly e-commerce applications, when a user clicks a button to submit an order, a message informs the user not to click the button twice; otherwise, the order may get corrupted or a double order may result. It would be nice to create an extender control that you can apply to a button that not only prevents the button from being clicked twice, but also provides enhanced feedback to highlight that fact. We will call the control the *SingleClickExtender*.

| Try It Out | Creating a New Project |

To begin, you must first create a new project:

1. Load Visual Studio 2005 and select File ➪ New ➪ Project from the menu. The Add New Project dialog box is displayed. Select your language, select Class Library, and then specify a name and directory location for the project. This should look similar to Figure 7-2.

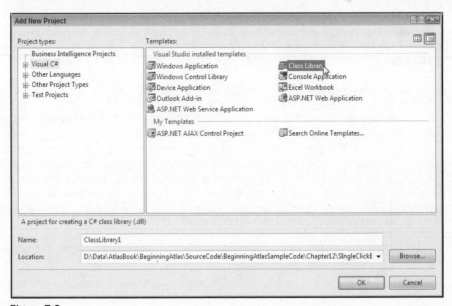

Figure 7-2

2. A blank project is created with a single class file. Rename the class file to `SingleClick.cs`.

3. Add references to the project to the `System.Web` and `System.Web.Extensions` assembly by right-clicking the References node and selecting Add Reference. You can locate both assemblies in the global assembly cache by clicking the .Net tab in the Add References dialog and scrolling through the entries listed. Alternatively, you can browse to the location on your file system and select the files by clicking the Browse tab.

How It Works

The `System.Web` assembly contains the types for all the base controls within ASP.NET on which you will be basing some of your code. The `System.Web.Extensions` assembly represents the ASP.NET 2.0 AJAX Extensions library and contains the `ExtenderControl` base class (among other things) on which you base your control. The ASP.NET 2.0 AJAX Extensions utilize types within the `System.Web` assembly. You will also be using some classes and types from within this assembly to assist in creating your extender control.

Try It Out   **Constructing the Server Component of Your Control**

Now that you have a blank project to work in, you can begin the actual task of coding your extender component:

1. In order to make easy use of the newly added references, you add two using statements to the top of your `SingleClick.cs` source code file, as shown in the following code sample:

```
using System.Web;
using System.Web.UI.WebControls;
using System.Web.UI;
```

2. As mentioned previously, you will be utilizing the `ExtenderControl` base class from which to base your custom extender control. To do this, you simply inherit from the `ExtenderControl` base class, as shown in the following code:

```
public class SingleClick : ExtenderControl
```

3. Extender controls typically target another control and extend its functionality. One of the nice features of the built-in framework is that you can specify what kinds of controls your extender will target. If the declaration of your control targets a control other than what you have specified, the runtime throws an exception notifying you of the error. This is useful because if you are targeting specific functionality of a type of control, such as a button in this instance, it makes no sense to allow your extender to target any type of control and not provide any functionality around it. The way you specify the type of control your extender will target is through the use of the `TargetControlType` attribute as shown in the following code:

```
[TargetControlType(typeof(Button))]
```

How It Works

Because you know that you will be extending a regular ASP.NET button control, you add the `TargetControlType` attribute just above the class declaration. You pass the attribute the type of the control to target using the `typeof` operator, passing it the `System.Web.UI.WebControls.Button` class. When a page is loaded with your extender on it, the ASP.NET AJAX runtime checks that the control your extender is targeting (as defined in the page markup) matches the type that is specified in the `TargetControlType` attribute. If not, an exception is raised. The code should look similar to the following snippet:

```
[TargetControlType(typeof(Button))]
public class SingleClick : ExtenderControl
{
}
```

If you now attempt to compile this project, you receive compilation errors stating the following:

```
'SingleClickExtender.SingleClick' does not implement inherited abstract member
System.Web.UI.ExtenderControl.GetScriptDescriptors(System.Web.UI.Control)'
'SingleClickExtender.SingleClick' does not implement inherited abstract member
System.Web.UI.ExtenderControl.GetScriptReferences()'
```

This is because in the base `ExtenderControl` class, these methods are marked as abstract and it is up to you, the control implementer, to provide functionality for these methods in your custom class.

Embedding Script Resources

Before you go about implementing the necessary abstract methods of your extender class, it is best to set up the resources that your extender requires, so that they can be referenced in the custom extender class. Because you are creating a component that dynamically interacts with the browser, the chances are good that you require some JavaScript to do some client-side work. The JavaScript code is typically placed within a JavaScript file within the project and you need to be able to reference this file from within your extender because both the JavaScript and the extender are reliant on each other.

You can instruct the runtime to load your scripts from an external file, or from an embedded resource within the assembly. The difference is that if you specify your script references as external files, those files must be present in the site that uses your component, and shipped with your component. When using embedded resources, the script files are embedded within the assembly itself. The runtime then embeds special `ScriptResource` requests within the page that trigger the extraction of your script from the assembly. This aids in packaging and deployment because you only have to ship an assembly. That assembly will contain all the code and embedded scripts necessary for your component to function. The embedding of script resources within the assembly produces something similar to the following within your web pages:

```
<script src="/YourSite/ScriptResource.axd?d=10sHVyrgzKXUmxInwW-Hfc5gY79_UvKol
AZluQbIPmcRnzTmYLBtfcW2cwQeBosDbN66O2Q6T3KXbLxkYIAjMFzeyRxr9xx4u5XOgaLY9F2uJp7
```

```
dfyONKo-xlF7jX905L29Zg8bo9xtt_CWXJ_fzAunseRu-wmQx409H_idqOpg1&amp;t=633001782125620
494" type="text/javascript"></script>
```

The embedding of script resources utilizes the same methods as embedding web resources within assemblies. Web resources are new to ASP.NET V2 and used heavily throughout the framework. For more information, see http://support.microsoft.com/kb/910442.

Before you go about embedding script resources and hooking them up to your components, you need to first create a script resource to use.

Try It Out   **Creating a Script Resource**

To create a script resource, follow these steps:

1. Right-click the `SingleClickExtender` project within the Visual Studio Solution Explorer and select Add ➪ New Item from the menu.

2. From the dialog box that is presented, select the JScript File option, type **SingleClick** into the Name text field, and then click Add, as shown in Figure 7-3. This adds a script file to your project named `SingleClick.js`.

3. In the Solution Explorer window, right-click the SingleClick.js file and select Properties from the menu. In the properties window that is displayed, select the Build Action drop-down list, and select the Embedded Resource option, as shown in Figure 7-4.

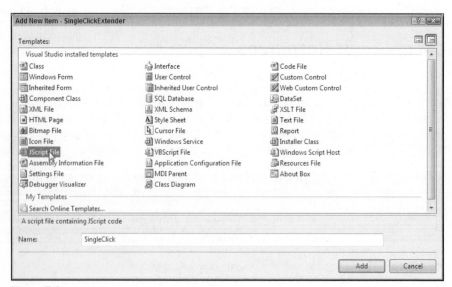

Figure 7-3

Figure 7-4

How It Works

When you set some content to be an embedded resource, whether it is an image or a script file as in this example, it causes the content of that resource to be embedded within the output assembly when the project is compiled. The resource is placed within the assembly as if it were just another piece of metadata with an entry within the assembly manifest pointing to this resource. This allows you to extract resource elements from the assembly using methods within the System.Resources namespace. For a web application, however, you need to add a special attribute to indicate that this will be a web resource, and this enables the runtime to generate a special URL making it possible to access this embedded resource directly from within a web page using a standard HTTP request. To enable your script file to be marked as a web resource you apply the following attribute:

```
[assembly: System.Web.UI.WebResource("SingleClickExtender.SingleClick.js",
"text/javascript")]
```

This attribute is typically placed above the namespace declaration within the class file. This can also be placed in an external file; however, items that relate to each other should be kept together rather than separated into different files. The code should now look similar to the following (without the using statements):

```
[assembly: System.Web.UI.WebResource("SingleClickExtender.SingleClick.js",
"text/javascript")]

namespace SingleClickExtender
{
    [TargetControlType(typeof(Button))]
    public class SingleClick : ExtenderControl
    {
    }
}
```

When a resource is embedded within the assembly, it is embedded with a name in the format `{namespace}`. `{filename}`. `{extension}`. When indicating your embedded resource is a web resource, you must reference it using that name. The web resource you saw previously requires the name of the embedded resource to be marked as a web resource (in this case `SingleClickExtender.SingleClick.js`) and the type of the web resource, which is this case is a regular JavaScript file as indicated by the `text/javascript` mime type.

Even though your script file contains nothing, it is now set up to be correctly embedded within the assembly on each compile and marked as a web resource ready for referencing within your web pages. The .NET framework provides a `System.Web.UI.ClientScriptManager.GetWebResourceUrl` method to allow you to obtain the specific URL required to access this resource from a web page. You saw an example of this previously that utilized the WebResource.axd handler. This manual step is not necessary, however, and is taken care of for you by the ASP.NET 2.0 AJAX Extensions framework when you implement the required abstract methods.

Implementing the Abstract Methods

You can now go about implementing the abstract methods necessary for your extender component. An easy way to start this process is to right-click the `ExtenderControl` base class name in the source code view, and select Implement Abstract Class from the context menu (see Figure 7-5).

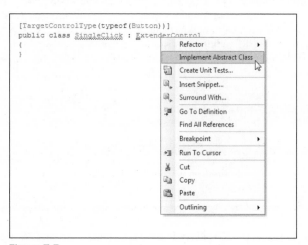

Figure 7-5

This automatically generates stub methods for each required abstract method. Stub methods are simply methods that contain no real implementation, but allow the class to compile correctly. The generated method code is shown in the following code:

```
protected override IEnumerable<ScriptDescriptor>
GetScriptDescriptors(System.Web.UI.Control targetControl)
{
```

```
        throw new Exception("The method or operation is not implemented.");
    }

    protected override IEnumerable<ScriptReference> GetScriptReferences()
    {
        throw new Exception("The method or operation is not implemented.");
    }
```

The project should now compile successfully. You still cannot use this component in a web page because exceptions will be generated from the previously generated stub methods, so now it is time to provide proper implementations for your abstract methods.

Try It Out   **GetScriptReferences Method**

As its name suggests, the `GetScriptReferences` method deals with the script references required for your component to function. Specifically, it returns references to any script files or resources that the custom extender class requires to function correctly. The runtime calls this method during the component creation to ensure that the requisite scripts are loaded.

Previously you have embedded your script file within the assembly, and indicated it should be accessed as a `WebResource` element. You now need to tell your extender component about this arrangement so that it can perform the correct actions and identify your script resource to the Microsoft ASP.NET AJAX framework. Examine the following code, which provides the implementation for your `GetScriptReferences` method:

```
    ScriptReference sr = new ScriptReference();
    sr.Name = "SingleClickExtender.SingleClick.js";
    sr.Assembly = "SingleClickExtender";

    yield return sr;
```

How It Works

In the preceding code you first construct a `ScriptReference` object, which is what you will be populating and returning to the caller (typically the Microsoft ASP.NET AJAX framework). Next you provide the name of the script resource. This is the same name that you defined in your `WebResource` attribute previously:

[assembly: System.Web.UI.WebResource("SingleClickExtender.SingleClick.js", "text/javascript")]

Next you provide the assembly that the script resource exists in. For this example, you use the same assembly as the main project assembly, but this does not always have to be the case. Finally, you return this `ScriptReference` object using the `yield` statement.

The `IEnumerable` interface easily allows custom collections to return values to the enumerator of that collection, within the iteration block. For more information on this, see http://msdn2.microsoft .com/en-us/library/9eekhta0.aspx.

Try It Out   **GetScriptDescriptors Method**

Now your extender knows what scripts are required to function and how to go about accessing them. You also need to provide some information about the extender's behavior so that the framework knows how to construct the appropriate JavaScript object specific to your extender, and also how to populate items such as properties and events.

Examine the following code, which provides the implementation for the `GetScriptDescriptors` method:

```
ScriptBehaviorDescriptor behavior = new
ScriptBehaviorDescriptor("SingleClickExtender.SingleClickBehavior",
targetControl.ID);
yield return behavior;
```

How It Works

In the preceding code, you first constructed a `ScriptBehaviorDescriptor` object, which is what the framework will use to determine what the behavior of your script object is, and how it maps to your extender control. The constructor for this object has the name of the behavior object for your extender. This object is a JavaScript object and will be contained within the JavaScript resource file you added previously. You have not defined this JavaScript object yet, though, which will become the next step in your implementation. In this instance you are specifying a script object called `SingleClickBehavior` that exists in the `SingleClickExtender` namespace. This is how the framework knows to create and associate a particular JavaScript component with your extender control.

Finally, in similar fashion to the `GetScriptReferences` method discussed previously, you return the `ScriptBehaviorDescriptor` object using the `yield` statement.

Providing the Implementation for Your Dynamic Behavior

With all the pieces now in place, you can now provide the actual JavaScript implementation for your extender control:

1. Open the `SingleClick.js` file within Visual Studio.

2. Define the namespace that the script behavior will use:

```
Type.registerNamespace('SingleClickExtender');
```

3. Create the constructor for the behavior:

```
SingleClickExtender.SingleClickBehavior = function(element) {
    SingleClickExtender.SingleClickBehavior.initializeBase(this, [element]);

    var _clickDelegate = null;
}
```

4. Create the prototype for the behavior with the minimum functions implemented for the behavior, which are `initialize`, `dispose`, and the custom event handler `onClickDelegate`:

```
SingleClickExtender.SingleClickBehavior.prototype = {

    initialize : function() {
        SingleClickExtender.SingleClickBehavior.callBaseMethod(this, 'initialize');

        var e = this.get_element();
        this._clickDelegate = Function.createDelegate(this,this._onClickDelegate);
        $addHandler(e,"click",this._clickDelegate);
    },

    _onClickDelegate : function() {
        alert("button has been clicked");
    },

    dispose: function() {
        $clearHandlers(this.get_element ());
        SingleClickExtender.SingleClickBehavior.callBaseMethod(this, 'dispose');
    }
}
```

5. Register the behavior class and define the class it inherits from, namely the `Sys.UI.Behavior` class:

```
SingleClickExtender.SingleClickBehavior.registerClass('SingleClickExtender
.SingleClickBehavior',  Sys.UI.Behavior);
```

The previous code represents a standard, albeit very plain, behavior defined using the Microsoft ASP.NET AJAX Client framework. Initially, you register the `SingleClickExtender` namespace, then begin to define the `SingleClickExtender.SingleClickBehavior` object by defining the constructor.

Next you define the initialize method on the behavior's prototype definition. The initialize method creates a delegate to point to the method that handles when the button is clicked. You then add that delegate as a handler for the button's `onclick` event. This is performed with the following code:

```
var e = this.get_element();
this._clickDelegate = Function.createDelegate(this,this._onClickDelegate);
$addHandler(e,"click",this._clickDelegate);
```

You provide a simple implementation of this handler by simply issuing an `alert` statement that displays the text *"button has been clicked"*. For now this is sufficient to ensure that everything is defined correctly.

```
_onClickDelegate : function() {
    alert("button has been clicked");
},
```

The preceding code is the only real piece of custom code within the behavior. All other methods defined are required, standard methods of a behavior, these being the constructor, `initialize`, `dispose` and `registerClass` implementations.

Finally, you provide an implementation of the `dispose` method to clean up any resources you have used, and register the class such that it inherits from the `Sys.UI.Behavior` component that is part of the Microsoft ASP.NET AJAX client framework.

Try It Out   **Testing the Extender Control**

You finally have a component you can use on a page. To verify its functionality, you need to create a web site that acts as a test harness for your new extender control:

1. With your custom extender control solution still loaded in Visual Studio, right-click the solution in the Solution Explorer window and select Add ➪ New Web Site. From the dialog that is presented, select ASP.NET AJAX-Enabled Web Site, specify a location to store the web site, and click OK.

2. You need to add a reference to your custom extender control project so that the web site knows about your new control. Right-click the root node of the newly added web site within the Solution Explorer window and select Add Reference, as shown in Figure 7-6.

3. When the dialog appears, select the Projects tab, ensure that the SingleClickExtender is highlighted, and click OK (see Figure 7-7).

4. Open the `Default.aspx` page within the web site so that it is open in the Visual Studio designer workspace and ensure you are in HTML source view.

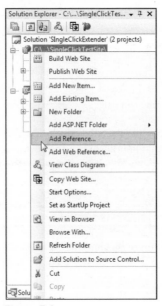

Figure 7-6

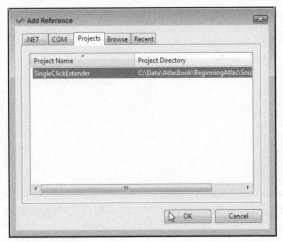

Figure 7-7

5. First you need to register your extender control for use within the page and provide an identifier to use on the page, in the form of a tag prefix. Add the following code declaration to the top of the page directly underneath the page directive as shown:

```
<%@ Page Language="C#" AutoEventWireup="true" CodeFile="Default.aspx.cs"
Inherits="_Default" %>
<%@ Register Assembly="SingleClickExtender" Namespace="SingleClickExtender"
TagPrefix="sce" %>
```

Here you registered your extender control by telling the page in what assembly and namespace to find your control. You also provided an identifier to use when specifying the control on the page, in this instance the "sce" tag prefix.

6. Now add some standard controls to the page, one of which is a button to enable you to utilize your extender control. Add the following markup to the page after the ScriptManager control declaration on the page:

```
<asp:ScriptManager ID="ScriptManager1" runat="server" />
<div>
    <asp:Label ID="lblField" runat="server" Text="Enter Some Text" />
    <asp:TextBox ID="txtField" runat="server" />
    <asp:Button ID="btnSubmit" runat="server" Text="Submit Data"
OnClick="btnSubmit_Click" />
    <br />
    <asp:Label ID="lblInfo" runat="server" Text="You Entered: " />
    <asp:Label ID="lblResult" runat="server" Text="{nothing yet}" />
</div>
```

7. In the code-behind file for the `Default.aspx` page, which is in the `Default.aspx.cs` file, enter the following code within the page class:

```
public partial class _Default : System.Web.UI.Page
{
    protected void btnSubmit_Click(object sender, EventArgs e)
    {
        System.Threading.Thread.Sleep(3000);

        lblResult.Text = txtField.Text;
    }
}
```

8. Ensure the test harness web site project is set to the startup project by right-clicking the project in the Solution Explorer window and selecting Set as Startup Project. Start a debug session by either pressing F5 or clicking the Start Debugging icon in the toolbar, as shown in Figure 7-8.

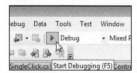

Figure 7-8

9. Because you have only a default `web.config` file currently in the project, debugging is not enabled. When you select to start a debugging session, a dialog opens and asks if you want to enable debugging in the `web.config`, as shown in Figure 7-9.

10. Click the OK button to enable debugging and continue. A simple page should be shown where you can enter text in the text entry field, click the Submit Data button, and after a delay of approximately 3 seconds, this text is displayed in the label below. The 3-second delay means that while the request is being sent to and processed by the server; you have the opportunity to click the button multiple times. This can easily occur before a response from the server is received by the browser. This is precisely the action you are trying to avoid with your custom extender, however for now, you just want to ensure you have everything hooked up right, and the extender is triggered at the appropriate time.

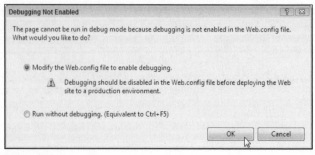

Figure 7-9

11. Now you can add your extender control into the page. Add the following markup to the page in the body of the HTML after the `ScriptManager` control:

```
<sce:SingleClick ID="sce1" runat="server" TargetControlID="btnSubmit" />
```

As you start typing this code, IntelliSense presents possible attributes to use in the markup for your extender control. Additionally, you have the ability to specify a `TargetControl` attribute (which is required for all extender controls) even though you did not explicitly define this in your extender. This is provided as part of the ASP.NET 2.0 AJAX Extensions framework.

Now when you start a debugging session to test this page, enter some text, and click the Submit Data button, an alert box is presented as defined in your extender control, JavaScript behavior. This verifies that everything is functioning as expected and you are attaching to the events correctly.

How It Works

There is no better way of testing a component than placing it into an application and seeing how it performs. That's exactly what you are doing by creating a new web site and placing the component within the site. You are simply registering the control within the application in a similar fashion to any other external control. You have added a reference to the control's assembly, and registered the control with an associated tag prefix within the page itself. The difference in this case is that you have a direct link to the control source code.

What is important here is properly simulating the scenario we are trying to address. Because this is a simplistic control, this is relatively easy by introducing a 3-second delay in the server-side `btnSubmit_Click` method event handler.

Additionally, you have kept things simple by not having a full suite of functionality to worry about. The development of the control is at such an early stage that there is nothing to really worry about in terms of functionality. At this stage, you are concerned only that the control is properly hooking into the click event. In other words, all the plumbing is in place and is working. Once this is verified, future testing need only be concerned with the new functionality that this control will be providing — namely, the "single click" feature.

Try It Out   **Providing the "Single Click Only" Functionality**

Now you can provide the necessary code that ensures your button is clicked only once:

1. In the `SingleClick.js` file, replace the implementation of the `_onClickDelegate` method with the following code:

```
_onClickDelegate : function() {
    this.get_element().disabled = true;
},
```

When you run the site, enter some text, and click the `SubmitData` button, the button is actually disabled as required! However, you are not there yet. You will notice that no postback has occurred. Once the button is disabled, it does not fire the rest of its click event, which would normally cause the form to be submitted. To get around this, you need to obtain the code required that would normally perform the postback and execute it once you have disabled the button. To do this, you add a property to your extender control.

3.   First you need to provide the ability in the JavaScript behavior itself to set the value of the property. In this instance, the property will be called `submitScript` and contain the JavaScript necessary to execute the required postback operation. Open the `SingleClick.js` file in the editor, and in the constructor for your behavior, add a private variable to hold the value of the property:

```
SingleClickExtender.SingleClickBehavior = function(element) {
    SingleClickExtender.SingleClickBehavior.initializeBase(this, [element]);

    var _clickDelegate = null;
    var _onSubmitScript = null;
}
```

4.   Next add the property *setters* and *getters* that act as the interface to allow values to be read and written to the private variable:

```
get_submitScript : function() {
    return this._onSubmitScript;
},

set_submitScript : function(value) {
    this._onSubmitScript = value;
}
```

5.   Add in the actual code in the click event handler that executes this code:

```
_onClickDelegate : function() {
    this.get_element().disabled = true;
    eval(this._onSubmitScript); },
```

6.   You now need to provide support for this property in the server portion of your extender. Open the `SingleClick.cs` file in the editor, and add a private field declaration to the `SingleClick` class as shown in the following code:

```
public class SingleClick : ExtenderControl
{
    private string _submitScript = null;
    // .... rest of class code omitted for brevity...
```

7.   Next, override the `OnLoad` method of the control to allow the extender to obtain the postback code before executing other methods and events. Add the following code to the `SingleClick` class:

```
protected override void OnLoad(EventArgs e)
{
    base.OnLoad(e);

    if (target != null)
        Control target = FindControl(this.TargetControlID);
    _submitScript = Page.ClientScript.GetPostBackEventReference(target, string.Empty);
}
```

8. The final piece of the puzzle is adding the `submitScript` property to the `ScriptDescriptor` object that you defined previously, with the value of the postback script in your private variable. This is shown in the following code:

```
protected override IEnumerable<ScriptDescriptor>
GetScriptDescriptors(System.Web.UI.Control targetControl)
{
    ScriptBehaviorDescriptor behavior = new
ScriptBehaviorDescriptor("SingleClickExtender.SingleClickBehavior",
targetControl.ID);
    behavior.AddProperty("submitScript", _submitScript);
    yield return behavior;
}
```

How It Works

In step 1, the code uses the Microsoft AJAX client framework to get a reference to the element and set its `disabled` property to `true`. The element in question is what your extender control is extending, or its `TargetControl`. The `disabled` property is a standard Document Object Model (DOM) property that controls whether the element is disabled or enabled.

The `OnLoad` implementation shown in the code first obtains a reference to the control for which you want to obtain the postback event. Next, you call the `Page.ClientScript.GetPostBackEventReference` method passing in the control and an argument of an empty string. The result of this method call is a string containing the necessary JavaScript to execute to perform the required postback operation. You then assign this to the private variable for later use.

The private variable, `_submitScript`, which contains the postback script, is then added to the list of properties for the `SingleClick` behavior in the `GetScriptDescriptors` implementation. The value of `_submitScript` is passed to the setter property of the behavior by the ASP.NET 2.0 AJAX Extensions for use by the client-side behavior.

The client-side behavior then executes the postback script after the button has been disabled to ensure a normal postback still occurs.

Here you have added one line to the `GetScriptDescriptor` interface method, which simply adds a property assignment to the descriptor object. The property has a name of *submitScript* and the value of that property is held in the private variable, `_submitScript`. In effect, when the behavior is created on the client, its `submitScript` property will be set to the value currently stored in `_submitScript`.

The Completed Extender

Your extender is finally complete. You now have a self-contained extender control that will extend any ASP.NET button to only allow a single click by disabling itself once clicked, then performing a normal postback.

It is apparent from the example shown that a majority of code goes toward setting up the basic pieces of the extender control so that it interacts correctly with the ASP.NET 2.0 AJAX Extensions framework. The framework itself provides much functionality in the form of base classes for both client- and server-side components; however, there is still a reasonable amount of code to write before even getting to the main functionality of the control. This is exactly the issue that the AJAX Control Toolkit was designed to solve.

The ASP.NET AJAX Control Toolkit

The ASP.NET AJAX Control Toolkit removes a large amount of effort to get a custom extender control up and running as quickly as possible. In this section, you create exactly the same control as shown in the previous example, but using the AJAX Control Toolkit.

Try It Out   **Creating an Extender Using the AJAX Control Toolkit**

You need to create a new project within the same solution you used in the previous example, so name this extender control the `ToolkitSingleClickExtender` to differentiate it from the previous extender control you created. What will be apparent throughout this exercise is how the AJAX Control Toolkit makes getting started and writing your own extender controls much quicker than doing it without using the Toolkit as shown in the previous example.

1.   In the Solution Explorer window, right-click the solution and select Add ➪ New Project. In the dialog that is presented, select the ASP.NET AJAX Control Project, change the name to **ToolkitSingleClickExtender**, specify a location to store the project, and click OK.

A new project is added to your solution with all the required references to the AJAX Control Toolkit assembly and Microsoft ASP.NET AJAX assembly, along with a set of files that contain a basic template for building an extender control (see Figure 7-10).

Figure 7-10

2.   Start with the server-side component first. Open the `ToolkitSingleClickExtenderExtender.cs` file in the Visual Studio editor and change all instances of the text `MyProperty` to **SubmitScript**. The class itself should now look similar to the following code:

```
public class ToolkitSingleClickExtenderExtender : ExtenderControlBase
{
    // TODO: Add your property accessors here.
    //
    [ExtenderControlProperty]
    [DefaultValue("")]
    public string SubmitScript
```

```
    {
        get
        {
            return GetPropertyStringValue("SubmitScript");
        }
        set
        {
            SetPropertyStringValue("SubmitScript", value);
        }
    }
}
```

An `ExtenderControlProperty` attribute is applied to the `SubmitScript` property you have defined. This indicates that this property should be associated to the same property in the associated JavaScript behavior class.

3.   You now also add the code that obtains the postback code required to trigger the button's submit postback event. This is shown in the following code:

```
protected override void OnLoad(EventArgs e)
{
    base.OnLoad(e);

    SubmitScript = Page.ClientScript.GetPostBackEventReference(this.TargetControl,
string.Empty);
}
```

Here you will notice that the code is somewhat simplified compared to the earlier example. There is no need to find the targeted control because there is a property supplied that already contains the target control reference. You assign the output of the `GetPostBackEventReference` method to your previously defined `SubmitScript` property. In the previous example, you defined a private field to hold this data.

That's all you need for your server-side portion. Now you can add the required functionality and properties to the JavaScript client-side behavior class.

4.   Open the `ToolkitSingleClickExtenderBehavior.js` class file in the Visual Studio editor. Replace the property getter and setter names with `get_SubmitScript` and `set_SubmitScript`, respectively. Replace all instances of the text `_myPropertyValue` with `_submitScriptValue`. The property definitions should now look similar to the following:

```
get_SubmitScript : function() {
    return this._submitScript;
},

set_SubmitScript : function(value) {
    this._submitScript = value;
}
```

5.   Define a private variable in the constructor of the class, as shown in the following code:

```
ToolkitSingleClickExtender.ToolkitSingleClickExtenderBehavior = function(element) {
```

```
        ToolkitSingleClickExtender.ToolkitSingleClickExtenderBehavior.initializeBase(this,
[element]);

        // TODO : (Step 1) Add your property variables here
        //
        this._submitScript = null;

}
```

6. Now you need to add in the functionality to trap the click event for the button, disable it, and then fire the normal postback event code. You achieve this as you did in the previous example. First you define a private variable to hold your delegate function within the constructor:

```
var _clickDelegate = null;
```

7. In the `initialize` method, you create a delegate that points to a custom handler and associate it with the click event for the target element, which is the button. This process is no different than if you were creating a standard non-Microsoft AJAX Toolkit behavior.

```
initialize : function() {
        ToolkitSingleClickExtender.ToolkitSingleClickExtenderBehavior.callBaseMethod(this,
'initialize');

        var e = this.get_element();
        this._clickDelegate = Function.createDelegate(this,this._onClickDelegate);
        $addHandler(e,"click",this._clickDelegate);
},
```

8. Finally, you provide the same implementation for the click handler as you did in the previous example:

```
_onClickDelegate : function() {
        this.get_element().disabled = true;
        eval(this._submitScript);
},
```

The only difference in the preceding code is the name of the private variable, _submitScript. In the previous example, it was named _onSubmitScript.

And that's it! The same extender as defined in the previous example is now defined using the AJAX Control Toolkit framework.

How It Works

Immediately after following step 1 in the example, you are provided with a usable but nonfunctional JavaScript behavior class, an extender designer code file, and the main server-side component of the extender control. As it stands, this project can be compiled and used on a web page; it just won't actually do anything because you haven't provided any custom functionality for your extender yet.

A quick look at both the client-side behavior file `ToolkitSingleClickExtenderBehavior.js` and the server-side extender file `ToolkitSingleClickExtenderExtender.cs` shows that each has the required class and attribute definitions, as well as a sample property that can be changed and used as a template for adding further properties.

The JavaScript resource file has already been set up for you as an embedded resource, with the appropriate attribute in the code to indicate the file is an embedded web resource, as shown in the following snippet:

```
[assembly: System.Web.UI.WebResource("ToolkitSingleClickExtender
.ToolkitSingleClickExtenderBehavior.js", "text/javascript")]
```

Some new attributes are also placed on the class definition, which you examine later.

Because the client-side behavior "plumbing" code has already been created on your behalf, you only need to supply the implementation required for your behavior. In this respect, the code required is identical to the code that was used when creating a standard, non-Microsoft AJAX Control Toolkit component.

Try It Out   Testing the Control Toolkit Extender Control

As with all development efforts, you need to test and verify that your code works. To do this, you will add your control to a web site and ensure it performs as expected:

1. First, add a reference to the `ToolkitSingleClickExtender` project to your web site that was added previously as a test harness for the original `SingleClickExtender` control.

2. To make use of this new extender control, you need to register a reference to the control and an associated tag prefix in the page. You can do this with the following code:

```
<%@ Register Assembly="ToolkitSingleClickExtender"
Namespace="ToolkitSingleClickExtender" TagPrefix="tsce" %>
```

3. You then add the following markup to the page that looks identical to the previous markup, except you make use of the new extender control:

```
<tsce:ToolkitSingleClickExtenderExtender ID="tsce1" runat="server"
TargetControlID="btnSubmit2" />
<asp:Label ID="lblFld2" runat="server" Text="Enter Some Text" />
<asp:TextBox ID="txtFld2" runat="server" />
<asp:Button ID="btnSubmit2" runat="server" Text="Submit Data (Toolkit Control
Test)" OnClick="btnSubmit_Click2" />
<br />
<asp:Label ID="lblInfo2" runat="server" Text="You Entered: " />
<asp:Label ID="lblResult2" runat="server" Text="{nothing yet}" />
```

4. Finally, you add the corresponding code to the code-behind class file to process the button click event:

```
protected void btnSubmit_Click2(object sender, EventArgs e)
{
    System.Threading.Thread.Sleep(3000);

    lblResult2.Text = txtFld2.Text;
}
```

You now have an extender control that operates in exactly the same manner as your previous `SingleClickExtender` control; however, you were able to do it with far less work. This was in part because of the already provided template components, such as the prefabricated class file with the basic method definitions, and support for linking properties to the associated JavaScript class behavior.

How It Works

In the same way that you added your standard extender control to a web site to test and verify its functionality, you have also added the AJAX Toolkit extender-based control to the same web site for the purposes of testing and verification.

Registration and usage of the control within a web site is the same regardless of how it was implemented.

From a technical perspective, this control works identically to a standard, non-Microsoft AJAX Control Toolkit control. That is, on the server side, the `GetScriptDescriptors` and `GetScriptReferences` methods are implemented as expected. However, you have not had to explicitly code those interface methods. Instead, you have decorated the server code with attributes like `ExtenderControlProperty` and `ClientScriptResource`, and the Microsoft AJAX Toolkit framework has provided the low-level implementation of the interface methods.

In addition, a majority of template, or "plumbing" code such as the basic behavior, has been provided for you by the AJAX Control Toolkit templates.

The main point here is that the underlying implementation is identical whether the control was developed using standard ASP.NET 2.0 AJAX Extensions or the ASP.NET AJAX Control Toolkit. Therefore, usage, and in this case testing, in a web application follows the same process.

Enhancing the Extender Using AJAX Control Toolkit Features

Because you are using the AJAX Control Toolkit to develop this extender, you can make use of some of the rich features it provides to enhance your extender. Instead of simply disabling the button when pressed, you can animate the button so that it can either fade out or shrink after it is clicked.

Try It Out   Enhancing the Extender Control with Animation Support

To enhance your component with animation support, you will define the kind of animation that can be performed, and also include the required script functionality from the AJAX Control Toolkit to facilitate that animation support:

1. First you need to add a property to your extender to specify what kind of animation to display. Start by adding a new class to the `ToolkitSingleClickExtender` project by right-clicking that project in the Solution Explorer window and selecting Add ⇨ Class. For the name of the class, enter **SingleClickAnimationTypes** and select Add.

2. In the newly created class file, remove the existing class definition and enter the following code to define your enumeration:

```
public enum SingleClickAnimationTypes
{
    None = 0,
    FadeOut = 1,
    Shrink = 2
}
```

3. Next, open the `ToolkitSingleClickExtenderExtender.cs` file in the Visual Studio editor, and add the following `RequiredScript` attribute declaration to the class definition:

```
[RequiredScript(typeof(AnimationScripts))]
public class ToolkitSingleClickExtenderExtender : ExtenderControlBase
{
    // ..... rest of class
```

The `RequiredScript` attribute tells the Toolkit framework that you need to utilize the animation scripts of the animation extender control within this custom extender control. The Toolkit framework takes care of loading and ensuring this script is available at runtime.

4. Add the following property definition to the class:

```
[ExtenderControlProperty]
public SingleClickAnimationTypes AnimationType
{
    get
    {
        return GetPropertyValue<SingleClickAnimationTypes>("AnimationType",
SingleClickAnimationTypes.None);
    }
    set
    {
        SetPropertyValue<SingleClickAnimationTypes>("AnimationType", value);
    }
}
```

Here you added a new property that exposes what type of animation to use when the button is clicked. Visual Studio takes care of exposing the enumeration as a drop-down list of animation types for a developer to choose in the markup, and the AJAX Control Toolkit takes care of hooking this property up to the JavaScript behavior counterpart. This is yet to be defined, though, and is the focus of the next few steps.

5. Open the `ToolkitSingleClickExtender.js` file in the Visual Studio editor, and add in the following private variable definition to the behavior class constructor:

```
var _animType = null;
```

6. Next you need to add the property setter and getter for this private variable to enable external parties access to setting this variable. Add the following code to the prototype class declaration of the behavior:

```
get_SubmitScript : function() {
    return this._submitScript;
},

set_SubmitScript : function(value) {
    this._submitScript = value;
},

get_AnimationType : function() {
    return this._animType;
},

set_AnimationType : function(value) {
    this._animType = value;
}
```

Note that there is now a comma after the `set_SubmitScript` declaration, and then the definition of the two new property getter and setter functions. This is important; otherwise, syntax errors, which can be hard to track down, result.

7. You also need to provide a client-side implementation of the `SingleClickAnimationTypes` enumeration defined in the server-side class. Place the following code at the bottom of the `ToolkitSingleClickExtender.js` file:

```
ToolkitSingleClickExtender.SingleClickAnimationTypes = function() {}
ToolkitSingleClickExtender.SingleClickAnimationTypes.prototype = {
    None : 0,
    FadeOut : 1,
    Shrink : 2
}
ToolkitSingleClickExtender.SingleClickAnimationTypes.registerEnum
("ToolkitSingleClickExtender.SingleClickAnimationTypes", false);
```

This is enough to correctly pass the enumeration between server-side markup and client-side behavior code. Now you need to provide only the functionality to perform the actual animation. Here you utilize the `AnimationExtender` functionality that is provided as part of the AJAX Control Toolkit. This was discussed in Chapter 6. In this example, you make programmatic use of the animation extender features.

8. Finally, change the implementation of the `_onClickDelegate` to look like the following:

```
_onClickDelegate : function() {
    this.get_element().disabled = true;
    if (this._animType != ToolkitSingleClickExtender.SingleClickAnimationTypes.None)
    {
        var anim;
        if (this._animType ==
ToolkitSingleClickExtender.SingleClickAnimationTypes.FadeOut)
```

```
                anim = new AjaxControlToolkit.Animation.FadeAnimation(this.get_element(),
    1, 30, AjaxControlToolkit.Animation.FadeEffect.FadeOut, 0, 1, true);
            else
                anim = new AjaxControlToolkit.Animation.ScaleAnimation(this.get_element(),
    1, 30, 0, "px",true,true,"px");
            anim.play();
        }
        window.setTimeout(this._submitScript,0);
    },
```

How It Works

Initially, you added an enumeration that defines the different types of animation to choose when the button is clicked. This was defined in both the server-side and client-side code. In the page markup, Visual Studio takes care of allowing you to choose an animation type based on this enumeration using a simple drop-down list. The AJAX Control Toolkit takes care of ensuring the selected value is propagated to the client-side behavior.

When defining a client-side enumerated type, specifically assigning the values of the enumerated values is not strictly necessary because the integer values of the server-side enumeration are passed to the property and you can simply test for those integer values. For example, the enumerated type None is assigned 0, FadeOut equals 1, and Shrink equals 2. However, providing an enumeration makes your code much easier to read and maintain, and also remains consistent with the server-side implementation.

On the definition of the extender class, you instructed the AJAX Control Toolkit to include the required scripts to support animation by using the following attribute:

[RequiredScript(typeof(AnimationScripts))]

With these functional elements in place, you then utilized the animation objects contained within the AJAX Control Toolkit scripts to invoke an animation on the button, based on what animation type was specified, using the enumerated property.

The animation code you created includes a check against the private variable _animType to see if it matches any of the values defined in the enumeration. If it is set to None, you proceed as normal without applying any animation. If _animType is set to FadeOut or Shrink, you create a behavior object based on the respective animation type that is defined within the AJAX Control Toolkit.

A Closer Look at the AJAX Control Toolkit Effects

The use of the AJAX Control Toolkit animation behaviors warrants some further explanation.

For the FadeOut effect, use a FadeAnimation type defined in the AjaxControlToolkit.Animation namespace:

```
anim = new AjaxControlToolkit.Animation.FadeAnimation(this.get_element(), 1, 30,
AjaxControlToolkit.Animation.FadeEffect.FadeOut, 0, 1, true);
```

For the `Shrink` effect, utilize a `ScaleAnimation`, also defined in the `AjaxControlToolkit.Animation` namespace:

```
anim = new AjaxControlToolkit.Animation.ScaleAnimation(this.get_element(), 1, 30,
0, "px",true,true,"px");
```

In both instances, the construction of the animation behavior object takes a similar but slightly different pattern. In each case, the three initial arguments in the construction of the animation represent the target element, the duration, and frames per second. So for each animation you construct, you are setting the target element as the same element that your extender is targeting through the `this.get_element()` reference. Next you set the duration to 1 second. In the third argument you set the frames per second to 30. At this point, the arguments to the animations become specific to the animation type.

For the `FadeAnimation`, the constructor signature is as follows:

```
FadeAnimation(target, duration, fps, effect, minimumOpacity, maximumOpacity,
forceLayoutInIE);
```

The first three arguments have already been discussed. `effect` represents the type of fade animation, whether fade in or fade out. In this example, you set this argument to the `FadeOut` enumerated value. The opacity settings represent the limit that the minimum and maximum opacity levels are allowed to reach, respectively. In this example, the `minimumOpacity` is zero, and the `maximumOpacity` is one. The last argument, `forceLayoutInIE`, deals with a bug that is specific to Internet Explorer and causes the background color and other attributes to remain fixed, which prevents display issues. You set this to `true` in this example.

For the `ScaleAnimation`, the constructor is as follows:

```
ScaleAnimation(target, duration, fps, scaleFactor, unit, center, scaleFont,
fontUnit);
```

Again, the first three arguments have already been discussed. `scaleFactor` is the target scaling factor, which in this instance, is zero because you are scaling down to eventually nothing. The `unit` represents the scaling units used. In this example, the units are pixels as denoted by `px`. The `center` parameter attempts to ensure the element remains centered as it is scaled. The `scaleFont` and `fontUnit` parameters deal with the scaling of fonts when scaling the associated element. This example specifies the font scale as the element that is scaled and the unit type as pixels.

You have seen how the use of the AJAX Control Toolkit framework makes it easier to define your own extenders, but also how you can use some of the included functionality of the toolkit to further enhance your extender controls.

Due to the specifics of each behavior contained within the toolkit, the reference documentation provided within the sample web site that is packaged with the Toolkit is an invaluable resource when trying to use those behaviors.

Advantages and Disadvantages of Using the AJAX Control Toolkit

So, why wouldn't you simply use the AJAX Control Toolkit in all cases when building a custom extender?

The simple answer is you can. The disadvantages to using the Toolkit are minimal, but still need to be considered.

First, there is a dependency on the `AjaxControlToolkit.dll` assembly that forms the Toolkit. This needs to be packaged and deployed with your application.

Second, some extra script file dependencies, which need to be downloaded at runtime, are used by the Toolkit. This follows the same caching strategy as all script files in that they are usually downloaded only once, and cached thereafter. In addition, the script files are relatively small (approximately less than 5k), so any negative effect is small.

The advantages to using the Toolkit are large and definitely outweigh the disadvantages.

First, they remove much of the manual code to associate server-side and client-side properties, and ensure the values are synchronized between the two. This was seen in the decreased time and effort it took to create the second example, using the Toolkit framework.

Second, they provide a rich framework that the developer can utilize. This comes in the form of the base classes and utility methods, as well as the existing controls and behaviors provided with the Toolkit. All of which can be utilized as you see fit, to create composite versions of the controls, or simply to comple-ment their own custom behaviors.

Another advantage of using the AJAX Control Toolkit, and one that hasn't been touched on yet, is that of debugging. The Toolkit provides support for debugging extender controls and, in particular, the JavaScript behaviors associated with them. This is provided in the form of the `ScriptPath` attribute on any extender control that you create using the AJAX Control Toolkit. Each extender control based on the AJAX Control Toolkit automatically has support for this property within the markup declaration for the control. This attribute tells the extender to *not* get the related JavaScript file from the assembly, where it is normally embedded as a `WebResource`, but rather from an explicit path. When a JavaScript file is embedded within an assembly, debugging often becomes difficult, because the URL to access that script is dynamic. Instead, you can specify a local path to access this script file, even though it may still be embedded in the assembly. Once you have finished developing the control and are happy with the script, you can simply copy the modified script back to the main project where it is embedded within the assembly, and remove the `ScriptPath` attribute. For example, the following declaration of your control specifies a `ScriptPath` that contains the path and name of the script file to use:

```
<tsce:ToolkitSingleClickExtenderExtender ID="tsce1" runat="server"
TargetControlID="btnSubmit2" AnimationType="None"
ScriptPath="~/TestScript/ToolkitSingleClickExtenderBehavior.js" />
```

The preceding declaration, when used within the test harness site you have developed, indicates that the runtime should try to load the associated JavaScript behavior file from the /TestScript directory, using a file named ToolkitSingleClickExtender.js. This much easier to debug and develop, and means that the control extender project need not be rebuilt just to include the modifications. You simply need to be sure that you copy any changes made in this local file to the code held in the control extender project, and then remove the ScriptPath attribute from the control declaration.

> *The* ScriptPath *attribute is part of the base class framework that the AJAX Control Toolkit provides, and you don't need to implement anything specific to gain this functionality within your own extender controls.*

Part of debugging your controls involves running tests against your controls. The AJAX Control Toolkit also comes with a comprehensive testing framework that is designed to test the dynamic capability of web-based interface controls, typical of those developed using the AJAX Control Toolkit. All the controls within the Toolkit have a series of tests defined in the provided test harness to verify their functionality. This test harness, though beyond the scope of this book, is a valuable resource that can be used within your own applications to create unit tests for your own components.

We have only touched on the surface of the existing Toolkit enhancements. In addition to all the included behaviors, there are many script enhancements, such as a common library of screen and formatting functions (which exist in common.js within the Toolkit) that can be used within your own code and behaviors.

Summary

The control extender concept within the ASP.NET 2.0 AJAX Extensions framework is a powerful one. It is something that developers can easily grasp, make use of within their applications, and neatly encapsulate that functionality into reusable components. The dynamic nature of AJAX-based applications and components can sometimes make this task difficult due to multiple dependencies on other libraries and multiple resources, such as script files, images, and other resources. The ASP.NET 2.0 AJAX Extensions provide a rich framework to allow you to build components, and package those components for deployment and use. Add in the AJAX Control Toolkit and you have a remarkable arsenal of functionality from which to enhance your applications and create your own extender controls. The AJAX Control Toolkit can save much of the drudgery and manual labor associated with creating your own extender controls.

This chapter looked at both approaches for developing extender controls: using the base framework and using the Toolkit. You also looked at the various features you can use in both approaches. Specifically, you looked at:

❑ General features of the extender controls and what the core ASP.NET 2.0 AJAX Extensions framework provides.

❑ Building an extender using the core features of the ASP.NET 2.0 AJAX Extensions. You looked at starting a brand new control extender project and how to build a completely encapsulated and reusable control. This includes the packaging of JavaScript resource files and associated dependencies required for the control extender to function.

❑ Building the same control extender as you did using the core framework features, but instead using the AJAX Control Toolkit to contrast the different approaches and highlight the improved productivity and features that the Control Toolkit can provide. By utilizing the AJAX Control Toolkit framework, you were able to easily create the basis for a control and add complex animation effects without the need to implement those effects directly.

❑ The advantages and disadvantages of both approaches. There is not a great deal of disadvantage to using the AJAX Control Toolkit and it will probably be the model of choice for most developers. However, restrictions based on policy on the types of libraries used may be the main obstacle in using the library within organizations, rather than any technical limitations or dependencies.

The control extender you built in this chapter is a relatively simple example of what can be achieved, however it does show the basic techniques involved in creating any control extender for use in your projects. Though the basic functionality of your control extender is simple, this can be expanded to be as complex as required to meet your personal or business needs.

There are still many aspects to developing custom extenders that begin to branch into complex areas of control development, and require a more thorough explanation that what can be presented within a single chapter. However, the information presented equips you with the tools and techniques to begin to experiment and create your own fully functional and usable extenders. In fact, it is recommended that you do just that — experiment, learn, and create your own controls — before embarking on more complex endeavors. This will make the whole process much clearer and allow a better understanding of ASP.NET AJAX control extender development in general.

JavaScript Enhancements

JavaScript is a very simple language for adding functionality to a web browser application. However, it is lacking in several areas that formal programmers consider important. With the introduction of ASP.NET AJAX, Microsoft has added enhancements for JavaScript, and these enhancements address the perceived shortcomings in JavaScript. Some of the enhancements you look at in this chapter include the following:

❑ Extended support for basic data types, such as numbers and strings

❑ The creation of namespaces and classes

❑ The notion of inheritance and interfaces

JavaScript has no concept of private members. There will be properties shown whose name starts with an underscore (_), and these properties are considered to be private. As a result, you should not use them in your code even though you can access them.

Data Types

JavaScript has support for data types, such as `Number()`, `String()`, and so forth. This allows methods of these data types to be used in ways that are particular to them.

JavaScript is also a prototype-based language. Without going into the specifics, this means that objects can be extended fairly easily through the following syntax:

```
myObject.prototype.GetData = function(param1)
{
      // do some work...
}
```

The calling syntax for a method implemented this way would be:

```
var obj = new myObject();
obj.GetData(param1);
```

This code would add the `GetData(param1)` method to an instance of `myObject` and show it being called. This is a different notation than most developers are used to because most developers are familiar with class-based development.

In addition to adding to the instantiated objects, it is possible to add what .NET developers might find similar to static (C#) or shared (VB.NET) members to the data types themselves. This is done through the following syntax:

```
Array.work = function(value)
{
    // do some work...
}
```

This code example shows that the `work()` method has been added to the `Array()` class so that the work method can be called without creating an instance of the `Array()` class. The calling syntax would then be:

```
Array.work(value);
```

This is referred to as a *static* method. From a developer's standpoint, an object does not have to be instantiated to call the method.

These data types/objects exist within an area that is sometimes referred to as the global namespace.

The Object() Object

The JavaScript `Object()` object is the primitive JavaScript object type. All JavaScript objects are descendants of `Object()`. Into the `Object()` class, the Microsoft AJAX Library provides support for the following two new static methods:

❑ `getType()` — This method returns the type of an instance of an object. The returned value may be simple, such as `String()`, or it may be complicated and return the complete listing of a class, such as with the `Sys.StringBuilder()` class.

❑ `getTypeName()` — This method returns the name of the type of an instance of an object. The returned value will be simple, such as `String` or `Sys.StringBuilder`.

Following is some example code that operates on an instance of type `Object()`:

```
var strOutput = "";
var strReturn = "<br />";
var obj = new Object();
strOutput += "Type: " + Object.getType(obj) + strReturn;
strOutput += "Name: " + Object.getTypeName(obj) + strReturn;
$get("Output").innerHTML = strOutput;
```

This code creates an instance of type `Object`, then obtains the `Type` and `TypeName` of the instance. The `Type` is obtained by calling `Object.getType()`. The `TypeName` is obtained by calling `Object .getTypeName()`. Figure 8-1 shows the output of this code.

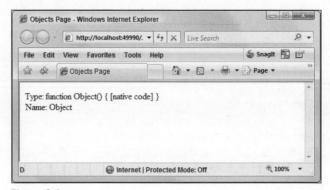

Figure 8-1

The `Type` of `Object()` shows that it is [native code]. This signifies that `Object()` is built into the JavaScript language.

The Boolean() Object

The `Boolean()` object is a wrapper around a Boolean value. The only new function that is added to the `Boolean()` object is the `parse()` method. The `parse()` method takes an input value while looking for a Boolean value. In the example that follows, the `parse()` method returns `true` when passed a string with the value of `true` inside of it.

The example code does the following:

❏   Returns the type of the object. In this case, it returns `Boolean(){[native code]}`. The "native code" refers to the fact that the `Boolean()` object is a native JavaScript object. This is performed by the call to `Object.getType(obj)`.

❏   Returns the object name. In this case, it returns `Boolean`. This is performed by the call to `Object.getTypeName(obj)`.

❏   Calculates and returns the parsed value that is passed in. In this example, this is performed by the call to `Boolean.parse('true')`, which returns a true value.

Figure 8-2 shows the output of the following code, which shows some simple examples with the `Boolean` object:

```
var obj = new Boolean(false);
strOutput += "Type: " + Object.getType(obj) + strReturn;
strOutput += "Name: " + Object.getTypeName(obj) + strReturn;
strOutput += "Parse(true): " + Boolean.parse('true') + strReturn;
strOutput += "Type Name (private): " + Boolean.__typeName + strReturn;
$get("Output").innerHTML = strOutput;
```

There is a "property" on the Boolean called _typeName. Although it is public, the underscore character means that it is private and not meant for public use even though the property is available to the public.

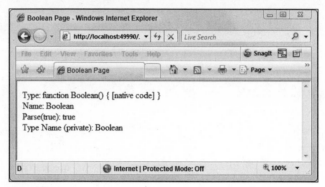

Figure 8-2

The Number() Object

The Number() object is a wrapper around a number value. Much like the additions to the Boolean() object, the Number() object adds the parse() and toFormattedString() methods to the Number object. In the following example, the parse() method returns the number 4.3 when passed a string with the value of "4.3j" inside of it. The toFormattedString() method is used to provide a formatted output.

This example code does the following:

❑ Returns the type of the object. In this case, it returns Number(){[native code]}. The "native code" refers to the fact that the Number() object is a native JavaScript object. This is performed by the call to Object.getType(obj).

❑ Returns the object name. In this case, it returns Number. This is performed by the call to Object.getTypeName(obj).

❑ Calculates and returns the parsed value that is passed in. In this example, this is performed by the call to Number.parse("4.3j"), which returns a true value.

❑ The call to format() formats the number in a predefined format. In this example, the "p" format specifies that the output is formatted in the percentage format.

Figure 8-3 shows the output of the code.

```
var strOutput = "";
var strReturn = "<br />";
var obj = new Number(1.234);
strOutput += "Type: " + Object.getType(obj) + strReturn;
strOutput += "Name: " + Object.getTypeName(obj) + strReturn;
strOutput += "Parse(4.3j): " + Number.parseLocale("4.3j") + strReturn;
strOutput += "Type Name (private): " + Number.__typeName + strReturn;
strOutput += ".format('p') of 1.234: " + obj.format('p') + strReturn;
$get("Output").innerHTML = strOutput;
```

The format() method takes the following options:

- ❑   d, D — The d and D parameters provide the standard decimal output.
- ❑   c, C — The c and C parameters output the value in the standard currency notation.
- ❑   n, N — The n and N parameters provide the standard numeric output.
- ❑   p, P — The p and P parameters provide the output in a percentage. This is featured in Figure 8-3.

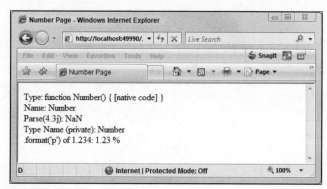

Figure 8-3

The String() Object

The processing of strings is a very important feature of any programming language. The need to process strings in JavaScript is no different. The Microsoft AJAX Library provides support for the following additional methods within an instance of the String() object:

- ❑   endsWith(value) — The endsWith(value) method takes a string value and returns a Boolean value that depends on whether or not the string ends in the string instance. A true means that the value ends within the String() object, and a false means that the string does not end within the String() object.

- ❑   startsWith(value) — The startsWith(value) method takes a string value and returns a Boolean value that depends on whether or not the string starts in the string instance. A true value returned means that the value starts within the String() object, and a false return value means that the string does not start within the String() object.

- ❑   trimStart() — The trimStart() method removes any leading spaces in the String() object.

- ❑   trimEnd() — The trimEnd() method removes any trailing spaces in the String() object.

- ❑   trim (value) — The trim() method removes any leading and trailing spaces in the String() object.

- ❑   format () — The format(stringToFormat, args) method is a static method on the String() object. The stringToFormat is passed a set of arguments and the method creates a string from the supplied format.

❑ localeFormat() — The localeFormat(stringToFormat, args) method is a static method on the String() object. This method takes the items to be formatted within a String object and replaces them with the text equivalent based on the passed arguments. With this method, culture information is used to create proper formatting.

The following code shows calling the methods supplied by the Microsoft AJAX Library to the String() object:

```
var strOutput = "";
var strReturn = "<br />";
var leftString = new String("    abcde");
var rightString = new String("12345    ");
strOutput += "leftString: " + escape(leftString) + (" <-- The %20 is there to show
the actual space.") + strReturn
strOutput += "rightString: " + escape(rightString) + (" <-- The %20 is there to
show the actual space.") + strReturn
strOutput += "Type: " + Object.getType(leftString) + strReturn;
strOutput += "Name: " + Object.getTypeName(rightString) + strReturn;
strOutput += "endsWith: " + leftString.endsWith("cde") + strReturn;
strOutput += "startsWith: " + rightString.startsWith("123") + strReturn;
strOutput += "trimStart(leftString): " + escape(leftString.trimStart()) +
strReturn;
strOutput += "trimEnd(rightString): " + escape(rightString.trimEnd()) + strReturn;
strOutput += "Trim(leftString + rightString): " + escape(leftString.trim() +
rightString.trim()) + strReturn;
strOutput += String.format("leftString: {0}", leftString);
$get("Output").innerHTML = strOutput;
```

In this example, various calls are made on the methods that are added to the String() object. Figure 8-4 shows example output from the preceding code.

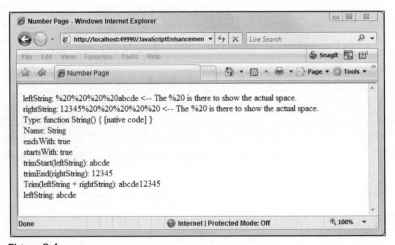

Figure 8-4

The Array() Object

The `Array()` object is analogous to the server-side .NET `ArrayList()` object. It has many of the same features in that it accepts objects and adds them to the `Array()` object. The Microsoft AJAX Library adds support for several new features to the JavaScript `Array()` object, including the following methods:

- ❏ `add(ArrayObject, item)` — The `add(ArrayObject, item)` method adds `item` to the `Array()` instance within `ArrayObject`. With the `add()` method, the `item` is added to the end of the `Array()` instance.

- ❏ `addRange(ArrayObject, items)` — The `addRange(ArrayObject, items)` method adds items to the instance of an `Array()` within `ArrayObject`.

- ❏ `clear(ArrayObject)` — The `clear(ArrayObject)` method clears the contents of the `ArrayObject`.

- ❏ `clone(ArrayObject)` — The `clone()` method makes a copy of the `ArrayObject`.

- ❏ `contains(ArrayObject, item)` — The `contains(ArrayObject, item)` method checks the `ArrayObject` for the item specified. A `true` is returned if the item is found within the `ArrayObject`.

- ❏ `forEach(ArrayObject, method, context)` — The `forEach(ArrayObject, method, context)` method performs the listed method on each element of the `ArrayObject`. This method is not consistent across all browsers.

- ❏ `indexOf(ArrayObject, item, startingIndex)` — The `indexOf(ArrayObject, item, startingIndex)` method returns the index within the array of `item`. The `startingIndex` value is optional.

- ❏ `insert(ArrayObject, index, object)` — The `insert(ArrayObject index, object)` method adds the `object` to the specified `ArrayObject` instance as the specified `index`.

- ❏ `parse()` — The `parse` method is a static method that parses the specified object into the `Array()` object.

- ❏ `remove(ArrayObject, object)` — The `remove(ArrayObject, object)` method removes the first occurrence of the specified object from the `ArrayObject` instance.

- ❏ `removeAt(ArrayObject, index)` — The `removeAt(ArrayObject, index)` method removes the object at location `index` within the `ArrayObject` instance.

The following example code uses the features added to the client-side `Array()` object:

```
var strOutput = "";
var strReturn = "<br />";
var obj = new Array();
var i = 0;
Array.add(obj, 123);
Array.add(obj, 456);
var objClone = Array.clone(obj);
strOutput += "Type: " + Object.getType(obj) + strReturn;
```

```
strOutput += "Name: " + Object.getTypeName(obj) + strReturn;
strOutput += "Length: " + obj.length + strReturn;
Array.clear(obj);
strOutput += "Length after clear: " + obj.length + strReturn;
strOutput += "Length of clone: " + objClone.length + strReturn;
obj = Array.clone(objClone);
strOutput += "Is 123 in array: " + Array.contains(obj, 123) + strReturn;
strOutput += "Is 1234 in array: " + Array.contains(obj, 1234) + strReturn;
strOutput += "Dequed value: " + Array.dequeue(obj) + strReturn;
Array.insert(obj, 2, 1235);
strOutput += "Insert length: " + obj.length + strReturn;
Array.remove(obj, "Hi there");
strOutput += "Length after call to .remove: " + obj.length + strReturn;
Array.removeAt(obj, 0);
strOutput += "Length after call to .removeAt: " + obj.length + strReturn;
strOutput += "Parse Array: " + Array.parse(1,2,3) + strReturn;
strOutput += "Array __typeName: " + Array.__typeName + strReturn;
for( i = 0; i < objClone.length; i++)
    strOutput += "  value of objClone at location " + i + ": " +
objClone[i] + strReturn;
$get("Output").innerHTML = strOutput;
```

Figure 8-5 shows example output from the preceding code.

Figure 8-5

The StringBuilder() Class

The Sys.StringBuilder() class that is implemented in the Microsoft AJAX Library is a similar concept to the StringBuilder within the .NET framework. The Sys.StringBuilder() class represents an object that is similar in concept to a String() object. The values within a Sys.StringBuilder() class may be modified after the object has been created. The values can be modified by adding, deleting, and replacing values on the Array() object that is set up for the StringBuilder() class.

The Sys.StringBuilder() class implements the following methods:

❑   append(value) — The append(value) puts the value into the internal array that holds the contents of the Array that contains the StringBuilder class's contents. This method is an instance method.

❑   appendLine(value) — The appendLine(value) method puts the value into the internal array that holds the contents of the Array and adds a "\r\n" as the next value into the Array(). This value results in a new line being created when the StringBuilder() is returned.

❑   clear() — The clear() method clears the contents of the internal Array() that holds the StringBuilder. The result is that the StringBuilder has no values in it and would result in an empty string being output from the StringBuilder.

❑   isEmpty() — The isEmpty() method returns a Boolean. If the value returned is true, the StringBuilder's internal Array has a length of zero. If the value returned is false, the StringBuilder's internal Array has a non-zero length.

❑   toString(value) — The toString(value) method returns the StringBuilder's contents as string. After each element in the Array is output to a string, each item is appended with the value, not including the extra line created by the appendLine() method.

Now that you have seen the functions specific to the Sys.StringBuilder() class, look at an example. This source code creates a StringBuilder() class, adds values through append() and appendLine(), and performs some additional operations:

```
var strOutput = "";
var strReturn = "<br />";
var obj = new Sys.StringBuilder("Hi There.");
obj.append("I'm Wally.");
obj.appendLine("This is a test.");
obj.appendLine("This is a second test.");
alert(obj.toString("<br />"));
strOutput += "Type: " + Object.getType(obj) + strReturn;
strOutput += "Name: " + Object.getTypeName(obj) + strReturn;
strOutput += "Type Name (private): " + Sys.StringBuilder._typeName + strReturn;
strOutput += "Text: " + obj.toString() + strReturn;
strOutput += "Is Empty: " + obj.isEmpty() + strReturn;
obj.clear();
strOutput += "Is Empty (after a call to .clear()): " + obj.isEmpty() + strReturn;
$get("Output").innerHTML = strOutput;
```

Figure 8-6 shows the output of the `alert()` box with the contents of the `StringBuilder()`. Note that the values added by the `appendLine()` method calls have a new line after them.

Figure 8-7 shows the output of the various calls to the `StringBuilder()` class. Note that the call to `Object.Type()` returns the definition of the class.

Figure 8-6

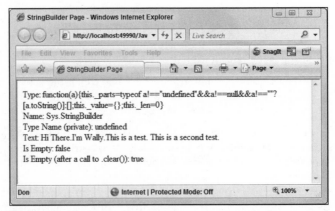

Figure 8-7

The Date() Object

The Microsoft AJAX Library provides additional support for the `Date()` object provided by JavaScript. This object provides support for creating date objects that can be used for various types of processing:

```
var strOutput = "";
var strReturn = "<br />";
var obj = new Date("10/10/2007");
strOutput += "Type: " + Object.getType(obj) + strReturn;
strOutput += "Name: " + Object.getTypeName(obj) + strReturn;
strOutput += "__typeName:" + obj._typeName + strReturn;
alert("hi");
strOutput += "Locale Format Date: " + Date.parseLocale("9/10/2007") + strReturn;
strOutput += "Custom Format Date: " + obj.format("dd-MMM-yy") + strReturn;
$get("Output").innerHTML = strOutput;
```

This object supports two types of formatting: standardized and custom.

The standardized formatting provides for the following formatting options:

❑   d — The d formatting option displays its output in the short date format.

❑   D — The D formatting option displays its output in the long date format.

❑   t — The t formatting option displays its output in the short time format.

❑   T — The T formatting option displays its output in the long time format.

❑   F — The F formatting option displays its output in the full date-time format.

❑   M or m — The M and m formatting options display their output in the month-day format.

❑   s — The s formatting option displays its output in the sortable date-time format.

❑   Y — The Y formatting option displays its output in the month-year format.

Figure 8-8 shows example output from the preceding code.

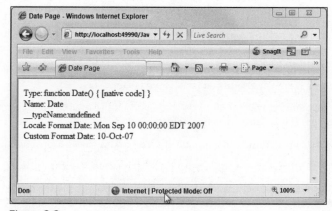

Figure 8-8

If the standard date formats don't meet your needs, custom date formats can be defined. These formatting options are made up from options that can be combined. These options are as follows:

❑   dddd — The dddd option displays the full name of a day.

❑   ddd — The ddd option displays the abbreviated name of a day.

❑   dd — The dd option displays the numeric value of a day with a leading zero if necessary.

❑   d — The d option displays the numeric number of a day with no leading zero.

❑   MMMM — The MMMM option displays the full name of the month within a Date object.

❑   MMM — The MMM option returns the abbreviated name of the month within a Date object.

❑   MM — The MM option returns the numeric value of the month within a Date object with a leading zero if necessary.

❑   M — The M option returns the numeric value of the month part of a Date object.

❑   yyyy — The yyyy option returns the full year of a Date object.

❑   yy — The yy option returns the last two digits of the year within a Date object. This includes any leading zeros necessary.

❑   y — The y option returns the last two digits of the year within a Date object. This option will not include any leading zeros.

❑   hh — The hh option returns the hour within a Date object along with any leading zeros as necessary. The value returned is between 1 and 12.

❑   h — The h option returns the hour within a Date object. The value returns without any leading zeros. The value returned is between 1 and 12.

❑   HH — The HH option returns the hour within a Date object. The value is returned with any necessary leading zeros. The value returned is between 00 and 23.

❑   H — The H option returns the hour within a Date object. The value is returned without any leading zeros. The value returned is between 0 and 23.

❑   mm — The mm option returns the minutes contained within a Date object along with any necessary leading zeros. The value returned is between 00 and 59.

❑   m — The m option returns the minutes contained within a Date object without any leading zeros. The value returned is between 0 and 59.

❑   ss — The ss option returns the seconds contained within a Date object along with any necessary leading zeros. The value returned is between 00 and 59.

❑   s — The s option returns the seconds contained within a Date object without any necessary leading zeros. The value returned is between 0 and 59.

❑   tt — The tt option returns the AM or PM designation as appropriate for the date.

❑   t — The t option returns A or P for AM or PM, respectively, for the date.

❑   fff — The fff option returns the milliseconds within a Date object. The value returned has necessary leading zeros to return three digits in the value.

❑   ff — The ff option returns the hundredths of a second within a Date object. No rounding to the nearest hundredth of a second is done.

❑   f — The f option returns the tenth of a second within a Date object. No rounding to the nearest tenth of a second is performed.

❑   zzz — The zzz option returns the time offset of the time as supplied to the browser by the host operating system. This value has any necessary leading zeros. An example value is +04:00.

❑   zz — The zz option returns the time offset of the time as supplied to the browser by the host operating system. This value has any necessary leading zeros. An example value is +04.

❑   z — The z option returns the time offset of the time as supplied to the browser by the host operating system. No leading zeros are added to the value. An example value is +4.

The Error() Object

The JavaScript Error() object has been modified within the Microsoft AJAX Library. This modification adds the static createError() method. This method takes three parameters, which are optional, and there is a test to determine whether the value is passed in. If the value does not exist, the property is not created. These parameters are the message, details, and the inner exception. The result of a call to this static method is an error object. The following code shows the use of the createError() method:

```
var strOutput = "";
var strReturn = "<br />";
var obj = Error.create("This is an example error", "Error details",
Error.create("Inner Error"));
strOutput += "Type: " + Object.getType(obj) + strReturn;
strOutput += "Name: " + Object.getTypeName(obj) + strReturn;
strOutput += "_typeName: " + Error._typeName + strReturn;
strOutput += "Error Details: " + obj.details + strReturn;
strOutput += "Error Description: " + obj.description + strReturn;
strOutput += "Error Message: " + obj.message + strReturn;
strOutput += "Error Name: " + obj.name + strReturn;
$get("Output").innerHTML = strOutput;
```

Figure 8-9 shows the output of the preceding code.

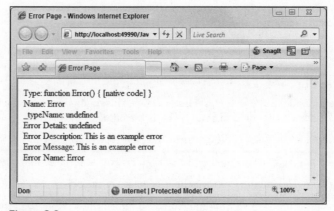

Figure 8-9

Code Management

.NET developers like to manage the code that they develop. To facilitate that, the .NET languages and framework offer support for namespaces, classes, inheritance, and interfaces.

Namespaces

A namespace is a concept for managing code. A namespace is a holder of one or more classes and other pieces of code, and these pieces of code are typically related in some way. With C#, a namespace and a class are defined according to this example:

```
namespace Test
{
  public class Example
  {
    public Example()
    {
    }
  }
}
```

The namespace keyword defines a namespace called Test in this example. Within the namespace is one class that is called Example.

To define a namespace within the Microsoft AJAX Library, execute the following command:

```
Type.registerNamespace("Test");
```

This is the command that defines a namespace called Test. The Type object contains a number of methods used for code management, including:

❑ callBaseMethod(instance, name, arguments) — This method calls a base method of the passed instance. The name is a string of the base type. The arguments are optional; they are an array of parameters to pass to the base method of the instance.

❑ getBaseMethod(instance, methodName) — This method returns the base method of the specified instance, where the methodName is the name of the method to retrieve.

❑ getBaseType() — This method returns the base type of the object.

❑ getInterfaces() — This method returns an array of interfaces that a type implements.

❑ getName() — This method returns the type name of the object.

❑ getRootNamespaces() — This static method returns an Array object that contains the root namespaces of an application. This method is called by Type.getRootNamespaces().

❑ implementsInterface(interface) — This method returns a Boolean indicating whether a class implements a specified interface.

❑ inheritsFrom(parent) — This method returns a Boolean indicating whether a class inherits from a specified class.

❑ initializeBase(instance, arguments) — This method initializes the base class of the specified instance and passes the arguments listed to that base class.

❑ isClass(specifiedType) — This method returns a Boolean that indicates whether the specifiedType is a class. The method is static and is called by Type.isClass(specifiedType).

❑ isImplementedBy(instance) — This method returns a Boolean representing whether the instance implements the interface.

❑ isInstanceOfType(instance) — This method returns a Boolean indicating whether an instance is of a specified type or a derived class.

❑ isInterface(type) — This is a static method that returns a Boolean indicating whether a type is an interface.

❑ isNamespace(object) — This is a static method that returns a Boolean indicating whether an object is a namespace.

❑ registerClass(className, inheritedClass, interfaceToImplement) — This static method will be used to register a class within a namespace.

❑ registerEnum() — This static method will be used to register an enumeration. Enumerations are a logical set of data that is grouped together.

❑ registerInterface() — This is a static method that will register an interface. Interfaces are helpful in projects with enforcing that classes implement certain specific functions.

❑ registerNamespace() — This is a static method that will register a namespace. By using namespaces, you will be able to group classes together in logical groups. This will be very helpful in large projects with a large amount of code.

❑ resolveInheritance() — This method will copy members from a base class to the associated prototype of the derived class.

These methods add features to JavaScript and client-side development that should allow developers to create applications that are conceptually similar to coding in the .NET framework.

Classes

A class is a programming object that contains a logical and singular object. For example, a customer or order is a logical object. JavaScript is a prototype-based language. Classes are not formally present in the JavaScript language; however, a similar concept is available.

In JavaScript, objects exist. These objects are extended through the cloning of existing objects, and the existing objects are referred to as *prototypes*. The Microsoft AJAX Library allows you to create an object that looks like a class using the functionality of a JavaScript prototype object.

Try It Out　　**Creating an Object**

Take a look at creating a prototype-based class in JavaScript. This class has a generic animal class that can represent an animal at a veterinarian hospital. This class has two fields that it stores — Name and Address — which are used to represent the name of the animal and the address where the animal lives, respectively. In addition, there are two additional methods that the class implements: dispose and toString. The dispose method is used for cleaning up when the class is completed. The toString method is used to display some standard text representation of the object.

```
Animal.Generic = function(Name, Address)
{
    this._Name = Name;
    this._Address = Address;
}
Animal.Generic.prototype = {
```

```
        get_Name: function()
        {
            return this._Name;
        },
        set_Name: function(val)
        {
            this._Name = val;
        },
        get_Address: function()
        {
            return this._Address;
        },
        set_Address: function(val)
        {
            this._Address = val;
        },
        dispose: function()
        {
            alert("disposing component with Animal Name:" + this.get_Name() + " @ " +
this.get_Address());
        },
        toString: function()
        {
            return this.get_Name() + " at " + this.get_Address();
        }
    }
```

How It Works

In this example, the code creates a class named `Animal.Generic`. The _Name and _Address properties are created when the object is instantiated. This class performs gets/sets through the get_Name, set_Name, get_Address, and set_Address methods, respectively. These methods are the JavaScript equivalent of property gets and sets in .NET. The get_Name() and get_Address() methods return the name and address values, respectively. The set_Name(value) and set_Address(value) set the name and address values to the value that is passed in, respectively.

Although the _Name and _Address methods are accessible from outside of this object, it is convention to not use them.

In the example code, note the creation of the dispose() method. Though it seems that the dispose() method would be unnecessary in a web page, web browsers are not the best citizens when it comes to cleaning up on the client side. As a result, the Microsoft AJAX Library implements a dispose method and an interface to implement in Sys.IDisposable.

The final piece to creating a class is to actually create the class. The Microsoft AJAX Library provides a registerClass() method to register the class. This registration takes a little bit of getting used to. The naming breaks down along the lines of ClassName.registerClass("ClassName", BaseClass, Interfaces). The calling sequence can be somewhat confusing as the in the previous example: Animal.Generic is the name of the class; therefore, it appears twice. The second parameter is any class that this class might inherit from. In this simple situation, it does not inherit from any class; therefore, a null is handed in. The final parameter is any interface that this class will implement. In this example, the class implements the `Sys.IDisposable` interface. To implement other interfaces, they may be specified by adding them in as additional parameters. For example,

```
ClassName.registerClass("className", BaseClass, Interface1, Interface2)
```

would implement `Interface1` and `Interface2`.

Inheritance

Inheritance is a programming mechanism that takes existing functionality and adds to it when you are creating a new object type. The example here uses an `Animal.Generic` class. This is what is referred to as the *base class*. You then create an `Animal.Cat` class. The `Animal.Cat` class inherits from the `Animal.Generic` class and adds additional pieces of functionality.

Try It Out   Using Inheritance

Try out an example of inheritance. This example uses the previous `Animal.Generic` example and inherits from it. The `Animal.Cat` class will inherit from the previous `Animal.Generic` class and add the `Parents` field along with the `get`/`set` for the field. Consider the following source code:

```
Animal.Cat = function(Name, Address, Parents)
{
    Animal.Cat.initializeBase(this, [Name, Address]);
    this._Parents = Parents;
}
Animal.Cat.prototype = {
    get_Parents: function()
    {
        return this._Parents;
    },
    set_Parents: function(val)
    {
        _Parents = val;
    },
    get_friendlyName: function()
    {
        return "Cat";
    }
}
Animal.Cat.registerClass('Animal.Cat', Animal.Generic, Animal.IPet);
```

How It Works

In this example, when the `Animal.Cat` class is instantiated, the base method is called with the appropriate parameters. The call to `registerClass()` passes in the name of the class, the class that is being inherited from, and a `null` signifying that no interfaces are used in this class.

Testing Inheritance

Along with the ability to inherit, there is a need to test for inheritance. There are two methods of interest: isInstanceOfType() and inheritsFrom(). Here is some example code:

```
if (Animal.Generic.isInstanceOfType(CatObj))
{
    str += "Cat object is of type Animal.Generic." + strReturn;
}
str += "Animal.Cat.inheritsFrom(Sys.IDisposable): " +
Animal.Cat.inheritsFrom(Sys.IDisposable) + strReturn;
str += "Animal.Cat.inheritsFrom(Animal.Generic): " +
Animal.Cat.inheritsFrom(Animal.Generic) + strReturn;
str += "Animal.Cat.inheritsFrom(Animal.Cat): " +
Animal.Cat.inheritsFrom(Animal.Cat) + strReturn;
```

The inheritsFrom() method enables you to test to determine if an object inherits from a specific base type. In this example, the Animal.Cat object does not inherit from Sys.IDisposable, so that call will return a false. The Animal.Cat object does inherit from Animal.Generic, so that will return a true.

The isInstanceOfType() method will return a Boolean value, allowing you to test to determine if an object is of a specific type. In this example, the Animal.Cat object is also of type Animal.Generic. As a result, the call to isInstanceOfType() returns a true.

Interfaces

Interfaces are a set of methods and properties that are defined. A child class is said to implement an interface when the child class implements the defined methods and properties within the interface and the class declares that it implements the interface. Defining the properties and methods within an interface gives you the ability to add and remove classes that implement a common interface.

The following code defines an interface:

```
Animal.IPet = function()
{
    this.get_friendlyName = Function.abstractMethod;
}
```

This example code shows that an interface named Animal.IPet requires the method get_friendlyName.

The use of I within an interface name is merely a convention and is not required. It is similar to the concept of using the underscore character (_) to denote that a variable is private.

The following code registers an interface with the Microsoft AJAX Library:

```
Animal.IPet.registerInterface('Animal.IPet');
```

The next step is for a class to declare that it implements an interface. This is done by using the registerClass() method, as shown in the following code:

```
Animal.Cat.registerClass('Animal.Cat', Animal.Generic, Animal.IPet);
```

In this example, the `Animal.Cat` class, which was defined earlier, is defined as implementing the `Animal.IPet` interface.

Another important part of interfaces is to verify that an object implements an interface. You can do this by using the `isImplementedBy()` method. The following is an example call:

```
if (Animal.IPet.isImplementedBy(CatObj))
{
    str += "Object does implement IPet." + strReturn;
    str += "This object has a friendly name of: " + CatObj.get_friendlyName() +
strReturn;
}
```

In this code sample, a test is performed to see whether an object, the `CatObj`, implements the `Animal.IPet` interface. If the test is positive, then one of the methods defined by the interface, `get_ friendlyName()`, is called.

Pulling Together Language Features

The following code shows an example of namespaces, classes, inheritance, and interfaces, as well as testing for these features. This example code builds on the code shown previously.

```
function GenerateClasses()
{
    var strReturn = "<br />";
    var str;
    var CatObj = new Animal.Cat("Wells", "Knoxville, TN", "Wally and Ronda");
    var GenObj = new Animal.Generic("Spot", "Atlanta, GA");
    str = "Cat's name: " + CatObj.get_Name() + strReturn;
    str += "Cat's Parents: " + CatObj.get_Parents() + strReturn;

    if (Animal.Cat.isInstanceOfType(CatObj))
    {
        str += "Cat object is of type Animal.Cat." + strReturn;
    }
    if (Animal.Generic.isInstanceOfType(CatObj))
    {
        str += "Cat object is of type Animal.Generic." + strReturn;
    }
    str += "Animal.Cat.inheritsFrom(Sys.IDisposable): " +
Animal.Cat.inheritsFrom(Sys.IDisposable) + strReturn;
    str += "Animal.Cat.inheritsFrom(Animal.Generic): " +
Animal.Cat.inheritsFrom(Animal.Generic) + strReturn;
    str += "Animal.Cat.inheritsFrom(Animal.Cat): " +
Animal.Cat.inheritsFrom(Animal.Cat) + strReturn;
    if (Animal.Cat.inheritsFrom(Animal.Generic))
    {
        str += "Cat object inherits from Animal.Generic." + strReturn;
    }
    if (Animal.IPet.isImplementedBy(CatObj))
    {
        str += "Object does implement IPet." + strReturn;
```

```
        str += "This object has a friendly name of: " + CatObj.get_friendlyName() +
    strReturn;
    }
    if (!Animal.IPet.isImplementedBy(GenObj))
    {
        str += "Animal.Generic does not implement the IPet interface.";
    }
    document.getElementById("Output").innerHTML = str;
}
```

The following steps are involved in this code:

1. An instance of the `Animal.Cat` object is created.

2. An instance of the `Animal.Generic` object is created.

3. A call is made to the `get_Name()` method of the `CatObj` object. This method is part of `Animal.Cat` object.

4. A call is made to the `get_Parents()` method of the `CatObj` object. This method is inherited from the base object `Animal.Generic`.

5. A call is made to test the `CatObj` object to see if it is of type `Animal.Cat`.

6. Three calls are made to test if `Animal.Cat` inherits from the various types. If the type inherits from the tested type, `true` is returned; otherwise, `false` is returned.

7. A call is made to test if the defined `Animal.Cat` type implements the specified interface. In this case, the test is made against the `Animal.IPet` interface.

Figure 8-10 shows the output of the preceding code.

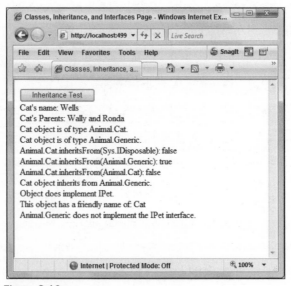

Figure 8-10

Enumerations

The Microsoft AJAX Library, like the .NET framework, provides support for enumerations — a mechanism to group a related set of constants. Look at a small code example to set up a listing of months:

```
Type.registerNamespace('BeginningAJAX');
BeginningAJAX.ExampleCalendarEnum = function(){};
BeginningAJAX.ExampleCalendarEnum.prototype=
{
    January:        0,
    February:       1,
    March:          2,
    April:          3,
    May:            4,
    June:           5,
    July:           6,
    August:         7,
    September:      8,
    October:        9,
    November:       10,
    December:       11
}
BeginningAJAX.ExampleCalendarEnum.registerEnum('BeginningAJAX.ExampleCalendarEnum')
;
```

In this example, an object is created (BeginningAJAX.ExampleCalendarEnum, in this case). The registerEnum() method is called. At this point, the month of July can be registered through the call BeginningAJAX.ExampleCalendarEnum.July. This code can be accessed in any other JavaScript code.

The registerEnum(enumName, true) method can be called with the second parameter being true if the enum that is being set up contains bit values.

Summary

The Microsoft AJAX Library adds several features to the JavaScript language. These features help in the area of code management and new features to the built-in JavaScript objects. This chapter discussed some of the new features, including the following:

❑   New methods and properties in some of the built-in objects. These include the String(), Number(), and other objects.

❑   The Sys.StringBuilder() class provides a client-side version of the .NET StringBuilder() class.

❑   Code management support through the inclusion of namespaces, classes, inheritance, and interfaces.

In the next chapter, you look at the classes that are provided by the Microsoft AJAX Library in more depth.

Microsoft AJAX Library

This chapter explains what the Microsoft AJAX Library is and how to use some of the classes. It goes over some of the more useful features of the Library you might use more often than others. The examples are going to be mostly in JavaScript because the way you call these from VB and C# is nearly identical. In fact, the only real difference is the first line of code in your .aspx page:

```
<%@ Page Language="C#" %>
```

or

```
<%@ Page Language="VB" %>.
```

The Microsoft AJAX Library is a set of classes that provide a rich framework that greatly simplifies web client programming with JavaScript. It contains several namespaces that are very helpful in creating clean client code that very much feels like what you are familiar with in C#. This chapter consists of a list and description of each namespace and class and then goes into several of the classes in the Sys.* namespaces. The "The Sys Namespace" section explains how to use a few of the popular classes including the Sys.EventHandler class and the Sys.Debug class, among others. The "The Sys.Net Namespace" section explains how to use the popular networking classes and how to manage communication between Microsoft ASP.NET AJAX client applications and web services on the server. The final section, "The Sys.Serialization Namespace," explains how and when you might want to serialize JavaScript types into JSON-formatted data.

In this chapter, you take a look at the following:

- ❑ A description of all the namespaces in the client library
- ❑ Which classes make up the Sys namespace
- ❑ Examples using the Sys.StringBuilder class
- ❑ How the underlying Sys.WebRequest class works
- ❑ JavaScript serialization
- ❑ Event handling in the Microsoft AJAX Library

Client Library Namespaces

The following are all the namespaces and classes in the Microsoft AJAX Library. Note that several chapters in this book cover many of the following classes in greater depth.

❑   Global namespace — Contains members and types that extend the base JavaScript objects and provide members that are familiar to .NET developers. This includes extensions for the JavaScript `Array`, `Number`, `Boolean`, `Error`, `Object`, and `String` types. This namespace also includes some global shortcuts to commonly used APIs, such as `$get`, `$find`, and `$addHandler`.

❑   `Sys` — This is the root namespace for the AJAX Library that contains all the fundamental classes and base classes. Some of the most-used classes are `StringBuilder`, `Debug`, and `Component`.

❑   `Sys.Net` — This namespace provides classes that communicate between the client application and web services. The two main classes you will use are `WebServiceProxy` and `WebRequest`.

❑   `Sys.Serialization` — This namespace contains the `JavaScriptSerializer` class, which enables you to serialize ECMAScript (JavaScript) types into JSON-formatted data and deserialize JSON-formatted data into JavaScript types.

❑   `Sys.Services` — This namespace contains types that provide client script access to the ASP.NET authentication service, profile service, and other application services.

❑   `Sys.WebForms` — This namespace contains classes related to partial-page rendering that is used with the `UpdatePanel` control.

❑   `Sys.UI` — This namespace contains types related to the user interface, such as controls, events, and UI properties. A couple of the base classes you will use are the `Behavior` and `Control` classes for creating behaviors and client controls, respectively.

Many of the namespaces are covered in other chapters, so this chapter does not cover all of them in detail. The following sections cover the namespaces and some useful classes in detail that have not been covered in this book.

The Sys Namespace

The `Sys` namespace is the root namespace for the Microsoft AJAX Library and contains all fundamental classes and base classes that are built on top of the new JavaScript Base Type Extensions mentioned in the previous chapter. These classes provide a JavaScript framework that feels very comfortable for people who use the .NET framework already, particularly C# because they use a very similar syntax. Some of the popular classes are `Sys.Debug` and `Sys.StringBuilder` along with the `Sys.WebService` and `Sys.WebServiceProxy` classes.

Before showing you what classes are in the `Sys` namespace, let's talk about why you would want to use these classes in the first place. If you are anything like me, it is hard to switch from a strongly typed, fully object-oriented language like C# to a dynamic, loose typed language like JavaScript. These classes help bridge the gap of differences between C# and JavaScript.

Types

Here is a table of all the classes for the `Sys` namespace.

Member Name	Description
`Sys.Application` class	Provides members that support client-component development.
`Sys.ApplicationLoadEventArgs` class	Provides a specialized event arguments collection for the load event of the `Application` class.
`Sys.CancelEventArgs` class	Used by event sources that enable the handler to cancel the operation in progress.
`Sys.Component` class	Provides the base class for the `Control` and `Behavior` classes, and for any other object whose lifetime should be managed by Microsoft ASP.NET AJAX.
`Sys.CultureInfo` class	Represents a culture definition that can be applied to other objects that accept a culture-related setting.
`Sys.Debug` class	Provides debugging and tracing functionality for client code. This is a static class that is invoked directly without creating an instance of the class.
`Sys.EventArgs` class	Used by event sources to pass event argument information.
`Sys.EventHandlerList` class	Creates a dictionary to hold client-script events and their associated handlers.
`Sys.IContainer` interface	Provides a common interface for all components that can contain other components.
`Sys.IDisposable` interface	Provides a common interface for application-defined tasks associated with closing, releasing, or resetting resources held by instances of a registered Microsoft AJAX Library class.
`Sys.INotifyDisposing` interface	Defines the disposing event.
`Sys.INotifyPropertyChange` interface	Defines the `propertyChanged` event.
`Sys.PropertyChangedEventArgs` class	Describes property changes.

Continued

Member Name	Description
Sys.Res object	Provides static, culture-neutral exception messages.
Sys.StringBuilder class	Provides an optimized mechanism to concatenate strings.
Sys Exception types	These exceptions are created dynamically by using the Error type extension functions and cannot be instantiated or invoked.

Three of my favorite classes in the Sys namespace are Sys.Debug, Sys.StringBuilder, and Sys.WebRequest. They bring so much functionality to JavaScript that it makes it much easier to write robust and testable applications.

Sys.Debug

The Sys.Debug class provides great debugging and tracing functionality for your JavaScript client code. How many times have you written alert("Hi, I am here") for debugging with JavaScript? Well, I will admit that I have. Now there is a much better way to debug your client-side script. With these members you have a much friendlier debugging experience. If you have previously installed beta versions of the Microsoft AJAX Library, make sure to uninstall and reinstall the 1.0 release; otherwise, the following classes will not work.

Member Name	Description
Sys.Debug.assert	Checks for a condition, and if it is false, it displays a message to users and prompts them to break into the debugger.
Sys.Debug.clearTrace	This method clears all the trace messages from the debugger output console. This only clears the HTML in the TraceConsole<textarea>.
Sys.Debug.fail	This method displays a message in the debugger's output window and breaks into the debugger.
Sys.Debug.trace	This method appends a text line to the debugger window and also to the TraceConsole<textarea> element, if it exists.
Sys.Debug.traceDump	This method dumps an object to the debugger window and also to the TraceConsole<textarea> element, if it exists.

There are plenty of examples in Chapter 12 on debugging toward the end of this book, so I will not elaborate anymore on the Debug class. Just know that it is there and use it. You will be very happy you did.

Sys.StringBuilder

The `Sys.StringBuilder` class provides a familiar way to concatenate strings similar to .NET. It has the basic functions you normally use, as described in the following table.

Member Name	Description
`StringBuilder.append`	Appends a string to the end of the `StringBuilder` instance.
`StringBuilder.appendLine`	Appends a new string with a line terminator to the end of the `StringBuilder` instance.
`StringBuilder.clear`	Clears the contents of the `StringBuilder` instance.
`StringBuilder.isEmpty`	Determines whether the `StringBuilder` instance has any content.
`StringBuilder.toString`	Creates a string from the contents of a `StringBuilder` instance.

The following example is not just about using the `StringBuilder` class, but also about how to write JavaScript classes that can be reused much as you can use them in .NET development. The class I wrote for this example is called `Samples.ListBuilder`, and basically allows you to create an HTML unordered list in memory and then draw it back to the screen using an update panel. The code in the .aspx page could have just as well have been normal HTML input and button tags, but because this is an ASP.NET AJAX book I thought it would be more appropriate to create the example using ASP.NET controls.

Try It Out Writing a Custom ListBuilder JavaScript Class

First, you need to create the JavaScript class file. I prefer to create my JavaScript classes in separate files for more reusability. For samples sometimes it is easier to create them in the .aspx page itself, but I believe that by forcing yourself to write your code in separate JavaScript files you will write better and cleaner code that can actually be reused. JavaScript is notorious for turning into spaghetti really fast, so be careful if you are writing an application that will need to be maintained.

First, create a file called `ListBuilder.js`. In this class, you are going to create a reusable class that will build an unordered list dynamically. The first thing you need to do is to register the namespace:

```
Type.registerNamespace('Samples');
```

In this example, I chose to use the name `Samples` for my namespace, but you could have just as easily used `Utilities` or whatever you want. So the class will be referenced as `Samples.ListBuilder`.

Next, you need to create the constructor. In the constructor you will create your properties that can be referenced later in methods of the class.

```
Samples.ListBuilder = function()
    {
        this._listTagStart = "<ul>";
```

```
            this._listTagEnd = "</ul>";
            this._listItemTagStart = "<li>";
            this._listItemTagEnd = "</li>";
            this._arrayOfItems = [];
            this._sb = new Sys.StringBuilder();
    }
```

Here is the whole class in its entirety:

```
    Type.registerNamespace('Samples');
    Samples.ListBuilder = function()
    {
        this._listTagStart = "<ul>";
        this._listTagEnd = "</ul>";
        this._listItemTagStart = "<li>";
        this._listItemTagEnd = "</li>";
        this._arrayOfItems = [];
        this._sb = new Sys.StringBuilder();
    }
    Samples.ListBuilder.prototype =
    {
        addToList: function(itemTitle)
        {
            try
            {
                // show different error exceptions that you can throw
                if (itemTitle === undefined) throw
Error.argumentUndefined('itemTitle');
                if (itemTitle === "") throw Error.argumentUndefined('itemTitle',
"You cannot add an item that is blank");
                if (itemTitle === null) throw Error.argumentNull('itemTitle');

                Array.add(this._arrayOfItems, itemTitle);
            }
            catch(e)
            {
                alert(e.message);
            }
        },
        buildListElement: function(itemTitle)
        {
            this._sb.append(this._listItemTagStart);
            this._sb.append(itemTitle);
            this._sb.append(this._listItemTagEnd);
        },
        buildList: function(updatePanel)
        {
            try
            {
                // clear the stringbuilder in case in use second time
                this._sb.clear();
                // add the beginning list tag
                this._sb.append(this._listTagStart);
                // Array.forEach(array, method, context);
                Array.forEach(this._arrayOfItems, this.buildListElement, this);
```

```
                            // add the list end tag
                            this._sb.append(this._listTagEnd);
                            // set the div element = to the list stringbuilder
                            updatePanel.innerHTML = this._sb.toString();
                }
                catch(e)
                {
                            alert(e.message);
                }
        },
        clearList: function(updatePanel)
        {
                try
                {
                            // clear the string builder
                            this._sb.clear();
                            // clear the array
                            Array.clear(this._arrayOfItems);
                            // empty the update panel
                            updatePanel.innerHTML = "";
                }
                catch(e)
                {
                            alert(e.message);
                }
        }
}
Samples.ListBuilder.registerClass('Samples.ListBuilder');
```

How It Works

There are a lot of things going on here. If you have read all the chapters up until this point you may already understand how to create classes. If you haven't, I highly suggest reading chapter 8 so that you can understand the following JavaScript code.

The first lines at the top of the file are comments with sample function calls so that people understand how to use your class. To me this is especially important when writing JavaScript classes because it is not as easy to read as .NET languages are and sometimes it is hard to know what types you need to pass in because it is a dynamic language:

```
// Samples.ListBuilder
// Samples.ListBuilder.addToList(string itemTitle);
// Samples.ListBuilder.buildList(DocElement updatePanel);
// Samples.ListBuilder.clearList(DocElement updatePanel);
Type.registerNamespace('Samples');
Samples.ListBuilder = function()
{
    this._listTagStart = "<ul>";
    this._listTagEnd = "</ul>";
    this._listItemTagStart = "<li>";
    this._listItemTagEnd = "</li>";
    this._arrayOfItems = [];
    this._sb = new Sys.StringBuilder();
}
```

Notice that I put all of my fields in the constructor. This is a best practice for organizing your variables within a class. Now once you have IntelliSense for JavaScript, it will be very easy to code these classes and reuse them. For now, you just have to look at the fields in the constructor to find your shared variables in the class.

Notice in the function `Samples.ListBuilder.addToList` that you are using the new `Array.add` function and three different error exceptions that you can catch found in the JavaScript Base Extensions. When you click the Add Item button in the form, leave the text field blank and you will see the `Error.argumentUndefined` with a custom message that gets sent to the user. This is very useful for simple parameter errors that you would like to handle separately. Putting all of this code in a try catch block allows the user to be notified if something unforeseen takes place. Which never happens, right? I highly suggest setting the debug level and turning alerts off if not in debug mode. Although some of these errors are friendlier than those generally used today, you do not want your users seeing every error in production if something goes wrong.

```
Samples.ListBuilder.prototype =
    {
        addToList: function(itemTitle)
        {
            try
            {
                // show different error exceptions that you can throw
                if (itemTitle === undefined) throw
Error.argumentUndefined('itemTitle');
                if (itemTitle === "") throw Error.argumentUndefined('itemTitle',
"You cannot add an item that is blank");
                if (itemTitle === null) throw Error.argumentNull('itemTitle');

                Array.add(this._arrayOfItems, itemTitle);
            }
            catch(e)
            {
                alert(e.message);
            }
        },
```

Notice the comma at the end of the function. You need to have a comma separating all the class methods if you have more than one. You do not need to have a comma after the last function in a class. IE will throw an exception if there is an extra comma either first or last.

Now on to the part where you use the `StringBuilder` class to append some strings when you want to build the list. Notice how you are passing in a reference to the `updatePanel` object so that you can set the `innerHTML` property equal to that of your built list HTML. First you clear the `StringBuilder` in case the object had already been used in a previous update on that client. Then you append the list start tag `<ul>` and start to create each item in the list by using the `Array.forEach` function. This has to be one of my favorite extensions to JavaScript so far. You are calling a method in the class called `buildListElement` that takes the item and appends it to a string for each element in the array. Lastly, you are appending the end list tag and calling `toString` on the `StringBuilder` class to set the `innerHTML` of the `updatePanel`:

```
buildList: function(updatePanel)
    {
        try
```

```
        {
            // clear the stringbuilder in case in use second time
            this._sb.clear();
            // add the beginning list tag
            this._sb.append(this._listTagStart);
            // Array.forEach(array, method, context);
            Array.forEach(this._arrayOfItems, this.buildListElement, this);
            // add the list end tag
            this._sb.append(this._listTagEnd);
            // set the div element = to the list stringbuilder
            updatePanel.innerHTML = this._sb.toString();
        }
        catch(e)
        {
            alert(e.message);
        }

    },
buildListElement: function(itemTitle)
    {
        this._sb.append(this._listItemTagStart);
        this._sb.append(itemTitle);
        this._sb.append(this._listItemTagEnd);
    },
```

As you can see, the `Array.forEach` function works very well with the `StringBuilder.append` function. Now onto getting this code to work with an .aspx page.

The following is the .aspx page that references the `ListBuilder.js` file shown previously and calls its methods from button presses and page load events:

```
<%@ Page Language="C#" AutoEventWireup="true"
CodeFile="StringBuilderExample.aspx.cs" Inherits="StringBuilderExample" %>

<!DOCTYPE html PUBLIC "-//W3C//DTD XHTML 1.0 Transitional//EN"
"http://www.w3.org/TR/xhtml1/DTD/xhtml1-transitional.dtd">

<html xmlns="http://www.w3.org/1999/xhtml" >
<head runat="server">
    <title>StringBuilder Example</title>
    <script language="javascript" type="text/javascript">
        // set listbuilder class to global
        var ListBuilderClass;

        function pageLoad()
        {
            ListBuilderClass = new Samples.ListBuilder();
            ListBuilderClass.addToList("Test1");
            ListBuilderClass.addToList("Test2");
            ListBuilderClass.buildList($get("MyList"));

        }
```

```
            function addValuetoList()
            {
                ListBuilderClass.addToList($get("NewListItem").value);
                ListBuilderClass.buildList($get("MyList"));
            }

            function clearItems()
            {
                ListBuilderClass.clearList($get("MyList"));
            }

      </script>
</head>
<body
      <form id="form1" runat="server">
      <div>
            <asp:ScriptManager ID="ScriptManager1" runat="server">
            <Scripts>
                <asp:ScriptReference Path="~/ListBuilder.js" />
            </Scripts>
            </asp:ScriptManager>
            <div ID="MyList"></div>

            <asp:TextBox ID="NewListItem" runat="server"></asp:TextBox>
            <asp:Button ID="ButtonAddItem" runat="server"
OnClientClick="addValuetoList();" Text="Add Item" CausesValidation="False"
UseSubmitBehavior="False" />
            <asp:Button ID="Button1" runat="server" OnClientClick="return
clearItems();" Text="Clear Items" CausesValidation="False"
UseSubmitBehavior="False" />
      </div>
      </form>
</body>
</html>
```

Notice here that the `ScriptReference Path` property is set in the `ScriptManager` control. The function `pageLoad()` will automatically get called after all the libraries are loaded. On the page load event it shows how to create an instance of the `Samples.ListBuilder` class and add items to build the unordered list:

```
// set listbuilder class to global
        var ListBuilderClass = "";

        function pageLoad()
        {
            ListBuilderClass = new Samples.ListBuilder();
            ListBuilderClass.addToList("Test1");
            ListBuilderClass.addToList("Test2");
            ListBuilderClass.buildList($get("MyList"));


        }
```

The `ListBuilder` class instance is set to be global so that other functions can access the same object in memory like this one does:

```
function addValuetoList()
{
    ListBuilderClass.addToList($get("NewListItem").value);
    ListBuilderClass.buildList($get("MyList"));
}
```

`$get("element")` is another one of my favorite JavaScript Base Extensions. It is the equivalent to `Sys.UI.DomElement.getElementById("element")`. Notice in Figure 9-1 the interface to add and clear items from a list.

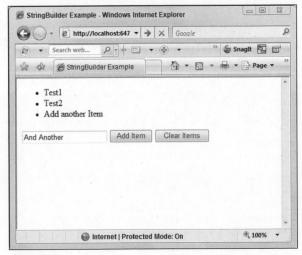

Figure 9-1

You learned how to create a `StringBuilder` class and make it a property of your own custom class that you can then access in a very familiar .NET development kind of way. Then you used some of the cool new JavaScript base extensions like `Array` and `$get` to pass around variables inside of your custom object.

After you get the hang of writing JavaScript this way, it will become easier and easier to write client-side code to do just about anything you want. Once you have your own libraries to do things that you want with the client, you will be able to create some very complex scenarios with clean, maintainable JavaScript.

The Sys.Net Namespace

The `Sys.Net` namespace contains classes that manage communication between Microsoft ASP.NET AJAX client applications and web services on the server. These can be simple web requests or more complex web service requests.

217

The different types inside of the `Sys.Net` namespace are shown in the following table.

Name	Description
`Sys.Net.WebServiceProxy` class	Enables calling a method of a specified web service asynchronously.
`Sys.Net.NetworkRequestEventArgs` class	Contains information about a web request that is ready to be sent to the current `WebRequestExecutor` instance.
`Sys.Net.WebRequest` class	Provides the script API to make a web request.
`Sys.Net.WebRequestExecutor` class	Provides the abstract base class from which network executors derive.
`Sys.Net.WebRequestManager` class	Manages the flow of web requests between the `WebRequest` object and the executor instance that makes the network requests.
`Sys.Net.WebServiceError` class	Represents the object type returned to the client when a web service issues an error.
`Sys.Net.XMLHttpExecutor` class	Makes asynchronous network requests by using the browser's `XMLHttpRequest` support.

The executor classes are the abstract base classes from which network classes like `WebRequest` derive. These classes have all the common network plumbing built in so that when you want to create a new type, you just derive from the `WebRequestExecutor` class or the `XMLHttpExecutor` class. The two classes you will most likely use are `Sys.Net.WebRequest` and `Sys.Net.WebServiceProxy`. A whole chapter is dedicated to calling web services, so I will show an example of how to use the `WebRequest` class to build your own cross-domain web proxy for the AJAX 1.0 library.

Sys.Net.WebRequest

The `Sys.Net.WebRequest` class provides a nice API to make a web request. There are several methods and properties in the following table that you should be aware of for when you need them.

Members	Description
`Sys.Net.WebRequest completed` method	Raises the completion event for the associated web request instance.
`Sys.Net.WebRequest add_completed` method	Registers an event handler to associate with the web request instance.

Members	Description
`Sys.Net.WebRequest.getResolvedUrl` method	Gets the resolved URL of the web request instance.
`Sys.Net.WebRequest invoke` method	Issues a network call for the web request instance.
`Sys.Net.WebRequest remove_completed` method	Removes the event handler associated with the web request instance.
`Sys.Net.WebRequest body` property	Gets or sets the HTTP body of the web request.
`Sys.Net.WebRequest executor` property	Gets or sets the executor of the associated web request instance.
`Sys.Net.WebRequest headers` property	Gets the HTTP headers for the web request.
`Sys.Net.WebRequest httpVerb` property	Gets or sets the web request HTTP verb used to issue the web request.
`Sys.Net.WebRequest timeout` property	Gets or sets the time-out value for the web request instance.
`Sys.Net.WebRequest url` property	Gets or sets the URL of the web request instance.
`Sys.Net.WebRequest userContext` property	Gets or sets the user context associated with the web request instance.

It is important to realize where this class came from. The `Sys.Net.WebRequest` class actually sits on top of the `XMLHttpRequest` object that almost all browsers have implemented in one way or another. Microsoft started using it in 1998 with its Outlook web access software. It was not known as AJAX at the time and did not really become popular until Google took advantage of it with its maps product. That's when people thought, wow, how did they do that?

Those out there who have written their own custom code to handle differences in browsers to talk to the `XMLHttpRequest` object will love this `WebRequest` class. It has become very easy to handle custom web requests because it is so similar if not easier than doing it in C#.

The first thing I tried to do with the demos was to request a web page that was not inside of my domain. To my disappointment, this did not work. It turns out that cross-domain calls are a security concern. Microsoft did have this working with a class called `iframexecutor`, but it was taken out before the release of the 1.0 version to avoid criticism on potential security issues. Now it does not make sense because cross-domain calls occur all the time with JavaScript from ad programs, stat trackers, and affiliate programs, all of which are inherently cross-domain calls. In the ASP.NET AJAX Futures CTP there is a bridge that will easily allow you to map an outside RSS feed or web service without having to write your own proxy. (For more information on the bridge, check out Chapter 13 and the online content.) Figure 9-2 shows the interface to get an external web page.

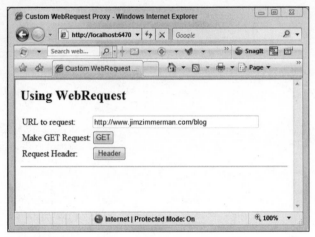

Figure 9-2

I hope Microsoft will consider putting it back in, but for now, there are other ways around this. If you really need access to an external web site or feed from within your AJAX application, you can call a proxy web page (which must reside on the caller's domain) that can route your web request through and then write it back to you. This example uses an .aspx page that will do the actual http request from the server and then return the data to the client. I created a JavaScript class called `MyWebRequest` and it can be reused very easily.

Try It Out   Creating a Custom WebRequest Class

1. First, create a class called `MyWebRequest` and make it part of the `Samples` namespace. You will want to make one method that will invoke a web request to your local web proxy and make a callback to a JavaScript function that you specify.

```
// Samples.MyWebRequest
// Samples.MyWebRequest.getFromOutsideUrl(string url, function callbackFunction);

Type.registerNamespace('Samples');
Samples.MyWebRequest = function()
{
    this._proxyPage = "http://localhost:52940/AJAXTestsWebsite/WebRequest/
GetOutsideDomainPage.aspx";
    this._displayElement = "";
}
Samples.MyWebRequest.prototype =
{
    getFromOutsideUrl: function(url, callbackFunction)
    {
        try
        {
            // show different error exceptions that you can throw
            if (url === undefined) throw Error.argumentUndefined('url');
```

```
            if (url === "") throw Error.argumentUndefined('url', "You cannot add an
url that is blank");
            if (url === null) throw Error.argumentNull('url');

            alert("Performing Get Web request.");
            var getPageUrl = "";
            // Instantiate the WebRequest object.
            var wRequest =  new Sys.Net.WebRequest();
            // Set the request Url.
            if (url != "")
            {
                getPageUrl = this._proxyPage + "?page=" + url;
            }
            alert(getPageUrl);
            wRequest.set_url(getPageUrl);
            // Set the request verb.
            wRequest.set_httpVerb("GET");
            // Set user's context
            wRequest.set_userContext("user's context");
            // Set the request handler.
            wRequest.add_completed(callbackFunction);
            // Execute the request.
            wRequest.invoke();
        }
        catch(e)
        {
            alert(e.message);
        }
    }
}

Samples.MyWebRequest.registerClass('Samples.MyWebRequest');
```

Keep in mind that you need to change the this._proxyPage to your own local web address
where the GetOutsideDomainPage.aspx file is located. The GetOutsideDomainPage.aspx
page will accept incoming requests for any URL and then make requests for that page and
return them to you.

2. Now, create a page called GetOutsideDomainPage.aspx or whatever you want to call it and
    put this code in the code-behind. This is an example of how to create a simple proxy service
    using a normal .aspx page. You obviously could add a lot to this, but for simplicity I have just
    made it work in a code-behind. It would be very easy to refactor from here.

```
protected void Page_Load(object sender, EventArgs e)
    {
        if (Request["page"] != null)
        {
            string pageUrl = Request["page"].ToString();
            string PageContents = this.GetFromURL(pageUrl);
            Response.Write(PageContents);
        }
    }
```

```
        public string GetFromURL(string url)
        {
            try
            {

                HttpWebRequest req = (HttpWebRequest)WebRequest.Create(url);
                req.AllowAutoRedirect = true;
                req.MaximumAutomaticRedirections = 3;
                req.UserAgent = "Mozilla/6.0 (MSIE 6.0; Windows NT 5.1;
.NET+CLR+1.1.4322)";
                req.KeepAlive = true;
                req.Timeout = 10000; // Timeout to 10 seconds
                // Get the stream from the returned web response
                HttpWebResponse webresponse = null;
                try
                {
                    webresponse = (HttpWebResponse)req.GetResponse();

                }
                catch (System.Net.WebException we)
                {
                    //remote url not found, 404, etc
                    return we.Message;
                }
                if (webresponse != null)
                {
                    // 1. Get the Stream Object from the response
                    Stream responseStream = webresponse.GetResponseStream();

                    // 2. Create a stream reader and associate it with the stream
object
                    StreamReader reader = new StreamReader(responseStream);
                    // 3. Read and return the entire stream
                    var responseString = reader.ReadToEnd();
                    reader.Dispose();
                    return responseString;
                }
                else
                {
                    return "No data found";
                }
            }
            catch (Exception ex)
            {
                return ex.Message;
            }
```

3.   Now create the web page that calls your MyWebRequest class. Notice that I put my JavaScript at the bottom of this page after everything else has been loaded. I ran into some issues of my $get('element') variables not being there yet when my globals executed. It would happen before the page rendered in the browser. It drove me nuts for an hour or two and then I realized

that the HTML elements and JavaScript libraries have to load before you can call or reference their objects. Now I realize that this why they created the `pageLoad` method I talked about earlier in the chapter. When you create a method called `pageLoad`, it will get called after the page and scripts are loaded. Hopefully that tip will save some people some time.

Here is the `WebRequestSample.aspx` page:

```
<%@ Page Language="C#" AutoEventWireup="true" CodeFile="WebRequestSample.aspx.cs"
Inherits="WebRequestSample" %>


<!DOCTYPE html PUBLIC "-//W3C//DTD XHTML 1.0 Transitional//EN"
"http://www.w3.org/TR/xhtml1/DTD/xhtml1-transitional.dtd">
<html xmlns="http://www.w3.org/1999/xhtml" >
    <head id="Head1" runat="server">

        <title> Custom WebRequest Proxy</title>
    </head>


    <body>

    <h2>Using WebRequest</h2>

        <form id="form1" runat="server">
            <asp:ScriptManager runat="server" ID="ScriptManagerId">
                <Scripts>
                    <asp:ScriptReference Path="MyWebRequest.js" />
                </Scripts>
            </asp:ScriptManager>

        <table>
            <tr align="left">
                <td>URL to request:</td>
                <td>
                    <asp:TextBox ID="TextBoxUrl" runat="server" Width="300"
Text="http://www.msn.com"></asp:TextBox>
                </td>
            </tr>
            <tr align="left">
                <td>Make GET Request:</td>
                <td>
                    <button id="Button1"
                        onclick="GetWebRequest()">GET</button>
                </td>
            </tr>
            <tr align="left">
                <td>Request Header:</td>
                <td>
                    <button id="Button7"
                        onclick="WebRequestHeader()">Header</button>
                </td>
```

```
                </tr>

         </table>


         <hr />
         <asp:UpdatePanel ID="UpdatePanelResults" runat="server">
         <ContentTemplate>

         </ContentTemplate>
         </asp:UpdatePanel>
         <div id="ResultId" style="background-color:Linen;"></div>


            </form>

   <script language="javascript" type="text/javascript">
         // globals
         var displayElement = $get("UpdatePanelResults");
         var textboxUrl = $get("TextBoxUrl");

         function GetWebRequest()
         {
             var MyWebRequest = new Samples.MyWebRequest();
             // $get("TextBoxUrl").value
             MyWebRequest.getFromOutsideUrl(textboxUrl.value,
OnWebRequestCompleted);

         }

         function OnWebRequestCompleted(executor, eventArgs)
         {
             if(executor.get_responseAvailable())
             {
                 alert("Received response");
                 var responseData = executor.get_responseData();

                 // cannot use innerHTML, will get unknown errors
                 if (document.all)
                         displayElement.innerText = responseData;
                 else
                 // Firefox
                         displayElement.textContent = responseData;
                         DisplayWebRequestStatus(executor);
                         DisplayWebRequestHeaders(executor);
                         DisplayWebRequestBody(executor);


             }
             else
```

```
            {
                if (executor.get_timedOut())
                    alert("Timed Out");
                else
                    if (executor.get_aborted())
                        alert("Aborted");
            }
        }


        // It displays the Web request status.
        function DisplayWebRequestStatus(executor)
        {
            displayElement.innerHTML +=
            "Status: [" +
            executor.get_statusCode() + " " +
            executor.get_statusText() + "]" + "<br/>"
        }
        // It displays Web request headers.
        function DisplayWebRequestHeaders(executor)
        {
            displayElement.innerHTML +=  "Headers: ";
            displayElement.innerHTML +=  executor.getAllResponseHeaders() + "<br/>";
         }

        // It displays the Web request body.
        function DisplayWebRequestBody(executor)
        {
            displayElement.innerHTML += "Body: ";
            if (document.all)
                displayElement.innerText += executor.get_responseData();
            else
                // Firefox
                displayElement.textContent += executor.get_responseData();
        }

    </script>
    </body>

</html>
```

In Figure 9-3 you can see the results from the web request put into the display element.

The reason I chose to put the response callback function in the web page is that it is much easier to modify UI logic inside the page you are modifying elements in. When I write these kinds of applications, I work much quicker when I create classes that are called from within the page where the logic of what to do with the data once received is also there. It makes it much easier to define element variables and modify them right inside the web page.

Figure 9-3

The Sys.Serialization Namespace

This namespace contains classes related to data serialization using JSON. You might not use this namepace much, but understanding how it works is a key to understanding how this AJAX architecture is set up.

Passing Complex Types Using JSON and Serialization

Sometimes it is very useful to pass a complex object to a web service and also return a complex object from the server. This allows you to write some very maintainable code both on the web service side and the JavaScript client side.

How this works is that you have to create a JSON object to pass to the web service. Now they make this very easy if you create the class in the web service and then reference it in the JavaScript. The serialization of the JavaScript happens automagically. Actually what they are doing that you don't see is using the `Sys.Serializer.JavaScriptSerializer` class. There are only two methods in this class and they are, as you might have guessed, `serialize` and `deserialize`. `serialize` converts the JavaScript object graph into a JSON string and `deserialize` converts the JSON string into a JavaScript object graph.

If you are not familiar with what a JSON object graph looks like, here is a very simple example:

```
{
"Year": 2007,
"Make": "BMW",
"Model": "325i",
"Colors": [
    "Grey",
    "Black",
    "Red"
    ]
}
```

So, if you wanted to you could call a normal web page that returns the object graph like the preceding one with code like the following:

```
var MyCar = Sys.Serialization.JavaScriptSerializer.deserialize(returnTextFromPage);

var MyMake = MyCar.Make;
var MyColorsArray = MyCar.Colors;
```

As you can see, this is much closer to the kind of code you actually like to write, except for the fact that it is not strongly typed. Some people do find that to be an advantage though.

If you do want to serialize and deserialize JavaScript objects into C# objects and the other way around, there is a great free open source utility that will do it at newtonsoft.com/products/json/.

Following is an example of how to serialize and deserialize a JavaScript object into a C# object and back again. First you need to create an .aspx page that will receive a JSON object and then look up the colors about that car and then return a JSON object back to the page:

```
using System;
using System.Data;
using System.Configuration;
using System.Collections;
using System.Web;
using System.Web.Security;
using System.Web.UI;
using System.Web.UI.WebControls;
using System.Web.UI.WebControls.WebParts;
using System.Web.UI.HtmlControls;
using Newtonsoft.Json;

public partial class json_ReturnCarObject : System.Web.UI.Page
{
    protected void Page_Load(object sender, EventArgs e)
    {

        if (Request["JsonCarObject"] != null)
        {
            string JavasScriptInput = Request["JsonCarObject"];
            Car DeserializedCar =
```

```
(Car)JavaScriptConvert.DeserializeObject(JavasScriptInput, typeof(Car));
            Car MyCar = new Car();
            MyCar.LoadColors(DeserializedCar);
            string output = JavaScriptConvert.SerializeObject(MyCar);

            Response.ContentType = "Content-Type: text/javascript";
            Response.Write(output);
        }

    }
}
// here is the car class

using System;

/// <summary>
/// Summary description for Car
/// </summary>
public class Car
{
    private string _Make;

 public string Make
 {
        get { return _Make;}
        set { _Make = value;}
 }

    private string _Model;

 public string Model
 {
        get { return _Model;}
        set { _Model = value;}
 }

    private string _Year;

 public int Year
 {
        get { return _Year;}
        set { _Year = value;}
 }

    private string[] _Colors;

    public string[] Colors
    {
        get { return _Colors; }
        set { _Colors = value; }
    }

public Car()
 {
```

```
    }

    public void LoadColors(Car MyCar)
    {
        // example of checking database for colors of car
        // string colors[] = DataAccessLayer.Car.GetCarColors(MyCar.Year,
MyCar.Make, MyCar.Model);

        this.Make = MyCar.Make;
        this.Model = MyCar.Model;
        this.Year = MyCar.Year;
        // Manually Add colors to Colors property for example
        this.Colors = new string[] { "Red", "Silver", "Green", "Black" };


    }
}
```

This uses a simple car class that has a method to look up in the database what colors that particular car would come in. Say you want to narrow it down in the future to the trim level. All you would need to do is add the trim property on both ends and then you could check for that value on the server and do a more precise lookup. This would be accomplished without having to add a parameter to the methods on the client or the server.

Here is the .aspx page that has the client JavaScript code that calls the .aspx page that generates the JSON object. Notice it uses the same Samples.MyWebRequest class from earlier to get the response from the web request.

```
<%@ Page Language="C#" AutoEventWireup="true"
CodeFile="JsonDeserialization.aspx.cs" Inherits="json_JsonDeserialization" %>

<!DOCTYPE html PUBLIC "-//W3C//DTD XHTML 1.0 Transitional//EN"
"http://www.w3.org/TR/xhtml1/DTD/xhtml1-transitional.dtd">

<html xmlns="http://www.w3.org/1999/xhtml" >
<head id="Head1" runat="server">
    <title>Deserialization Example</title>

</head>
<body>
    <form id="form1" runat="server">
        <asp:ScriptManager runat="server" ID="ScriptManagerId">
        <Scripts>
                <asp:ScriptReference Path="MyWebRequest.js" />
            </Scripts>
        </asp:ScriptManager>

        <input type="button" id="btn" onclick="return GetWebRequest();" value="Get
Colors" />

        <asp:UpdatePanel ID="UpdatePanelResults" runat="server">
            <ContentTemplate>
            </ContentTemplate>
        </asp:UpdatePanel>
    <div>
```

```
        </div>

        </form>
        <script language="javascript" type="text/javascript">
        var displayElement = $get("UpdatePanelResults");

        function GetWebRequest()
            {
                var MyWebRequest = new Samples.MyWebRequest();

                var baseUrl =
"http://localhost:64702/AJAXTestsWebsite/json/ReturnCarObject.aspx";
                var jsonCarObject = '{"Year": "2007","Make": "BMW","Model": "325i"}';
                var newUrl = baseUrl + "?JsonCarObject=" + jsonCarObject;
                MyWebRequest.getFromLocalUrl(newUrl, OnWebRequestCompleted);

            }

        function OnWebRequestCompleted(executor, eventArgs)
        {
            if(executor.get_responseAvailable())
            {
                alert("Received response");
                // Clear the previous results.
                var responseData = executor.get_responseData();

                var Car =
Sys.Serialization.JavaScriptSerializer.deserialize(responseData);

                displayElement.innerText = "The " + Car.Year + " " + Car.Make + " "
+ Car.Model + " has these colors: " + Car.Colors;

            }
            else
            {
                if (executor.get_timedOut())
                    alert("Timed Out");
                else
                    if (executor.get_aborted())
                        alert("Aborted");
            }
        }
        </script>
</body>
</html>
```

Figure 9-4 shows that I have an alert that shows what the URL looks like that is posted back to the server.

What you have just learned is how the underlying magic works. You do not need to call web services in order to talk back and forth to the server. When you are calling web services in the AJAX Library, underneath it is actually doing the deserialization for you. The default protocol is JSON with the AJAX Library.

You may be asking yourself why you would ever do it this way instead of the web service way. Well, sometimes you may not have the ability to create web services or you have code that is already spitting out JSON objects, but you want to move to the AJAX Library and do not want to have to rewrite anything.

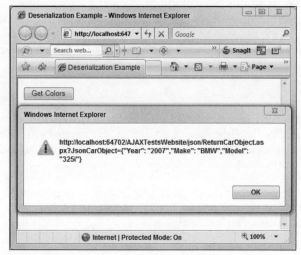

Figure 9-4

Event Handling in the Microsoft AJAX Library

Several useful event handling techniques are built into the framework. You can easily add handlers for events such as a mouse click event or a key press event. A quick and easy way to add a handler event is to use the $addHandler method found in the global shortcuts. This is an alias for Sys.UI.DomEvent .addHandler.

Here is an example of how you would use it:

```
$addHandler($get("Button1"), "click", processEvent );

function processEvent(eventElement)
{
        alert("Processed Event");

}
```

The eventName *parameter should not include the* on *prefix. For example, specify* click *instead of* onclick.

This is a simple example, but it shows how simple it is to add an event handler to an HTML element on the page.

After adding an event handler, you can unhook an event using the `$removeHandler` method. For instance, you should do that from your dispose methods to break circular references between your JavaScript objects and the DOM and to prevent memory leaks. Have you ever seen you IE process using way more memory than it should? Maybe you were on a page that had some JavaScript memory leaks. You want to make sure this is not your page that is causing this problem. You may also want to change an event attached to a button dynamically and maybe remove the event handler after it has fired the first time.

Here is an example of how you would remove an event handler using the shortcut method:

```
// $removeHandler(element, eventName, handler);
$removeHandler($get("Button1"), "click", processEvent);
```

In the real world you usually put an `onclick="javascriptfunction()"` inside of the element properties on the HTML page. Now with the use of the `$addHandler` method you can more easily attach handlers to events dynamically, which will produce cleaner code. This also allows you to change the interface at runtime and attach handlers to events as you need them.

In a lot of cases I still prefer setting the `onclick` property of the element in the actual page, but there are times when it is so much smarter to add the handler at runtime. This allows you to change the event handler of each event based on certain rules.

Summary

This chapter has covered several of the underlying classes of the AJAX framework that are used to do a lot of the plumbing of AJAX. This chapter covered the following:

❑ The `Sys` namespace and its classes

❑ How to use the `StringBuilder` class

❑ How to make your own web requests using the `Sys.WebRequest` class

❑ How to send complex JSON objects back and forth using serialization

❑ How to use event handling in the AJAX Library

Now that you understand how to make these requests at a lower level, you can customize your application in almost any way you see fit. The information presented on why and how to create reusable JavaScript classes will help your development in JavaScript and make it much more fun to do. You noticed how in the examples that there was some code reuse using the `Samples.MyWebRequest` class. Feel free to add to that class functions that you think might be useful. It is far from complete and needs work, but is a decent place to start.

You also learned how event handling will help to keep your code maintainable when encountering complex dynamic scenarios, especially when writing your own controls and behaviors. It is also very important to remove the handlers because your web application will create a memory leak in the user's browser. Handlers are your friend and you should try to use them when possible.

When you understand how things work beneath the surface, you will have better ideas and multiple solutions to the same problem. It also builds confidence that you can write whatever you want and can fix it and debug it. I have a feeling that there are going to be some very cool JavaScript applications once this stuff goes mainstream.

User Interface Design

By this point in the book you should have a good understanding of how ASP.NET 2.0 AJAX makes it easy to provide functionally enhanced user interfaces to end users. This chapter focuses more on the visual enhancements that ASP.NET 2.0 AJAX provides and explains how they work. It just so happens that one of the best visual enhancements is also one of the best functional enhancements. ASP.NET AJAX asynchronous postbacks are not only useful and efficient, but also pleasing to the eye. With a little effort, however, they can be made even more pleasing. Here's a summary of the topics covered in this chapter:

❑ Understanding the differences between asynchronous and synchronous postbacks

❑ Notifying users during asynchronous postbacks

❑ Using the `UpdatePanelAnimation` extender

❑ Providing feedback during ongoing operations

❑ Aborting operations

❑ Handling exceptions gracefully

Asynchronous vs. Synchronous Postbacks

ASP.NET 1.x is considered to be synchronous. From a user's perspective, "synchronous" means that he or she clicks a submit button and the page stops responding while the browser makes a round trip to the server for a new version of the entire page and then redraws it element by element. Displaying custom status bars or animated .gifs is usually not feasible during this postback process. This process happens even in situations where only a single element on the page needs updating. This technique lacks efficiency and annoys users who have to wait around for postbacks to complete.

From a programmer's perspective, the term "synchronous" usually means that processing on the current thread stops until a function call returns. In situations where this is undesirable, multithreading is often used to execute function calls on a separate helper thread. The current thread is often notified of completion by having a specified function "called back" upon the termination of the helper thread. In an ASP.NET environment, such an asynchronous solution may be a good way to make efficient use of server resources, but it does little to pacify a user who is sitting around waiting for the final response from a postback to the server.

Although classic multithreading techniques work well for addressing a programmer's asynchronous needs, AJAX provides the solution we've all been seeking for addressing a web user's asynchronous demands. It essentially allows web applications to respond more like Windows applications do.

ASP.NET AJAX provides asynchronous communication with the server, meaning that data is passed transparently in the background, allowing the page to remain responsive and dynamically refresh only pieces of the page as needed. Such asynchronous postbacks (also known as partial-page postbacks) are a great way to keep a responsive interface in front of the user at all times.

The primary technology used to provide this functionality is AJAX, which stands for Asynchronous JavaScript And XML. As is standard with most classic AJAX solutions, the built-in browser object XMLHTTP is used by client-side JavaScript code to execute server requests instead of doing old-fashioned full-page postbacks.

The XMLHTTP object is essentially the core of AJAX. Although you can use this object directly via JavaScript, ASP.NET AJAX encapsulates such calls so that you don't need to use it directly. Instead, you need only concentrate on using the ASP.NET AJAX object model, and all the messy networking functionality is handled automatically.

> It's worth noting that Internet Explorer uses the XMLHTTP object, whereas other browsers use the similar XMLHttpRequest object. However, the ASP.NET AJAX framework abstracts the minor differences between these two models, so you needn't worry about such trivia.

User Notification of Processing

It's quite nice that ASP.NET AJAX allows the user to keep working with a web page even while it's communicating with the server in the background. However, it's often necessary (or at least desirable) that users be informed of currently processing operations. Sometimes you might even need to block the user from interacting with all or parts of the page during such operations. In such a case you may be tempted to resort to a standard full-page postback instead of using AJAX, but that still results in an ugly user experience while the page blanks out and gives no real indication to the user of what's happening or how long it might take.

Conversely, a properly developed Windows application would likely display some kind of progress bar to give feedback to the user during such long-running operations. That's exactly the kind of rich user feedback that the `UpdateProgress` control provides. The `UpdateProgress` control has the unique properties defined in the following table.

Property	Type	Description
AssociatedUpdatePanelID	String	An `UpdateProgress` control can optionally be associated with a single specific `UpdatePanel` control. To enable such functionality, set this property to the ID of the `UpdatePanel`.
DisplayAfter	Integer	An `UpdateProgress` control can optionally be set to only appear if a partial-page postback takes longer than a specified time period. To enable such functionality, set this property to the number of milliseconds desired for the delayed appearance.
DynamicLayout	Boolean	Determines whether space should be preserved on the page for the `UpdateProgress` control or whether space should be created dynamically at runtime on the client side, as needed. The default value is `True`.

The `UpdateProgress` control can be defined as follows:

```
<asp:UpdateProgress ID="UpdateProgress1" runat="server"
    AssociatedUpdatePanelID="UpdatePanel1" DynamicLayout="True">
    <ProgressTemplate>
      Update in progress...
    </ProgressTemplate>
</asp:UpdateProgress>
```

Essentially, the `UpdateProgress` control outputs the contents of the `ProgressTemplate` into a `div` element, and automatically (using client-side script) makes the `div` element visible only while an `UpdatePanel` is doing a partial-page postback.

Using the preceding declaration, the "Update in Progress..." message will appear when `UpdatePanel1` initiates a partial-page postback. When the partial-page postback is complete and the controls within `UpdatePanel1` have been updated, this progress indicator is automatically hidden. If the `AssociatedUpdatePanelID` property is left blank, the `UpdateProgress` control activates for every `UpdatePanel` on the page, not just `UpdatePanel1` as is specified here. If the `AssociatedUpdatePanelID` property is set to an invalid control name or the `ProgressTemplate` is empty, no progress indicator will ever be shown.

In Design mode the page looks roughly like Figure 10-1.

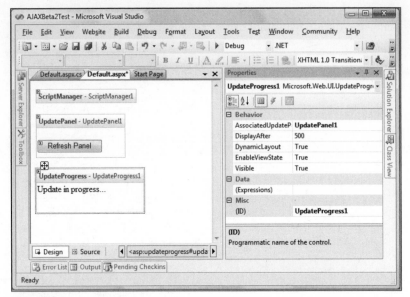

Figure 10-1

Try It Out   Using the UpdateProgress Control

1. Create a new Visual Studio ASP.NET AJAX-enabled web site.

2. Add a `ScriptManager` to a new web form:

```
<asp:ScriptManager ID="ScriptManager1" runat="server"/>
```

3. Add an `UpdatePanel` control to the web form, and place a `Button` control inside of it:

```
<asp:UpdatePanel ID="UpdatePanel1" runat="server">
    <ContentTemplate>
        <asp:Button ID="Button1" runat="server"
        Text="Button" OnClick="Button1_Click" />
</ContentTemplate>
    </asp:UpdatePanel>
```

4. Add a delay to the button's server-side click event:

```
protected void Button1_Click(object sender, EventArgs e)
{
    System.Threading.Thread.Sleep(3000); //Simulate processing
}
```

5. Add an `UpdateProgress` control to the web form. Add some text to its `ProgressTemplate`, such as "Update In Progress…":

```
<asp:UpdateProgress ID="UpdateProgress1" runat="server">
    <ProgressTemplate>
```

```
                    Update in Progress...
                </ProgressTemplate>
            </asp:UpdateProgress>
```

6. Run the project, click the button, and observe how the UpdateProgress notification text automatically appears during the asynchronous postback.

How It Works

The Button control inside the UpdatePanel control invokes a server-side sleep event. Normally, you'd never intentionally cause an artificial delay such as this, but in this case it acts as a good simulation of server-side processing and allows for a nice clean look at the display from the UpdateProgress control during the asynchronous postback.

———————————

If an UpdatePanel is nested (placed within) another UpdatePanel, an update of the parent UpdatePanel will show all UpdateProgress controls assigned to the parent UpdatePanel and child UpdatePanel. However, if only the child UpdatePanel is updating, only its UpdateProgress control will be shown and the parent's UpdatePanel (if any) will not be shown.

Any HTML content can be placed inside the ProgressTemplate element; for example, an animated gif could be displayed like this:

```
<asp:UpdateProgress ID="UpdateProgress1" runat="server"
    AssociatedUpdatePanelID="UpdatePanel1" DynamicLayout="True">
    <ProgressTemplate>
        <img src="MyAnimated.gif" alt="In Progress..." />
    </ProgressTemplate>
</asp:UpdateProgress>
```

Using the previous declarations, whenever a partial postback occurs the user is presented with a friendly animated processing indicator. This kind of responsive feedback is virtually impossible during old-fashioned full-page postbacks.

All the previous code in this chapter works great when all relevant controls are placed within an UpdatePanel control. However, there may be times when you need or want to use the UpdateProgress control in other ways, such as interacting with it directly using client-side code.

For example, if a Button control is added to the previous example (outside the bounds of UpdatePanel1) and its click event is configured to be a trigger for UpdatePanel1, the UpdateProgress control won't be automatically shown during the partial-page postback. Another case in which the UpdateProgress control fails to show automatically would be when you're not using an UpdatePanel. Virtually any web control can be configured to trigger asynchronous postbacks, but the UpdateProgress control won't be automatically activated unless it is partnered with an UpdatePanel control.

You can activate the UpdateProgress control manually in such scenarios with a small amount of code. Because the UpdateProgress control is rendered as a div element at runtime, its Visibility or Display styles can be toggled with client-side code just like any other div. This may sound like standard stuff if you're an experienced JavaScript developer, but there are a few ASP.NET AJAX tidbits you'll need to know to get things working optimally.

In some situations it doesn't make much sense to use the UpdateProgress control at all. For example, if you have no UpdatePanels on your page, there is little point in having an UpdateProgress control on the page because its primary function is to partner with UpdatePanel controls. In such a case you might be better off just using a standard div (or similar element) instead of the UpdateProgress control.

The trick to displaying any kind of processing notification is to hook into the correct client-side events so that the visibility of the element can be toggled at the appropriate times. The PageRequestManager's beginRequest and endRequest events are ideal for this scenario because they are fired just before and just after all asynchronous postbacks, respectively.

First, you'll need to create a couple of JavaScript functions to handle the beginRequest and endRequest events. The following code does just that:

```
function beginRequestHandler(sender, args)
{
    $get("UpdateProgress1").style.display = "block";
}

function EndRequestHandler(sender, args)
{
    $get("UpdateProgress1").style.display = "none";
}
```

When the BeginRequestHandler function is called, it displays the UpdateProgress control, and when the EndRequestHandler function is called, it returns the UpdateProgress control to its invisible state.

Now all that's left to do is to explain to ASP.NET AJAX that these custom functions are intended to handle the beginRequest and endRequest events. A few more lines of JavaScript are all that's needed to accomplish that goal:

```
var prm = Sys.WebForms.PageRequestManager.getInstance();
prm.add_beginRequest(BeginRequestHandler);
prm.add_endRequest(EndRequestHandler);
```

The preceding code gets an instance of the PageRequestManager and then instructs it to call your two new custom functions in response to beginRequest and endRequest events.

The following code shows the complete page with the JavaScript highlighted:

```
<!DOCTYPE html PUBLIC "-//W3C//DTD XHTML 1.1//EN"
"http://www.w3.org/TR/xhtml11/DTD/xhtml11.dtd">
<html xmlns="http://www.w3.org/1999/xhtml">
<head id="Head1" runat="server">
  <title>Manual Progress Page</title>
</head>
<body>
    <form id="form1" runat="server">
        <asp:ScriptManager ID="ScriptManager1" runat="server" />
        <div>
        <asp:UpdatePanel ID="UpdatePanel1" runat="server" UpdateMode="Conditional">
            <ContentTemplate>
                <%=DateTime.Now.ToString() %>
```

```
            <br />
            <asp:Button ID="Button2" runat="server" Text="Refresh Panel" />
        </ContentTemplate>
        <Triggers>
         <asp:AsyncPostBackTrigger ControlID="Button1" EventName="Click" />
        </Triggers>
    </asp:UpdatePanel>
    <asp:UpdateProgress ID="UpdateProgress1" runat="server"
        AssociatedUpdatePanelID="UpdatePanel1">
        <ProgressTemplate>
            Update in progress...
        </ProgressTemplate>
    </asp:UpdateProgress>
    <br />
    <asp:Button ID="Button1" runat="server" Text="Button" />
    <br />
    </div>
</form>
<script type="text/javascript" language="javascript">
    function BeginRequestHandler(sender, args)
    {
        $get("UpdateProgress1").style.display = "block";
    }

    function EndRequestHandler(sender, args)
    {
        $get("UpdateProgress1").style.display = "none";
    }

    var prm = Sys.WebForms.PageRequestManager.getInstance();
    prm.add_beginRequest(BeginRequestHandler);
    prm.add_endRequest(EndRequestHandler);
</script>

</body>
</html>
```

Animating Asynchronous Postbacks

Although it's nice to be able to display static text and animated images during partial-page postbacks, the ASP.NET AJAX Control Toolkit (detailed in Chapter 6) provides the capability to declare custom animations that are executed on-the-fly in response to predefined events.

Although the Toolkit provides a variety of controls and control extenders, the UpdatePanelAnimation extender is one of the most useful for providing feedback during partial-page postbacks.

Control extenders enhance existing controls, providing them with extra functionality. The UpdatePanelAnimation extender is intended to enhance the UpdatePanel control with the ability to execute animations in reaction to its OnUpdating and OnUpdated events. The OnUpdating event is raised just before a partial-page postback is sent to the server, and the OnUpdated event is raised after the server's response is received by the client. An animation can be linked to one or both of these events.

The following page is a variation on the previous examples. This example includes an UpdatePanelAnimation extender that fades the target UpdatePanel to invisible as the partial-page postback begins, and fades it back in again once the postback is complete:

```
<%@ Page Language="C#" %>
<%@ Register Assembly="AjaxControlToolkit"
Namespace="AjaxControlToolkit" TagPrefix="cc1" %>

<!DOCTYPE html PUBLIC "-//W3C//DTD XHTML 1.0 Transitional//EN"
"http://www.w3.org/TR/xhtml1/DTD/xhtml1-transitional.dtd">

<script runat="server">

    protected void Page_Load(object sender, EventArgs e)
    {
        Label1.Text = DateTime.Now.ToString();
        if (this.IsPostBack)
        {
            //Simulate processing
            System.Threading.Thread.Sleep(3000);
        }
    }
</script>

<html xmlns="http://www.w3.org/1999/xhtml">
<head runat="server">
    <title>Untitled Page</title>
</head>
<body>
    <form id="form1" runat="server">
        <div>
            <asp:ScriptManager ID="ScriptManager1" runat="server">
            </asp:ScriptManager>
            <asp:UpdatePanel ID="UpdatePanel1" runat="server">
                <ContentTemplate>
                        <asp:Label ID="Label1" runat="server" Text="Label"/>
                        <br />
                        <asp:Button ID="Button1" runat="server"
                        Text="Server Refresh" />
                </ContentTemplate>
            </asp:UpdatePanel>
        </div>
        <cc1:UpdatePanelAnimationExtender
            ID="UpdatePanelAnimationExtender1" runat="server"
            TargetControlID="UpdatePanel1">
            <Animations>
                <OnUpdating>
                    <FadeOut Duration=".5" Fps="20" />
                </OnUpdating>
                <OnUpdated>
                    <FadeIn Duration=".5" Fps="20" />
                </OnUpdated>
            </Animations>
        </cc1:UpdatePanelAnimationExtender>
```

```
        </form>
    </body>
    </html>
```

As is common with all extenders, the `TargetControlID` property specifies which control is to be extended. In this case the `UpdatePanel` named `UpdatePanel1` is the target of the animation. As the partial-page update begins, a fade-out animation executes for half a second, at a rate of approximately 20 frames per second (FPS). When the response is received from the server, the `UpdatePanel` gradually fades back into visibility over the same time period and with the same frames per second.

Although a variety of animations are available besides fade in and out, the `UpdatePanelAnimation` extender supports their initiation only via the `OnUpdating` and `OnUpdated` events.

The following declaration fades the background color of the `UpdatePanel` to gray during a partial-page postback, giving it a disabled look. When the server response is received, the background color fades back to the original white color:

```
<cc1:UpdatePanelAnimationExtender
    ID="UpdatePanelAnimationExtender1" runat="server"
    TargetControlID="UpdatePanel1">
    <Animations>
        <OnUpdating>
            <Color
              Duration="1"
              StartValue="#FFFFFF"
              EndValue="#999999"
              Property="style"
              PropertyKey="backgroundColor"
            />
        </OnUpdating>
        <OnUpdated>
            <Color
              Duration="1"
              StartValue="#999999"
              EndValue="#FFFFFF"
              Property="style"
              PropertyKey="backgroundColor"
            />
        </OnUpdated>
    </Animations>
</cc1:UpdatePanelAnimationExtender>
```

The color animation has several properties to specify the starting and ending colors and how long it will take to fade from the starting color to the ending color. In this example, `PropertyKey` specifies that the background's color should be affected by this animation (instead of the font color, for example.)

More than a dozen different animations are available for use in the Toolkit in addition to the fade and color animations shown previously. In case that's not enough, these animations can be combined in a variety of ways to create unique and custom animations. For example, the following declaration declares a sequence of animations:

```
<cc1:UpdatePanelAnimationExtender
    ID="UpdatePanelAnimationExtender1" runat="server"
```

```
         TargetControlID="UpdatePanel1">
         <Animations>
             <OnUpdating>
                 <Sequence>
                     <Color
                         Duration="1"
                         StartValue="#FFFFFF"
                         EndValue="#0000FF"
                         Property="style"
                         PropertyKey="backgroundColor"
                     />
                     <Color
                         Duration="1"
                         StartValue="#0000FF"
                         EndValue="#FF0000"
                         Property="style"
                         PropertyKey="backgroundColor"
                     />
                 </Sequence>
             </OnUpdating>
             <OnUpdated>
                 <Sequence>
                     <Color
                         Duration="1"
                         StartValue="#FF0000"
                         EndValue="#0000FF"
                         Property="style"
                         PropertyKey="backgroundColor"
                     />
                     <Color
                         Duration="1"
                         StartValue="#0000FF"
                         EndValue="#FFFFFF"
                         Property="style"
                         PropertyKey="backgroundColor"
                     />
                 </Sequence>
             </OnUpdated>
         </Animations>
     </cc1:UpdatePanelAnimationExtender>
```

Similar to the previous example, this declaration fades the background color of the specified `UpdatePanel` to blue (#0000FF) when the partial-page update begins. However, once that animation completes the sequence then continues to change the color to red (#FF0000). When the client receives the server's response, the animation sequence reverses, changing from red to blue and then back to the original color of white (#FFFFFF).

Using sequences such as this, animations can be strung together in a nearly infinite variety of ways. Alternatively, animations can be configured to run conditionally or in parallel instead of sequentially.

See Chapters 6 and 7 for more information about the AJAX Control Toolkit, animations, and extenders.

Providing Feedback during Ongoing Operations

Although the `UpdateProgress` control is great for informing users about a pending partial-page post-back, it's no help for displaying the progress of a long-lasting, ongoing operation.

For example, a button click might trigger a series of database updates on a background thread or Windows service. If this process is time consuming, it's nice to be able to keep the user informed of the ongoing progress of this operation.

Although no built-in control handles this situation, it doesn't take much to put together a solution by gluing together a few controls and sprinkling in a little code.

Try It Out   Creating Custom Progress Bars

The following page uses an `UpdatePanel`, `Button`, `Label`, `Timer`, and a `div` nested inside another `div`:

```
<%@ Page Language="C#" %>

<!DOCTYPE html PUBLIC "-//W3C//DTD XHTML 1.0 Transitional//EN"
"http://www.w3.org/TR/xhtml1/DTD/xhtml1-transitional.dtd">

<script runat="server">
    protected void Timer1_Tick(object sender, EventArgs e)
    {
        int Status = GetStatus();
        ProgressDiv.Style["width"] = Status.ToString() + "%";
        lblStatus.Text = ProgressDiv.Style["width"];
    }

    protected void btnSubmit_Click(object sender, EventArgs e)
    {
        //In a real project this event might also
        //kick off the long operation on a background thread
        //or Windows service.
        Timer1.Enabled = true;
    }

    //Simulates getting the status of a long-running process.
    //Normally this might get a value from a file or database
    //that represents the current status of an ongoing operation.
    protected int GetStatus()
    {
        int Status = 0;
        if (Session["status"] != null)
        {
            Status = (int)Session["status"];
        }
```

```
            Status += 10;
            Session["status"] = Status;
            if (Status >= 100)
            {
                Timer1.Enabled = false;
                Session["status"] = 0;
            }
            return Status;
        }

</script>

<html xmlns="http://www.w3.org/1999/xhtml" >
<head runat="server">
    <title>Untitled Page</title>
</head>
<body>
    <form id="form1" runat="server">
    <div>
        <asp:ScriptManager ID="ScriptManager1" runat="server">
        </asp:ScriptManager>
            <asp:UpdatePanel ID="UpdatePanel1" runat="server">
            <ContentTemplate>
                    <asp:Button ID="btnSubmit" runat="server"
                    Text="Submit" OnClick="btnSubmit_Click" />
                    <div style="text-align:center;">
                        <asp:Label ID="lblStatus" runat="server" Width="200px"/>
                    </div>
            <div style="width:200px; border-right: black 1px ridge;
            border-top: black 1px ridge; border-left: black 1px ridge;
            border-bottom: black 1px ridge;">
                <div runat="server" id="ProgressDiv"
                style="width:1%;background-color: blue;"> 
                </div>
            </div>
            <asp:Timer ID="Timer1" runat="server" Interval="2000"
                OnTick="Timer1_Tick" Enabled="False"/>
                </ContentTemplate>
                </asp:UpdatePanel>
    </div>
        <br />
         
    </form>
</body>
</html>
```

How It Works

When the user clicks the button, the timer is enabled and the start of the ongoing operation is simulated. Normally this background operation might run on a separate thread or in another process such as a Windows service. This background operation must periodically update its status in a location where

ASP.NET can check it, such as in a file or database. The `GetStatus` function simulates such a check, even though in this simple example it actually just increments a session variable.

The `Timer1_Tick` event calls the `GetStatus` function and updates the width of the `ProgressDiv` element. This `ProgressDiv` element has its background color set to blue, and it's nested inside another `div` with a visible border. Together these two `div`s look like a standard Windows progress bar at run-time. As the timer ticks and the `ProgressDiv`'s width increases, the progress bar appears to advance every time the `UpdatePanel` refreshes, as shown in Figure 10-2.

Using techniques like this, you can keep the user up-to-date about the progress of long-running, ongoing operations.

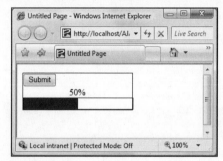

Figure 10-2

Aborting Operations

Users like to be in the driver's seat. They don't like to sit around twiddling their thumbs during long-running operations without an option to cancel the request if they feel it's taking too long to be worth their time. Therefore, a cancel button of some kind is essential for a user-friendly web application.

The `PageRequestManager` exposes the required method for aborting partial-page postbacks. Its `abortPostBack` method can be called to immediately cancel the partial postback operation:

```
Sys.WebForms.PageRequestManager.getInstance().abortPostBack();
```

The following page displays a clickable hyperlink during partial-page postbacks that allows a user to cancel the pending transaction, which also immediately hides the `UpdatePanel`:

```
<%@ Page Language="C#" %>

<!DOCTYPE html PUBLIC "-//W3C//DTD XHTML 1.0 Transitional//EN"
"http://www.w3.org/TR/xhtml1/DTD/xhtml1-transitional.dtd">
```

```
<script runat="server">
    protected void Page_Load(object sender, EventArgs e)
    {
        Label1.Text = DateTime.Now.ToString();
        if (this.IsPostBack)
        {
            //Simulate processing
            System.Threading.Thread.Sleep(3000);
        }
    }
</script>

<html xmlns="http://www.w3.org/1999/xhtml" >
<head runat="server">
    <title>Untitled Page</title>
</head>
<body>
    <form id="form1" runat="server">
    <asp:ScriptManager ID="ScriptManager1" runat="server"/>
    <div style="width:200px;border-right: black thin outset; border-top: black thin
outset; border-left: black thin outset; border-bottom: black thin outset;">
        <asp:UpdatePanel ID="UpdatePanel1" runat="server">
            <ContentTemplate>
                <asp:Label ID="Label1" runat="server" Text="Label"></asp:Label>
                <br />
                <asp:Button ID="Button1" runat="server" Text="Server Refresh" />
            </ContentTemplate>
        </asp:UpdatePanel>
    </div>
        <br />
        <asp:UpdateProgress ID="UpdateProgress1" runat="server"
        AssociatedUpdatePanelID="UpdatePanel1">
            <ProgressTemplate>
                <asp:Label ID="Label2" runat="server" Text="Updating..."/>
                <br />
              <div style="color: blue;cursor:hand; text-decoration: underline;"
onclick="Sys.WebForms.PageRequestManager.getInstance().abortPostBack();"
                >
                <asp:Label ID="Label3" runat="server" Text="Cancel"/>
                <br />
                </div>
            </ProgressTemplate>
        </asp:UpdateProgress>
    </form>
</body>
</html>
```

This is a fairly standard example page with a ScriptManager, UpdatePanel, and UpdateProgress
control. A standard ASP.NET Button and Label control are placed inside the UpdatePanel to trigger
the partial-page postback and display the current server time, respectively. There are only two lines of
server-side code: one to update the label with the current time and another that simulates a longer running server operation. (Normally, you'd never put an artificial delay like this in production code, but it
serves well for the purposes of this demonstration.)

Notice the highlighted line that calls the client-side `abortPostBack` method when the Cancel label is clicked. This is all that's required to cancel a pending asynchronous operation. In this case it's cancelled in response to a user's click, but it could be just as easily be called in response to any other logical client-side trigger that you could imagine. Figure 10-3 shows the page in action at runtime.

Figure 10-3

In the previous example, a request was sent to the server but the user is allowed to cancel out, effectively ignoring any response that may have eventually been generated from the server. In other words, the request was initiated but was cancelled before it finished.

It's also possible to cancel a pending partial postback operation before it even starts — from within the client-side `initializeRequest` event. Because the `initializeRequest` event is raised before any data is sent to the server, at this point it is possible to cancel the request and prevent anything from being sent across the wire. From the server's perspective it's as if nothing ever happened.

To do this, simply set the `initializeRequest`'s `Cancel` argument to `true`. For example, the following example ensures that only one partial postback operation is active at a time.

Try It Out   Cancelling Duplicate Asynchronous Postbacks

1. Create a new Visual Studio ASP.NET AJAX-enabled web site.

2. Add a `ScriptManager` to a new web form:

```
<asp:ScriptManager ID="ScriptManager1" runat="server"/>
```

3. Add an `UpdatePanel` control to the web form, and place a `Button` control inside of it:

```
<asp:UpdatePanel ID="UpdatePanel1" runat="server">
    <ContentTemplate>
```

```
        <asp:Button ID="Button1" runat="server"
        Text="Button" OnClick="Button1_Click" />
</ContentTemplate>
    </asp:UpdatePanel>
```

4. Add a delay to the button's server-side click event:

```
protected void Button1_Click(object sender, EventArgs e)
{
    System.Threading.Thread.Sleep(3000); //Simulate processing
}
```

5. Add an `UpdateProgress` control to the web form. Add some text to its `ProgressTemplate`, such as "Update In Progress...":

```
<asp:UpdateProgress ID="UpdateProgress1" runat="server">
    <ProgressTemplate>
        Update in Progress...
    </ProgressTemplate>
</asp:UpdateProgress>
```

6. Add the following JavaScript code block to the end of the HTML page:

```
<script type="text/javascript" language="javascript">
  var prm = Sys.WebForms.PageRequestManager.getInstance();
  prm.add_initializeRequest(CheckRequest);

function CheckRequest(sender, e)
  {
    if (prm.get_isInAsyncPostBack())
    {
      e.set_cancel(true);
      alert('request cancelled - another operation is already in progress.');
    }
  }
</script>
```

7. Run the page and click the button. During the asynchronous postback (while the "Update in Progress" message is displayed), click the button again to cause a second asynchronous postback.

How It Works

The JavaScript `If` block (in step 6) checks to see whether another asynchronous operation is already in progress. If so, the new pending asynchronous operation is cancelled and the user is informed. (It's worth noting that the framework inherently ensures that only one postback is active at a time, but normally it's the first postback that's cancelled, and the user is not notified.) Figure 10-4 shows this code functioning at runtime.

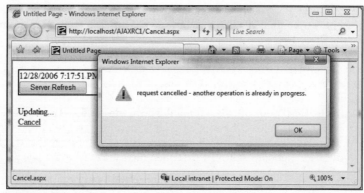

Figure 10-4

Gracefully Handling Exceptions

By this point in the book you should have a fairly good understanding of how ASP.NET AJAX works under normal conditions, but what about when things go wrong?

In any complex software system glitches can occur from time to time, both expected ones and unanticipated ones. Luckily, ASP.NET AJAX has a rich set of error-handling features that enable you to plan for such unfortunate incidents and handle them gracefully.

The `ScriptManager` component has several members that are useful for dealing with server-side exceptions during a partial-page postback. These members are listed in the following table.

Exception Member	Type	Description
AllowCustomErrorsRedirect	Property (Boolean)	If set to its default value of `True`, exceptions during partial-page postbacks cause the user to be redirected to the page specified by the `defaultRedirect` attribute of the `customErrors` element in the `web.config` file.
AsyncPostBackErrorMessage	Property (String)	Gets or sets the error message that will be sent to the client in response to a server-side exception during a partial-page postback.
AsyncPostBackError	Event	This server-side event is called when an unhandled exception occurs during a partial-page postback. It's a good place to set the `AsyncPostBackErrorMessage` property.

249

The ASP.NET 2.0 `customErrors` section of the `web.config` is unchanged by ASP.NET AJAX. This `web.config` element is used by ASP.NET AJAX in several different ways depending on how it's configured and how the preceding properties are set.

When an exception is thrown during a partial-page postback, there are several ways the error can be handled:

❑ **A message box (alert) pops up, displaying the error message** — This is the default behavior when the `customErrors` section of the `web.config` is missing or turned off. If the `ScriptManager` `.AsyncPostBackErrorMessage` property is set, that is the message that will be displayed to the user; otherwise the standard ASP.NET exception message will be displayed.

❑ **A message box (alert) pops up, displaying this generic error message** — `Sys.WebForms` `.PageRequestManagerServerErrorException: An unknown error occurred while processing the request on the server. The status code returned from the server was: 500.`

 Because this message is not very user friendly, this approach is not recommended. This is the default error response when `customErrors` is turned on in the `web.config` and one of the following two conditions is also true: The `defaultRedirect` attribute of the `customErrors` `web.config` element is missing or the `AllowCustomErrorsRedirect` property of the `ScriptManager` is set to `False`.

❑ **The user can be automatically redirected to the error page specified in the `defaultRedirect` attribute of the `customErrors` element of the `web.config` file** — This happens automatically and by default when `customErrors` is turned on and the `customErrors` element has its `defaultRedirect` attribute set. To enable this functionality, the `AllowCustomErrorsRedirect` property of the `ScriptManager` must also be set to its default value of `True`. If the value is `False`, the `web.config` `customErrors` element is ignored.

❑ **A custom action can be taken by writing some JavaScript code to handle any errors detected in the `EndRequestHandler` client-side event** — For example, the following page displays a red error message below the `UpdatePanel` when an exception is raised:

```
<%@ Page Language="C#" %>

<!DOCTYPE html PUBLIC "-//W3C//DTD XHTML 1.0 Transitional//EN"
"http://www.w3.org/TR/xhtml1/DTD/xhtml1-transitional.dtd">

<html xmlns="http://www.w3.org/1999/xhtml" >
<head runat="server">
    <title>Untitled Page</title>
</head>
<body>
<form id="form1" runat="server">
<div>
  <asp:ScriptManager ID="ScriptManager1" runat="server"
  OnAsyncPostBackError="ScriptManager1_AsyncPostBackError"/>
</div>
<div style="width: 200px; border-right: black thin outset;
border-top: black thin outset;border-left: black thin outset;
border-bottom: black thin outset;">
        <asp:UpdatePanel ID="UpdatePanel1" runat="server">
            <ContentTemplate>
```

```
            <asp:Label ID="Label1" runat="server" Text="Label"/>
            <br />
            <asp:Button ID="btnException" runat="server"
            Text="Throw Exception" OnClick="btnException_Click" />
            <br />
            <asp:Button ID="btnNoException" runat="server"
            Text="No Exception" OnClick="btnNoException_Click" />
        </ContentTemplate>
      </asp:UpdatePanel>
</div>
<asp:Label ID="lblError" runat="server" Font-Bold="True" ForeColor="Red"/>
</form>
</body>
</html>

<script runat="server">
    protected void btnException_Click(object sender, EventArgs e)
    {
        //Simulate an error
        throw new Exception();
    }

    protected void btnNoException_Click(object sender, EventArgs e)
    {
        Label1.Text = DateTime.Now.ToString();
    }

    protected void ScriptManager1_AsyncPostBackError(object sender,
    AsyncPostBackErrorEventArgs e)
    {
        ScriptManager1.AsyncPostBackErrorMessage = "Oops, an error occurred!";
        Label1.Text = ""; //ignored because of the exception
    }
</script>

<script type="text/javascript" language="javascript">
Sys.WebForms.PageRequestManager.getInstance().add_endRequest(EndRequestHandler);
function EndRequestHandler(sender, args)
{
    if (args.get_error() != undefined)
    {
        $get('lblError').innerHTML = args.get_error().message;
        args.set_errorHandled(true);
    }
    else
    {
        $get('lblError').innerHTML = '';
    }
}
</script>
```

When the Throw Exception button is clicked, a server-side exception is thrown during the partial-page postback. The server-side `AsyncPostBackError` event is raised in response, which sets the `AsyncPostBackErrorMessage` property. (When a server-side exception is thrown, the `UpdatePanel` does not update. Thus the line that sets the label text is ignored.)

The client-side `EndRequestHandler` event is called when a partial-page postback has completed, regardless of whether or not an error was thrown. The arguments passed to this function are examined to determine if an error occurred. If the `error` property returns a value, its message is displayed in the designated label (as shown in Figure 10-5); otherwise, the label text is cleared because no error was detected. The `errorHandled` argument is set to `true`, because otherwise the default ASP.NET AJAX message box would still pop up (which would be redundant in this case).

Using these coding and configuration techniques, ASP.NET AJAX partial-page postback errors can be handled gracefully in an unlimited number of ways.

Figure 10-5

Summary

Asynchronous postbacks are one of the greatest new benefits that ASP.NET AJAX gives us. They provide not only functional enhancements, but also visual enhancements. These visual enhancements can be gussied up even further with a little bit of know-how.

The `UpdateProgress` control is a simple and efficient way to provide feedback to users during asynchronous postbacks. Its configurability makes it a snap to use with no code necessary. Client-side coding techniques can optionally be used to display the `UpdateProgress` control (or similar elements) on demand.

The ASP.NET AJAX Control Toolkit provides configurable animation capabilities including the `UpdatePanelAnimation` extender that make it reasonably simple to provide a variety of alluring animations during asynchronous postbacks.

To provide feedback during ongoing operations other than asynchronous postbacks, a little custom coding is necessary. You've seen how to use ASP.NET AJAX to create and display a custom progress bar to display the status of long-running operations.

You've also seen how to put users in control of their experience by providing them with the ability to cancel out of partial-page postbacks. The `abortPostBack` method of the `PageRequestManager` is usually all that's needed. Alternatively, a partial-page postback can be cancelled before it even gets started by setting the cancel argument of the `initializeRequest` event.

Exceptional circumstances require exceptional handling, and users will expect nothing less. Luckily, ASP.NET AJAX provides a plethora of techniques for handling exceptions in nimble ways. The `ScriptManager` component provides several members that make error handling easy. In cases where the default ASP.NET AJAX error management does not suffice, there are a variety of techniques for displaying custom messages or sending users to custom error pages.

In total, this all amounts to the ability to provide constant, uninterrupted two-way interaction with the user at all times, resulting in communication abilities that come closer to perfection than web applications have ever been able to achieve before.

Security and Integration

Some of the most valuable features of ASP.NET 2.0 are the Membership and Profile services APIs. Saving developers countless hours of development time, these services are an extensible foundation for identifying and authorizing users of a web application and persisting personal preferences. This chapter teaches you how to use Microsoft ASP.NET 2.0 AJAX integration with ASP.NET services to provide AJAX-style login and user-customized experiences.

The following topics are covered in this chapter:

❑   How to enable your site for AJAX support of ASP.NET application services

❑   How to use Microsoft ASP.NET 2.0 AJAX to build login, logout, and profile features for your web site

Understanding How Integration Works

Microsoft ASP.NET 2.0 AJAX ships with web services that act as an interface into the ASP.NET services. Once these services are enabled in your application you can provide AJAX-enabled custom profile and membership features.

The Microsoft ASP.NET 2.0 services model is built on top of the security model. For client-side access, the ASP.NET 2.0 AJAX Extensions 1.0 comes with a number of JavaScript objects that encapsulate the calls to the web services. Pages are secured so only identified users are granted access to the page. Once a user is identified, the application has enough information to provide customized experiences for the user.

Before you begin working with the ASP.NET services integration, however, you must enforce a security context for the web site.

Securing Web Applications

One of the most important features of a web site is security. When an application is accessible to anyone in the world via the Web, web site owners must include security measures to ensure only authorized persons access critical areas of a web site.

The ASP.NET security model is driven by user authentication. Security is enforced when the ASP.NET engine intercepts requests from pages to detect whether a user is authenticated. If the user is not identified, a challenge is issued to provide a valid set of credentials. Once the user provides valid credentials, the user is authorized and granted access to the site.

There are two ways an application can be secured in ASP.NET: either using Windows authentication or using Forms authentication. Windows authentication requires access to internal network resources and is best suited for intranet or corporate extranet environments. In this book you are building a publicly available web site, therefore the security model of choice is Forms authentication.

Forms Authentication

How does Forms authentication work? When a page is secured by Forms authentication and a user requests the page, ASP.NET will first look to see if the user is authenticated. If the authentication request fails, the browser is redirected to the login page and the originally requested page's URL is passed along to the login page in the query string. Once the user provides a valid set of username and password credentials, the application will log the user in to the system. When the user is logged in, a cookie is written on the user's system to store the authentication status and then the user is redirected to the page originally requested.

Forms authentication can be enabled with a few simple updates to the web.config. To secure your application, open the web.config and enter the following markup, replacing the existing authentication tag within the system.web tag:

If your web.config does not have an existing authentication tag, place the following markup after the opening of the system.web tag.

```
<authentication mode="Forms">
  <forms loginUrl="Login.aspx" />
</authentication>
<authorization>
  <deny users="?"/>
</authorization>
```

This change secures the all files in the application by denying access to all pages unless the user is authenticated. The one page that users will be able to get to is the Login.aspx page. ASP.NET will allow access to whatever page is defined in the loginUrl attribute even if all files in the application are secured.

The authorization section designates which users are allowed into the secure areas. In this case you are only allowing authenticated users. To achieve this restriction the deny tag includes users="?". Using the question mark indicates that unauthenticated users are denied access to the areas secured by the security definition.

Exceptions to the Rule

The changes you made to the security rules in the previous section deny access to all pages to any unauthenticated users. What if your application has pages that do not require authenticated access? You can change the security context on a folder or page level.

Before you move on to add the first user to your application, you must first open up a page from the security context that allows you to add that user. Enter the following markup directly after the close tag of <system.web>:

```
<location path="NewUser.aspx">
  <system.web>
    <authorization>
      <allow users="*" />
    </authorization>
  </system.web>
</location>
```

The location tag as you have entered it here allows read access to all users who request it. Obviously this is not a recommended security model, but necessary until you get your first user created. Once you have created the first administrative user, you should return to the web.config and remove this location tag.

ASP.NET Membership Services

ASP.NET 2.0 also includes an API to help you manage user accounts, profiles, and roles. Before Microsoft added these features to the .NET framework, developers were forced to implement basically the same logic over and over again for dealing with user information. The built-in membership services provide an extensible framework that includes the API for programmatic access to the data store and ASP.NET server controls to interface with the API. Using the controls that interface with the membership services are a delight in that they often do not require any additional code for seamless operation with the membership services.

> *For an in-depth discussion on ASP.NET membership services, read Scott Mitchell's series at*
> http://aspnet.4guysfromrolla.com/articles/121405-1.aspx.

Microsoft ASP.NET 2.0 AJAX has extended this framework by further allowing access to the membership API through a number of web services. Once these web services are enabled, you can use JavaScript to access the membership store.

The following section walks you though the steps to creating a membership store within your application. As you set up membership services, you create a user account used to access the membership services with Microsoft ASP.NET 2.0 AJAX.

Try It Out   Creating Sample Data

In order to create samples that will allow you to use ASP.NET's security model, you will have to add membership services support to your application and set up a user. The following steps lead you through the process to add a new user to your application.

These steps use the membership database created in Chapter 2. Make sure you follow the steps in Chapter 2 to create the ASP.NET membership database.

1. Begin by adding a new file to the solution and name it `NewUser.aspx`. Open the HTML editor and enter the following markup between the `<div>` tags:

```
<asp:CreateUserWizard runat="server">
    <WizardSteps>
        <asp:CreateUserWizardStep runat="server" />
        <asp:CompleteWizardStep runat="server" />
    </WizardSteps>
</asp:CreateUserWizard>
```

2. Launch this page in the browser and create a new user. For your purposes throughout the rest of this chapter, enter the User Name as **admin** and the Password as **P@ssw0rd**. Then enter any valid values into the rest of the fields.

3. Once you click the Create User button your account is created and you are redirected to a confirmation screen. You can now close this browser window and return back to Visual Studio 2005.

Figure 11-1 shows how you will fill out the form.

Before proceeding to implement integration with the Microsoft ASP.NET 2.0 AJAX controls, you first create a test page to ensure your user account is set up correctly.

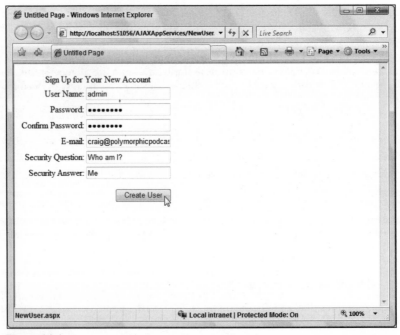

Figure 11-1

Creating a Test

Follow these steps to create your test page:

1. If your application does not have a default page yet, add a new web form to your application and name it `Default.aspx`. Open the HTML editor and enter the following markup some-where between the `<body>` tags:

```
<h1>Default</h1>
```

2. Add a new web form to your project and name it `Login.aspx`. Open the HTML editor window and enter the following markup between the `<div>` tags:

```
<asp:Login runat="server" />
```

3. Launch your application in the browser and attempt to view the `Default.aspx` page. Forms authentication redirects the browser to the login page and gives you a chance to log in. If you set up your user account correctly you will be able to log in successfully with the *admin/P@ssw0rd* credentials and be redirected to the `Default.aspx` page. If your login fails, review the previous steps to make sure you configured the membership services support correctly.

The rest of this chapter guides you through the process of using the Microsoft ASP.NET 2.0 AJAX controls to interface with the ASP.NET membership services.

Using Microsoft ASP.NET 2.0 AJAX

Now that you have the foundation set for granting access to a known user to your web site, you can begin using the Microsoft ASP.NET 2.0 framework to provide membership and profile support.

The ASP.NET application services integration is divided into two sections: the authentication service (or membership support) and the profile service. The authentication service provides AJAX features to help you create client-side login and logout screens. The profile service allows you to read and write user profile information. Profile information is a set of data unique to each user, giving the developer an opportunity to create a custom experience for each user.

Authentication Service

The authentication service is available through `Sys.Services.AuthenticationService`. With the two functions on the service, `login` and `logout`, you have read-only access to the membership store. The authentication service does not ship with a way to create new users or add new roles.

Before you begin coding login features, the next section reviews the JavaScript functions involved in detail.

Login Function

When the `login` function is called and successfully logs in a user, the Forms authentication cookie is set and then a user can travel throughout a secured ASP.NET application just as if the user had logged into the application using a traditional server-based login screen.

The following table explains the purpose for each argument that the `login` function requires.

`login` Function Argument	Purpose
Username	The account username.
Password	The account password.
isPersistent	A Boolean flag to signal to the login function whether to save the user's login status in a cookie so they are not required to log in when returning to the site.
redirectUrl	The location of where the user is directed to after a successful login.
customInfo	Reserved for future use.
loginCompletedCallback	The name of the function the script will call when the login is complete.
failedCallback	The name of the function the script will call if the login fails.
userContext	An instance of any JavaScript primitive type, object, or array that is passed to the callback function in the matching `userContext` argument.

Logout Function

When the `logout` function is complete, the Forms authentication cookie is cleared and the user is restricted from secure areas of the site just as if he had logged out of the application using a traditional server-based logout screen.

The following table details the arguments involved in the `logout` function.

`logout` Function Argument	Purpose
redirectUrl	The location the browser redirects to upon a successful logout.
logoutCompletedCallback	The name of the function the script calls when the logout is complete.
failedCallback	The name of the function the script calls if the logout fails.
userContext	An instance of any JavaScript primitive type, object, or array that is passed to the callback function in the matching `userContext` argument.

Now that you have an overall familiarity with the authentication service functions, use the following sections to try out the implementation.

Enable Authentication Services

Before you are able to use the Microsoft ASP.NET 2.0 AJAX authentication service, you must update the `web.config` file to grant access from the application to the services. The required change is to uncomment a line of code in the `web.config` that Microsoft has already written for you.

Open the `web.config` and uncomment the line that exposes the membership services to the client. The following code listings show you how your `web.config` looks before and after your changes.

Before:

```
<!--
   <authenticationService enabled="true" requireSSL="true|false"/>
-->
```

After:

```
<authenticationService enabled="true" requireSSL="false"/>
```

Notice that in addition to uncommenting the `authenticationService` line you must instruct the application whether to require a secure socket layer (SSL). SSL is the transport encryption mechanism used on the Web to protect passwords and other in-transit data. For your purposes here you want to set this attribute to `false`.

Try It Out   Building a Login Screen

Be sure you have secured your application with the instructions found in the "Forms Authentication" section and set up a sample account as directed in the "Creating Sample Data" Try It Out.

1. Begin by opening the `Login.aspx` page. Open the HTML editor and remove the `<asp:Login>` tag you added earlier in the chapter. Implement an AJAX login by entering the following markup between the `<div>` tags:

```
<asp:ScriptManager
    runat="server" />

User Name:
<input
    type="text"
    id="txtUserName"
    name="txtUserName"
    value="admin" />

<br />

Password:
<input
    type="password"
```

```
        id="txtPassword"
        name="txtPassword"
        value="P@ssw0rd" />

<br />

<input
    type="button"
    value="Login"
    onclick="btnLogin_Click();" />

<div
    id="divMessage"
    style="visibility:hidden">
    Attempting Login...
</div>
```

2. The first control you add to the page is the `ScriptManager` control. The `ScriptManager` is essential on any Microsoft ASP.NET 2.0 AJAX page in order to make decisions about what scripts to load in the page.

After the `ScriptManager` are a set of HTML controls that will allow the user to enter in a username and password as well as a button to initiate the login request.

The final element on the page is a `<div>` that is programmatically displayed and hidden in order to provide feedback to the user about what is happening when the login button is clicked. The next section guides you though how to implement the JavaScript to interact with the Microsoft ASP.NET 2.0 AJAX application services integration.

Notice that the input controls declared on this page are standard HTML input controls and not server-side `<asp:>` controls. The fact that you are using HTML controls is important for two reasons. The first reason is that you must add the `name` and `id` attributes with identical values for full browser support (ASP.NET does this for you when you use server controls). The second reason is to point out that you are strictly using client-side scripting to interact with the ASP.NET Member Services API.

3. The next listing details the JavaScript you must implement to complete the login feature. The goal of the JavaScript you implement is to notify the user of what is happening and perform the action of logging a user into the system.

```
<script type="text/javascript">

var message      = $get("divMessage");

function btnLogin_Click(sender)
{
    var authService = Sys.Services.AuthenticationService;
    var userName    = $get("txtUserName").value;
    var password    = $get("txtPassword").value;

    authService.login(
        userName,        // userName
        password,        // password
```

```
                false,              // isPersistent
                null,               // redirectUrl
                null,               // customInfo
                OnComplete,         // loginCompletedCallback
                OnFail,             // failedCallback
                null                // userContext
        );

        message.style.visibility = "visible";
    }

    function OnComplete(result)
    {
        message.style.visibility = "hidden";

        if(result)
        {
            alert("You are logged in!");
        }
        else
        {
            alert("Login failed.");
        }
    }

    function OnFail(response)
    {
        message.style.visibility = "hidden";
        alert("There was an error while trying to login." + response.get_message());
    }

</script>
```

4. To test this page, run the application and navigate to the `Login.aspx` page. Attempt to log in using the `admin` and `P@ssw0rd` credentials.

Figure 11-2 shows how the page will look if have implemented the login correctly.

How It Works

The first part of the script in step 3 creates a reference to the `<div>` on the page that has the message to the user. Using the `$get()` function is cross-browser shorthand for the standard JavaScript `document .getElementById()` function to reference an element on the page. Once this reference is established you use it to display and hide the message to the user at the appropriate time.

The next section of the script is the function associated with the click event of the input button. The `btnLogin_Click()` function implements the work of sending a login request to the server via Microsoft ASP.NET 2.0 AJAX. The implementation begins by setting up some variables to make your code easy to understand. The `authService` variable makes reference to the `Sys.Services.AuthenticationService` static object. This object is available to the page because you have included a `ScriptManager` control on the page in the markup. The next two lines create references to the username and password input values on the page. You will use this information to pass to the `authService` to log in the user.

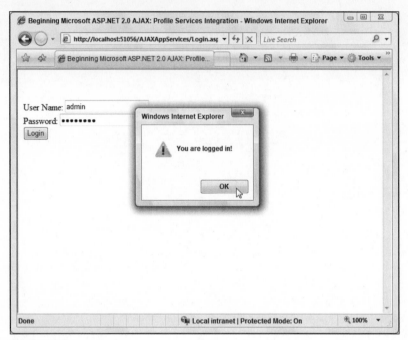

Figure 11-2

Before attempting to log the user into the system, the script displays a message to the user by setting the style sheet `visibility` property to `visible`. Later, when the script calls back to the client you hide this message, signaling the login request is complete.

When calling the login function you pass in the username and password as entered by the user. In this instance you will pass a `false` into the `isPersistent` argument. The only other arguments required for this example are to give function names for a complete and failed login. If the login is complete the callback will run the `OnComplete` function, and if the login fails, the `OnFail` function will be executed. All other arguments receive a `null` value because they are not required.

The `OnComplete` function will run if the login request is complete. Please note that there is a distinction between the login request being complete and the login being complete. When the request is complete, the script calls back to the `OnComplete` function. To determine if the login action is complete you must check the `result` argument's value. If the `result` is `true`, the user is logged in. If the `result` is `false`, the login request completed, but the login failed for some other reason. An example of why the login may fail might include the user providing mismatched security credentials.

The `OnFail` function runs if the script cannot establish the right connections or fails in some other way while trying to submit a login request.

In both the `OnComplete` and `OnFail` functions you set the `visibility` property to `hidden` in order to hide the login message from the user.

Try It Out **Building a Logout Screen**

Be sure you have secured your application with the instructions found in the "Forms Authentication" section and set up a sample account as directed in "Creating Sample Data."

1. Begin by adding a new web form to your project and name it Logout.aspx. Open the HTML editor and enter the following markup between the <div> tags:

```
<asp:ScriptManager
    runat="server" />

<input
    type="button"
    value="Logout"
    onclick="btnLogout_Click();" />
```

As always, when building a Microsoft ASP.NET 2.0 AJAX page, you will need to add a ScriptManager to the page. The only other element on the page is a button used to initiate the logout request.

2. Next, enter the JavaScript required to implement the logout:

```
<script type="text/javascript">

var authService = Sys.Services.AuthenticationService;

function btnLogout_Click()
{
    authService.logout(
        "Login.aspx",    // redirectUrl
        OnComplete,      // loginCompletedCallback
        OnFail,          // failedCallback
        null             // userContext
    );
}

function OnComplete(response)
{
    if(!authService.get_isLoggedIn())
    {
        alert("Logout complete.");
    }
    else
    {
        alert("Logout failed.");
    }
}

function OnFail(response)
{
    alert("Logout failed: " + response);
}

</script>
```

3. Test your code by starting your application in a web browser, logging in, and then attempting to log out.

Figure 11-3 shows you how the page will look if you have implemented the logout correctly.

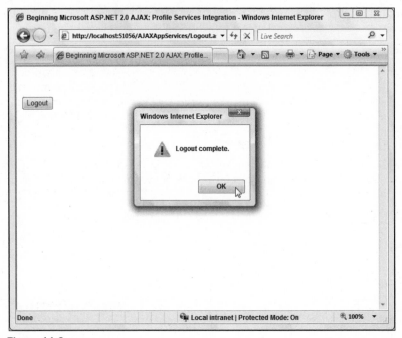

Figure 11-3

How It Works

Just as in the login screen, you begin by creating a reference to the `AuthenticationService` object.

The `btnLogout_Click()` function tells the authentication service to redirect to the `Login.aspx` page when the logout is complete. This function also tells the script to call the `OnComplete` function when the logout is complete and the `OnFail` function if the logout fails.

The `OnComplete` function must first check the `authService` object's `get_isLoggedIn()` function to see if the user is still logged in. If this function returns `false`, the user has successfully logged out of the system. If the user is still logged in, the logout attempt has failed.

You might think that checking a value in the `response` *argument would make the most sense in evaluating whether the user is logged in. Though this would be a natural inclination, the* `response` *argument returns* `null`. *To interrogate the system to see if the user is still logged in you must use the* `Sys.Services.AuthenticationService.get_isLoggedIn()` *function.*

What You Have Learned

The authentication service features of Microsoft ASP.NET 2.0 AJAX add web services and JavaScript objects that act as the glue between the client and the ASP.NET membership store. These objects give you a read-only view of the membership data.

Profile Services

Using profile services allows you to easily configure and store information about individual users in order to create a custom user experience. The profile service is available through ASP.NET 2.0 AJAX Extensions 1.0 using the `Sys.Services.ProfileService` class. The user profile information is defined in the `web.config`. (See "Defining User Profiles" in a following section for setup details.)

When you set up profile properties in the `web.config` you designate which properties are restricted to read-only and which are open to read/write access. While using the Microsoft ASP.NET 2.0 AJAX profile service you can read and write to the defined properties values, but you cannot add new properties. A final restriction is that the profile services don't allow you to change which properties are available to read or write.

The next section explains the function and fields involved in developing features using the profile service.

Properties Field

The `Sys.Services.ProfileService.properties` field contains JavaScript wrappers for each property defined in the `web.config` under the `profileService` tag in the `web.config`. (See the "Enabling Profile Services" section for setup details).

Load Function

When the `load` function is called, the values associated with the user's profile are loaded into the associated properties field values.

The following table details the arguments involved in the `load` function.

`load` Function Arguments	Purpose
`propertyNames`	An array of property names to load.
`loadCompletedCallback`	The name of the function the script calls when the load completes.
`failedCallback`	The name of the function the script calls if the load fails.
`userContext`	An instance of any JavaScript primitive type, object, or array that is passed to the callback function in the matching `userContext` argument.

Save Function

When the `save` function is called the profile service stores the latest values of the properties that match what you pass in the `propertyNames` array. If you make a change to a profile property and do not include the property name into the `propertyNames` array, that value isn't saved.

The following table details the arguments involved in the `save` function.

`save` Function Arguments	Purpose
`propertyNames`	An array of property names to save.
`saveCompletedCallback`	The name of the function the script calls when the save completes.
`failedCallback`	The name of the function the script calls if the save fails.
`userContext`	An instance of any JavaScript primitive type, object, or array that is passed to the callback function in the matching `userContext` argument.

Enabling Profile Services

Just as you did for the authentication service, before you are able to use the Microsoft ASP.NET 2.0 AJAX profile service, you must update the `web.config` to expose the profile service.

Open the `web.config` and uncomment the line that exposes the profile services to the client. The following code listings show you how your `web.config` looks before and after your changes.

Before:

```
<!--
<profileService enabled="true"
                readAccessProperties="propertyname1,propertyname2"
                writeAccessProperties="propertyname1,propertyname2" />
-->
```

After:

```
<profileService enabled="true"
                readAccessProperties="IsPremiumMember"
                writeAccessProperties="IsPremiumMember" />
```

The `readAccessProperties` attribute holds a comma-delimited list of properties that the client may read. The `writeAccessProperties` has the list of properties to which the client may write values. The lists in these attributes are not required to match. You may want to allow read-only access to some profile values.

Now that you have enabled the application to use profile services you must define at least one profile property to store user data. The next section demonstrates how to create profile properties in the `web.config`.

Defining User Profiles

In the following examples you implement pages to read and write profile information. Often web site owners want different information displayed to paying members of the site than to nonpaying web surfers. For example purposes, you create a single profile entry `IsPremiumMember`. You use this profile definition to store this setting for each user to the site.

To add profile definitions, open the `web.config` file and enter the following markup after the start of the `<system.web>` tag:

```
<profile enabled="true">
 <properties>
            <add name="IsPremiumMember" type="System.Boolean"
defaultValue="false"/>
 </properties>
</profile>
```

Now that the services are available to the application and you have a profile property defined, you can try out reading profile information using AJAX.

Try It Out   Reading Profile Information

Be sure you have secured your application with the instructions found in the "Forms Authentication" section and set up a sample account as directed in "Creating Sample Data."

1. Begin by adding a new web form to your application and name it `ProfileRead.aspx`. Open the HTML editor and enter the following markup between the `<div>` tags:

```
<asp:ScriptManager
    runat="server" />

<input
    type="button"
    value="Load Profile"
    onclick="btnLoadProfile_Click();" />

<div
    id="divMessage"
    style="visibility:hidden;">Loading profile...</div>
```

This page follows the same form you used in the previous examples. The `ScriptManager` is on the page to marshal the required JavaScript; the input button exists as a way to initiate the call to read the profile service. The `<div>` at the end of the markup is displayed to the user while the system is reading the profile information in order to give the user a signal as to what is happening.

2. Now you are ready to implement the JavaScript to access the profile service:

```
<script type="text/javascript">

var message        = $get("divMessage");
var profService    = Sys.Services.ProfileService;
var authService    = Sys.Services.AuthenticationService;
```

```
var propertyNames = new Array();

propertyNames[0] = "IsPremiumMember";

function btnLoadProfile_Click()
{
    message.style.visibility = "visible";

    profService.load(
        propertyNames,   // propertyNames
        OnComplete,      // OnLoadComplete callback
        OnFail,          // OnFail callback
        null             // userContext
        );
}

function OnComplete(result)
{
    var negate = " ";

    message.style.visibility = "hidden";

    if(!profService.properties.IsPremiumMember)
    {
        negate = " not ";
    }

    if(result)
    {
        alert("Your profile is loaded. You are" +
            negate + "a premium member.");
    }
    else
    {
        alert("Your profile did not load.");
    }
}

function OnFail(result)
{
    message.style.visibility = "hidden";
    alert("Error while trying to read profile." + result);
}

</script>
```

3. Test your page by launching it in the browser and clicking the Load Profile button.

Figure 11-4 shows how the page will look when you have implemented the read profile feature correctly.

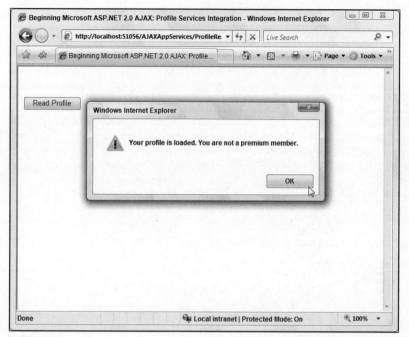

Figure 11-4

How It Works

The script begins by creating a reference to the status message on the page by using the Microsoft ASP.NET 2.0 AJAX $get() function. Next, references are made to the ProfileService and AuthenticationService objects.

A new object named propertyNames is created to hold a list of the profile properties you pass to the load function. This array is fed the names of the properties you want to load for the user. In this instance you load the IsPremiumMember profile property.

The btnLoadProfile_Click() function reads the user's profile and provides some feedback. First, the function checks to see if the user is logged in. If the user is logged in, the property names are passed to the load method, and the names of the functions to call when the load is complete and if the load fails are provided to the function.

If the load completes, the OnComplete function runs. The OnComplete function queries the profile service object to find out the value of the IsPremiumMember property. Finally, a message is displayed to the user reflecting the value of the profile property.

Try It Out   **Writing Profile Information**

Be sure you have secured your application with the instructions found in the "Forms Authentication" section and set up a sample account as directed in "Creating Sample Data".

1. Begin by adding a new web form to your application and name it `ProfileWrite.aspx`. Open the HTML editor and enter the following markup between the `<div>` tags:

```
<asp:ScriptManager
    runat="server" />

<input
    type="button"
    value="Make Non-Premium Member"
    onclick="btnNonPremium_Click();" />

<input
    type="button"
    value="Make Premium Member"
    onclick="btnPremium_Click();" />

<div
    id="divMessage"
    style="visibility:hidden;">Writing profile...</div>
```

2. This form has the familiar `ScriptManager` and message `<div>`. Also included on the page are a check box to gather user input indicating whether to set the current user as a premium member and a button to initiate the call to write to the profile service:

```
<script type="text/javascript">

var message       = $get("divMessage");
var profService   = Sys.Services.ProfileService;
var authService   = Sys.Services.AuthenticationService;
var propertyNames = new Array();

function btnNonPremium_Click()
{
    Save(false);
}

function btnPremium_Click()
{
    Save(true);
}

function Save(isPremiumMember)
{
    if(authService.get_isLoggedIn())
    {
        message.style.visibility = "visible";

        profService.properties.IsPremiumMember = isPremiumMember;
```

```
            propertyNames[0] = "IsPremiumMember";

            profService.save(
                propertyNames,   // property names
                OnComplete,      // load complete callback
                OnFail,          // fail callback
                null             // user context
                );
        }
        else
        {
            alert("You must be logged in to access your profile.");
        }
    }

    function OnComplete(result)
    {
        message.style.visibility = "hidden";

        if(result)
        {
            alert("Your profile is updated.");
        }
        else
        {
            alert("Your profile is not updated.");
        }
    }

    function OnFail(result)
    {
        message.style.visibility = "hidden";
        alert("Error while trying to write to your profile." + response);
    }

</script>
```

3.   Test this page by launching it in the browser and clicking the Make Premium Member button.

Figure 11-5 shows how the page will look if you have implemented the write to profile feature correctly.

How It Works

Just as you implemented in `ProfileRead.aspx`, the script begins by creating a reference to the status message on the page and setting references the `ProfileService` and `AuthenticationService` objects. Lastly, `propertyNames` is an array created to hold a list of the profile properties you pass to the `save` function.

The `btnNonPremium_Click()` and `btnPremium_Click()` functions pass the appropriate argument to the `Save()` function. The save process first checks to see if the user is logged in to the system. If the screen detects that a user is unauthenticated, he sees an alert box asking him to log in before trying to save profile information. If the user is logged in, the first action is to hide the message, signaling to the user that the page is writing the profile information.

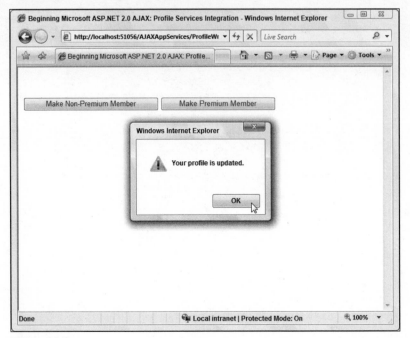

Figure 11-5

Next, the `profService.properties.IsPremiumMember` property is set on the value from the `isPremiumMember` argument. Then the array is loaded with the profile property name that is intended to be saved. Finally, you pass in the names of the functions to call when the save is complete or if the action fails.

The profiles defined in the `web.config` are available to page developers through the `Sys.Services` `.ProfileService` object. When defining the profile members, you might decide which items are read-only and which items are read/write. Using the profile service on the page enables you to customize the user experience based on the setting saved per user in the profile items.

Using User Context

As stated earlier in the chapter, user context is an instance of any JavaScript primitive type, object, or array that is passed from a calling function to a callback function. Until now you have seen only place-holders for the `userContext` argument in the examples showing you how to use the functions to interface with ASP.NET application services.

The following example shows you how to use the `userContext` argument in your pages.

The following implementation uses a profile read operation for example purposes only. You can use the `userContext` *argument in much the same way whether you are reading profile information or logging a user into the system.*

Try It Out   **Using User Context**

1.   Begin by adding a new web form to your project and naming it `UserContext.aspx`. Open the HTML editor and enter the following markup between the `<div>` tags:

```
<asp:ScriptManager
    runat="server" />

<input
    type="button"
    value="Read User Context Argument"
    onclick="btnReadUserContext_Click();" />

<div
    id="divMessage"
    style="visibility:hidden;">Reading User Context...</div>
```

The page starts by including the required `ScriptManager` control. The next control is a button that will requisition the call to read a profile property. The final element is a message that reports back to the user that an operation is in progress.

2.   Enter the required JavaScript:

```
<script type="text/javascript">

var message      = $get("divMessage");
var profService  = Sys.Services.ProfileService;
var authService  = Sys.Services.AuthenticationService;
var propertyNames = new Array();

propertyNames[0] = "IsPremiumMember";

function btnReadUserContext_Click()
{
    var userContext = "User Context String";

    message.style.visibility = "visible";

    profService.load(
        propertyNames,    // propertyNames
        OnComplete,       // OnLoadComplete callback
        OnFail,           // OnFail callback
        userContext       // userContext
        );
}

function OnComplete(result, userContext)
{
    message.style.visibility = "hidden";
    alert(userContext);
}

function OnFail(result)
```

```
{
        message.style.visibility = "hidden";
        alert("Error while trying to read profile." + result);
    }
</script>
```

The preceding code is much like what you implemented while reading profile information in the last section. The item to note in this page is that you are giving the `userContext` variable a value before passing it to the `load` function. Once the load is successful, the contents of `userContext` are available to the `OnComplete` function.

3. Test your code by starting your application in a web browser and clicking the Read User Context Argument button.

Figure 11-6 shows you how the page will look if you have implemented the context argument correctly.

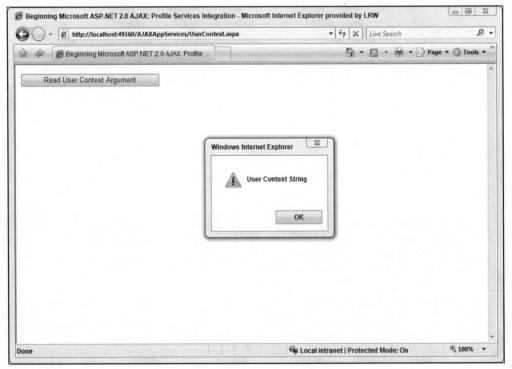

Figure 11-6

How It Works

The `userContext` argument is available throughout the functions that interface with ASP.NET application services. You can pass any JavaScript primitive type in this argument. Often you will use this method to pass data from the calling function to the callback function as a way to reduce the need for redundant `if/then` logic by making decisions ahead of time and placing the result in the `userContext` argument.

Summary

You have had an opportunity to learn how Microsoft ASP.NET 2.0 AJAX integrates with ASP.NET services. Integration with ASP.NET is found within two main areas: authentication and profiles.

The authentication service has the features needed to create AJAX login and logout features. These features are available once you expose them through a setting in `web.cofing` and have users in the membership database.

The profile service allows you to read and write profile information on a page using AJAX. Profiles must be defined in `web.config`.

The next chapter steps you through the details of how to debug your Microsoft ASP.NET 2.0 AJAX web applications.

Debugging

So you have written your first ASP.NET AJAX application or you have upgraded an existing web site to utilize some features of ASP.NET AJAX and it all works straight away, without issue, right? Unfortunately, this is rarely the case, and at some point in time in any form of application development, AJAX or otherwise, you need to debug your application.

Debugging is the art of identifying and removing problematic code within your applications. Every developer has been required to perform some degree of debugging within their applications, at some point in time.

ASP.NET is predominately a server-side development technology and support for debugging of applications within ASP.NET is quite extensive. ASP.NET AJAX applications introduce some new aspects, which in turn introduce some new debugging challenges. The extensive use of JavaScript, and the fact that custom data may be transferred through the use of asynchronous postbacks, means that attention needs to be paid to these significant areas to deal with the challenges that are introduced when debugging AJAX-type applications with ASP.NET.

This chapter examines the various aspects of debugging ASP.NET AJAX applications and covers the following topics:

- ❑ General server-side ASP.NET debugging
- ❑ General JavaScript debugging
- ❑ Specific debugging support provided by the ASP.NET AJAX Extensions
- ❑ HTTP debugging — examining what gets transferred asynchronously

Server-Side Debugging

ASP.NET is a server-based development environment and the ASP.NET runtime engine parses and compiles virtually all web pages and code into .NET assemblies.

When an ASP.NET web page is requested (for example, `www.SomeSite.com/SomePage.aspx`), the ASP.NET runtime engine parses the web page and also the code that is associated with the page. This is usually in the form of a code-behind file present in the `App_Code` directory of a web site, or the code can be embedded within the web page (ASPX) itself. The web page and code are compiled into a .NET assembly and loaded into the assembly cache for execution.

.NET assemblies form a very rich unit of deployment, in that it can contain an extensive amount of information that allows it to be self-describing. This means that the ASP.NET runtime can interrogate the assembly and obtain a large amount of information about the assembly, such as security requirements and other operating parameters. In addition, special debugging information can be included when the assembly is compiled. As a result of this, the debugging experience on the server for ASP.NET applications can be very rich and interactive.

First, look at how debugging support and information can be enabled so that you can utilize the debugging features available on the server.

Debugging support needs to be enabled specifically before debugging can be used. For ASP.NET web applications, this means including the following `<compilation>` setting within the `web.config` web application configuration file:

```
<configuration>
  <system.web>
    <compilation debug="true">
    </compilation>
  </system.web>
</configuration>
```

If you try to run a web application using Visual Studio 2005 in debug mode, and the `<compilation debug="true" />` configuration entry has not been set, you are prompted to enable debugging support with the dialog box shown in Figure 12-1.

When creating a new web site project using the ASP.NET AJAX Extensions project template, the debug mode will be set to `false`, *and running the application in debug mode causes the dialog shown in Figure 12-1 to be displayed.*

For other project types, such as class libraries, debugging must be selected as the active configuration within Visual Studio 2005, as shown in Figure 12-2.

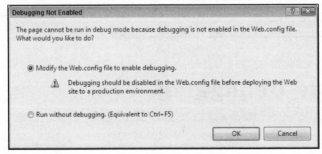

Figure 12-1

In either case, when the application files are compiled, special debugging information and symbols are produced that enable the Visual Studio 2005 debugger to track and accurately show what lines are being executed. You can see this by having a look at the output directory of the respective application you are compiling. If the "debug" build has been selected, or debugging is enabled via the web.config setting mentioned previously, there will be debug symbol files present, which have a .pdb file extension.

For example, if your project produces a MyApp.exe assembly, a corresponding MyApp.pdb file is produced.

Figure 12-2

Using Breakpoints

Now that debugging has been enabled, application execution can be tracked on the server. The easiest way to do this is to set a breakpoint.

A *breakpoint* is a marked line of code that tells the debugger to pause execution at the line indicated by the breakpoint, when program execution reaches that line. A breakpoint is indicated by a red dot to the left of the line, with the entire line itself also highlighted in red. Figure 12-3 illustrates what a breakpoint looks like.

```
namespace ConsoleApplication1
{
    class Program
    {
        static void Main(string[] args)
        {
            Console.WriteLine("My application is about to start...");
            InitialiseApp();
            Console.WriteLine("Application Initialised successfully.");
            PerformWork();
            Console.WriteLine("Application is terminating.");
        }
    }
```

Figure 12-3

This figure shows a breakpoint set on the line that executes the PerformWork() method.

When the application is run, execution is paused at the breakpoint. When this occurs, the application is literally suspended, enabling you to examine various aspects of the program's execution such as values of variables. You can choose to continue execution step by step and examine the changing values of variables as the program executes each step. This can be accomplished by pressing the F10 function key, or selecting the Debug menu, then selecting the Step Over menu option. When a method is encountered during debugging, you may opt to continue execution past the method using the Step Over option previously mentioned, or you can "drill into" the execution of each step within the method by selecting either the F11 function key or selecting the Debug menu option, then selecting Step Into.

This debugging environment is very rich and allows a huge amount flexibility when it comes to inspecting and evaluating the state of your application. In Figure 12-4, the debugger displays the value of a variable when the mouse hovers over that variable during a debugging operation.

This is one of the many ways you can interact with the server-side debugger within Visual Studio 2005.

For an exhaustive explanation of debugging applications, visit
`http://msdn2.microsoft.com/en-us/library/awtaffxb.aspx.`

This method of debugging should be reasonably familiar to most Visual Studio developers. One of the reasons it is so rich and powerful is because it exists within the domain and execution control of ASP.NET. Visual Studio 2005 has intimate knowledge of .NET runtime execution and can therefore offer a richer environment.

Breakpoints are active whether the request from the browser is a regular postback or an asynchronous request. From a debugging perspective, both requests are the same. The runtime parses the HTTP request (postback or asynchronous), and the IDE will pause on any breakpoints and allow the developer to examine and modify variable values during execution.

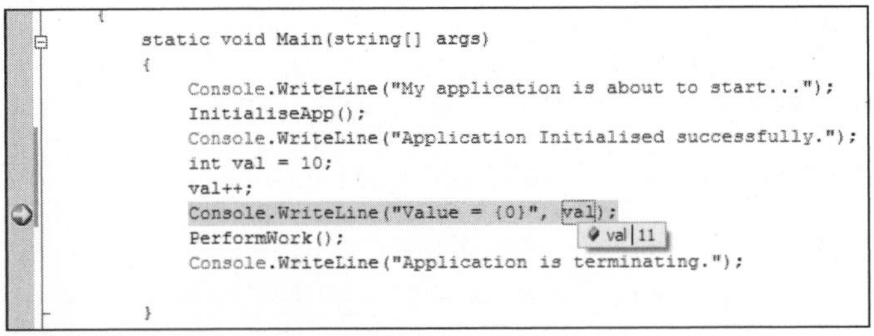

```
        {
⊟           static void Main(string[] args)
            {
                Console.WriteLine("My application is about to start...");
                InitialiseApp();
                Console.WriteLine("Application Initialised successfully.");
                int val = 10;
                val++;
⊕               Console.WriteLine("Value = {0}", val);
                PerformWork();                      ⚲ val  11
                Console.WriteLine("Application is terminating.");

            }
```

Figure 12-4

JavaScript Debugging

JavaScript is the core scripting language utilized within the browser to achieve the AJAX functionality that the ASP.NET Extensions provide. Without it, almost all the functionality within ASP.NET AJAX would be impossible to achieve. Because JavaScript is a client-side language and executes within the context of the browser, you need to instruct the browser that you want to perform debugging operations. Visual Studio 2005 provides support for interactively debugging JavaScript within the browser context in a similar fashion to traditional server-side debugging discussed previously.

JavaScript itself does not offer any real support for debugging. The best you can hope to do is to make use of display constructs such as the `Alert` statements to display program variables during execution. This has definite limitations though. Examine the following code:

```
function TestAlert()
{
    // Create a string object
    var s = new String("Hello");
```

```
    alert("'s' object is: " + s);

    // Create a custom object
    var o = new Object();
    o.someValue = 100;
    o.someString = "someText";
    alert("'o' object is: " + o);
}
```

When this code is executed within a browser, a dialog box first displays the value of the string variables as you would expect (see Figure 12-5).

However, the next dialog shows that o is an object, and does not display any further information about the object (see Figure 12-6).

This is clearly not very useful because you already know that you are dealing with an object. As objects in your applications become more complex, particularly when dealing with objects within the ASP.NET AJAX Extensions framework, you need to know a lot more about your objects.

Figure 12-5

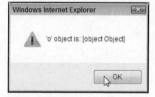

Figure 12-6

Try It Out   Enabling Visual Studio Script Debugging

Having a rich debugging environment, similar to the server-side environment, is possible. It does require some interaction between the browser and Visual Studio 2005; therefore, some configuration is required to enable this support, which is not normally enabled by default.

Internet Explorer needs to be configured to allow debugging to take place. By default, debugging is not enabled within Internet Explorer. To enable this feature, follow these steps:

1. Within Internet Explorer, select the Tools menu option, and select the Internet Options menu option.

2.   A dialog box is presented with a number of tab options. Select the Advanced tab to access a number of options, as displayed in Figure 12-7.

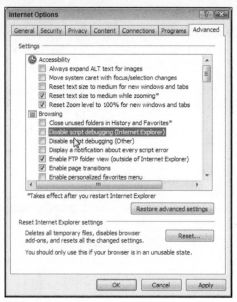

Figure 12-7

3.   Ensure both the Disable Script Debugging (Internet Explorer) and Disable Script Debugging (Other) are unchecked. Strictly speaking, only the Disable Script Debugging (Internet Explorer) needs to be unchecked for script debugging to work. Deselecting the Disable Script Debugging (Other) option means that debugging is enabled for scripts hosted outside of Internet Explorer, such as Microsoft Outlook, for example.

4.   That's all the configuration required to enable script debugging. To test this, create a new web site project within Visual Studio 2005. Create a new web form/ASPX page, or alternatively edit the `Default.aspx` page within the project. Remove the existing <html></html> declaration and everything contained within those tags, and replace it with the following code:

```
<html xmlns="http://www.w3.org/1999/xhtml" >
<head runat="server">
    <title>Test Script Debugging</title>

    <script type="text/javascript">
    function DoSomeWork()
    {
        var cntrl = document.getElementById("txtInput");
        var number = cntrl.value;
        number++;

        var newValue = DoSomeMoreWork(number);

        alert("New Value = " + newValue);
```

```
    }

    function DoSomeMoreWork(arg)
    {
        // Do some calculations
        arg = arg * 2 + 32;
        arg = arg + 18 / 2;
    }
    </script>

</head>
<body>
    <form id="form1" runat="server">
    <div>
        <input type="text" id="txtInput" value="test" />
        <input type="button" value="Submit value" onclick="DoSomeWork();" />
    </div>
    </form>
</body>
</html>
```

5. Ensure that the newly created page is set as the Startup Page within Visual Studio by right-clicking the page and selecting Set as Start Page.

6. Ensure that the active configuration is set to Debug.

7. Click the Play button or press F5 to start the application in debug mode.

8. Click the Submit Value button to see an alert box similar to the one shown previously in Figure 12-8.

Figure 12-8

Try It Out   **Setting a Breakpoint**

This behavior is not what is desired and typically you would expect something more than a message saying your value is *undefined*. To fix this, you are going to debug the client-side script within this application. You set a breakpoint early in the script's execution to see what is going on within the code.

1. Leave the Internet Explorer browser instance running and click the OK dialog box button if it is still displayed.

2. Switch to Visual Studio 2005 (while Internet Explorer is still running) and select Debug ➪ Windows ➪ Script Explorer, as shown in Figure 12-9.

Once the option has been selected, a Script Explorer window will be displayed within Visual Studio. If your window layout is at the default settings, the Script Explorer window should appear on the right side of the screen, as shown in Figure 12-10.

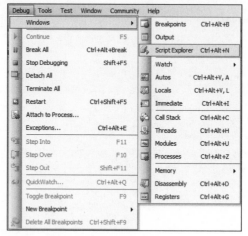

Figure 12-9

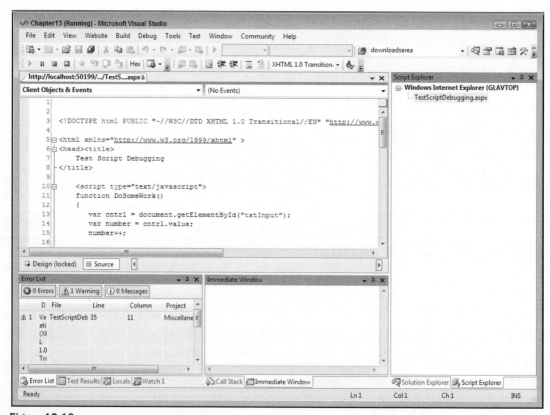

Figure 12-10

3. In the Script Explorer window, you will notice one ASPX page listed, which is the one currently being executed. Double-click that page within the Script Explorer window. This lists the page within the editor window and looks very similar to the page at design/development time.

The big difference is that you can now set breakpoints and examine variable values as the code is executing in almost exactly the same way that is performed with server-side code.

4. Within the editor window where the web page is displayed, navigate to the first line within the DoSomeWork JavaScript function and press F9 or click the left-side gray sidebar to place a breakpoint on the line. The editor window should now look similar to Figure 12-11.

5. Now switch back to the running instance of the browser that is executing the web page. Click the Submit Value button. Visual Studio should automatically become the active window and execution of the web page pauses on the line that the breakpoint is on. The line will be highlighted, as shown in Figure 12-12.

6. Press the F10 button to advance the execution to the next line. The next line is highlighted. Position the mouse pointer above the cntrl variable definition on the line that reads:

```
var cntrl = document.getElementById("txtInput");
```

A small dialog box is displayed showing the cntrl variable with an option to expand the values of this variable by clicking the + symbol, similar to Figure 12-13.

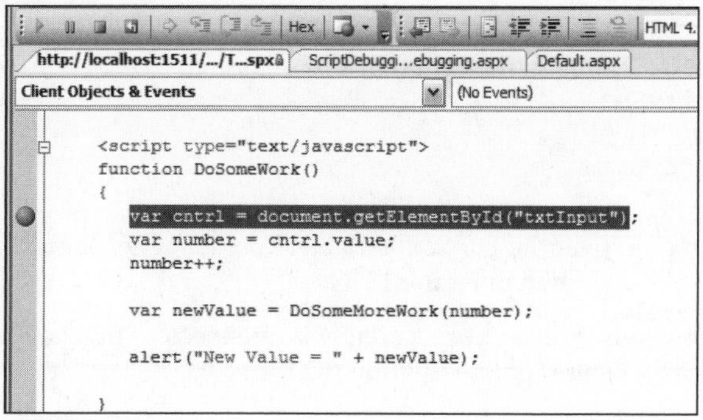

Figure 12-11

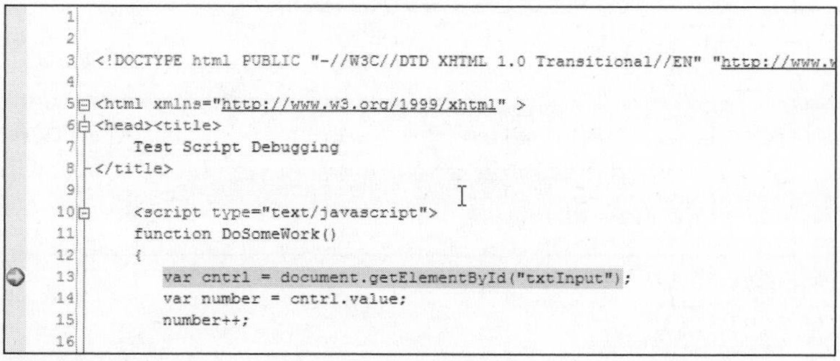

Figure 12-12

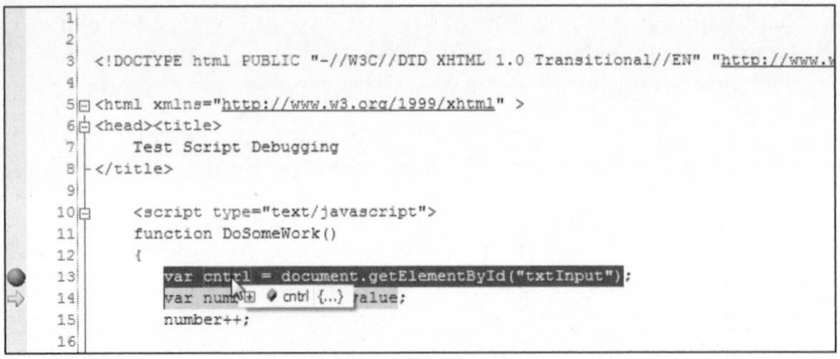

Figure 12-13

Clicking the + symbol allows you to examine the value of that variable and to drill down into the properties of that variable at the current position within the program's execution. This method of examining a variable is very similar to the debugging experience with server-side code.

Right-clicking the `cntrl` variable brings up a context menu, again similar to the menu presented to the user when debugging server-side code. Traditional debugging mechanisms are available, such as *Add watch* to add the display of the `cntrl` variable to the Watch window at the bottom of the display. Alternatively, you can open a *Quick watch* window. From there you can open a dialog box that allows easy examination of the variable's contents. These features are discussed further later in this chapter.

7. Press F10 again to advance the program's execution to the next line. Program execution should now be paused on the line that reads:

```
number++;
```

8. Position the mouse over the `number` variable. The debugger should display the value of the `number` variable, as shown in Figure 12-14.

   Currently, the value of the `number` variable is as expected, that is, it is equal to the contents of the input text box control defined within the form.

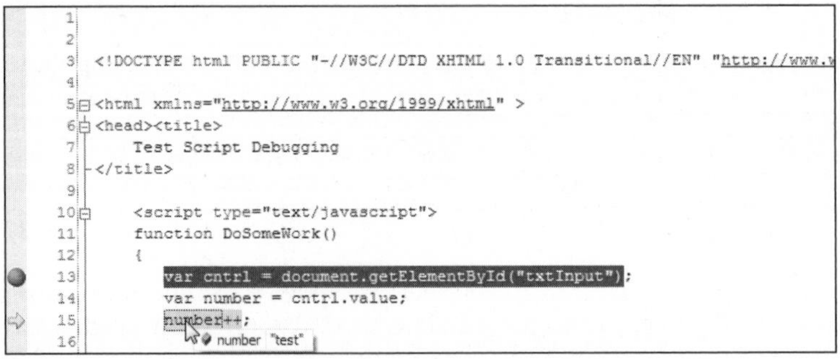

Figure 12-14

9. Press the F10 key again to cause the debugger to execute the next line of execution. The debugger should now be paused/positioned on the line that reads:

```
var newValue = DoSomeMoreWork(number);
```

10. Position the mouse over the newValue variable to display its current value. The display should look similar to Figure 12-15.

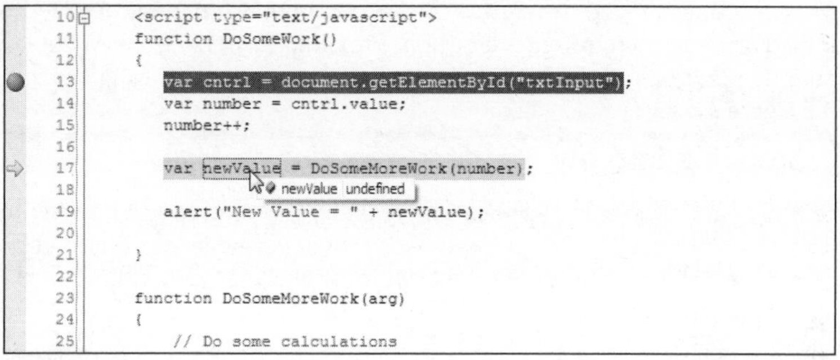

```
10   <script type="text/javascript">
11       function DoSomeWork()
12       {
13           var cntrl = document.getElementById("txtInput");
14           var number = cntrl.value;
15           number++;
16
17           var newValue = DoSomeMoreWork(number);
18               ⊗ newValue  undefined
19           alert("New Value = " + newValue);
20
21       }
22
23       function DoSomeMoreWork(arg)
24       {
25           // Do some calculations
```

Figure 12-15

How It Works

You now can see the exact point at which the variable value is turned into something invalid. It is apparent that the value of the number value was in fact a textual value of test. The next point of execution attempts to perform a mathematical operation on that string value, which of course is invalid. JavaScript is not like the traditional strongly typed server-side languages such as VB.NET and C#. This apparently invalid operation does not yield an exception, but rather, the value of the number variable is now flagged as NaN. The NaN value is a JavaScript special value indicator that means *Not a Number*. This value cannot be used for numerical calculations, which results in the value of newValue being calculated as undefined.

Pressing the F5 key (or clicking the Play button) allows execution to continue as normal, which yields the result seen previously.

You have successfully debugged the script code and identified why the web application behaves in the way it does. Debugging in this manner is a very powerful and intuitive way of examining the execution of script-based applications. Applications can be examined with intricate detail allowing very accurate determination of any problems within the code's execution.

The previous technique works great; however, it assumes that the application starts okay, and then you can set breakpoints to debug into the operations required. What if you wanted to start debugging the code immediately, or examine the code as it was starting?

You can do this by starting the application using the F10 key, or by choosing the Debug ➪ Step Over menu option. Normally, this is used to advance the debugger to the next step in the code's execution or to *step over* the current instruction. Using this step over technique to start the application starts the application as if you had pressed F5 to start it in debug mode, but will immediately pause execution on the first instruction, rather than stopping only on a breakpoint.

So far, you used F10 to advance the debugger's execution. As mentioned in the previous paragraph, this steps over the next line of code. If the debugger encounters a function to execute, pressing the F10 key calls the function, but doesn't step through each line within that function. In order to do that, use either the F11 key or the Debug ➪ Step Into menu option. Pressing the F11 key when you are about to execute a function or call out to another method will have the effect of stepping through each line of that method.

Try It Out   **Stepping into the Method Execution**

1. To see this in action, run the application again by pressing the F5 key. Switch back to Visual Studio and ensure that the Script Explorer window is visible, as described previously. Double-click the page within the Script Explorer window and place a breakpoint on the line that reads:

```
var newValue = DoSomeMoreWork(number);
```

If you find you are unable to place a breakpoint on a line, it is most likely that you have not double-clicked the page within the Script Explorer window, and you are simply examining the source code of the page in the standard Visual Studio 2005 display window.

The breakpoint is placed on the line that calls the DoSomeMoreWork() method. Switch to Internet Explorer (which is running the web page) and click the Submit Value button. Visual Studio 2005 switches to the foreground and execution pauses on the line with the breakpoint.

2. Press the F10 key. Notice that execution is now paused on the next line, which reads:

```
alert("New Value = " + newValue);
```

The method has been executed, and you are now positioned on the next line in the codes sequence. Here you have *stepped over* the execution of the DoSomeMoreWork() method. Instead, you want to examine execution of the code within that function.

3. Press F5 to allow execution of the code to continue, and the *alert* box is displayed as shown previously. Click OK in the alert box, and then click the Submit Value button once more. Execution should again pause on the line with the breakpoint.

4. This time, press the F11 key. Notice that the debugger has now jumped to the first line within the DoSomeMoreWork() method and is paused on that line. Hovering the mouse over the arg variable shows a value of *NaN* (JavaScript's method of indicating the value is *Not a Number*). From here you can continue to step through the execution of the code, and the debugger returns to the original place where the method was called and continues execution.

Other Ways of Invoking the Debugger

Previously, this chapter discussed placing breakpoints in code to pause the debugger at certain positions within the code. Although this is a great and easy technique to use, it does have some limitations.

When JavaScript has been generated and registered on the client, it becomes a little more difficult. The JavaScript may be executed on startup and be sufficiently long and complex that you don't want to step through the entire section of code from the beginning using the technique described previously, where the application is launched by pressing the F10 key to invoke the debugger.

Using the debugger Keyword

Another way to invoke the debugger is to make use of the debugger keyword in your script. In the following example, the code-beside file is registering the JavaScript for immediate execution within the web page. The web page itself contains nothing different than a newly added web form within Visual Studio 2005. Examine the web page and code-beside file in Listing 12-1 and the code-beside file in Listing 12-2.

Listing 12-1: Web Page / ASPX Page

```
<%@ Page Language="C#" AutoEventWireup="true" CodeFile="DebuggerKeword.aspx.cs"
Inherits="ScriptDebuggingSample_DebuggerKeword" %>

<!DOCTYPE html PUBLIC "-//W3C//DTD XHTML 1.0 Transitional//EN"
"http://www.w3.org/TR/xhtml1/DTD/xhtml1-transitional.dtd">

<html xmlns="http://www.w3.org/1999/xhtml" >
<head runat="server">
    <title>Debugger Keyword Test Page</title>
</head>
<body>
    <form id="form1" runat="server">
    <div>

    </div>
    </form>
</body>
</html>
```

The markup code represents a new page that is created when you add a new page item using Visual Studio. The code is the initial markup provided by Visual Studio.

Listing 12-2: Code File / Code-Beside File

```
using System;
using System.Data;
using System.Configuration;
using System.Collections;
using System.Web;
using System.Web.Security;
using System.Web.UI;
using System.Web.UI.WebControls;
using System.Web.UI.WebControls.WebParts;
using System.Web.UI.HtmlControls;

public partial class ScriptDebuggingSample_DebuggerKeword : System.Web.UI.Page
{
    protected void Page_Load(object sender, EventArgs e)
```

```
        {
            string script = @"
                var val1 = 10;
                var val2 = 20;
                var result1 = AddValues(val1,val2);
                alert('Sum of values 1 & 2 = ' + result1);
                var val3 = 30;
                var result2 = AddValues(result1,val3);
                alert('Sum of previous values and Value 3 = ' + result2);
                ";
            string addFunction = @"
                function AddValues(v1, v2)
                {
                  return v1 + v2;
                }";

            Page.ClientScript.RegisterStartupScript(this.GetType(), "startupCode",
        script,true);
            Page.ClientScript.RegisterClientScriptBlock(this.GetType(), "addMethod",
        addFunction,true);
        }
    }
```

This example registers all the required JavaScript to execute from the Page_Load event of the code file. Running this code (by pressing F5 to execute in debug mode) produces two alert boxes displaying the sum of some values. You can alter this code to automatically invoke the debugger just prior to the first invocation of the AddValues method.

To accomplish this, you insert the debugger keyword as part of the generated script. Examine the following code, which just shows the Page_Load method and highlights the modifications:

```
        protected void Page_Load(object sender, EventArgs e)
        {
            string script = @"
                var val1 = 10;
                var val2 = 20;
                debugger;
                var result1 = AddValues(val1,val2);
                alert('Sum of values 1 & 2 = ' + result1);
                var val3 = 30;
                var result2 = AddValues(result1,val3);
                alert('Sum of previous values and Value 3 = ' + result2);
                ";
            string addFunction = @"
                function AddValues(v1, v2)
                {
                  return v1 + v2;
                }";

            Page.ClientScript.RegisterStartupScript(this.GetType(), "startupCode",
        script,true);
            Page.ClientScript.RegisterClientScriptBlock(this.GetType(), "addMethod",
        addFunction,true);
        }
```

Now execute this application using F5 to start the application in debug mode. The application starts as normal, but then jumps to the debugger screen and pauses execution of the code on the line with the `debugger` keyword, as shown in Figure 12-16.

It's important to note that the `debugger` keyword is an Internet Explorer–only feature. If you intend to use this form of debugging across other browsers, you can test whether the browser supports the `debugger` keyword feature using the `Sys.Browser` object, which contains capabilities of the current browser. In particular, you can use the hasDebuggerStatement property to test for this support. The following code shows an example of this:

```
if (Sys.Browser.hasDebuggerStatement)
    debugger;
```

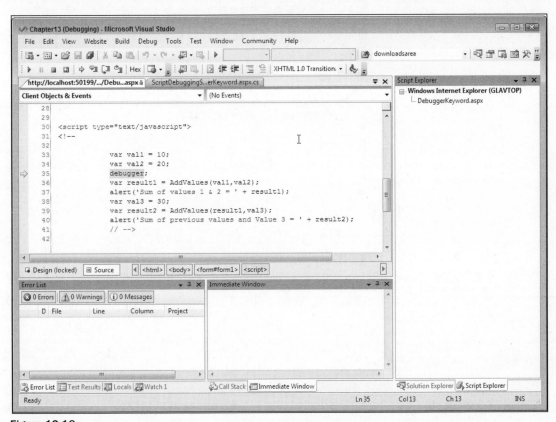

Figure 12-16

Other Ways of Inspecting the Value of Variables

As mentioned previously, when in debug mode, you can simply hover the mouse over a variable to display its current value. However, having to do this for a range of variables constantly as each line of code is executed can be cumbersome.

In similar fashion again to server-side debugging techniques, you can apply a watch to variables to monitor your values, and interactively perform computations against variables within your application.

Using the previous code example, press F5 to launch the application, which should automatically pause at the `debugger` keyword. When Visual Studio 2005 displays the debugger window, right-click the `result1` variable. This brings up a context menu. Select the Add Watch option, which will add the `result1` variable to the Watch window. The Watch window is typically located on the bottom left of the Visual Studio 2005 environment, as shown in Figure 12-17.

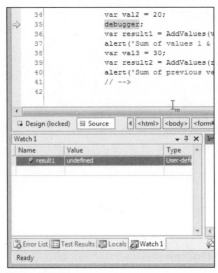

Figure 12-17

Notice that the `result1` variable is displaying a value of *undefined* in the Watch window. Pressing F10 twice to advance the program's execution past the call to the `AddValues` method causes the value of the `result1` variable to be updated within the Watch window according to the operation within the code's execution.

Multiple items can be added to the Watch window to enable so you can track the values of variables as execution progresses.

Alternatively, you might want to evaluate conditions as the code is executing that are not part of the program itself, or even execute Visual Studio commands. To accomplish this, you can make use of the Command, Immediate, and Locals windows. These windows allow interactive evaluation of ad-hoc statements and variable values within the context of the application's execution, at the point in time that it has been paused.

The Command and Immediate windows are very similar in operation and both can perform the same operations. The Command window is geared toward issuing Visual Studio commands (such as saving a file), whereas the Immediate window is geared toward immediate evaluation of variables as a program is executing. In either window, it is possible to switch to the other window easily, or even to execute the same commands.

You can display the Command window by selecting the View ⇨ Other Windows ⇨ Command Window menu option (or by pressing Ctrl+Alt+A). The Immediate window can be shown by selecting Debug ⇨ Windows ⇨ Immediate (or by pressing the Ctrl+D+I key combination).

The most obvious difference between the Command window and the Immediate window is simply the focus of execution. As already mentioned, the Command window is geared toward issuing Visual Studio commands. To do this, commands must be prefixed with the > symbol. The Command window always provides this prompt, whereas the Immediate window does not. To issue Visual Studio commands from the Immediate window, you must manually type the > character. For example, to make the debugger step into the next statement from the Immediate window (normally performed by pressing F11 while execution is paused at a breakpoint), you would need to issue the following command:

```
>Debug.StepInto
```

To issue the same command from the Command window, issue the following:

```
Debug.StepInto
```

As you can see, the difference is minimal. To further blur the difference, from the Command window it is perfectly valid to display a variable's value by issuing a command such as this:

```
? variable1
```

Because both windows are so similar in operation, you can assume that whatever operation is covered in one window can also be performed in the other.

The Locals window displays variables local to the current context or scope of execution. These variables will change as the scope of execution changes. This window is very handy to give a quick and concise view of the current state of execution of an application.

Try It Out   Using the Command and Locals Windows

To demonstrate this, follow these steps:

1. Run the previous application by pressing the F5 key to start the application in debug mode. The application presents the debug screen within Visual Studio with execution paused on the `debugger` statement.

2. Ensure the Command window is visible by clicking the Command Window tab (typically located on the bottom right of the Visual Studio 2005 environment) or by selecting the View ⇨ Other Windows ⇨ Command Window menu option (or by pressing the Ctrl+Alt+A key combination).

3. The Command window has a > symbol as the prompt. In the Command window, type the following command and press Enter:

```
? val1 + val2
```

4. A value of 30 should be displayed. Now try typing the following command:

```
? AddValues(81,42)
```

A value of 123 should be displayed. The Command window should now look like Figure 12-18.

5. Click the Locals window tab (also typically located on the bottom of the Visual Studio environment near the Command window tab). Your display should now show a list of variables within the current scope of execution and their respective values. The Locals window should look similar to Figure 12-19.

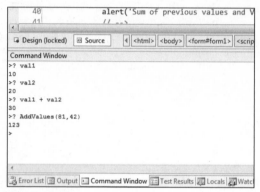

Figure 12-18

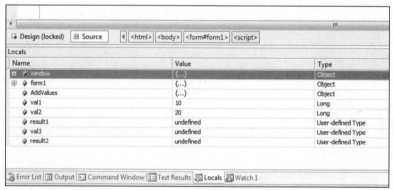

Figure 12-19

Here you are interactively evaluating variables and executing methods within the application. The question mark (?) symbol is shorthand for *display* or *print*. This technique is an extremely powerful way of evaluating different conditions within your script applications at various points within the script's execution.

How It Works

Visual Studio maintains the debugging environment of your application and allows you to query the value of variables at any time during an application's execution. In order to do this at any particular time, you need to set a point at which execution can pause, and allow you to query values of variables. At the breakpoint, you have access to the values of all variables that are within the current scope of execution. This is regardless of whether the execution process is within server-side code or client-side code, as the example in this case shows. Visual Studio has the ability to leverage Internet Explorer during the course of execution, to extract the value of variables, and allow inspection or even modification.

The various windows and options to view the application's current state are simply different ways of looking at the same data. It is important to experiment with these options to get a feel for the situations where they are best used, and also to develop your own preferences when debugging and viewing debug information.

ASP.NET AJAX Debugging Support

So far, you have seen how to perform debugging on the server side, as well as on the client side within the browser. These are all general debugging techniques for interrogating a program's execution as it occurs; however, ASP.NET AJAX Extensions offers some specific support for debugging purposes.

Using Sys.Debug

ASP.NET AJAX provides a Debug object that can be used within your JavaScript code to output the contents of variables and perform assertions in a fashion similar to the way you perform them on the server side.

Within any ASP.NET AJAX-enabled application, a Debug object is created within the Sys namespace. This object can be accessed using the following JavaScript code:

```
Sys.Debug
```

This object has several methods and a single property to assist in debugging. The single property available on the debug object is isDebug. This is a Boolean property and represents whether the application is running in debug mode or release mode. This is roughly equivalent to whether debug mode is enabled in the web.config file via the following switch:

```
<compilation debug="true">
```

In the previous example, the isDebug property would be equal to true. This property can be used to first determine whether the application is running in debug mode, and only output the appropriate debugging information if debugging is enabled. The following code demonstrates this:

```
if (Sys.Debug.isDebug) {
    //.... debug code ...
}
```

For the output of debugging information, the Debug object provides the three methods detailed in the following table.

Method	Purpose
Sys.Debug.trace(string text);	This statement simply outputs whatever string contents are supplied as the argument text.
Sys.Debug.traceDump(object obj, string name);	This statement recursively lists each property and associated value for the given object obj. The name parameter is used to display the name of the object.
Sys.Debug.clearTrace()	This statement simply clears the trace information from the trace console element.

Before looking at code examples showing how the Debug object works, it is worth noting that the information that is output via the trace commands shown in the preceding table can be displayed on different display devices. By default, the trace information is displayed in the Output window within Visual Studio; however, it can also be displayed in a TextArea HTML element on the web page. The trace information can also be output to the JavaScript console present in the Firefox, Safari, and Opera browsers. There is nothing specific that the developer needs to set in order for this output to be directed to a specific browser's display mechanism. The Microsoft AJAX Library directs output to the appropriate device depending on the browser being used.

Try It Out   Displaying Trace Information

To see the debugging support in action, you will create a simple application that uses the Sys.Debug object to output some simple debugging text. To demonstrate this, follow these steps:

1. Within Visual Studio, create a new web site using the ASP.NET AJAX Web Site template.

2. Create a new web form, or open the existing Default.aspx page within the editor.

3. Enter the following JavaScript code within the <head> section of the page:

```
<script type="text/javascript">
    function RunSimpleTest()
    {
      // Create a string object
      var s = new String("Hello");
      //alert("'s' object is: " + s);

      // Create a custom object
      var o = new Object();
      o.someValue = 100;
      o.someString = "someText";

      if (Sys.Debug.isDebug) {
          Sys.Debug.trace("---Outputting Trace Information ---");
          Sys.Debug.trace("Value of variable 's' is: " + s);
          Sys.Debug.traceDump(o,"Object Named 'o':");
      }
```

```
        }

    </script>
```

4. Within the empty `<div>` section in the page markup, enter the following code:

```
<button id="btn" onclick="RunSimpleTest();">Do Some Debugging</button>
```

Your page should now contain the following code:

```
<%@ Page Language="VB" AutoEventWireup="false" CodeFile="DebugStatement.aspx.vb"
Inherits="ASPNETAJAXSupport_DebugStatement" %>
<!DOCTYPE html PUBLIC "-//W3C//DTD XHTML 1.0 Transitional//EN"
"http://www.w3.org/TR/xhtml1/DTD/xhtml1-transitional.dtd">

<html xmlns="http://www.w3.org/1999/xhtml" >
<head runat="server">
    <title>Untitled Page</title>
    <script type="text/javascript">
        function RunSimpleTest()
        {
          // Create a string object
          var s = new String("Hello");
          //alert("'s' object is: " + s);

          // Create a custom object
          var o = new Object();
          o.someValue = 100;
          o.someString = "someText";

          if (Sys.Debug.isDebug) {
              Sys.Debug.trace("---Outputting Trace Information ---");
              Sys.Debug.trace("Value of variable 's' is: " + s);
              Sys.Debug.traceDump(o,"Object Named 'o':");
          }
        }
    </script>
</head>
<body>
    <form id="form1" runat="server">
    <asp:ScriptManager ID="sm1" runat="server" />
    <div>
        <button id="btn" onclick="RunSimpleTest();">Do Some Debugging</button>
    </div>
    </form>
</body>
</html>
```

5. Ensure that the page you created in the preceding steps is set as the startup page within the project.

6. Run the application in debug mode.

7. Click the Do Some Debugging button and examine the output in the Output window within Visual Studio.

When this code is run within Visual Studio in debug mode, the Output window contains output similar to Figure 12-20.

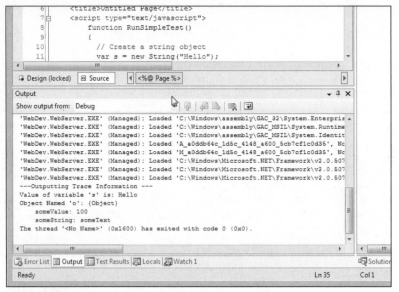

Figure 12-20

How It Works

The preceding JavaScript code example creates a string and a custom object in a similar fashion as was created at the beginning of this chapter for the Alert dialog box examples. However, instead of using the alert statement, you are using a series of Sys.Debug.trace statements to display your variable data.

First, you determine if the application is running in debug mode:

```
if (Sys.Debug.isDebug) {
```

Next, you output a simple string to identify that you are about to output more debug tracing information:

```
Sys.Debug.trace("---Outputting Trace Information ---");
```

Next, you display the value of the s string variable:

```
Sys.Debug.trace("Value of variable 's' is: " + s);
```

Finally, you display the o object variable, including all properties and their values:

```
debug.traceDump(o,"Object Named 'o':");
```

In Figure 12-20, you will notice that each property of the object o and the value of that property has been listed as part of the trace output. In one statement, you have recursively listed all the property values, along with the property names of an object. This is very handy because it gives a concise view of the state of an object.

This feature also supports client-side output, in addition to the server-side output console. If using the Mozilla Firefox browser, trace output is also sent to the Firebug console. Firebug is a popular add-on for the Mozilla Firefox browser and can be downloaded from `https://addons.mozilla.org/firefox/1843/`.

In addition, if using Internet Explorer, output is also directed to the Internet Explorer Web Development Helper tool, which can be downloaded and installed separately from `http://projects.nikhilk.net/Projects/WebDevHelper.aspx`.

> *The Web Development Helper tool is a separate add-in that does not come with Internet Explorer and was developed independently by a Microsoft employee named Nikhil Kothari. Nikhil is very active within the ASP.NET AJAX development team. His blog and web site are located at* `www.nikhilk.net/`.

In addition to outputting the trace information to the various consoles described previously, trace information can also be displayed on the web page itself. This requires the placement of an HTML `<textarea>` control on the page, with a specific ID of *TraceConsole*.

Try It Out — Displaying Trace Output in a Web Page

In this section, you supplement your previous tracing example by adding a `<textarea>` HTML element to the page named *TraceConsole*.

1. Add the following code to the page in the previous example after the `<button>` markup declaration:

```
<%@ Page Language="VB" AutoEventWireup="false" CodeFile="DebugStatement.aspx.vb"
<button id="clr" onclick="ClearTrace();">Clear Trace Info</button>
<hr />
<textarea rows="10" cols="40" id="TraceConsole"></textarea>
```

The web page code should now comprise the following:

```
<!DOCTYPE html PUBLIC "-//W3C//DTD XHTML 1.0 Transitional//EN"
"http://www.w3.org/TR/xhtml1/DTD/xhtml1-transitional.dtd">

<html xmlns="http://www.w3.org/1999/xhtml" >
<head runat="server">
    <title>Untitled Page</title>
    <script type="text/javascript">
        function RunSimpleTest()
        {
          // Create a string object
          var s = new String("Hello");
          //alert("'s' object is: " + s);

          // Create a custom object
          var o = new Object();
          o.someValue = 100;
          o.someString = "someText";
```

```
            if (Sys.Debug.isDebug) {
                Sys.Debug.trace("---Outputting Trace Information ---");
                Sys.Debug.trace("Value of variable 's' is: " + s);
                Sys.Debug.traceDump(o,"Object Named 'o':");
            }
        }

        function ClearTrace()
        {
            Sys.Debug.clearTrace();
        }
    </script>
</head>
<body>
    <form id="form1" runat="server">
    <asp:ScriptManager ID="sm1" runat="server" />
    <div>
        <button id="btn" onclick="RunSimpleTest();">Do Some Debugging</button>
        <button id="clr" onclick="ClearTrace();">Clear Trace Info</button>
        <hr />
        <textarea rows="10" cols="40" id="TraceConsole"></textarea>
    </div>
    </form>
</body>
</html>
```

2. Run the application in debug mode or in release mode.

3. Click the Do Some Debugging button.

Now when this page is executed, whether or not it is in a debug session, you receive output similar to Figure 12-21.

Clicking the Clear Trace Info button now clears the `<textarea>` element of all trace information it is currently displaying.

How It Works

This web page now contains a simple declaration for a `<textarea>` HTML element:

```
<textarea rows="10" cols="40" id="TraceConsole"></textarea>
```

In addition, you have added an extra function, `clearTrace`, that simply executes one statement, `Sys.Debug.clearTrace();` (which, as the name suggests, clears the trace output):

```
function ClearTrace()
{
    Sys.Debug.clearTrace();
}
```

The Microsoft AJAX Library knows explicitly about tracing to an element named `TraceConsole`. This element ID is coded within the debugging runtime support of the Microsoft AJAX Library. By simply including it within your page, the Microsoft AJAX Library can locate and utilize this element for debugging purposes.

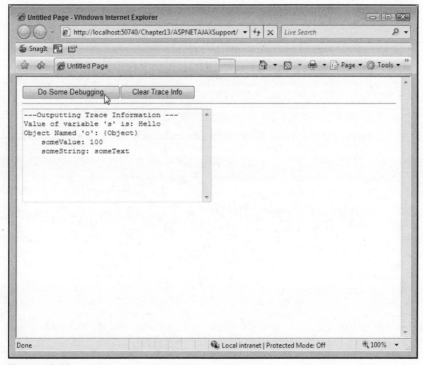

Figure 12-21

Assertions and Failures

Further debugging support is provided within ASP.NET AJAX through the provision of *assertions* and *failures*.

Using Sys.Debug.assert

An *assertion* is simply a statement that checks a condition, or "asserts" a condition, and takes action if that condition is not met. In the case of ASP.NET AJAX, you have the Sys.Debug.assert method, which checks for a condition, and if false, displays a message and breaks into the debugger.

Try It Out   **Using Sys.Debug.assert Method**

This section demonstrates very simple usage of the Sys.Debug.assert functionality to assert a value that is entered within a textual input field.

1. Within Visual Studio, create a new web site using the ASP.NET AJAX Web Site template.

2. Create a new web form, or open the existing Default.aspx page within the editor.

3. Enter the following JavaScript code within the <head> section of the page:

```
function TestAssertion()
{
    var e = document.getElementById('txt');
    Sys.Debug.assert(e.value == "Wiley","Text is not equal to 'Wiley'!");
    alert('Test Complete');
}
```

4. Enter the following markup within the empty <div> section in the page markup:

```
<body>
    <form id="form1" runat="server">

    <asp:ScriptManager ID="sm1" runat="server" />
    <div>
        <label id="lbl">Enter the text 'Wiley': </label>
        <input type="text" id="txt" /><br />
        <button id="btn" onclick="TestAssertion();">Test Debug.Assertion</button>
    </div>
    </form>
</body>
```

With this example, if a user enters any text other than Wiley, the message shown in Figure 12-22 is displayed.

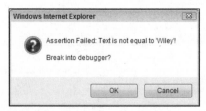

Figure 12-22

How It Works

In this example, the following code:

```
Sys.Debug.assert(e.value == "Wiley","Text is not equal to 'Wiley'!");
```

checks whether the variable `e.value` (the value of the text box) is equal to a value of `Wiley`. If not, the dialog box shown in Figure 12-22 is displayed with the text specified as the second argument of the `Sys.Debug.assert` statement. If it is, no dialog box is displayed.

Using Sys.Debug.fail

The `Sys.Debug.fail` command accepts a string message as its single function parameter, and displays that message in the debugger's output console or window, and then breaks into the debugger. There is no conditional logic built into this command. It simply outputs the message and then enters the debugger.

Try It Out **Using Sys.Debug.fail**

To try out using `Sys.Debug.fail`, follow these steps:

1. Expanding on the previous `Sys.Debug.assert` example, add the following code to the page:

```
function TestFail()
{
    var e = document.getElementById('txt');
    if (e.value != "Wiley")
        Sys.Debug.fail("A debug failure!");
    alert('Test Complete');
}
```

2. Similarly, you can add a button to invoke this function:

```
<button id="btn2" onclick="TestFail();">Test Debug.Fail</button>
```

How It Works

Here you manually test for the value of the text box being equal to Wiley using standard JavaScript `if/then` constructs, and if this condition is false, you execute the `Sys.Debug.fail` command, and pass a string message to display in the debugger output console or window.

Both of these statements, the `Sys.Debug.assert` and `Sys.Debug.fail`, are only useful when the application is running within the Visual Studio debugger, in a debugging session. This is because, even though a dialog may be displayed in the case of the `Sys.Debug.assert` statement, the IDE will not break into the debugger.

ScriptManager Debugging Support

The `ScriptManager` control also provides some basic support around debugging features. This control automatically detects whether the application is running in debug or release mode. If the application is running in debug mode, the debug version of the ASP.NET AJAX runtime scripts are loaded. These include extensive comments as well as tracing and assertion code. The release version of these scripts does not contain all the debugging support statements, and is far less readable due to all comments and whitespace being removed. This is primarily to reduce size, decrease load times, and increase performance.

It is possible to manually override the automatic detection of debug mode by the ScriptManager. This is possible using the ScriptMode attribute of the ScriptManager class. Figure 12-23 shows the possible values.

The possible values for the ScriptMode attribute are Auto (the default), Debug, Inherit, and Release. Specifying Debug or Release causes the ScriptManager control to load the respective version of the runtime scripts regardless of what mode the application is running in. This can be useful if you want to ensure the debug version of the ASP.NET AJAX runtime scripts are loaded, even though your application may be running in release mode. Be aware, though, that the debug versions of the scripts are larger in size and, therefore, slower to load.

The inherit setting of the ScriptMode attribute tells the ScriptManager to inherit the application state (whether in debug or release) from the page itself and is effectively the same as using the Auto setting.

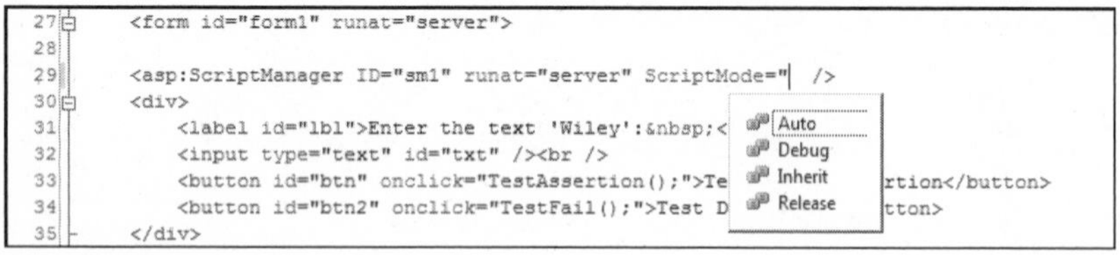

```
27    <form id="form1" runat="server">
28
29    <asp:ScriptManager ID="sm1" runat="server" ScriptMode="| />
30    <div>
31        <label id="lbl">Enter the text 'Wiley': <     Auto
32        <input type="text" id="txt" /><br />               Debug
33        <button id="btn" onclick="TestAssertion();">Te      Inherit      rtion</button>
34        <button id="btn2" onclick="TestFail();">Test D     Release        tton>
35    </div>
```

Figure 12-23

The Man in the Middle

So far, you have seen how to debug applications on the server side and how to debug applications on the client side within the browser. But what about what happens in between? Using AJAX, a large amount of information can be flowing asynchronously between the client and server. Using certain tools, you can inspect this traffic to ensure it is what you expect it to be. Many tools and network monitors are available that allow you to examine network traffic in various forms. However, the actual function of sending data over the network (whether that network is the Internet or a local intranet) relies on many layers of networking components and protocols acting together.

Web developers are typically interested in only the traffic pertinent to their web application. One such tool that effectively provides this functionality is called *Fiddler*.

Fiddler

Fiddler is a freely available tool that installs as a component that can be activated from within Microsoft Internet Explorer, and allows the HTTP traffic between a browser and a server to be easily viewed, examined, and manipulated — or *fiddled* (hence, the name Fiddler).

The Fiddler home page, where a copy can be downloaded, is located at www.fiddlertool.com/fiddler.

A full set of documentation, instructions, and tutorials exist on the Fiddler site. This section is not intended to be detailed instructions for using Fiddler. However, it is worth discussing how you can use this tool to assist the debugging process within a web application, specifically using AJAX techniques.

Try It Out   **Using Fiddler**

After you have downloaded and installed Fiddler, follow these steps:

1. Create a new web site project within Visual Studio 2005 and add a new page (or modify the existing Default.aspx page).

2. Place the markup in Listing 12-3 within the page (.aspx file):

Listing 12-3: TestFiddler.aspx — Web Form

```
<%@ Page Language="C#" AutoEventWireup="true" CodeFile="TestFiddler.aspx.cs"
Inherits="FiddlerExamples_TestFiddler" %>

<!DOCTYPE html PUBLIC "-//W3C//DTD XHTML 1.0 Transitional//EN"
"http://www.w3.org/TR/xhtml1/DTD/xhtml1-transitional.dtd">

<html xmlns="http://www.w3.org/1999/xhtml" >
<head runat="server">
    <title>Test Fiddler</title>
    <script type="text/javascript">
    function OnCallComplete(arg,ctx)
    {
        var dataReturned = arg.split(";");
        var cnt = 0;
        for (var cnt=0; cnt < dataReturned.length;cnt++)
        {
            alert("Data #" + cnt + " returned was: " + dataReturned[cnt]);
        }
    }
    </script>
</head>
<body>
    <form id="form1" runat="server">
    <div>
        <button onclick="DoCallback(null,null);">Do Async Callback</button>
    </div>
    </form>
</body>
</html>
```

3. In the code-behind file/code-beside file for the preceding page, enter the code shown in Listing 12-4:

Listing 12-4: TestFiddler.aspx.cs — Code-Beside File

```
using System;
using System.Data;
using System.Configuration;
using System.Collections;
using System.Web;
using System.Web.Security;
```

```
using System.Web.UI;
using System.Web.UI.WebControls;
using System.Web.UI.WebControls.WebParts;
using System.Web.UI.HtmlControls;

public partial class FiddlerExamples_TestFiddler : System.Web.UI.Page,
 ICallbackEventHandler
{
    protected void Page_Load(object sender, EventArgs e)
    {
        string js = Page.ClientScript.GetCallbackEventReference(this, "arg",
"OnCallComplete", "ctx", true);
        string jsFunction = "function DoCallback(arg,ctx) { " + js + " } ";

        Page.ClientScript.RegisterClientScriptBlock(this.GetType(), "Callback",
jsFunction,true);
    }


    #region ICallbackEventHandler Members

    public string GetCallbackResult()
    {
        System.Threading.Thread.Sleep(2000);
        string[] dataToReturn = new string[] { "Data1", "DataPart2", "SomeData3" };
        // return a hardcoded string array as a single string
        return string.Join(";", dataToReturn);
    }

    public void RaiseCallbackEvent(string eventArgument)
    {
        // Do nothing here
    }

    #endregion
}
```

4.   Ensure that the application runs by right-clicking the modified page and selecting View in Browser. A simple web page should be displayed with a single button labeled Do Async Callback. Clicking the button should result in a short two-second delay, and then three alert boxes displaying the returned data values of Data1, DataPart2, and SomeData3.

This page is obviously not very complex, but does utilize an asynchronous postback to execute a server-side method, and retrieve some data for display.

5.   Now access the Fiddler tool by selecting the Tools ➪ Fiddler menu option.

This displays a new dialog. Ignore it for now, but do not close it. Select the previous browser window (that is running the web page previously listed) and click the Do Async Callback button. You should see the same results within the browser — that is, the display of the three result values.

6. Bring the Fiddler window to the foreground by clicking in the window or selecting it in the Microsoft Windows taskbar.

All requests made by the browser are now logged in the Fiddler window. These include the original request for the page as specified in the address bar, but also any additional requests for images, script libraries, and other resources that the page loads as part of its functionality and display.

The Fiddler screen should now look similar to Figure 12-24.

7. The asynchronous request issued by the browser has been logged in the Fiddler window in the left-hand pane (indicated in the preceding diagram by the `localhost:1511` entry; the port number may be different on different systems). Select this entry by clicking it with the mouse. The right-hand section of the display should now show some details about the request.

This initial display shows some simple performance timings as well as the total bytes for the request and response itself.

8. Click the Session Inspector tab in the right-hand pane. This will initially display the HTTP headers that were sent as part of the HTTP request in the top right-hand pane. The bottom right-hand pane will automatically have the Transformer section selected. Select the Headers tab in the bottom right-hand pane. This displays the HTTP headers that were sent from the web server as part of the response.

The Fiddler display window should now look similar to Figure 12-25.

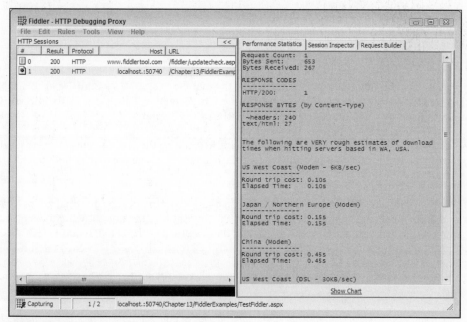

Figure 12-24

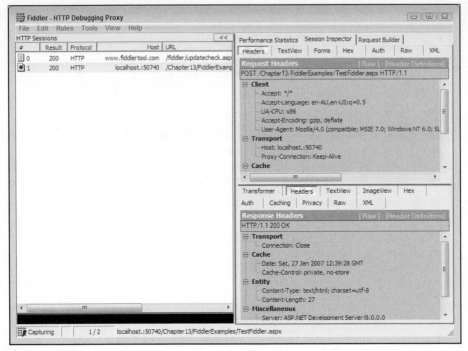

Figure 12-25

How It Works

This is useful for examining the HTTP headers of the request/response sequence to ensure that the correct headers are being set in an easy-to-view treeview-type display. This is especially important when formulating your own SOAP requests (as demonstrated in Chapter 4).

However, one of the most useful aspects of Fiddler is to examine the raw contents of the request/response sequence. With the Fiddler display still showing the headers, click the Raw tab in both the top and bottom right-hand panes.

This display shows the entire request and response data, including header information, as it would be sent by the client and received from the server. In the top right-hand pane showing the request, you can see the HTTP headers and also the associated data payload of the HTTP request. This should equal something similar to the following text:

```
__EVENTTARGET=&__EVENTARGUMENT=&__VIEWSTATE=%2FwEPDwUJNzgzNDMwNTMzZGRyE%2BruV%2BBh77
fo76pKQAZFknAX7Ag%3D%3D&__CALLBACKID=__Page&__CALLBACKPARAM=null
```

For a view of the payload that does not contain all the header information, and is a little cleaner to look at, you can select the TextView, which displays only the payload of the request and response.

From this, you can get an idea of how asynchronous client script callbacks notify the server of what control generated the callback, and what the argument of the call is (via the _CALLBACKID=__Page and __CALLBACKPARAM=null arguments, respectively).

The request data in the bottom right-hand pane shows the HTTP headers that form the response, and also response data that has been sent back as a result of your asynchronous request. The response data should look similar to the following:

```
0|Data1;DataPart2;SomeData3
```

This enables you to verify that what is being displayed within the browser through the application code is in fact what has been returned by the server.

> *Internet Explorer 7 was changed such that all requests to either 127.0.0.1 or localhost now bypass the proxy. Because this is the mechanism by which Fiddler intercepts calls (by acting as a proxy), debugging applications on your local system, or debugging applications that make calls to your local system, may not be intercepted by Fiddler. This means that running your applications using the local web server within Visual Studio 2005 will cause Fiddler to not capture the associated traffic. The easiest way to make this work is to simply append a period (.) to the host address. For example,* `http://localhost:1234/ SomePage.aspx` *becomes* `http://localhost.:1234/SomePage.aspx`. *This forces Internet Explorer 7 to proxy the request, and thus Fiddler can intercept and examine the traffic.*

It is also important to note that although Fiddler integrates well with Internet Explorer, it can also be used with the Firefox browser as well. However, for this to work, you need to set up Firefox to use a proxy server, in particular the proxy address that Fiddler listens on. To do this within Firefox, simply select the Tools ➪ Options menu option and select the Network tab. Then specify **127.0.0.1** and port **8888** as your HTTP proxy. With this setting, and Fiddler running, you can now inspect all traffic through the Firefox browser. Figure 12-26 illustrates the settings.

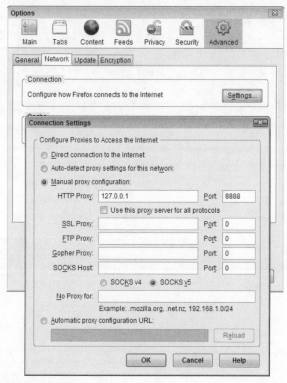

Figure 12-26

Using the Web Development Helper

A Microsoft employee, Nikhil Kothari, has created a tool for Internet Explorer that also allows traffic to be inspected as it flows between the server and the client. The tool is called the WebDevHelper and can be downloaded at `www.nikhilk.net/Project.WebDevHelper.aspx`. It is installed as an add-in within Internet Explorer and once installed can be activated by going to the Tools ➪ Web Development Helper menu option. This will create a console window at the bottom of the Internet Explorer browser window, as shown in Figure 12-27.

This tool provides the ability to view the traffic as it is sent and received from the client and server. This can be achieved by simply enabling the Enable Logging option. In addition, this tool provides the ability to view the Document Object Model (DOM) of the page, examine script execution, and execute arbitrary script through its provided script window.

ASP.NET AJAX itself supports this tool by providing the ability to output trace information to the WebDevHelper console if it is present.

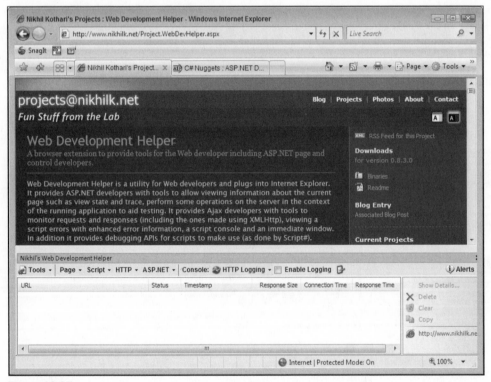

Figure 12-27

Try It Out   **Using the Web Development Helper**

This section offers a quick look at using WebDevHelper.

1. Ensure that the WebDevHelper tool window is shown by selecting Tools ⇨ Web Development Helper from the Internet Explorer menu. Select the Enable Logging option and ensure it is enabled. Load a page into the browser. The example in Figure 12-28 shows the home page of the WebDevHelper tool listed previously.

    A series of entries, listing the page traffic, will be displayed within the WebDevHelper console window (see Figure 12-28).

2. Double-click any entry within the WebDevHelper tool console window to view information about that particular request.

3. One particularly useful feature is the DOM Inspector tool. This enables you to examine the DOM structure of the page and is very useful when the DOM is being dynamically manipulated. This can be accessed from the Page ⇨ DOM Inspector menu option. Selecting this option displays a dialog similar to that shown in Figure 12-29 and allows you to examine the DOM structure in detail.

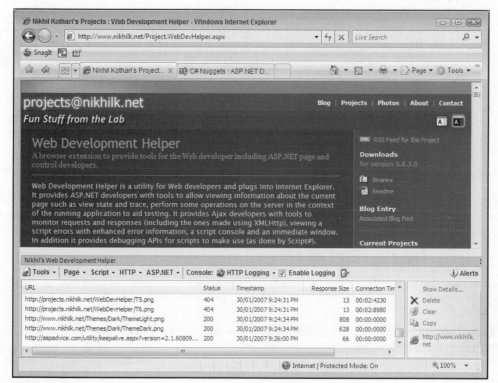

Figure 12-28

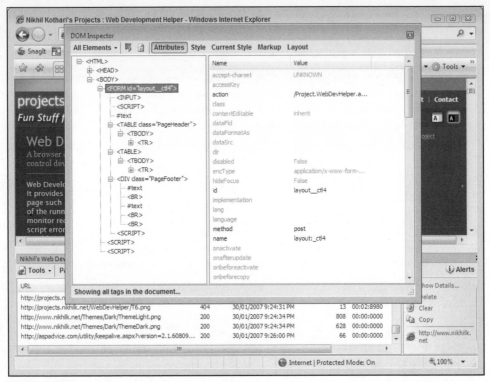

Figure 12-29

A full tutorial on this tool is beyond the scope of this chapter; however, the most useful functions are easily accessible via its simple menu interface, and provide an extremely useful companion to ASP.NET AJAX development.

A Firefox browser version of this tool can also be downloaded from www.thundermain.com/ aspnetdevhelper.xpi. An information page about the Firefox version of this tool can be accessed from http://aspadvice.com/blogs/rbirkby/archive/2005/05/12/2418.aspx.

Debugging in Firefox

The Firefox browser provides some built-in capability for debugging via its JavaScript console and the included DOM Inspector.

When Firefox is installed, an option is provided to install a set of developer tools. Selecting to install these tools provides the user with a menu option Tools ⇨ DOM Inspector. Selecting this menu option displays a window that will look similar to the screen shown in Figure 12-30.

The DOM Inspector tool available within the Firefox browser is very similar to the IE Developer Toolbar in that it allows you to view the structural and style elements of a web page, and any associated attributes or contextual items. The tool also allows some degree of manipulation to certain elements within the page.

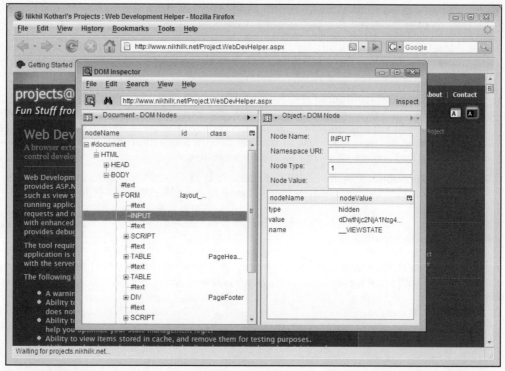

Figure 12-30

Firefox also provides a convenient JavaScript error console that displays any errors and warnings encountered while processing the JavaScript code within a web page, in addition to also displaying any CSS (Cascading Style Sheet) errors that are encountered.

Selecting the Tools ⇨ Error Console menu option displays a window showing any JavaScript or CSS errors encountered thus far in the page's execution, and looks similar to Figure 12-31.

The JavaScript console provides a convenient and easy-to-use method for viewing and collecting any JavaScript errors that have occurred during the processing of a page.

Firebug

Firebug is an add-on for the Firefox browser and can be downloaded from `www.getfirebug.com/`. Firebug integrates tightly with Firefox and contains a huge array of functionality to allow you to debug and tweak almost any aspect of a web page.

Some of the features of Firebug include:

- ❑ **Inspecting and editing HTML within any page with section highlighting and immediate feedback** — You can scroll through a hierarchical display of all the elements within your web page, and select and edit the item — all with feedback immediately shown on the page.

❑ **Inspecting and editing of CSS within a web page** — Editing and tweaking of all styles within a web page and immediate updates of any changes you make in real time.

❑ **Monitoring of network activity** — You can easily see how long components of the page take to load when accessing the network and analyze what parts of the page may be taking a long time to load.

❑ **Debugging and profiling of JavaScript** — Firebug will debug JavaScript within the page as it executes, allowing you to easily place breakpoints and view variables as the page executes. Additionally, full profiling of JavaScript functions showing how long a function takes make fine-tuning the pages very easy. You can easily see errors within the JavaScript code as well as evaluate and execute JavaScript in an ad-hoc fashion.

❑ **Document Object Model browse and edit** — You can easily browse the DOM within the web page and make changes, with the effects being shown immediately within the page.

After you have downloaded and installed Firebug, you can access it with the Tools ➪ Firebug menu option, as shown in Figure 12-32.

Selecting the Open Firebug menu option will display the Firebug console within Firefox (see Figure 12-33) and allow you to utilize all the features previously mentioned and apply them to any web page loaded within Firefox.

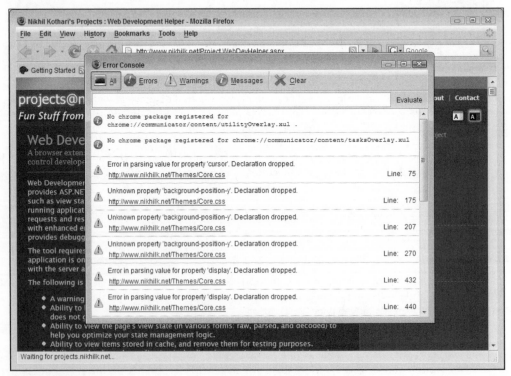

Figure 12-31

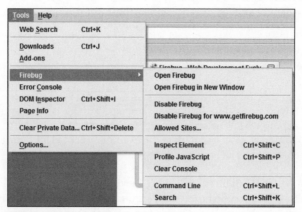

Figure 12-32

Figure 12-33

Firebug is an extremely comprehensive debugging suite. The range of features and functionality are very large and to discuss them in any detail is beyond the scope of this book. It is a very valuable and capable tool that should be a part of any web developer's toolkit.

Summary

This chapter has provided a broad look at how to debug ASP.NET AJAX applications. This ranged from general debugging techniques on the server and client side, to ASP.NET AJAX-specific debugging support, and finally to looking at tools to facilitate the examination of HTTP traffic and Document Object Model (DOM) elements within the browser. Specifically, the areas covered were as follows:

❑ **Server-side ASP.NET debugging** — This looked at the basic techniques to debug server-side code and although not specific to AJAX applications, or even web applications, is an important piece of the debugging concept. Developers need a thorough understanding of these techniques regardless of what development they are undertaking.

❑ **General JavaScript debugging** — JavaScript debugging has traditionally been a difficult task because the tools to support this have not provided the same level of functionality as their server-side counterparts. You examined how Visual Studio goes a long way toward narrowing that gap and providing server-side debugging capabilities within the browser, for JavaScript client code. This is often crucial in AJAX applications and ASP.NET AJAX makes extensive use of JavaScript to achieve its functionality.

❑ **Specific debugging support provided by the ASP.NET AJAX Extensions** — ASP.NET AJAX enhances the support that Visual Studio provides by providing specific debugging commands to allow the developer to easily output debug and trace information. You looked at how the debug support within ASP.NET AJAX provides a consistent output mechanism so that developers can actually build debugging support into their applications. You also looked at how the `ScriptManager` control automatically detected release or debug mode and loads the appropriate version of the ASP.NET AJAX runtime scripts.

❑ **HTTP and client-side debugging** — Finally, you examined some of the tools available that allow you to view the HTTP request information as it traverses from client to server and back again. Asynchronous postbacks happen invisibly in the background and being able to monitor this information and ensure it is correct is very important in AJAX applications. In addition, you saw how these tools can also allow you to examine the basic Document Object Model (DOM) of the page within the browser. This can allow you to interactively view the effects of your code.

Debugging is often considered a "black art" and there is still a vast amount of information needed to truly be a master of the art. This chapter has provided a broad spectrum of techniques, tools, and tips to allow you to debug your applications effectively. You are encouraged to continue to experiment with the tools and techniques provided within this chapter to refine your debugging skills.

No one can escape the fact that applications they write need to be debugged at some point, particularly with today's complex applications, and mastering the art of debugging can make your life a lot easier.

ASP.NET AJAX Futures CTP: Online Content

Microsoft's ASP.NET AJAX framework consists of three parts. So far this book has talked about the main features of the Core bits and the AJAX Control Toolkit. This chapter provides an overview of the last set of features, collectively part of the ASP.NET AJAX Futures CTP — we will be making updates to the code samples online (www.wrox.com) as the CTPs change. Nothing is guaranteed to be in the Futures CTP, and based on feedback and testing, some bits will be cut out and not put into the next release.

The following are the main features of the ASP.NET AJAX CTP as it exists at the time of the ASP.NET AJAX 1.0 release:

❑ XML-Script
❑ Data binding
❑ Drag and drop
❑ Bridging
❑ Silverlight with AJAX

One of the goals of this book is to allow a beginner to run the code with as little modification as possible. Because we are unable to know what changes are in store for the features within the ASP.NET AJAX Futures CTP, we decided not to cover these features in the printed book. Instead, we felt it best to provide some simple examples in the online content that goes with this book. To access the online content, go to www.wrox.com and search for "Beginning ASP.NET 2.0 AJAX."

XML-Script

With the release of ASP.NET AJAX 1.0, there was hand-coding of events and behaviors into applications. XML-Script is a declarative script format for defining script object instances, their property values, and how they wire up to each other. One of the ideas behind this script markup is to allow you to define the behavior of your application and its user interface as a separate layer that is attached to the content and style layers. Why not just write imperative code? Well, there are some advantages to doing it declaratively:

❑ Declarative markup is more designable than code. This approach will facilitate tool development in the future.

❑ Declarative markup enables you to tell the application what it should do, but not necessarily how to do it. Frameworks can take advantage of this by having the ability to interpret semantics and do some different things, such as running script functionality on the server to generate a view of the page more suitable for search engines.

You do not have to write any JavaScript to call a web service and then populate a control using XML-Script. The JavaScript to write that is not difficult, but it does require knowledge of the library and of JavaScript, which not everyone has.

XML-Script is very simple to understand and as soon as IntelliSense works for this stuff, you will be able to write this declarative code easily. This kind of scripting language will also give you tools that can generate this kind of code easily. With.client-side data binding, you will have a powerful solution for creating applications without any managed code besides the `ScriptManager` control. I don't know if I would suggest doing it this way for all your applications, but it could work nicely in certain situations — for example, when you need a more modern and cross-browser version of DHTML applications. With client-side data binding, your final site will include pages that have a thick layer of JavaScript and/or XML-Script and virtually no managed code except for the `ScriptManager` control.

By using the XML-Script markup, you don't need to learn how to code JavaScript. JavaScript can be difficult to write and requires some time for the learning curve. For example, you need to learn how to call and use the DOM (Document Object Model) and also how to write script that should work for different browsers, and so on. By using the XML-Script markup, you can easily bind controls to each other and call methods without worrying about writing client-side script that should be compatible with other browsers. This is taken care of for you by the Microsoft AJAX Library.

Data Binding

Data is the basis for all major applications that developers build today. Every developer knows and understands the concepts of taking data in the form of objects as well as DataSets and displaying it to the user by means of some type of control. This capability is in Windows Forms development as well as ASP.NET. ASP.NET AJAX extends the capability of working with data within a web browser and a set of user interface controls.

Chapter 4 discussed calling a web service. When calling a web service, you can pass some parameters to a web service and get back a custom business object. The question comes up as to why can't you get the DataSet/DataTable back from a query and send that through to the client browser over a web service. After all, a DataSet is serializable. As a result, one would think that a DataSet or DataTable could be sent over ASP.NET AJAX. Unfortunately, the ASP.NET 2.0 AJAX 1.0 Extensions does not provide the ability to process a DataSet/DataTable being sent across a web service to a web browser client. The ASP.NET AJAX Futures CTP provides the ability to serialize DataSets/DataTables over a web service and be processed on the web browser.

You can view client-side data binding as an extension to the classic JavaScript runtime and DOM. In a purely client-side programming style, you connect to a remote endpoint, download data, and bind it to a DOM subtree. The structure of the template remains on the client, along with some state information, and only raw data is moved from the server to the client.

You will need .NET Framework 3.5 Beta 1 in order to play with dynamic data controls.

Two client-side controls are written entirely in AJAX JavaScript to implement template-based binding:

❑   `ListView` — For multiple-records view

❑   `ItemView` — For single-record view

These two controls are combined together with client data source and filtering components. When using client-side data binding, you use XML-Script to declaratively tell the client where to get the data.

Data binding allows a developer to associate user interface elements and data sources. Without having to write all that client code and code-behind to do the binding from the server, you save a lot of time and the application feels faster to the user. This will not only speed up development, but will speed up the application from the client's point of view.

For more information on data binding, see Appendix B of the online content.

Drag and Drop

Windows Forms developers have long had the capability to grab an object and move it around within an application. Developers working in a web environment haven't had the luxury of that feature without the use of client-side libraries from numerous third parties. With the ASP.NET AJAX CTP, this capability is now included in a set of libraries supplied by Microsoft.

The model that it uses is patterned after the old OLE drag-drop model, in which drag sources implement the `IDragSource` interface, drop targets implement the `IDropTarget` interface, and the system provides a `DragDropManager` class from `Sys.UI.DragDropManager` to connect drag sources to drop targets. Some examples you will see in the online content include creating your own drag-and-drop control by implementing the `IDragSource` interface, which is defined in `PreviewDragDrop.js`. You will also implement the `IDropTarget` interface to allow different kinds of scenarios, including changing colors of the drop target when dragging the drag source control over the target (known as *drag highlighting*). Because you will have such granular control over the drag-and-drop events and properties, you will be able to create some very fancy UI interfaces that previously were only possible using Windows Forms applications. Imagine a drag-and-drop shopping cart or an admin panel that allows you to drag and drop members from one list to another.

A good example of the kinds of drag-drop scenarios that `DragDropManager` enables can be found in the ASP.NET AJAX Control Toolkit. For example, the `ReorderList` control uses its own copy of `DragDropManager` to implement a list whose items can be rearranged using drag-drop. It uses its own specific version of `DragDropManager` instead of the one in the Futures CTP so that the Toolkit can be used without the CTP.

As of this writing (and I would assume in the future), there are different ways to implement drag and drop with the Futures CTP:

❑ **Declarative drag and drop** — First you want to make a `<div>` element and create a drag handle. Then you will add XML-Script to the page, which makes the `<div>` element draggable. The example will demonstrate the simplicity and ease of using the declarative model with the client library. Basically, you will use declarative markup to add floating behavior to an HTML element.

❑ **Imperative drag and drop** — You can use JavaScript to do the same thing you do in XML-Script. You just need to create a floating behavior using the `Sys.Preview.UI.FloatingBehavior` class. This will probably change in the final release, but the examples online will stay up-to-date as new CTPs roll out. One reason why you would want to use the imperative way to create drag-and-drop behaviors is when you want to create DOM objects dynamically. A limitation of the declarative model is that you can only work with objects that are on the page initially. When you add objects to the page dynamically, you cannot add the floating behavior to them using the declarative model.

❑ **Dropzones** — Being able to drag elements around a page and have them stay where you leave them is very useful. You should have an event be thrown when the drop occurs to add a richer UI experience. You also want the event that is thrown to depend on where the drop occurs. There needs to be a behavior that can be added to a given element that will turn it into a "dropzone" or a "drop target," the same way that the floating behavior can be added to a `<div>` tag to turn it into a drag-and-drop element. For example, you can have a dropzone highlight when you mouse over the dropzone with your drag-and-drop element and make it turn another color when it is dropped.

For more information on drag and drop, refer to Appendix C of the online content.

Bridging

Mashups are increasingly becoming commonplace applications, thanks to Microsoft, Yahoo!, Amazon, and Google exposing data through web services. The problem with a web browser directly calling these web services is that web browsers are only allowed to call back to the web sites that are loaded into them at that moment. Though each vendor has ways around this, it would be nice if it were possible to call the web services provided by these major vendors. The `Bridge` control will provide that ability to call from a client browser to the web site that has loaded it, and then have the web site call the web service and have the data flow back to the web browser through the web server.

Chapter 9 showed an example of how to create your own proxy to allow your client-side script to call outside web services. It is definitely a hack, and it will be nice to have the bridging feature built into the next release. The way the `Bridge` control handles the outside domain web service calls is quite simple and powerful at the same time. It also can call REST services and map them like web services. The proxy is basically built for you and by using a simple configuration file you can easily map an outside service.

The `Bridge` control is an XML file with an extension of *.asbx*. The `Bridge` control can also have a code-behind file. The `Bridge` control file is converted to C# code by a custom build provider, which is specified in the config file. In the current CTP this is called the BridgeProvider, but could change by the next CTP. The C# code is then compiled into an assembly by the ASP.NET runtime.

To get IIS to recognize the .asbx file extension, you need to edit the properties of the web site you want to put the `Bridge` control in, as follows:

1. On the Home Directory tab in the properties window, click Configuration.

2. In the Application Configuration dialog box, click Add.

3. In the Add/Edit Application Extension Mapping dialog box, add the .asbx extension, and in the Executable box, browse to and select the `aspnet_isapi.dll`. You can look at how the .aspx extension is mapped to see an example.

4. Add the build provider and `httpHandlers` entries to the `<system.web>` element in the `web.config` file:

The examples in Appendix D of the online material include how to create mashups using the Flickr, Amazon, and Virtual Earth services, along with calling outside RSS feeds. There are so many potential applications that can be written once you see how easy it is to mash up data from many different web services.

Silverlight

Silverlight is a cross-platform, cross-browser .NET plug-in that will help designers and developers work better together to deliver rich Internet applications (RIAs). Silverlight XAML elements are scriptable via the browser script engine (JavaScript). It currently supports Firefox, Safari, and IE browsers on both the Mac and Windows.

Silverlight 1.0 should be released sometime in the summer of 2007. The size of the plug-in will be around 1.2 MB and will install seamlessly in the browsers, making it a very viable solution to adding a rich UI experience to your projects. It will consist of the following features:

❑ Media support for playing WMV and VC-1 video along with MP3 and WMA audio in the browser

- ❑ UI controls such as text boxes, drop-down lists, and buttons
- ❑ Support for creating complex animations
- ❑ DOM API controlled by JavaScript
- ❑ XAML declarative markup language for creating UI elements and many other features

Silverlight provides a nice API to the HTML DOM, allowing easy integration of HTML elements. The Silverlight scriptable objects are obtained via findName and can be controlled via properties and methods. findName is the equivalent to document.getElementById(). This models JavaScript and HTML DOM interaction. You can set the position of the object using Canvas.Top and Canvas.Left. Here is a very simple example of how you would control a Silverlight object via JavaScript:

```
function onLoad(sender, args, root) {
    var mainObject = root.findName("mainObject");
    mainObject["Canvas.Left"] = 250;
}
```

This simple example shows how easy it is to access the properties of a Silverlight object.

For more information on Silverlight integration, refer to Appendix E of the online content.

Resources

Here is a sampling of the links you should visit to learn more about ASP.NET AJAX. Start your journey at `http://ajax.asp.net/`, the official ASP.NET AJAX site.

- **ASP.NET AJAX Control Toolkit**
  - *ASP.NET AJAX Control Toolkit site* (`http://ajax.asp.net/toolkit/default.aspx`) — The main page for the ASP.NET AJAX Control Toolkit.
  - *CodePlex repository* (`www.codeplex.com/Wiki/View.aspx?ProjectName=AtlasControlToolkit`) — This link is the location for the AJAX Control Toolkit repository on the CodePlex community site.
  - *Downloads* (`http://ajax.asp.net/downloads/`) — AJAX and AJAX Control Toolkit downloads.
  - *IEnumerable interface* (`http://msdn2.microsoft.com/en-us/library/9eekhta0.aspx`) — A support article detailing the features and requirements of the `IEnumerable` interface.
  - *Shawn Burke Blog* (`http://blogs.msdn.com/sburke/`) — Shawn Burke, one of the main Microsoft contributors and managers of the ASP.NET AJAX Control Toolkit project, has a blog that contains a large amount of information related to AJAX Control Toolkit usage and development.
  - *Web Resource support article* (`http://support.microsoft.com/kb/910442`) — This support article details the functionality and features of Web Resource handling within ASP.NET 2.0.
  - *WinMerge* (`http://winmerge.org/`) — An extremely powerful and easy-to-use file comparison and merging utility.
  - *WinRAR* (`www.rarlab.com/download.htm`) — A very popular file compression and decompression utility.
  - *WinZip* (`www.winzip.com/downwz.htm`) — One of the most popular file compression/decompression utilities.
- **ASP.NET AJAX documentation** (`http://ajax.asp.net/documentation/`) — The documentation covers all the major classes and members of the ASP.NET AJAX framework. Every ASP.NET AJAX developer should be familiar with this valuable resource.

❑ **ASP.NET AJAX Under the Hood Secrets** (`www.codeproject.com/Ajax/ aspnetajaxtips.asp`) — This meaty article covers all kinds of tips and tricks for manipulating ASP.NET AJAX in unusual and interesting ways to squeeze optimal performance out of it.

❑ **Blogs**

    ❑ *ASP.NET Blogs* (`http://weblogs.asp.net/`) — Here you can find the blogs of several members of the ASP.NET team. You will get information about undocumented features in ASP.NET AJAX as well as future features and interesting facts.

    ❑ *Burke, Shawn* (`http://blogs.msdn.com/sburke/`) — Shawn Burke, one of the main Microsoft contributors and managers of the ASP.NET AJAX Control Toolkit project, has a blog that contains a large amount of information related to AJAX Control Toolkit usage and development.

    ❑ *Guthrie, Scott* (`http://weblogs.asp.net/scottgu/`) — Scott Guthrie is one of the primary geniuses behind the architecture of ASP.NET AJAX. Nobody knows more about ASP.NET AJAX than Scott. Get the inside scoop directly from him here.

    ❑ *Kothari, Nikhil* (`www.nikhilk.net`) — Nikhil is an architect in the ASP.NET team. He has blogged about many of the features of the `UpdatePanel` and other features of ASP.NET AJAX.

❑ **Configuration documentation** (`http://ajax.asp.net/docs/ ConfiguringASPNETAJAX.aspx`) — Visit this page for a description of the elements in the `web.config` file that support ASP.NET AJAX.

❑ **Debugging**

    ❑ *Debugging Managed Code* (`http://msdn2.microsoft.com/en-us/library/ awtaffxb.aspx`) — This article contains extensive links to information regarding general server-side debugging techniques.

    ❑ *Fiddler* (`www.fiddlertool.com`) — The official home page and download location for Fiddler, an HTTP network traffic monitoring tool.

    ❑ *Firebug add-on download* (`https://addons.mozilla.org/firefox/1843/`) — This link is the official add-on download location for the Firebug debugging utility that can be installed within Mozilla Firefox.

    ❑ *Firebug official home page* (`www.getfirebug.com/`) — The official home page and also additional download location of the Firebug tool.

    ❑ *Nikhil's Home Page* (`www.nikhilk.net`) — Nikhil Kothari's home page contains links to other resources related to general web development.

    ❑ *Web Development Helper* (`http://projects.nikhilk.net/Projects/ WebDevHelper.aspx`) — The download location for Nikhil Kothari's popular Web Development Helper utility that installs within Internet Explorer.

    ❑ *Web Development Helper Firefox version* (`www.thundermain.com/ aspnetdevhelper.xpi`) — The install location for a Mozilla Firefox version of Nikhil Kothari's popular Web Development Helper utility. You can find more information about this version at `http://aspadvice.com/blogs/rbirkby/archive/2005/05/12/ 2418.aspx`.

❑ **Forums** (`http://forums.asp.net`) — The forums at ASP.NET hold discussions about numerous issues, with the `UpdatePanel` being the most discussed single component. The forums of interest are:

  ❑ *AJAX Control Toolkit* — This forum is for discussing the ASP.NET AJAX Control Toolkit.

  ❑ *AJAX Discussion and Suggestions* — This is a general forum for discussing ASP.NET AJAX.

  ❑ *AJAX Networking and Web Services* — This forum is for discussing the network subsystem of ASP.NET AJAX and the web services that will be called on the server side.

  ❑ *AJAX UI* — This forum is for discussing the user interface issues of ASP.NET AJAX-based applications.

❑ **Installation documentation** — `http://ajax.asp.net/docs/InstallingASPNETAJAX.aspx`

❑ **JavaScript** (`http://ajax.asp.net/docs`) — The ASP.NET AJAX site contains documentation on the additions to the JavaScript global namespace.

❑ **Microsoft AJAX Library**

  ❑ *Client Reference* (`http://ajax.asp.net/docs/ClientReference/default.aspx`) — This link details the entire client library.

  ❑ *Json.NET* (`http://newtonsoft.com/products/json/`) — Great open source libraries that allow the simple and safe reading and writing of JSON objects from .NET.

❑ **Podcast** (`www.aspnetpodcast.com`) — The ASP.NET Podcast discusses many ASP.NET and ASP.NET AJAX features.

❑ **Security and Integration**

  ❑ *Official ASP.NET AJAX documentation* (`http://ajax.asp.net/docs/tutorials/ASPNETApplicationServicesTutorials.aspx`) — This is the official home for documentation on how to interface ASP.NET 2.0 AJAX with ASP.NET application services.

  ❑ *Examining ASP.NET 2.0's Membership, Roles, and Profile* (`http://aspnet.4guysfromrolla.com/articles/120705-1.aspx`) — A series by Scott Mitchell exploring the details of ASP.NET application services. This is a great foundational article to learn about application services before you begin extending their access with AJAX interfaces.

❑ **Starter kits** (`http://asp.net/downloads/starterkits/`) — This link points to the ASP.NET 2.0 Starter Kits for Visual Web Developer.

❑ **User interface design**

  ❑ *AjaxLoad.info* (`www.ajaxload.info/`) — This handy web site helps you to create custom animated images for display during asynchronous postbacks. Use it to give your users a pleasant and entertaining visual experience while they wait.

  ❑ *ModalUpdateProgress control* (`www.codeproject.com/Ajax/ModalUpdateProgress.asp`) — This open source control easily allows other controls on the page to be disabled during asynchronous postbacks.

  ❑ *UpdateProgress control documentation* (`http://ajax.asp.net/docs/overview/UpdateProgressOverview.aspx`) — This page acts as the online documentation's starting point for learning all about the properties, events, and methods of the `UpdateProgress` control.

❑ *Using the UpdateProgress Control* (`http://aspalliance.com/1013_Video_Using_ the_Atlas_UpdateProgress_Control`) — If you learn well by example, this online video could help you to understand details about the `UpdateProgress` control.

❑ **Videos**

❑ `www.asp.net/learn/videos/` — If you learn well by watching demonstrations, this collection of online "How Do I?" demonstration videos could be an essential resource for learning all about ASP.NET AJAX.

❑ `http://aspalliance.com/1013_Video_Using_the_Atlas_UpdateProgress_ Control` — This online video can help you understand the details about the `UpdateProgress` control.

Index

Index

V

ValidatorCallout control, 129
variables, values, 293–297
ViewState, synchronizing, 80–81

W

web pages, controls, adding, 140–145
web services
    encapsulating, .aspx page, 75–76
    page-based, 75–76
web sites
    AJAX Library, 327
    ASP.NET AJAX functionality, 137–138
    configuration documentation, 326
    Control Toolkit, 325
    creating, controls and, 130–136
    debugging, 326
    forums, 327
    under the hood secrets, 326
    installation, 327
    integration, 327
    JavaScript, 327
    security, 327
    starter kits, 327
    user interface design, 327–328
    videos, 328
Web.Config file, 45–51
    ASP.NET AJAX Support, 24–27
WebDevHelper, 312–314
WebRequest class, creating custom, 220–226
writing controls, 107
    initializing script, 109–110
    registering script, 108–109

X

XAML (Extensible Application Markup Language), 5
XML, XML-based languages, 5
XML-Script, 63
    Futures CTP, 320
XUL (XML User Interface Language), 5